GROCERY

MW00785278

★

TEXAS

ON *the* TABLE

Terry Thompson-Anderson

TEXAS
ON *the* TABLE

PEOPLE, PLACES, *and* RECIPES
Celebrating the Flavors of the Lone Star State

PHOTOS BY
Sandy Wilson

UNIVERSITY OF TEXAS PRESS 🐂 AUSTIN

The publication of this book was made
possible by the generous support of Ellen
and Ed Randall and is dedicated to David
Middleton and Edward Randall IV and
Michael Rohan, in grateful appreciation
for many memorable meals.

Copyright © 2014 by Terry Thompson-Anderson and Sandy Wilson
All rights reserved
Printed in China
First edition, 2014

Requests for permission to reproduce material from this work
should be sent to:
    Permissions
    University of Texas Press
    P.O. Box 7819
    Austin, TX 78713-7819
    http://utpress.utexas.edu/index.php/rp-form

♾ The paper used in this book meets the minimum requirements
of ANSI/NISO Z39.48-1992 (R1997) (Permanence of Paper).

LIBRARY OF CONGRESS CATALOGING-IN-PUBLICATION DATA

Thompson-Anderson, Terry, 1946–   author.
   Texas on the table : people, places, and recipes celebrating the
flavors of the Lone Star State / by Terry Thompson-Anderson ;
photos by Sandy Wilson. — First edition.
       pages   cm
   Includes index.
   ISBN 978-0-292-74409-7 (cl. : alk. paper)
1. Cooking, American—Southwestern style.   2. Cooking—Texas.
3. Terroir—Texas.   I. Wilson, Sandy, 1952–   illustrator.   II. Title.
   TX715.2.S69T558   2014
   641.5976—dc23
                                                    2013048386
doi:10.7560/744097

CONTENTS

ACKNOWLEDGMENTS

A WRITER FERVENTLY HOPES that each new book he or she writes is better than the last, as I do with this book. There have been so many, many people and events that led, over the years, to the writing of this book, and I have been shaped by each of them.

I am in debt to all of the many people who appear in the pages of this book. Many I have known for years and watched their progress in their particular agricultural endeavors. Others I met through this book and have been greatly touched by their stories. Thanks to all of you who took the time to tell those stories and make room in your busy schedules for Sandy to photograph you at work. I sincerely hope that we did you all justice.

My husband, Roger, has shared some of life's best things with me. He taught me how to fish and gave me a profound love and understanding of the waters and the creatures that dwell in them. He taught me how to grow things, opening a new world of flavor with his homegrown tomatoes and other vegetables and fruits. He introduced me to the incredible taste of a potato freshly dug from the black soil of his garden.

My sister, Sandy Wilson, has lent her enormous talents as a photographer to two of my books now, and her carefully studied images give life to my one-dimensional words. Her stunning food shots give the recipes a compelling vitality, and I am honored to work with her. Thanks to my brother-in-law, Steve Freeman, for muddling through Sandy's many absences as she traveled the great state of Texas shooting photos.

Marla Camp, the publisher of the incredible *Edible Austin* magazine, was invaluable in the writing of this book with her assistance in seeking out all the best artisan producers in Texas. Thanks to Marla, I have met so many dedicated, hardworking people who are trying to turn the tide of unsustainable food practices and provide good, healthy, and safe food for all of us.

I have enjoyed more than a few wonderful glasses and bottles of wine, and some great meals, with my friend Russ Kane, one of the best wine authorities I know, and his wife, Delia. Russ helped me choose those Texas wineries that we felt best represented the Texas wine industry and those that are forging new paths for the Texas wine industry.

Julie Hettiger, food stylist extraordinaire, has been a longtime friend, lending her tremendous talent to make my recipes jump off the pages in photographs. And a big thanks to Julie's husband, Ken Nelson, who patiently tolerated his home being turned into a commercial kitchen/photography studio for weeks at a time.

Doug Clark, my back-fence neighbor and fellow food and wine lover; his wife, Angie; and their children, Zack and Lainey, have been a godsend in the writing of this book. Not only did they taste and evaluate recipes but they fed my chickens and my persnickety cat when I had to travel to work on the book.

My profound thanks to Matt Weissler for making this book happen.

It takes an entire team to make a good book. Our editor at the University of Texas Press, Casey Kittrell, is the best. He pushed mercilessly to extract the very best work from me and was patient as I scoured my brain to deliver it. And thanks to the great design staff at UT Press for making this book so great.

I've saved some of the most important people for last. It indeed takes a big team to produce a book like this, most of them behind the scenes. I am grateful to the many women who cooked, chopped, sliced, minced, and diced, washed dishes, watched simmering pots, ran to the grocery store, and a million other things during the food photography weeks of this book.

TERRY THOMPSON-ANDERSON
Fredericksburg, Texas, 2013

A BOOK LIKE THIS cannot be undertaken without the support of more people than I ever imagined, and I am extremely grateful to each of them. There is our editor, Casey Kittrell of UT Press, without whom I would never have had the opportunity to share in all these experiences. I absolutely could not have done this project without my sister-author, Terry Thompson-Anderson, who managed to schedule access to all the many venues and people throughout this huge state with the least amount of driving possible and the help of food stylist Julie Hettiger.

There are literally hundreds of people throughout this great state of Texas without whose cooperation this book would not have been possible. They are the growers, producers, and restaurant and winery owners who let me follow them around, photographing them—often getting in their way. I have to single out Neal and Janice Newsom in Plains, who offered me a wonderful five-day window into the grape harvest in West Texas by letting me stay in their B&B and tag along through four days and nights of harvest.

Many people stepped forward to help with the food photography in Houston. My longtime assistant, Janet Lenzen, always came through to help when needed. My friend and pastry chef Yvonne Sternes cooked, tasted, and loaned her beautiful kitchen for an entire Thanksgiving meal; and my dear French friend Marie Noelle Garbey tirelessly chopped, diced, stirred, and washed dishes many days with us.

We also found along the way many helpers among Julie's colleagues: Sharon Kuhner, Mary Stork, Sherri Atlas, Sarah Darnielle, Cherri Gossett, Lucy Keeper, Kuhl Linscomb, Stacy Neal, Vicki Shafer, and Marian Tindall.

I am very grateful to my friends—Thelma Coles, Sue Heatly, Cynthia Jones Miller, among them—whose generosity provided not just a bed for the night but the comfort of shared food and conversation during my many days away from home. Thanks also to my neighbor Cindy Goldblatt for looking after my sweet dog, Lola, during my travels.

Special thanks go to my husband, Steve Freeman, who not only endured my prolonged absences but flew me back and forth in his plane, accompanying me for "just one more photo," saving me long hours on the roads of this vast state.

SANDY WILSON
Houston, Texas, 2013

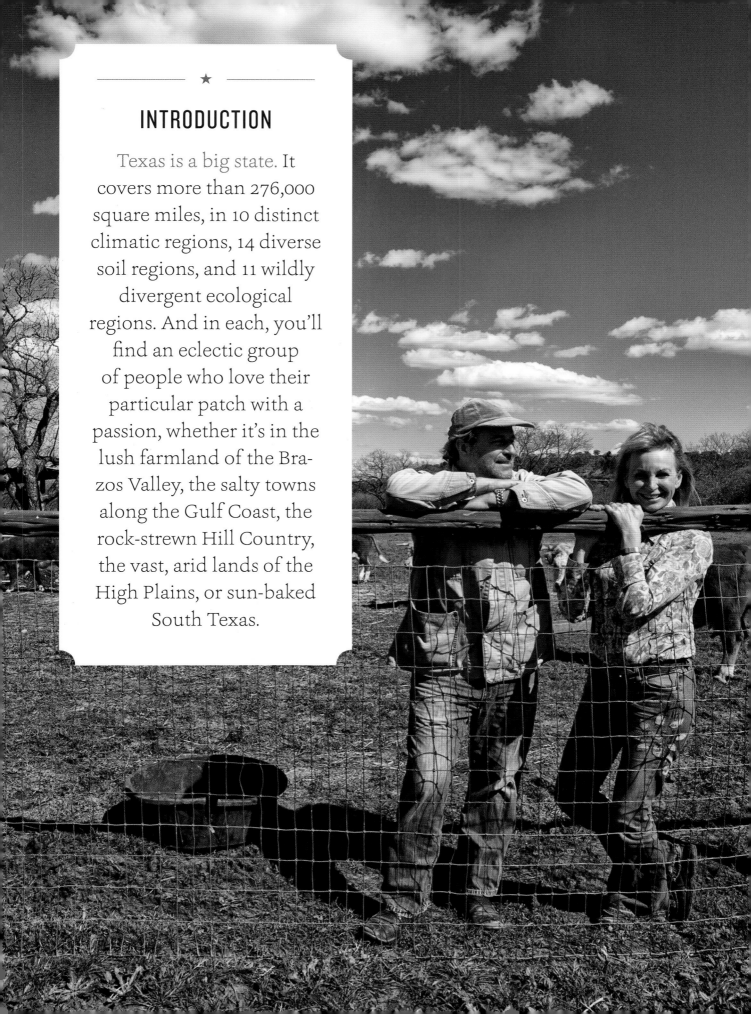

INTRODUCTION

Texas is a big state. It covers more than 276,000 square miles, in 10 distinct climatic regions, 14 diverse soil regions, and 11 wildly divergent ecological regions. And in each, you'll find an eclectic group of people who love their particular patch with a passion, whether it's in the lush farmland of the Brazos Valley, the salty towns along the Gulf Coast, the rock-strewn Hill Country, the vast, arid lands of the High Plains, or sun-baked South Texas.

It's a very exciting time to be cooking in Texas. This book offers up a collection of new and classic Texas recipes and tells the stories of the people—the farmers, ranchers, shrimpers, cheesemakers, winemakers, and chefs—who inspired so many of them and who are changing the taste of Texas food. It's all about *terroir*, a French term that originally applied to wine but has become more broadly used to describe "a taste of place." It refers to the scientific factors—climate, soil, and so on—that affect the way living things grow and thrive but also the cultural conditions that determine the unique flavor of the final product. Simply put, one of the things I discovered in writing this book is that the Texas terroir produces a taste like that nowhere else.

People in every state have begun to embrace the idea that locally grown food tastes better. The agriculturally inclined men and women of Texas have responded in kind (though in some cases they were there all along). In the Hill Country where dairy cows and goats range on green pastures, artisan cheesemakers collect milk from their herds to make a variety of exceptional cheeses. In and around the little town of Medina, a vital apple industry has grown up based on fruit from dwarf trees.

In South Texas, a thriving olive industry has taken root, with new orchards and tasty new varieties of olives being planted every year.

On the coast, oystermen have begun selling their catch by appellation, charging premium prices for oysters from the best reefs. This practice is allowing them to earn a decent living.

Humanely harvested game from Broken Arrow Ranch is sought by chefs from around the country, and local lamb, bison, rabbit, quail, and duck are now as likely as beef to be on the menu at the state's best restaurants.

One of the most exciting agricultural industries in Texas today is the wine business. There are almost 300 wineries, in all corners of the state. While the modern Texas wine industry is young compared with those of Europe and California, it's catching up fast. Viticulturalists and winemakers are experimenting with grapes from around the world, especially those native to the Mediterranean. Texas actually encompasses such a large area—equivalent to several of the wine-producing regions of the Mediterranean—that winemakers have the flexibility to produce a wide variety of wines and wine styles, from Spain's Tempranillo to Germany's Riesling. Grapes that originated in southern France, Spain, Portugal, Italy, and Sardinia are flourishing in the Texas heat and growing in abundant supply. For most winemakers, these are the grapes of the Texas wine industry's future.

Many wineries are creating great wines from native American grapes, with blanc du bois, which thrives in Texas, becoming increasing popular in producing many styles of wine, including Madeira. Hybrid grapes are being grown, too, a cross between European *Vitis vinifera* and native American grapes, such as chambourcin, Salado, Lenoir (or black Spanish, or Jacquez), and Cynthiana (or Norton). As the right grapes are being grown in the right conditions, we're starting to best competitors from other states and countries.

Thirty years ago no one would have believed that Texas might someday become known for its *wine*. But it certainly is a true statement today, and one that provides encouragement for the younger, but rapidly growing spirits movement in the state and the resurgence of the craft beer industry, which actually dates to the mid-1800s.

The wineries featured in this book are scattered throughout the various chapters. I consulted with the winemakers, asking them to pair their wines with recipes from the chapter in which their feature occurs or, in some instances, with dishes from other chapters that particularly begged for a wine from that winery. Wine pairing is an art, and one that is personal, so the pairings are merely suggestions or starting points rather than precise prescriptions to be followed to the letter.

The growth of the wine industry doesn't mean that Texas and Texans have given up beef. Or chili. Or even ruby red grapefruit or San Saba pecans. Far from it. The old foodways, from African American barbecues, to German-style sausage shops, to Mexican taco carts and Czech bakeries, are thriving still. The difference is that some of us now buy grass-fed beef for our chili. We shop for it—and most of the rest of our food—every week at our local farmers' market. And it tastes better.

Sandy and I traveled thousands of miles while researching this book. Some of the people you'll meet in these pages were old friends; others were strangers who welcomed us into their lives and work. They taught us how grasses and grains differ, and when a grape is ripe for harvest, or how to separate the curds from the whey.

Many of the places we visited are family-run, even multigenerational, farms or food businesses. Many were started by retirees or refugees from the corporate world, finally doing what they really want to do. It shows. These folks don't sell anything they don't put on their own tables. They don't take shortcuts. They treat their animals well. Many of their businesses are certified organic, an expensive and bureaucratic process. The hard part was trying to fit in as many as we could—there are many more. We hope you'll find them as inspiring as we did. What I learned in writing this book proves the time-honored adage that *what grows together, goes together*.

1

FINGER FOODS

and

FIRST COURSES

★

Finger foods fit the Texas lifestyle, where we "graze" at many social functions. The host or hostess will arrange small finger foods or dips around the party area, and folks just mosey leisurely around the room, selecting from the many delicious offerings, then move on to another dish and another conversation. Some dishes are served hot in a chafing dish or perhaps a Crock-Pot if it's a casual get-together. Others may be served cold or even in bowls over ice, like boiled, peeled shrimp with red cocktail sauce, long a Texas party favorite. Still others might be served at room temperature. But there's one common thread that you will encounter woven into finger foods at Texas parties that stems from the Mexican heritage of our foods. They all have a little zing of spice lurking inside. Sometimes it's quite subtle, kind of like a warm glow in the back of your throat after you swallow. But then, the spice can be quite an up-front hit, as in many of our beloved salsas and pico de gallo.

Often having friends over for dinner in Texas involves some dishes that will be cooked outside on the pit or grill and some cooked inside in the kitchen, so finger foods will simply be set out on the kitchen counters or island as some of the guests congregate in the kitchen. Outside, some good smoked sausage might be grilled up, sliced, and simply set out on a plate for those gathered around the grill to enjoy as the main course cooks slowly.

I experiment a lot with finger foods and often turn them into first courses for a seated meal by adding some garnishes or other flavor and/or texture elements. Some work fine as first courses just the way they are, only served on individual plates. Let the seasons dictate first courses. In the spring, you might serve first courses created from fresh vegetables and leafy greens and fresh berries. In the summer, first courses might contain fresh fruits and shrimp and crabmeat. In the fall and winter, Gulf oysters are at their salty best, so first courses at my house in the colder months will be a celebration of both raw and cooked oyster half-shell dishes or other cooked oyster dishes.

Salsa Chilo

A SIMPLE MEXICAN TABLE SALSA

I probably use this zesty, vibrant-tasting simple salsa as much as any other condiment. It will forever be named after my friend and fabulous chef Cecilio Solis, who created it. However, it makes a great flavor addition to many culinary creations that need a little jazz. Or just serve a bowl of it with your favorite corn tortilla chips.

MAKES 2 CUPS.

---

1 can (15 ounces) plum tomatoes and their juice

1 cup loosely packed cilantro tender top sprigs and leaves

2 large garlic cloves, peeled and trimmed

1½ tablespoons chopped chipotle chiles in adobo sauce

Kosher salt, to taste

Combine all ingredients in the container of a high-speed blender. Beginning on low, begin to puree the mixture, gradually increasing speed to high. Puree until very smooth. Refrigerate in a container with tight-fitting lid until ready to use.

Green Salsa

This salsa is definitely a seasonal summer dish, when green tomatoes are available. So don't be tempted to make it using red tomatoes. It won't be the same. Just get your fill of it in the summer!

MAKES ABOUT 4 TO 5 CUPS.

3 medium-sized green tomatoes, preferably homegrown, coarsely chopped

4 large tomatillos, husks removed and discarded, scrubbed well, and coarsely chopped

2 to 3 jalapeños, stems removed, coarsely chopped, including seeds, depending on desired level of heat

3 small garlic cloves, peeled and trimmed

3 medium-sized ripe Hass avocados, peeled, pitted, and cut into medium dice

6 large cilantro sprigs

1 tablespoon freshly squeezed lime juice

1 teaspoon kosher salt, or more

1½ cups sour cream

Good-quality white corn tortilla chips

Combine the green tomatoes, tomatillos, jalapeños, and garlic in a small, heavy-bottomed saucepan over medium-high heat. Bring the mixture to a boil—the tomatoes will provide the liquid—stirring often to prevent sticking. Reduce heat to a bare simmer and cook for 10 to 15 minutes, stirring frequently. The tomatoes and tomatillos will be completely broken down and pulpy. Remove from heat and set aside to cool.

Combine the green tomato mixture with the avocados, cilantro, lime juice, and salt in the work bowl of a food processor fitted with the steel blade. Process until smooth. Turn out into a bowl and whisk in the sour cream. Taste for salt, adjusting as desired, but remember that salt is nature's natural flavor enhancer. So if the salsa tastes a little flat, then add a bit more salt, and it should come to life. Refrigerate until ready to serve. Serve with corn tortilla chips.

Avocado-Tomatillo Guacamole

Nobody in Texas would dare have a major get-together without serving guacamole. This is my favorite recipe. It contains only the real nitty-gritty ingredients, and the taste is as clean and straightforward as a summer breeze on the upwind side of the corral. Serve with your favorite store-bought corn chips (my favorite brand is Tia Rosa), or make your own. (See recipe for Chorizo Con Queso Dip with Handmade Tortilla Chips on page 7.)

MAKES ABOUT 4 CUPS.

---

3 serrano chiles, seeds and veins removed, roughly chopped

½ cup firmly packed cilantro tender top stems and leaves, roughly chopped

1 small white onion, peeled and roughly chopped

8 ounces tomatillos, husked, well rinsed, and roughly chopped

3 ripe large Hass avocados, peeled, seeds removed, and cut into chunks

Kosher salt

Shredded iceberg lettuce and tomato wedges as garnish

Place the serrano chiles, cilantro sprigs, and onion in the work bowl of a food processor fitted with the steel blade. Process until the vegetables are pureed and smooth. Add the tomatillos and process until broken up into small bits. Add the avocado chunks and process to desired consistency. Some people like it really smooth, or you can leave some small chunks of the avocado. To leave chunks, use the pulse feature, pulsing until it looks the way you like it. Turn the mixture out into a bowl and add salt to taste. Don't be stingy with the salt, or your guacamole will have a flat, one-dimensional taste. The salt turns up the volume on the taste, bringing all of the component flavors to life.

An old trick for storing guacamole before serving is to place the seeds from the avocados on the surface of the mixture and push them in slightly. Cover tightly with plastic wrap and refrigerate until ready to serve. The seeds will prevent drastic color change for about 4 hours.

To serve, arrange the shredded lettuce in the center of a serving platter and turn the guacamole out onto the lettuce. Place tomato wedges around the edge of the guacamole as a garnish, if desired.

Chorizo con Queso Dip with Homemade Tortilla Chips

Like guacamole, don't even think about having a party in Texas without queso, or you might be mistaken for a Yankee. Don't try to fancy it up by using some gourmet variety of real cheese. It won't be Texas chile con queso if you do. Just use plain old pasteurized processed cheese—the kind that comes in rectangular blocks. Trust me, I am an ingredient purist, but I don't mess with a Texas tradition like chile con queso!

DIP:

6 ounces Mexican, bulk-style chorizo

1 pound pasteurized processed cheese

1 medium onion, chopped

1 large garlic clove, minced

2 teaspoons dark chili powder

1 can Ro-Tel Diced Tomatoes & Green Chilies

½ cup evaporated milk

Begin by cooking the chorizo. If you can only find links of chorizo, squeeze it out of the casings. Place the sausage in a nonstick skillet over medium-high heat. Cook, breaking up the sausage into small, crumbly bits with the back of a wooden spoon, until browned. The sausage will render a lot of fat as it cooks. Drain into a wire-mesh strainer, pressing down on the sausage to squeeze out as much fat as possible. Combine the sausage and all other dip ingredients in the top of a double boiler over simmering water. Cook, stirring often, until cheese has melted and mixture is creamy. Continue to cook for 20 more minutes.

Serve hot with tortilla chips. When I serve this dip at a "grazing" event, I will put it in a Crock-Pot if the event is informal, or a chafing dish if it's classier.

HOMEMADE TORTILLA CHIPS:

6-inch thin flour tortillas, cut into 6 wedges

Canola oil for deep-frying, heated to 350°F

Cut as many tortilla wedges as desired, but make enough for all of your guests to eat up that chile con queso. Fry the chips in batches, taking care not to crowd the oil. Cook just until they are crisp and light golden in color. Drain on absorbent paper towels set on a wire rack over a baking sheet. Lightly salt the chips and serve them warm. They're best eaten the same day they are fried.

A BRIEF HISTORY OF THE TEXAS WINE INDUSTRY

I<small>T'S HARD TO</small> live in Texas today and not be aware of the state's rapidly growing wine industry. As of 2012, the total number of wineries in Texas was climbing toward 300. With wine trails in every region of the state, there's a Texas wine for every taste.

Few realize that wines were being produced in Texas a good hundred years before the first grape grew in California. Most think that the industry began in the state in the mid-1970s. We've merely rekindled our love affair with the fruit of the vine that began when the Spanish padres first introduced winemaking about 1659 to what is now the El Paso area, when they established a mission there. As additional missions were founded, each friar brought cattle and sheep, wheat for making bread, and rootstock for planting vineyards to make sacramental wine. As European immigrants began to enter Texas, they established wineries in many regions of the state, using native mustang grapes to make their wines. German immigrants planted vineyards in the Hill Country. During the 1870s and 1880s, Italian immigrants established wineries in Bowie, Montague, and Nocona.

The most well known of the Italian winemakers was Frank Qualia, who emigrated from northern Italy and founded the Val Verde Winery in Del Rio in 1883. As of 1910, grapes were being produced in all but 29 of Texas's 254 counties. But the death knell for winemaking sounded in 1919 with the ratification of the Eighteenth Amendment to the US Constitution, prohibiting the manufacture, transport, and sale of alcoholic beverages in the entire country. Wineries across the state closed. Val Verde was the only winery that survived, by growing grapes for the table and for making jams and jellies, and by making wines for sacramental and medicinal purposes. Val Verde is the oldest winery in the state and is still run by the Qualia family, who kept the Texas history of viticulture alive.

In the 1970s, a new group of wine pioneers began to reestablish the wine industry in Texas,

including George Ray McEachern of Texas A&M University; Bobby Cox, who founded the Pheasant Ridge Vineyards in Lubbock in conjunction with the Texas A&M Agricultural Experiment Station; Bob Oberhellmann of Oberhellmann Vineyard, now known as Bell Mountain Winery, in Fredericksburg; Ed and Susan Auler of Fall Creek Vineyards; and Clinton (Doc) McPherson and Bob Reed, two Texas Tech professors who founded Llano Estacado Winery. The pair convinced several local cotton farmers that they could make more money by growing grapes on their land. They found investors and opened the first modern Texas winery. Soon their wines were winning awards and acclaim against wines from around the globe. Llano brought the first Double Gold Award to Texas for its 1984 Chardonnay at the prestigious 1986 San Francisco Fair wine competition. It was considered a major feat for the young industry.

Ed and Susan Auler took a trip to France in 1973 to buy cattle. Ed is the fifth generation to raise cattle on his family's Fall Creek Ranch. As Ed tells the story, the pair spent three days looking at cattle and two weeks visiting wineries. The couple noticed how similar the soil, terrain, and microclimate of France's famed wine regions were to those of their own ranch. They planted their first vineyard and produced a wine in 1979. The couple went on to experiment with varietals and finally concentrated on growing vinifera grapes, or old-world-style grapes. An attorney by trade, Ed Auler was responsible for getting several pieces of legislation passed in Texas that allowed the Texas wine industry to grow and flourish.

From its small beginning, the Texas wine industry has grown. In 2011, the industry brought $1.75 billion to the Texas economy and provided hundreds of jobs. There have been some casualties along the road, with many of the original wineries having gone out of business, but it has been a learning experience. There were varietals planted by the dozens that did not thrive in Texas and that did not make very good wine here. Slowly, the industry has begun to focus on the Mediterranean varietals that thrive in Texas and produce some great wines. The industry has also developed a number of good wines using native American and hybrid grapes such as Norton, blanc du bois, chambourcin, lamonto, and Lenoir, also sometimes called "black Spanish." These are grapes that grow and thrive in any region of the state and have proven to be disease resistant. Raymond Haak of Haak Winery and Vineyard has garnered both national and international attention for his wines made from native varietals, including an award-winning Madeira that he makes from both blanc du bois and Lenoir grapes—in Santa Fe, a mere 15 miles from the Gulf of Mexico, a location that scoffers said would never produce wine grapes.

The native American varietals owe their modern legacy to Thomas Volney Munson, a lifelong student of viticulture. Munson moved to Denison in 1876. He became interested in Texas while doing his master's thesis on the trees and forests of the state. An 1873 visit to a Texas vineyard began his interest in grape growing. Munson's experiments with grapes took him all over the United States. He gathered grape specimens and studied the soils and climates of the regions where they grew. He settled on a piece of property on the Red River, where he spent the rest of his life developing more than 300 wine grape varieties. He helped establish wineries across the southern United States and eventually founded a nursery, shipping rootstock around the country. He became the leading authority on native wild grapes in North America—sort of a Johnny Appleseed of grapes. Among those varietals were insect- and disease-resistant rootstocks that led to his most famous achievement.

In the 1860s, the French vineyards began to die. French scientists could find no cause and couldn't isolate the disease as it ravaged the famous old vineyards. Finally, a French professor of pharmacy isolated the culprit, a tiny louse that fatally

attacked the roots of the vines. He named it *Phylloxera vastatrix*, the "devastator." Hundreds of measures were tried to eradicate the pest, but to no avail.

In Texas, Munson began to experiment with grafting French rootstock onto his phylloxera-resistant native American rootstock, sharing his research with the French grape experts. In the 1880s and 1890s, French grape growers began to import Munson's Texas (and other) American rootstock, which they grafted onto their *Vitis vinifera* vines. The grafted vines thrived, and Munson was credited with saving the French wine industry.

It's an exciting time in Texas winemaking. Winemakers are producing stellar wines from obscure Mediterranean varietals that are thriving in Texas. As the industry moves forward, it is attracting a new breed of winemakers—young, industrious, and enthusiastic people who have studied the history of winemaking in Texas. Many are not folks who have retired from careers in other fields, with nest eggs in their pockets. These winemakers have chosen to live an agrarian lifestyle, fully informed of the pitfalls often associated with any type of farming endeavor. They are starting new wineries with a focus on the Mediterranean grapes that

their predecessors, through costly trial and error, have proven thrive best and produce the best wines in Texas. So they can concentrate on finding even more of those hot-weather varietals that are creating a unique niche for Texas wines. And they're making some outstanding blends using those varietals. It's a very promising sign for the future of the Texas wine industry, and one that will result in growth founded on the wisdom, tenacity, and errors of the industry pioneers.

Texas wines are attracting the attention of an increasing number of Texas chefs, who see great food-pairing possibilities with the wines and foods grown in Texas. It seems that the wine and culinary industries in Texas are beginning to work in harmony to make the enjoyment of Texas wine *with* Texas food a fully rounded experience, proving that what grows together goes together. In Fredericksburg, chef Ross Burtwell went out on a limb and changed his wine list to an all-Texas list, then created new menu offerings of Texas-sourced foods to pair with the wines. Although he didn't know what the public reaction would be, his wine sales have steadily increased. Today, Ross's Cabernet Grill is a destination for those wanting to try his totally Texas menu.

Romano Cheese and Pepita Spread

Pepitas, or pumpkin seeds, are an ingredient widely used in Mexican cooking. They have also crossed into many of the dishes that would be considered purely *Texan*. The seeds have a unique, woodsy kind of flavor with a hint of nuttiness that results in a really great little flavor combination with the Romano cheese in this spread. It's a perfect party dish, and I've also spread it on French bread as an accompaniment to simple salads.

MAKES ABOUT 1 QUART OF SPREAD.

2 large jalapeños, seeds and veins removed, roughly chopped

1½ cups grated Pecorino Romano cheese

½ cup toasted pepitas (pumpkin seeds)

1 cup firmly packed cilantro leaves and tender top stems

⅓ cup sour cream

1½ cups mayonesa (lime-flavored mayonnaise)

1 tablespoon fresh lemon juice

¼ teaspoon kosher salt

¾ teaspoon cayenne

French bread rounds, sliced about ½-inch thick

Combine all ingredients, except French bread rounds, in the work bowl of a food processor and process until smooth. Refrigerate. Serve at room temperature with French bread rounds for spreading.

CKC FARMS

ALTHOUGH I HAVE NO research to back it up, I feel confident in saying that Chrissy Omo was the youngest person in Texas to start a commercial cheesemaking operation. Chrissy was just 15 when her family moved from San Antonio to a rural home outside the sleepy little Hill Country town of Blanco. Her parents urged her to do what the Blanco kids did, so she joined the Ag kids and raised two Boer wether goats to show at the county fair. She won Grand Reserve for Ozzy, one of her goats. Most of the other kids "floored" their goats after the competition, but Chrissy had become way too emotionally attached to them. So Ozzy and his pal went home with the family, where they lived out the rest of their days munching on grass and getting daily doses of love.

During a family vacation to Italy in 2004, Chrissy got her first taste of fresh Italian goat cheese curd. "My goodness. We were all in heaven. I'll never forget the taste of that cheese or that little farm," Chrissy recalled. She talked to more Italian farmers, who showed her the basic steps to making the fresh cheeses, as language barriers would allow.

When the family returned home, Chrissy went to work for Sara Bolton at Pure Luck to learn what running a dairy really entailed. With her parents' approval, Chrissy withdrew money from her college fund to purchase seven pregnant does. The family built a commercial cheesemaking facility on the property, and Chrissy named the operation after herself (C), and her two brothers, Kenny (K), and Conner (C), both of whom work in the operation.

The family agreed at the beginning of the operation that it would be run as a business and that its profits would pay for Chrissy to go to college. In the spring of 2012, she graduated from Texas State University in San Marcos, thanks, she says, to her wonderful goats.

Herb-Baked Texas Goat Feta with Garlic, Olives, and Almonds

This quick and easy recipe makes a delicious snack when friends drop by for a glass of wine and conversation. It also makes a nice communal first course for a meal. Chrissy Omo's CKC Farms goat feta is especially good in the dish, as its rich, tangy flavor blends with the assertiveness of the garlic and bold-flavored herbs.

SERVES 6 TO 8.

8 ounces CKC Farms Texas goat feta cheese, cut into ½-inch cubes

16 pitted kalamata olives, roughly chopped

¼ cup whole, skin-on, sliced almonds

5 large garlic cloves, peeled and sliced thin

1 cup Texas extra-virgin olive oil

1 teaspoon minced fresh rosemary

1 teaspoon minced fresh thyme

1 tablespoon minced flat-leaf parsley

1¼ teaspoons freshly ground black pepper

Kosher salt

French baguette, sliced into rounds ½-inch thick

Preheat oven to 425°F. Spread the cheese cubes around an ovenproof 8- to 10-inch oval gratin dish. Scatter the olives, almonds, and garlic around the dish. In a medium-sized bowl, combine the olive oil, rosemary, thyme, parsley, and pepper; whisk to blend well and flavor the oil. Pour the oil mixture evenly over the cheese. Scatter a little salt over the top. Place dish in preheated oven and bake for about 15 minutes, or until cheese is very lightly browned and oil is bubbling. Let mixture cool for about 5 to 6 minutes before serving. Serve with a basket of baguette slices and a spoon for spreading the cheese and herbs and moistening the bread with the flavorful oil.

Queso Blanco with Pebre Sauce and Warm Tortillas

Queso blanco is a tangy white Mexican cheese that's known as the "frying cheese." It's usually seared on an oiled comal or flat griddle over fairly high heat, then eaten as a snack. It also makes a nice lagniappe, Cajun for "a little something extra," on the side of a salad, with a bowl of soup, or on a Tex-Mex combo plate. The Mozzarella Company in Dallas makes one of the best queso blanco cheeses. It browns nicely without melting, and the flavor is really incredible. It makes a very popular finger food when served with warm corn tortillas and a Latino-style pebre sauce, which resembles chimichurri sauce. Be sure to serve the pebre the same day that it's made, as it tends to get soggy and the flavor wanes by the next day.

SERVES 10 AS FINGER FOOD.

CHEESE:

1 pound (2 rounds) Mozzarella Company queso blanco, cut into small wedges

Olive oil to grease comal or flat griddle

20 to 25 warm white corn tortillas

PEBRE SAUCE:

MAKES ABOUT 2 CUPS.

1 cup peeled, seeded, and diced homegrown or heirloom tomatoes

¼ cup finely chopped fresh cilantro leaves

1 cup finely chopped flat-leaf parsley

2 teaspoons Texas extra-virgin olive oil

1 teaspoon minced garlic

1 teaspoon red wine vinegar

1 teaspoon freshly squeezed lime juice

2 serrano chiles, seeds and veins removed, minced

1 green onion, finely chopped

Kosher salt and freshly ground black pepper

Make the pebre sauce by combining all ingredients in a bowl and stirring to blend. If not serving right away, store it in the refrigerator tightly covered.

To fry the cheese, liberally oil a comal or flat griddle with olive oil over medium-high heat. When the comal is quite hot, lay the cheese slices in a single layer in the sizzling oil. Cook until caramelized to a rich golden brown, about 2 to 3 minutes; then flip the slices and brown the other side. Serve in a shallow casserole dish alongside a bowl of the pebre sauce and the tortilla warmer filled with warmed corn tortillas. To heat the tortillas, stack them in the tortilla warmer and microwave on high for about 1½ minutes.

Spicy Boiled Shrimp with Jalapeño Remoulade

Chilled boiled shrimp is a time-honored dish to serve at Texas parties—and why not, since Texas is among the top three shrimp-producing states, along with our neighbor, Louisiana, and Alaska. Boiled shrimp are generally served with a red cocktail sauce, but here I've paired them with a Texanized version of remoulade sauce laced with jalapeños.

SERVES 8 TO 10.

SHRIMP:

¼ cup cayenne

⅓ cup kosher salt

3 large lemons, quartered

1 onion, peeled and roughly chopped

2½ pounds large (16 to 20 count) shrimp, peeled and deveined, with tail sections left intact

Large bowl of ice water (with ice) and ½ cup kosher salt or fine sea salt

Shredded romaine lettuce, if serving as a first course

JALAPEÑO REMOULADE:

2 large garlic cloves, peeled and trimmed

3 tablespoons minced flat-leaf parsley

2 large jalapeños, roughly chopped

2 teaspoons minced lemon zest

2 anchovy fillets, minced

2 tablespoons ketchup (made without high-fructose corn syrup)

1 tablespoon whole-grain mustard

1 teaspoon champagne vinaigrette

2 tablespoons dry sherry

1 cup real mayonnaise, preferably homemade

½ teaspoon kosher salt

1 teaspoon freshly ground black pepper

Additional minced parsley as garnish

Begin by boiling the shrimp. Fill a heavy-bottomed 8-quart soup pot ⅔ full of water. Add the cayenne, salt, lemons, and onion. Bring to a boil, then lower heat and simmer for about 25 minutes to develop a bold, spicy court bouillon. Be sure to turn on the vent hood over your stove, as the mixture is quite spicy and tends to cause sneezing! Add the shrimp and stir to mix them into the broth. Cook just until the shrimp turn a rich coral-pink color, about 3 to 5 minutes. Drain into a colander, then immediately plunge the shrimp into the salted ice water to stop the cooking process. (The salted water also sweetens up the taste of the shrimp.) When shrimp are completely chilled, drain them, pat them dry using absorbent paper towels and refrigerate until ready to serve.

To make the jalapeño remoulade, place the steel blade in the work bowl of a food processor. With processor running, drop the garlic cloves through the feed tube to mince. Stop and scrape down the sides of the bowl. Add all remaining ingredients and process until smooth and well blended. Turn out into a bowl, cover tightly, and refrigerate until chilled.

To serve, fill the bottom of a large decorative bowl with ice. Cover the ice with plastic wrap. Transfer the jalapeño remoulade to a serving bowl and nest it in the center of the large bowl in the ice. Garnish the dip with a scattering of minced parsley. Scatter the boiled shrimp on the ice around the bowl of sauce and serve at once.

To serve as a first course, line large, stemmed margarita-style glasses or martini glasses with some of the shredded romaine lettuce. Place a generous dollop of the sauce in the center, and arrange the boiled shrimp around the rim of the glass with the tail sections on the outside of the glass.

Kitchen Pride Braised Mushrooms with Garlic and Olives

This is one of my favorite spring and summer finger foods. Lots of bright, fresh tastes skipping around in this dish! If you want to serve the dish as a communal party food, then simply do the marinating in an attractive shallow casserole dish and serve it in the same dish with a basket of thin-sliced baguettes alongside. Sometimes I like to serve it in tiny ramekins as a side dish to a luncheon entrée. Then I usually just put a couple of the baguette slices in the ramekin. Either way, it's a welcome and refreshing little nibble. The dish can be cooked and assembled up to 3 days ahead of time, then refrigerated. Bring to room temperature before serving.

SERVES 10 AS FINGER FOOD.

Braised Mushrooms (recipe follows)
½ pound mixed pitted olives, such as picholine, arbequina, kalamata, and oil-cured, or others of your choosing
Herb-Roasted Garlic (recipe follows)
2 teaspoons minced fresh basil leaves
1 tablespoon fresh rosemary leaves, whole

3 fresh thyme sprigs
2 tablespoons minced flat-leaf parsley
1 teaspoon crushed red pepper flakes
¼ cup good-quality red wine vinegar
1 cup Texas extra-virgin olive oil
½ teaspoon freshly ground black pepper
Kosher salt
Thin slices of French baguettes

BRAISED MUSHROOMS:

1 teaspoon whole black peppercorns

2 large fresh bay leaves

½ teaspoon crushed fennel seeds

1 teaspoon toasted whole coriander
seeds

2 cups water

¼ cup Texas extra-virgin olive oil

Grated zest of 1 large lemon

3 tablespoons freshly squeezed
lemon juice

½ pound small white mushrooms,
whole, or quartered if you can't
find small ones

½ pound Texas Pride crimini, or
baby bella, mushrooms, whole,
or quartered if you can't find
small ones

HERB-ROASTED GARLIC:

3 heads garlic

1 cup Texas extra-virgin olive oil

1 tablespoon minced fresh basil leaves

1 tablespoon minced fresh rosemary

Kosher salt and freshly ground black
pepper

Begin by braising the mushrooms. Tie the spices in a square of cheesecloth, securing with cotton twine. Place the bag in a heavy-bottomed 4-quart pot and add the water, olive oil, lemon zest, and lemon juice. Bring to a boil over medium-high heat; then reduce heat to medium low and simmer, covered, for 15 minutes to make a flavorful court bouillon. Add the mushrooms, stirring well. Cook, covered, for about 10 minutes, or just until mushrooms are tender. Drain and set aside until cool. Discard spices.

Roast the garlic. Preheat oven to 350°F. Cut the top ½ inch off each garlic head to expose the cloves. Place the garlic in a small casserole dish with shallow sides. Drizzle the olive oil over the garlic. Scatter each head with a portion of the herbs; season liberally with salt and pepper. Cover tightly with foil and roast in preheated oven for 30 to 45 minutes, or until the garlic cloves are browned and tender. Remove from oven and set aside until garlic is cool enough to handle. When garlic has cooled, separate the cloves and squeeze gently to remove the garlic cloves without smashing them. Set aside.

Combine the braised mushrooms, olives, and roasted garlic cloves in a shallow dish. In a separate dish, combine the fresh basil, rosemary leaves, thyme sprigs, chopped parsley, red pepper flakes, and red wine vinegar. Whisk to blend well, then drizzle in the olive oil as you whisk, until all is incorporated. Season to taste with salt and black pepper and pour over the mushroom mixture. Cover and refrigerate at least 6 hours, or overnight, before serving. Serve at room temperature with picks and thin rounds of French bread.

MARFA MAID DAIRY

ARFA MAID, a dairy owned by Allan McClane and Malinda Beeman, is located in Antelope Hills, two miles east of Marfa in the Big Bend country of West Texas. It is the only Grade A goat's milk dairy in the region. Although the dairy has been licensed only since 2010, its goat cheese products have become staples with cheese connoisseurs, caterers, specialty markets like the Get-Go in Marfa, and restaurants in the Big Bend area.

Marfa Maid cheeses have a sweet and clean-tasting flavor that the couple attributes to making the cheese right after the goats are milked. The animals also have an excellent diet of local alfalfa, grass, and grains. Herbs used to flavor their cheese spreads are grown organically on the property, as is the lavender used in their "herbs de Provence" spice mix.

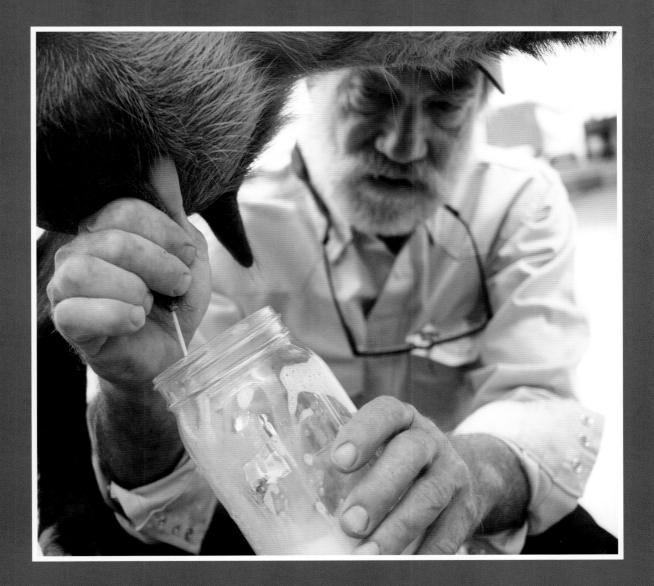

Pickled Red Onions

Pickled red onions, which are widely used in Mexican cuisine, are a favorite condiment in Texas cooking as well. They can be served with barbecued and grilled meats, on tacos, on chalupas, or wherever you'd like to enjoy their taste. People pile them on anything or just eat them with their fingers. I always had trouble with the red onion's color bleaching out from the vinegar until I learned a trick from Austin's legendary chef Miguel Ravago of Fonda San Miguel. Miguel slices a red beet into the original marinade, which preserves the color of the red onions. (Actually, they look better than their original color!) The onions will last for about a month in a tightly sealed container, like a French canning jar, in the refrigerator—but they're never around that long at my house!

MAKES ABOUT 1½ CUPS.

1 large red onion, peeled and sliced into very thin rings, using a mandoline or other type of slicing box

2 cups red wine vinegar

1 tablespoon sugar

1 teaspoon whole cumin seeds

1 dried chile de arbol

3 large garlic cloves, sliced

1½ teaspoons kosher salt

2 teaspoons whole black peppercorns

1 fresh red beet, peeled and sliced

Place the sliced red onion in a saucepan and add cold water to cover. Bring to a full boil over high heat, then remove immediately from heat and drain. Shake out all of the water and place the onions in a single layer in a baking dish; set aside.

Combine all remaining ingredients, except the sliced beet, in a saucepan. Bring to a boil, then lower heat and simmer for about 10 minutes.

Add the sliced beet to the baking dish with the sliced onion. Strain the vinegar mixture into the baking dish, covering the onions and beet slices. Discard solids from strainer. Set aside at room temperature for 2 hours, then remove and discard the beet slices. When the onions are cool, store them in a tightly sealed container in the refrigerator. Serve at room temperature.

Texas Goat Cheese with Sun-Dried Tomato Relish and Cayenne Toasts

This relish can be made in advance and stored up to a week in the refrigerator. In fact, it tastes better when made at least a day ahead of time, allowing time for the flavors to blend together well. The cayenne toasts can also be made in advance and stored in zip-sealing bags or frozen. If you freeze them, crisp them up in a 350°F oven for about 5 minutes before serving. A warning: they're addictive, albeit somewhat spicy.

MAKES ABOUT 30 FINGER-FOOD SERVINGS.

8 ounces plain goat cheese

SUN-DRIED TOMATO RELISH:
1 jar (8 ounces) oil-packed sun-dried
    tomatoes and their oil
1 cup Texas extra-virgin olive oil
½ cup (loosely packed) fresh basil
    leaves
½ cup sliced ripe olives
¼ cup (loosely packed) flat-leaf parsley
2 large garlic cloves, peeled
½ teaspoon kosher salt
½ teaspoon sugar
2 green onions, coarsely chopped,
    including green tops

CAYENNE TOASTS:
1 French-style baguette loaf, sliced
    into rounds ¼-inch thick
1½ cups Texas extra-virgin olive oil
2 teaspoons cayenne
1½ teaspoons kosher salt
2 teaspoons sugar
1½ teaspoons finely ground black
    pepper
1½ teaspoons paprika
1½ teaspoons granulated garlic
1½ teaspoons onion powder
1 teaspoon dried leaf oregano

Make the tomato relish first. Combine all ingredients except goat cheese in the work bowl of a food processor fitted with the steel blade and process until all ingredients are minced. You'll get the best results by using the pulse feature on the processor, pulsing until you get the right consistency. It should not be totally pureed but should not have large chunks of ingredients. Refrigerate until ready to serve.

To make the toasts, preheat oven to 250°F. Lay the bread slices on baking sheets; set aside. Combine remaining ingredients in a small bowl and whisk to blend well. Using a pastry brush, paint one side of each bread round with the oil mixture. Rewhisk the oil often, as the seasonings have a tendency to settle to the bottom. Place baking sheets in preheated oven and cook for about 45 minutes, or until toasts are dry and crisp. Cool on wire racks. When toasts are completely cool, store in zip-sealing bags if not serving right away.

To serve, place the goat cheese in a shallow bowl and pour the tomato relish over the top. Serve with a spreading knife and a basket of the cayenne toasts.

RED CABOOSE WINERY AND VINEYARD

THE RED CABOOSE VINEYARD in Meridian sits at the upper reaches of the Texas Hill Country on limestone rock. "There's very little soil in which to plant the vines," explains Evan McKibben, winemaker and vineyard manager. "We use a rock saw to cut grooves in the rock about 32 inches deep, then backfill with the rock debris and plant the vines." The McKibbens laughingly remember when they first started digging the vineyard. "The locals thought we were crazy. We understand that they were betting as to whether or not we'd make it," recalls owner Gary McKibben (Evan's father).

The winemaking philosophy at Red Caboose is old school. "Our wines are similar to those you might have experienced in the 1700s," explains Evan. "Our reds are unfiltered and oaked in American oak barrels for 12 to 24 months, depending on what we want to achieve with a particular wine."

The winery itself, however, is new school. Gary McKibben has advocated sustainability at his architectural firm in Dallas since the 1970s, long before green practices became widespread. He designed the winery, which utilizes geothermal energy for heating and cooling and for cold stabilization of their white wines. Solar panels generate electricity, and rainwater collection tanks gather as much as 19,000 gallons of water to irrigate the vineyard.

Pair the Red Caboose Tempranillo with the Spanish Chorizo in Tempranillo Broth (page 30). With its smoky nose and flavor, this wine exhibits wonderful mineral notes from the limestone rock in which it's planted. The Red Caboose Lenoir/Tempranillo blend, one of the winery's most distinctive wines, is also a very good match to the dish.

The Texas Goat Cheese with Sun-Dried Tomato Relish and Cayenne Toasts (page 23) is quite nice served with the Red Caboose Viognier. The wine combines a fruity nose and the characteristic dry white flavors of this grape. The wine holds its own with the strong taste of the goat cheese, while enhancing the tomato relish flavors.

MILL-KING MARKET AND CREAMERY

THE MILL-KING MARKET AND CREAMERY is operated by three generations of the Miller family in the small town of McGregor, just west of Waco. It's a bucolic setting with the family's small, whitewashed farm store and cows grazing lazily in the lush grass. And the operation is truly a family enterprise, with all family members living on or around the dairy.

Mill-King Market and Creamery produces a number of incredibly good cheeses, including Asiago, Manchego, Cheddar, Mexican mozzarella, fromage blanc, and a variety of flavored cheese curds. The creamery also produces quark, a soft, fresh, white unaged cheese that is used extensively in Germany in baking and in dessert making. I've used quark in some pastries with wonderful, tasty results.

Vaudeville Bistro's Crispy Heirloom Tomato with Wild Boar Rillettes, Herb Salad, and Gazpacho Sorbet

The Texas Hill Country has experienced an influx of talented young chefs who have been lured to the scenic area by both the rising bar of culinary awareness and, well, the scenery. Jordan Muraglia, a Denver, Colorado, native, is one of those chefs. His family acquired a ranch outside Fredericksburg, and Jordan couldn't pass up the opportunity to be in close proximity to such a plethora of all-natural agricultural products. So he and his partner, Richard Boprae, moved to Fredericksburg and opened their own home accessory/design center/bistro on the town's bustling Main Street. They named it Vaudeville, and it was an instant success.

This dish has great eye appeal, with a fusion of flavors and textures, cooked and uncooked, hot and cold. Jordan says the dish is a testament to his version of the Hill Country experience. The dish is component driven, pulling from his own garden and utilizing local game. The various parts of the dish can also be well matched in many other applications. The wild boar rillettes are perfect to set out with some grilled bread and pickled cherries for a casual appetizer or on a charcuterie board. They can also be fried with sweet potatoes in a Sunday-morning hash and topped with a poached egg. The gazpacho sorbet is amazing on a lump crabmeat salad or shaken with vodka for a gazpacho martini that is sure to replace your Bloody Mary habit! The crispy heirloom tomato really goes with just about anything and can even replace a hamburger patty for a vegetarian sandwich. Or it can replace a plain tomato slice *on* the hamburger. Great components make great dishes!

SERVES 10.

WILD BOAR RILLETTES:

1 wild boar shoulder, about 5 to 6 pounds (Jordan uses Broken Arrow Ranch)

6 whole garlic heads, cut in half horizontally

10 sprigs fresh thyme

2 tablespoons freshly ground black pepper

¼ cup kosher salt

2 cups rendered duck fat

2 tablespoons bacon fat

GAZPACHO SORBET:

1 cucumber

1 onion

4 ripe tomatoes

1 red bell pepper

1 garlic clove

Juice of 1 lemon

1 tablespoon Texas extra-virgin
   olive oil

1 teaspoon fine sea salt

1 teaspoon champagne vinegar

1 teaspoon agave nectar

½ cup water (or more if you
   are using a blender)

CRISPY HEIRLOOM TOMATO:

2 cups panko bread crumbs

Zest of one lemon

¼ cup chopped flat-leaf parsley

2 tablespoons minced fresh thyme
   (about 8 large sprigs)

3 tablespoons plus 1 tablespoon
   Texas extra-virgin olive oil, divided

2 teaspoons freshly ground black
   pepper

2 teaspoons fine sea salt

5 medium-sized heirloom tomatoes

HERB SALAD:

Leaves from 1 head of celery

Small fresh basil leaves

Fresh chives

Fresh tarragon

Texas extra-virgin olive oil for drizzling

Freshly ground black pepper

Begin by making the wild boar rillettes. Cut the boar shoulder into 3-inch cubes and place in a bowl with the garlic cloves and thyme. Place in the refrigerator for 1 to 3 days, stirring often. Remove from refrigerator and rub the meat with the salt and pepper. Preheat oven to 300°F. Place the meat mixture and fat in a shallow pot or baking dish (cast iron works very well) and cover. Cook the boar in preheated oven for approximately 4 hours, or until the meat is tender and will shred easily. Cool to room temperature in the fat. When meat has cooled, strain the fat through a fine strainer, reserving it for another use. Reserve 8 ounces of the fat. (You can use the remaining fat to make duck confit, to fry potatoes or eggs, or to make biscuits. Duck fat is amazing and delicious.) Shred the boar meat and cover with the reserved duck and bacon fat, which will preserve the meat—the original intention of this technique. Refrigerate while preparing the other components.

Make the gazpacho sorbet. Start by peeling and roughly chopping the cucumber. Chop the rest of the fruits and vegetables into the same-sized pieces. For this gazpacho Jordan uses a juicer, or you can use a high-speed blender, but remember to add a bit more water. Process all of the fruits and vegetables through the juicer or blender, and then add the rest of the ingredients. Add water as needed until it blends easily. Taste and adjust seasoning as desired. Pour the gazpacho into ice-cube trays and freeze until solid. To finish the sorbet, place the frozen ice cubes in the food processor, adding lemon juice if needed to loosen them. Blend until smooth, then pour into a storage container, cover tightly, and place back in the freezer. Remove the sorbet 5 minutes before you will arrange the plates.

To make the crispy heirloom tomatoes, combine all of the ingredients, except tomatoes, reserving 1 tablespoon of the olive oil and 1 teaspoon each of the salt and pepper. Pulse until well blended. Transfer the panko mixture to a shallow pan; set aside. Slice the tomatoes ¾-inch thick and lay the tomato slices flat in the panko mixture, pressing down gently to be sure they are well coated. Only one side of the tomato will be breaded. Place an empty nonstick skillet over medium-high heat 10 minutes before you are ready to fry the tomatoes. When it begins to smoke, add the remaining tablespoon of olive oil. Fry the tomatoes quickly, breaded sides down, in the olive oil. This should take only 30 seconds to reach the desired golden brown crispness. Remove quickly from the pan; flip the tomatoes so that the breaded sides are up when assembling the dish.

Make the herb salad. Jordan uses the listed herbs because he always has them on hand, but you can use any leafy herbs you wish to create the salad. Just be sure that you include celery leaves in the mix to prevent the herb flavors from being overpowering. Trim the celery leaves from the stalks and put them in an ice bath. Pull the small basil leaves from the stems. Chop the chives into pieces ½-inch long. If you have chive flowers, they are also wonderful to use in this salad. Remove the tarragon leaves from the stems. Toss the herbs together; set aside.

To assemble the dish, roll the rillettes into ten 1½- to 2-ounce balls (Jordan uses a medium-sized ice-cream scoop to consistently portion the balls). There will be enough rillettes left for another use. Sear the rillettes in a smoking-hot cast-iron skillet. You don't need to add oil to the pan, as residual fat will render from the rillettes. Press down on the rillettes to create patties. Brown the rillettes on both sides, turning once; then remove from pan and set aside to keep warm. Sear the tomatoes in the hot olive oil.

Place the tomatoes, breaded sides up, in the center of individual plates. Top each with a rillette patty, followed by a little nest of the salad. Place a small scoop of the sorbet on top of each serving. Drizzle the plate with a good-quality extra-virgin olive oil and grind a bit of black pepper on top. This is definitely a dish your guests won't forget!

Spanish Chorizo in Tempranillo Broth

Leslie Horne, the charcuterie genius who created Aurelia's Authentic Spanish Chorizo, has become a dear friend. Her chorizo is truly so authentic and such a savory delight to my palate that I never tire of using it in new and different ways from breakfast through dinner. This preparation is a traditional Spanish-style tapas dish, but, of course, Texas Tempranillo reflects the taste of our Texas dirt, or terroir, giving the dish a true taste of Texas. Not that Tempranillo from Spain's Rioja isn't quite good also; it just lacks that very characteristic minerality inherent in Texas wines. This dish is very quick and easy to prepare, but the flavor will wow your guests. I like to serve the dish with a basket of rustic bread slices and the excellent artisan Manchego cheese produced by Mill-King Market and Creamery in McGregor.

SERVES 10 AS FINGER FOOD.

2 tablespoons Texas extra-virgin olive oil
1 package (3 links) Aurelia's Authentic Spanish Chorizo
12 large garlic cloves, peeled and sliced thin

1 bottle Texas Tempranillo wine
6 fresh bay leaves
½ teaspoon cayenne
Rustic bread slices
Manchego cheese

Heat the olive oil in a heavy-bottomed skillet over medium heat. When the oil is hot, add the chorizo links. Cook, turning often, for about 5 minutes to render some of the fat. Add the sliced garlic and cook just until the garlic is very lightly golden in color, about 3 minutes. Carefully drain the fat from the skillet, taking care not to pour out any of the garlic. Return the pan to medium-high heat and pour in the Tempranillo, stirring to scrape any browned bits from the bottom of the pan. Add the bay leaves and cayenne. Reduce heat to medium, cover the pan, and simmer for about 15 minutes, or until the chorizo have plumped. Uncover the pan and remove from heat; allow to sit for about 5 minutes.

Remove the chorizo from the skillet, retaining the broth and garlic, and cut the links on the bias into slices ¼-inch thick. Return the sliced chorizo to the broth in the skillet; simmer on low heat for 5 minutes.

To serve, use a slotted spoon to transfer the chorizo and garlic into a shallow serving dish. Pour enough of the broth over the chorizo just to cover the slices. Serve with cocktail picks, a basket of rustic bread slices, and Manchego cheese—the perfect Spanish tapa!

Boiled Texas Shrimp and Blue Crabmeat with Chipotle and Cucumber Dip

The classic shrimp cocktail as we all know it—the one served with a red, ketchup-based sauce—still shows up on an occasional menu or in some version at parties where delectable boiled Texas Gulf shrimp are piled around bowls of the sauce on platters. And it's still a favorite. I developed this version, combining Texas Gulf shrimp and succulent lump blue crabmeat with a unique sauce that plays the zesty heat of chipotle chiles off the cool, refreshing meat of cucumbers, with a spike of capers, as an alternative. It's become my updated version of the old standby.

SERVES 6 AS A FIRST COURSE.

----

2 pounds peeled and deveined large (16 to 20 count) Texas Gulf brown shrimp, boiled and chilled (recipe follows)

1½ pounds jumbo lump Texas blue crab meat, well chilled (purchase from seafood market)

Chipotle and Cucumber Dip (recipe follows)

Shredded romaine lettuce

Lemon wedges and curly parsley sprigs as garnish

BOILED SHRIMP:

1 package (3 ounces) crab and shrimp boil

3 lemons, cut into quarters

3 bay leaves

2 tablespoons cayenne

1 cup kosher salt, divided

2 tablespoons whole black peppercorns

4 gallons water, divided

2 quarts ice cubes

CUCUMBER AND CHIPOTLE DIP:
MAKES ABOUT 2 CUPS.

2 to 3 canned chipotle chiles in adobo sauce, or more, depending on desired heat level

1 tablespoon adobo sauce from the chiles

1 medium-sized cucumber, peeled, pulp and seeds removed, roughly chopped

1½ cups sour cream

¼ cup minced fresh cilantro

3 tablespoons freshly squeezed lime juice

2 tablespoons well-drained capers

Kosher salt

Begin by making the cucumber and chipotle dip. Combine all ingredients except capers and salt in the work bowl of a food processor fitted with the steel blade; process until smooth. Turn out into a bowl and stir in capers; add salt to taste. Refrigerate, covered, until ready to use.

Boil the shrimp. Combine crab and shrimp boil, lemons, bay leaves, cayenne, ½ cup of the salt, peppercorns, and 2 gallons of the water in a heavy-bottomed 12-quart pot over high heat. Bring to a swift, rolling boil, then reduce heat to medium and simmer for about 20 minutes to make a spicy court bouillon. While the court bouillon is simmering, place the remaining 2 gallons of water in a large bowl and add the salt. Stir to dissolve salt, then add the ice cubes; set aside. Bring the court bouillon back to a full boil and add the shrimp, stirring them down into the broth quickly. Cook just until all shrimp turn a rich coral-pink, about 3 minutes. Drain immediately, shaking to expel the hot water. Quickly plunge the shrimp into the salted ice water, stirring them around to submerge them. Let stand until shrimp are completely chilled, about 10 minutes. Drain and refrigerate until ready to serve.

Serve in short, footed cocktail glasses or the large margarita "bowl"-type stemmed glasses. Line the glasses with shredded romaine and spoon a generous portion of the dip in the center of each glass. Mound ½ cup of the crabmeat on the dip in each glass. Arrange the shrimp around the rim of the glass. Garnish each serving with a lemon wedge and parsley sprig. Serve well chilled.

KITCHEN PRIDE MUSHROOMS

In the early 1970s, Darrell McLain went to work for a large multinational company that was in a period of diversification. The company wanted to build a division to provide fresh mushrooms to markets at a time when only canned mushrooms were available. Darrell became general manager for one of the first mushroom farms, learning the business, literally, from the ground up. By the mid-1980s, he wanted to start his own operation and selected Texas as an underserved mushroom market.

After buying a property in Gonzales, the McLains went to banks to obtain financing. They were met with blank stares, or even chuckles, then the question: "You want to start—a what?" It was not exactly a Texas banker's idea of a farm, but they got just enough money to make a start.

The first couple of years were tough. Of the 50 people required to operate the farm, only Darrell and his son Greg had any mushroom experience. And it's not exactly like growing other vegetables. Although the 12-week process starts outdoors with a compost pile, most of the growing takes place indoors under temperature-controlled conditions, and harvesting must be done by hand.

"Growing mushrooms is a challenging business," says Greg. "But it's something that gets in your blood. And it's a rewarding business when you see a huge room full of mushrooms on the bed." Needless to say, the McLains succeeded in building a market for their mushrooms and have expanded several times since founding the business. Today, Kitchen Pride grows several varieties and harvests nearly a million pounds of mushrooms every month.

Crisped Kitchen Pride Portabella Mushrooms with Red Pepper Aioli and Pico de Gallo

This visually attractive dish makes a delicious first course. It's a symphony of flavors and textures. All of the component parts can be made earlier in the day, and even the mushrooms can be breaded ahead of time and fried just before serving. I've also served these mushrooms as a luncheon entrée by scattering a few shrimp that have been pan-seared in olive oil with some spicy Cajun-style seasoning or jumbo lump crabmeat on top after slicing the mushrooms. Then add the red pepper aioli and pico de gallo.

SERVES 4.

MUSHROOMS:

4 fairly small portabella mushrooms, about 3½ inches in diameter

Egg wash made from 4 eggs beaten with 3 cups whole milk

3 cups panko bread crumbs, seasoned with ⅓ cup Cajun-style seasoning

Oil for deep-frying, heated to 350°F

Romaine lettuce, sliced into thin julienned strips

Red Pepper Aioli (recipe follows)

Pico de Gallo (recipe follows)

RED PEPPER AIOLI:

3 large garlic cloves

3 eggs

1½ tablespoons whole-grain mustard

1½ teaspoons kosher salt

½ teaspoon cayenne

3 tablespoons red wine vinegar

1⅔ cups grapeseed oil

⅓ cup Texas extra-virgin olive oil

PICO DE GALLO:

6 homegrown Roma tomatoes, cut into ¼-inch dice

½ small red onion, cut into ¼-inch dice

2 serrano chiles, seeds and veins removed, minced

Juice of ½ medium-sized lime

1 cup cilantro sprigs, chopped fine

Kosher salt

Begin by making the aioli. Place the steel blade in the work bowl of a food processor. With processor running, drop the garlic cloves through the feed tube to mince. Stop machine and scrape down sides of bowl. Add all remaining ingredients except the oils. Process until mixture is smooth and eggs are thickened and light lemon-yellow in color, about 2 minutes. Combine the grapeseed and olive oils. With processor running, add the oils in a slow, steady stream through the feed tube until all has been added. Process an additional 15 to 20 seconds to form a strong emulsion. Refrigerate in a tightly sealed container until ready to use. Do not keep homemade mayonnaise longer than 3 days if you don't use it all.

Make the pico de gallo. Combine all ingredients in a medium-sized bowl and toss to blend well. Refrigerate, covered, until ready to use. The pico de gallo can be made the morning before you will use it in the evening, but don't add the salt until you're ready to serve it, or the salt will cause the tomatoes to weep, watering down the pico and wilting the tomatoes.

To cook the mushrooms, carefully remove the large stems without tearing or breaking the mushroom caps. Wipe the tops with a slightly damp paper towel. Dredge the mushrooms in the egg wash, coating them well on both sides. Next coat them with the seasoned panko crumbs, pressing the crumbs into both sides of the mushrooms. Shake off excess crumbs.

Fry the mushrooms in preheated oil until golden brown on both sides, turning once, for a total of about 5 minutes. Drain on a wire rack set over a baking sheet.

To serve, transfer the aioli to a squeeze bottle; set aside. Place a portion of the shredded romaine on each serving plate. Cut the mushrooms into slices ¼-inch thick, cutting at a slight angle. Fan the slices out, slightly overlapping, over the lettuce on the plates, one mushroom per plate. Squiggle a liberal portion of the aioli over the top of the mushrooms. Place a hefty spoonful of the pico de gallo in the center of each serving. Serve at once.

Oysters on the Half Shell with Bloody Mary Granité and Horseradish

Being an ardent oyster lover, I created this dish one Christmas when my daughter Cory and her family were coming to visit, knowing that she and her husband, Darrin, also love oysters. We had the oysters for breakfast Christmas morning, and they were such a treat. The oysters that we loved and a bit of Bloody Mary—all in one bite. I've since served them many times.

When you buy Texas Gulf oysters in the shell and see a lot of deep purple coloring on the inside of the shells, according to Misho Ivic, founder of Misho's Oysters in San Leon, it means that the oyster is absorbing minerals and will be very tasty. "The perfect oyster," Misho says, "grows in an area that has *brackish* water, where fresh water and salt water mingle. As the weather gets colder and the water chills, the oysters get fatter and sweeter."

Hence the theory that oysters should be eaten only in the colder months, those with an *r* in their names. It's still okay to eat them year-round; they just don't taste as good. Off-season oysters are best in cooked dishes.

MAKES 12 HALF SHELL SERVINGS.

12 freshly shucked oysters in the half shell

1 quart V-8 brand vegetable juice, or your favorite Bloody Mary mix

¼ cup freshly squeezed lemon juice

1½ tablespoons Worcestershire sauce

¼ teaspoon kosher salt

½ cup Texas vodka

Horseradish (see recipe for Maiya's Restaurant Saarin's Salad on pages 136–138)

Lemon wedges

Drain the oysters into a covered container and keep them chilled in the refrigerator. Reserve the bottom shells. Combine the V-8 juice, lemon juice, Worcestershire sauce, salt, and vodka in a bowl and whisk to blend well. Turn the mixture out into a shallow dish or rimmed baking sheet so that it is no deeper than ½ inch. Place the dish on a level surface in the freezer and allow the mixture to freeze until it is getting stiff and grainy, about 1½ hours. Using the tines of a fork, scrape the mixture, fluffing it into crystals. Be sure to get into all of the corners of the pan. Smooth the mixture out over the pan and return to the freezer. Continue to fluff with the fork every 15 minutes for another 45 minutes, or until the mixture is very grainy and holds together as a nice granité. Transfer to a covered container and leave in freezer until ready to use, up to 30 minutes. Don't let the granité freeze solid.

To serve the oysters, spoon a generous portion of the granité into each oyster shell. Set an oyster on top and spoon desired portion of the horseradish on each oyster, but use caution as it's the kind of hot that sets your nose ablaze if you get too much in one bite. Place on a platter with lemon wedges and serve at once.

Browned Butter Oysters

If you're an oyster lover like me, then you're always seeking out new and different ways to serve them. I created this dish as a first course. I cook and serve the oysters in Chinese soup spoons on a long rectangular plate. In the center of the plate I put a little mound of Roasted Beet Salad with Peppered Bacon and Goat Cheese (see recipe on pages 119–120), with two of the oysters on each side. It's a colorful and visually interesting dish—and the flavors, as they play off one another, are stellar. The oysters can be assembled a few hours before serving, arranged on a baking sheet, and refrigerated until you're ready to broil and serve them.

MAKES 12 OYSTERS.

12 Texas Gulf oysters and their liquor
1½ sticks unsalted butter
1 teaspoon Tabasco
1½ teaspoons minced lemon zest
1 heaping tablespoon minced flat-leaf parsley

½ teaspoon kosher salt
½ cup unseasoned bread crumbs
3 tablespoons grated Romano cheese
Lemon wedges as garnish

Preheat broiler and position oven rack 6 inches below heat source. Arrange 12 Chinese soup spoons on a baking sheet. Place one oyster in each spoon along with a little of the oyster liquor. Set aside.

Combine the butter, Tabasco, lemon zest, parsley, and salt in a small saucepan; cook to melt the butter. Stir in the bread crumbs and cheese, blending well. Divide the buttery crumb mixture among the oysters, topping each oyster with a little pile of it. Place the baking sheet under the preheated broiler and cook for 4 minutes, or until topping is golden brown and bubbly. Serve at once with lemon wedges.

Cat New's Fresh Spring Rolls with Bison and Peanut Sauce

Chef Cat (Catherine) New grew up in San Antonio with a single mom. Cat credits her mom and the foods of San Antonio as being the biggest influences on her style of cooking. The smoky-sweet-roasted flavors of Southwest cooking are a pretty constant note in the dishes that she creates.

Cat started working in the food business when she was 14, eventually making her way into the kitchen, where she learned the necessary skills by trial and error. She tried her hand at private catering for a few years, during which time she sourced bison, her favorite red meat, from Thunder Heart Bison. She and Patrick Fitzsimons of Thunder Heart Bison often talked about opening a food trailer, and the pair made it happen in November 2011, with the opening of Thunder Heart Bison: Ranch to Trailer. Cat had some stringent core requirements for the venture, including that all ingredients would be sourced locally.

MAKES A DOZEN SPRING ROLLS.

BISON:

2 pounds bison rib eye or sirloin

½ cup rice wine

1 tablespoon tamari

2 tablespoons sesame oil

SPRING ROLLS:

Rice papers

1 package rice noodles, boiled
and held in ice water

1 head romaine or large green leaf
lettuce, thick midribs removed

1 bunch fresh mint

1 cup julienned carrots

PEANUT SAUCE:

⅛ cup toasted sesame oil

⅛ cup plain sesame oil

1 tablespoon freshly crushed
coriander seeds

1 tablespoon freshly minced ginger

½ teaspoon cayenne

1 tablespoon sambal oelek

1 tablespoon tamari

1 tablespoon toasted sesame seeds

1 tablespoon hoisin sauce

Juice and zest of 1 lime

1 tablespoon rice wine vinegar

¾ cup all-natural peanut butter—
the only ingredients should be
peanuts and salt

1 cup hot water

Begin by making the peanut sauce. Combine the sesame oils, coriander seeds, ginger, and cayenne in a heavy-bottomed 2-quart saucepan over medium-low heat. Cook slowly until a good aroma emanates from the pan. Remove from heat and set aside.

Place the peanut butter in the work bowl of a food processor fitted with the steel blade. Process until very smooth. Add the heated oil and spice mixture; process until thoroughly blended, then add all remaining ingredients except hot water.

With processor running, add the hot water in a slow stream through the feed tube until the desired texture and thickness are achieved and the sauce is very smooth. Turn the sauce out into the saucepan and simmer 15 to 20 minutes to add a greater depth of flavor to the sauce. Serve at room temperature.

Remove steak from marinade and trim off excess fat and tendons. Sear or grill the steak in olive oil to your preference, but rare to medium rare is recommended for bison. Allow the steak to rest for 5 minutes, then slice into long, thick strips, allowing one strip per spring roll.

Heat a large skillet full of water to just before boiling for cooking the rice papers. Have all of the ingredients for the rolls organized and allow plenty of working space close to the pot of water.

Using a pair of chef's tongs, submerge the rice paper, one at a time, into the skillet of water, holding it just long enough to make the edges of the paper curl in. Remove from water with tongs and lay flat on work surface. You may need to drizzle some water on the work surface to keep the papers from sticking. Working very quickly, place a lettuce leaf in the center of the rice paper, then layer the remaining ingredients into the wrap, ending with the steak. Roll the short ends of the paper tightly over the ends of the filling, then roll the closest side of the paper tightly up over the filling, and then roll tightly toward the other edge of the paper, completely enclosing the filling. Serve immediately with the peanut sauce for dipping.

Randy Evans's Country-Fried Chicken Livers with Biscuits and Andouille Gravy

The culinary world can be thankful that Randy Evans didn't wind up becoming a doctor as he intended when he entered Baylor University as a biology major. Randy grew up near his grandfather's farm, eating fresh, seasonal produce and vegetables. He has fond memories of large family dinners and remembered that he loved to be in the kitchen, where he'd stand, hands gripping the edge of the counter, looking eye level at the bowls in which his mother was mixing ingredients for mouthwatering down-home desserts. He didn't realize how much the food he had grown up eating had influenced him. But in college, he was always cooking dinners for friends and began to amass a sizable library of cookbooks. His friends loved his cooking, and over time Randy realized that the kitchen was where he really belonged.

He worked his way through cooking school and prestigious restaurants and eventually opened the restaurant of his dreams in Houston. In fact, he named it Haven. In homage to his grandparents' farm, and philosophy for Haven, Randy planted an organic garden beside the restaurant. He said, "I'm doing what my grandparents did—using seasonal, fresh ingredients. We don't have much waste here, as we have multiple purposes for our ingredients. When we purchase an animal from a farmer, we use the whole animal, as this recipe using the chicken livers demonstrates, rather than just the choice cuts. We can and pickle vegetables and fruit. We cure and smoke our own bacon. We don't take shortcuts by using commercially processed ingredients."

Evans is on a mission to help create a demand for local, seasonal products and, in turn, bring about the return of small farmers to the land. He figures that he takes a cut in profit at Haven by making menu items more affordable than normal food cost–to–profit ratios would dictate in order to spread the word of how *good* real, unadulterated food tastes.

- -

SERVES 4.

- -

16 chicken livers, deveined
1 cup whole buttermilk (not low fat)
1 tablespoon Crystal Hot Sauce
Kosher salt and freshly ground
   black pepper

Canola oil for deep-frying, preheated
   to 350°F
Fresh parsley sprigs as garnish

BUTTERMILK BISCUITS:

1 cup all-purpose flour

½ teaspoon baking powder

¼ teaspoon baking soda

¼ teaspoon kosher salt

2 tablespoons cold shortening

½ cup cold whole buttermilk
   (not low fat)

ANDOUILLE GRAVY:

8 ounces andouille, cut into
   very small dice

¼ cup all-purpose flour

2½ cups whole milk

Kosher salt and freshly ground
   black pepper

Marinate the chicken livers. Combine the livers, buttermilk, and hot sauce in a bowl, tossing to blend. Cover and refrigerate for at least 4 hours, or overnight.

Begin by making the gravy. Cook the sausage in a heavy-bottomed 10-inch skillet over medium heat for 5 minutes to render out the fat. Using a slotted spoon, remove the sausage pieces from the skillet and set aside, leaving the rendered fat. Whisk the flour into the hot dripping until smooth; cook, whisking constantly, for 1 minute. Slowly whisk in the milk, whisking constantly, and cook for 5 to 7 minutes, or until thickened. Stir in the reserved sausage and cook on low heat for 30 minutes. Season to taste with salt and pepper. Keep warm.

Preheat oven to 325°F. Line a baking sheet with parchment paper; set aside. Make the biscuits. In a medium bowl, combine the dry ingredients. Using your hands or a pastry blender, cut in the shortening until the mixture resembles coarse meal. Add the buttermilk and mix just until combined. Turn out onto a work surface and knead gently 3 or 4 times to form a cohesive dough. Don't overwork the dough, or the biscuits will be tough. Roll the dough out on a floured work surface to ½-inch thick. Cut out the biscuits using a 1-inch-diameter cutter. Place biscuits on prepared baking sheet and bake in preheated oven for 20 minutes. Set aside to keep warm.

To fry the chicken livers, remove them from the buttermilk mixture and season with salt and pepper. Dredge the livers in seasoned flour, coating well and shaking off excess flour. Fry the livers in batches in the preheated oil until they float to the top and are cooked through. Take care not to crowd in the oil, or the livers will stick together. Place on a wire rack set over a baking sheet to drain. Repeat with remaining livers.

To plate and serve, split the biscuits in half and toast for a minute. Spoon some of the gravy down the center of long, narrow plates. Place four toasted biscuit halves on each plate and spoon more of the gravy over the biscuits. Place livers on the smothered biscuits and top each with a fresh parsley sprig. Serve at once.

PERISSOS WINERY

ETH AND LAURA Martin knew the name Perissos would ignite many conversations, as it is not a familiar word. But it is a word. *Perissos* is a Greek word (from Ephesians 3:20–21) meaning "exceedingly abundant, beyond what is expected, imagined, or hoped for." It is the Martins' sincere aspiration to craft wines that live up to that description.

Although the winery's name is ancient, Seth and Laura Martin are a good example of younger winemakers who have studied the industry in Texas and chosen to focus on the hot-weather varietals that thrive here. Perissos wines are made from 100 percent Texas fruit, which is processed in a state-of-the-art facility. After harvesting, the grapes are instantly refrigerated to bring the temperature below 55°F so that native yeasts will not start fermenting. This is a process known as cold soaking, which makes it possible to control the fermentation temperatures. A long and cooler fermentation allows for greater extraction of delicate flavors and aromas from the grapes prior to pressing.

"It all boils down to a simple philosophy," says Martin. "We work hard to draw forth the best product the land—or vineyard in our case—allows us, and then we protect that product throughout the entire winemaking process and, ultimately, present it in the bottle."

The bulk of the Perissos wines are made in a traditional dry style. The Martins, who both love beef marrow, recommend their Perissos Malbec with the Grilled Beef Marrow Bones with Herbed Toasts (pages 46–47).

The Perissos Roussanne, with its crispness and citrus flavor, greatly complements the Browned Butter Oysters (page 38).

Grilled Beef Marrow Bones
with Herbed Toasts

In addition to being a great source of dense protein, bone marrow is delicious. Humans have eaten it for eons, and there's even a special spoon, called appropriately, a marrow spoon, for scooping the marrow out of the bones. I've loved it since I was a kid, savoring every creamy bite with its subtle nuttiness and decadent richness. Besides, bones are very inexpensive compared to other meats and don't require a lot of complex preparation and few ingredients. I believe bones from grass-fed beef have superior taste and may be healthier than those from grain-fed cattle. I love to serve marrow bones as finger food with herbed crusty bread for sopping up savory juices from the plate. Unfortunately, I don't have a set of marrow spoons, although I look in the nooks and crannies of every antique shop I visit, so I serve them with tiny seafood forks.

SERVES 4 TO 6.

----

12 center-cut beef marrow bones, cut about 2 inches long (about 4 pounds)

2 cups Texas extra-virgin olive oil, divided

2 teaspoons freshly squeezed lemon juice

3 teaspoons minced fresh rosemary, divided

2 shallots, minced

Kosher salt

⅔ cup minced flat-leaf parsley

2 teaspoons minced lemon zest

2 large garlic cloves, minced

3 green onions, roughly chopped, including green tops

1 teaspoon kosher salt

8 to 12 slices rustic crusty bread, brushed lightly with olive oil on one side

Combine 1 cup of the olive oil, lemon juice, 2 teaspoons of the minced rosemary, the shallots, and salt to taste in a small bowl and whisk to blend well. Place the bones in a zip-sealing plastic bag and pour the mixture over the marrow bones, turning the bag to coat well. Refrigerate overnight or set at room temperature for 2 hours.

Preheat a gas grill to medium high or build a hardwood charcoal fire and allow the coals to burn down to the point where they are glowing red, covered by a layer of white ash. Line a small rimmed baking sheet with a triple layer of foil extended slightly over the rim of the baking sheet; set aside.

In the work bowl of a food processor fitted with the steel blade, combine the remaining cup of olive oil, 1 teaspoon of minced rosemary, parsley, lemon zest, green onions, and additional 1 teaspoon salt. Process until smooth. Turn out into a bowl and set aside.

When you're ready to grill and serve the marrow bones, remove them from the bag and set them on the prepared baking sheet, large ends up. Pour the marinade from the bag over them. Salt the bones to taste. (They need a dose of surface salt, which will melt into the marrow as it cooks.) Carefully remove the foil with the bones and marinade; place directly on the hot grill. Keep the baking sheet handy to remove the bones. Grill for about 30 to 35 minutes, or just until the marrow begins to melt and pulls away from the side of the bones. The marrow will begin to turn from opaque white to translucent. Don't overcook, or the marrow will all melt!

About 5 minutes before the marrow is done, lay the bread slices, oiled sides down, on the grill. Turn once and toast until well marked, about 5 minutes.

Remove the marrow bones and juices, using the foil, and place on a baking sheet. To serve, spread the bread slices with the reserved herb mixture. Arrange the bones on a platter and drizzle the pan juices over them. Add additional salt if needed. Arrange the herbed toasts in a separate basket or bowl and serve. Scoop the marrow from the bones and spread on the toasts.

2

GREAT BOWLS OF SOUP
and
COMFORTING BREADS

★

---★---

I've always loved soup. It's probably my ultimate comfort food. I have childhood memories of the soups that my mother would make. She didn't cook a great deal, but her soups were especially good—hearty vegetable soup in the fall with meaty beef shank bones that simmered for hours on the stovetop, developing an aroma and flavor that I would savor all day as those great bouquets wafted round the kitchen. When she served the soup to the family, I always begged for everyone's shank bones after they had eaten the meat. My favorite part was the wonderful little nugget of marrow in the center of each bone.

The key to making great soups is using the best and freshest ingredients possible. And when a soup calls for stock, whether chicken, beef, seafood, game stocks, lamb stock, or other flavors, always try to make it from scratch. If not, many of our new charcuterie markets and seafood markets are making fabulous stocks from the supply of bones that are a natural by-product of their businesses. Being concerned with sustainability issues, these folks want to use all parts of the animal. Making stock is a great way to use the final product—the bones. So always check with the artisan charcuterie markets and seafood markets. You may find a ready source for made-from-scratch stocks.

I know that there are people who believe that soups are only for the colder months. While I certainly agree that a steaming bowl of chili on a cold and dreary winter day seems to brighten everyone's mood, I also think those folks are missing out on some very tasty light meals during the warmer months. In Texas we have such a bountiful supply of fresh fruits, berries, and vegetables year-round. Chilled soups can be the perfect luncheon or dinner solution for those times when the heat is wretched and the very thought of turning on a stove for an extended period of time is unbearable. And making chilled soups offers yet another way to use the harvest from the garden and the orchard.

Nothing goes better with a nice bowl of soup, or stew, or chili, than bread. The artisan bread movement in America has taken off big-time. In Texas we have many fine bakers making wonderful breads of every description. But making your own bread is a relaxing pursuit with a little physical energy expended kneading that dough. And the results are well worth the effort. Nothing smells better than bread baking in the oven.

Avocado Cream Soup with Crispy Tortilla Strips and Shrimp Pico de Gallo

This chilled soup tastes like the very essence of summer in Texas. It's sultry and spicy, smooth, with crisp highlights from the shrimp pico de gallo, and it will make you feel good—just like summer in Texas.

There is an art to seasoning foods that will be served cold, such as this soup. Cold dulls the senses of hot, sweet, salty, and spicy on our tongues. Therefore, you should slightly overseason foods that will be served cold, or they will taste very bland once they have been refrigerated. After the food has been chilled, it is very hard to adjust the seasonings. A good example is to think about the times you may have tasted melted ice cream. Remember how extremely sweet it tasted? Yet when it was frozen, it was just perfect. Ice cream is oversweetened before freezing so that it will be just right once it is frozen. So don't be stingy with the salt in this soup, or it just won't reach its full flavor potential.

SERVES 8 TO 10.

4 large ripe Hass avocados,* peeled, seeded, and cut in 1-inch cubes
½ cup firmly packed cilantro leaves and tender top stems
3 serrano chiles, seeds and veins removed, roughly chopped
1 quart good-quality chicken stock, preferably homemade
1 cup whipping cream
¼ cup freshly squeezed lime juice
1 teaspoon ground ancho chile powder
Kosher salt
Sour cream
Tortilla Strips (recipe follows)
Chopped cilantro leaves
Shrimp Pico De Gallo (recipe follows)

TORTILLA STRIPS:

10 white corn tortillas, cut in half, then cut into strips about ¼-inch wide
Canola oil for frying, heated to 350°F

SHRIMP PICO DE GALLO:

3 ripe Roma tomatoes, preferably homegrown, cut into tiny dice, about ¼-inch square
2 serrano chiles, seeds and veins removed, minced
¼ cup finely diced red onion
2 tablespoons chopped cilantro
12 medium shrimp, peeled, deveined, boiled, and chopped
2 teaspoons freshly squeezed lime juice
Kosher salt

To make the soup, combine the avocado, cilantro, serrano chiles, and 1½ cups of the chicken stock in a high-speed blender. Blend until mixture is very smooth. Transfer to a medium-sized bowl and whisk in the remaining chicken stock, whipping cream, lime juice, and ancho chile powder. Add salt to taste and whisk to blend well. Taste for seasoning, adding additional salt if the soup tastes flat and boring. Cover and refrigerate until well chilled before serving.

Fry the tortilla strips in preheated oil until crisp and very lightly browned, about 3 to 4 minutes. Use a slotted spoon or flat wire skimmer to remove the tortilla strips and drain on a wire rack set over a baking sheet; set aside.

To make the shrimp pico de gallo, combine all ingredients except salt in a small bowl and toss to blend well. Season to taste with the salt and refrigerate until ready to use.

To serve, ladle a portion of the soup into shallow, rimmed soup plates; then top with a dollop of sour cream in the center of the bowl. Nest some of the tortilla strips on the sour cream, then scatter some of the chopped cilantro over the whole surface of the soup, and finish with a generous portion of the pico de gallo over the tortilla strips.

----

* When choosing avocados, be sure to purchase the small Hass avocados with very dark brown, bumpy skins. This avocado has flourished in the lush countryside of Michoacán, west of Mexico City, for thousands of years. The avocados you choose at the market should never be hard but should yield slightly to the touch. Reject those that are very soft and squishy. To peel and seed an avocado, cut lengthwise around the pit, and gently twist the two halves to separate. Strike the pit with the blade of sharp knife (taking care to hit the pit and not your hand), then twist to remove the seed. Using a spoon, scoop out the avocado flesh. It should come out in one piece.

Chilled Fredericksburg Peach Soup

Many states have peach-producing regions, and I'm sure I have tried most all of them, but I have to say that the very best peaches are the ones grown in the tight little region of the Central Texas Hill Country around Stonewall and Fredericksburg. The bounty of the crop is celebrated each July in Stonewall with the annual Peach Jamboree, complete with parade, Peach Queen, and mountains of fresh peach concoctions—everything from peach cobbler, peach pie, peach fried pies, to my favorite, fresh peach ice cream. Peach stands line the highways in the region during the summer, often also selling an array of peach preserves made by the orchard owner's wife from an old family recipe. Several farms offer "pick-your-own" peaches by the basket or bushel, so you can haul them home and make own preserves.

While the peaches last, I love to make fresh chilled peach soup to celebrate the taste of the peach at its best. This version of the soup has a little touch of Gewürztraminer, a white wine that ranges in taste from off dry to sweet, as in dessert-wine sweet. *Gewürz* means "spice" in German, and the wine does have a little nip of spice (aromatic spice, not heat spice), which makes it a great companion flavor to the peaches.

SERVES 4 TO 6.

2 cups water

¼ cup raw turbinado sugar

1 teaspoon whole cloves

Dash of freshly ground allspice berries

¼ cup cornstarch dissolved in 2 cups chilled Gewürztraminer*

2½ pounds peeled, pitted, and roughly chopped fresh peaches

GARNISH:

3 ounces cream cheese, softened

2 tablespoons powdered sugar

2 cups Mexican crema fresca

1 cup fresh blueberries or blackberries, rinsed and drained well

Mint sprigs, if desired

To make the soup, combine the water, sugar, all seasonings, and Gewürztraminer/cornstarch mixture in a heavy-bottomed 3-quart saucepan over medium heat. Bring the mixture to a boil; then reduce, cover, and simmer gently for 15 minutes, or until the mixture is thickened and glossy. Strain through a fine-mesh strainer into a bowl; discard cloves. Set aside to cool. Puree the peaches in a high-speed blender until very smooth. Pour the peach puree into the wine mixture, whisking to blend well. Chill thoroughly, at least 4 hours, before serving.

While the soup is chilling, prepare the garnish. Combine cream cheese, powdered sugar, and Mexican crema fresca in the work bowl of a food processor fitted with the steel blade. Process until the mixture is smooth. Turn out into a bowl and stir in the blueberries or blackberries, distributing them well. Refrigerate until ready to use, but bring to room temperature before serving so that it will be soft.

To serve, ladle a portion of the soup into individual bowls and place a generous dollop of the garnish in the center of each bowl. Nest a mint sprig in the crema, if desired.

* To develop this recipe, I tried several varieties of white wine to get the perfect match to the Fredericksburg peaches. The excellent Gewürztraminer produced by the Fredericksburg Winery made the peaches dance and gave the soup exactly the flavor I was seeking. Often, looking in one's own backyard is not only the easiest but the best place to find exactly what you need!

Chilled Yellow Squash and Poblano Chile Soup with Lime and Chile Crema

This soup is one of my rewards to myself for tending my vegetable garden. When I pick a bounty of yellow squash fresh from the creeping vines in the early morning, I often make a batch of it for a light summer supper, serving it with a simple green salad, some good bread, and a glass of chilled Texas Viognier or Sauvignon Blanc. The buttermilk gives the soup a nice tang, but don't worry if you hate buttermilk, as I do, because its flavor is diluted so much that only the nice acidity is left.

SERVES 4 TO 6.

SOUP:

3 tablespoons Texas extra-virgin olive oil

1 sweet Texas 1015 onion, chopped

2 garlic cloves, minced

4 cups yellow squash, about 1½ pounds, sliced

2 poblano chiles, blistered, peeled, seeded, and roughly chopped

1 cup chicken stock, preferably homemade

1 cup buttermilk

1 tablespoon minced cilantro

Kosher salt and freshly ground black pepper

LIME AND CHILE CREMA:

½ cup Mexican crema fresca

1 teaspoon ground cumin

½ teaspoon lime zest

2 teaspoons freshly squeezed lime juice

1 teaspoon Cholula Hot Sauce

¼ teaspoon kosher salt

To make the soup, heat the olive oil in a heavy-bottomed 4-quart saucepan over medium-high heat. When the oil is hot, add the onion and garlic. Cook, stirring often, until onion is wilted and transparent but not browned, about 5 minutes. Reduce heat to medium and add the squash and poblano chiles; cover and cook until squash is very wilted, about 10 minutes. Transfer to a high-speed blender and puree, adding the chicken stock a little at a time. Add the buttermilk and cilantro to the blender and puree until very smooth. Season to taste with salt and pepper. Refrigerate until well chilled before serving.

Make the lime and chile crema. Combine all ingredients in a medium bowl and whisk until smooth and well blended. Refrigerate, tightly covered, until chilled before serving.

To serve, spoon chilled soup into individual soup plates. Spoon a dollop of the lime and chile crema in the center of each bowl and serve.

Summer Squash Bisque

Anyone who has ever planted a vegetable garden during a Texas summer knows that squash is a very prolific vegetable, even if you plant a small crop of it. My neighbors often get to the point where they don't answer their doors when they see me coming up their sidewalks bearing gifts of more squash. But it's a tasty and versatile vegetable that can be combined with myriad seasonings to create a side dish for just about any entrée. One of my personal favorite uses for summer squash is this flavorful soup. It's really easy to prepare, yet it has a taste that seems much more complex than the sum of its simple ingredients. The swirl of smoked paprika garnish adds an exotic note that marries perfectly with the creamy vegetables. The soup freezes well, so you can use up the last of the summer bounty of squash by making enough to enjoy through the winter. And those neighbors always answer the door when I come bearing a quart of the soup in the dead of winter!

SERVES 8 TO 10.

6 tablespoons unsalted butter
1 large onion, chopped
2 medium baking potatoes, peeled and sliced about ¼-inch thick
2 medium carrots, peeled and sliced
4 cups yellow summer squash, about 1½ pounds, sliced
3 tablespoons all-purpose flour

1½ quarts chicken stock, preferably homemade
Kosher salt
¼ teaspoon cayenne
1 cup whipping cream
¼ teaspoon freshly grated nutmeg
Smoked Spanish paprika

Melt the butter in a heavy-bottomed 6-quart soup pot over medium-high heat. Add the onion and sauté until wilted and transparent, about 5 minutes. Add potatoes, carrots, and squash; toss to coat with butter. Add the flour all at once; stir to blend well. Cook, stirring constantly, for 3 to 4 minutes. Slowly stir in the chicken stock. Add salt to taste and cayenne. Cover pot and cook until all vegetables are fork tender, about 45 minutes. Puree the soup in batches in a blender or food processor until it is very smooth. Return soup to pot and stir in the cream. Taste for seasoning, adjusting as needed. Cook just to heat the cream. Stir in the nutmeg; cook 3 to 4 minutes. Ladle the soup into individual bowls and float about ⅛ teaspoon of the smoked paprika in the center of the bowl. Using a spoon, swirl the paprika around the bowl to create an attractive pattern. Serve hot.

Cream of Mostly Asparagus Soup

Fresh asparagus at the farmers' market is the harbinger of spring. I perceive that asparagus is the essence of the taste of spring, just like that special vibrant, light green color of the newly sprouting leaves on trees is the special color reserved only for heralding the arrival of the vernal equinox. When selecting asparagus, look for spears with straight stalks and a uniform green color. The tips should be compact and pointed. The freshest asparagus will be crisp to your fingernails. Select spears that are no thicker than a ball-point pen, with woody ends no longer than an inch. The taste of this soup is almost purely the taste of asparagus, with just a hint of the one herb that I think does it justice, fresh marjoram, with a garnish of fresh lemon zest, which sets it to music. For this soup you must use only fresh asparagus, and they must be peeled. Julia Child was a stickler for peeling the thin, tough skin, which is very hard to digest, from asparagus spears, and I never thought of doing otherwise. The peeled spears are much more tender.

SERVES 6 TO 8.

2 pounds fresh asparagus spears
6 tablespoons unsalted butter
1 medium onion, chopped
1 tablespoon minced fresh marjoram
1 teaspoon freshly ground black pepper
⅛ teaspoon red (cayenne) pepper
2 quarts plus 2 cups chicken stock
⅓ cup whipping cream
Kosher salt
2 teaspoons minced lemon zest

Snap off the woody, whitish bottom portion of the asparagus spears and discard. (I slice them thin for my chickens, who love them!) Using a sharp vegetable peeler, peel a thin layer of the thick skin and scales from each spear, beginning about an inch below the tips of the spears. Roughly chop the spears and set aside. Melt the butter in a heavy-bottomed 6-quart soup pot over medium heat. Sauté the onion, marjoram, black pepper, and cayenne until onions are wilted and transparent, about 10 minutes. Add the chopped asparagus, tossing to moisten the pieces with the butter. Add the chicken stock and stir to blend. Cover and simmer the soup for 45 minutes.

Remove pan from heat and puree the soup in batches in a high-speed blender. Don't fill the container more than half full. Place the lid securely on the blender and cover the top with a kitchen towel. Hold your hand on the lid and begin to blend on low speed to prevent an eruption. Increase speed to high and puree until very smooth. Repeat with remaining soup. Return soup to medium-low heat and simmer, uncovered, for 20 minutes. Stir in the whipping cream and add salt to taste. Cook just to heat through. Serve hot, garnishing each bowl with about ¼ teaspoon of the minced lemon zest.

Mushroom and Texas Port Wine Soup

Nothing warms the body and delights the palate more than a steaming bowl of good mushroom soup on a blustery winter day. This particular soup derives a dose of hefty flavor from a little bulk-style pork sausage and good Texas mushrooms, mellowed by the rich, full-bodied taste of Texas ruby port.

SERVES 10 TO 12.

2 tablespoons Texas extra-virgin olive oil
1 medium onion, chopped
5 ounces bulk-style pork breakfast sausage
1 pound Kitchen Pride white mushrooms, stems and caps, roughly chopped
3 medium garlic cloves, minced
1½ cups Texas ruby port wine
2 cups chicken stock
2 cups beef stock
Kosher salt and freshly ground black pepper
⅛ teaspoon ground cloves
1 tablespoon Asian chili paste with garlic

2 cups whipping cream
Butter Roux (see recipe below)
Flavor Garnish (see recipe below)

BUTTER ROUX:
½ cup unsalted butter
½ cup all-purpose flour

FLAVOR GARNISH:
¼ pound (1 stick) unsalted butter
2 large shallots, cut into tiny dice
6 ounces fresh shiitake mushrooms, stems removed, caps sliced thin
Kosher salt and freshly ground black pepper
Sour cream

Heat the olive oil in a heavy-bottomed 8-quart soup pot over medium heat. Add the onion and sausage. Simmer until the onions are wilted and transparent, about 7 minutes. Use the back of a spoon to keep the sausage broken into small pieces. Add the mushrooms and cook until the mushroom liquid is released. Add the garlic and cook slowly until mushroom liquid has evaporated. Do not allow the garlic to brown. Quickly add the port wine, stirring rapidly to scrape up all browned bits from the bottom of the pan. Cook to reduce the port by half. Add the chicken and beef stocks and seasonings. Cover and simmer about 30 minutes. Remove soup from heat and puree in batches in a blender until smooth.

To make the butter roux, melt the butter in a heavy-bottomed 10-inch skillet over medium heat. Whisk in the flour all at once and cook until the roux reaches a light almond color. Remove from heat and transfer to a small bowl until ready to use. *Note:* The roux, or any that is left over, may be refrigerated for use another time.

Return pureed soup to a clean soup pot and stir in the whipping cream, blending well. Bring the soup to a full, rolling boil. Whisk in the butter roux a little at a time until desired consistency is reached. Taste for seasoning and adjust as needed. Keep warm while making the flavor garnish.

To prepare the flavor garnish, melt butter in a heavy-bottomed 10-inch skillet over medium-high heat. When butter has melted and foam subsides, stir in the shallots and mushrooms. Cook, stirring often, until shallots are wilted and transparent and mushrooms are lightly browned, about 8 minutes. Season to taste with salt and pepper. Keep warm until ready to serve.

To serve, ladle the soup into individual shallow, rimmed soup plates. Spoon a dollop of sour cream in the center of each serving and scatter a portion of the mushroom flavor garnish around it. Serve hot.

VELDHUIZEN FAMILY FARM

CONNIE AND STUART Veldhuizen used to think cheesemaking was for the French, or the Swiss, or folks in Wisconsin or Vermont. Stuart's dad was a dairyman, and, as a young married couple, Stuart and Connie followed suit. But after years of freezing Minnesota winters they began to think about the places where cows could graze all year. But mainly they just wanted to be warm. So they packed up their kids, tucked in Grandma and Grandpa for good measure, and headed south.

The family arrived in Texas in 1990 and set up a traditional dairy operation near Dublin. When their herd became established, they were milking 200 cows twice a day. They sold their milk to the dairy co-op for whatever it would pay. The milk was pooled with that from other farms, then sent off for pasteurization, bottling, and shipment to grocery stores. The family had no say in the final product or the price they would receive for their hard labor.

Market fluctuations would hit them hard. Stuart began to dream about a small, family-run dairy and cheesemaking operation. He wanted to make a living with 40 cows instead of 200.

Their new business began with 20 baby Jersey calves. The entire family, including Grandma and Grandpa, is involved in the business. Sustainability is very important to the Veldhuizens, who get as much of their feed from grasses grown on the farm as possible. No growth hormones or antibiotics are used on the cattle, and no chemicals in the pastures. Production has increased to more than a dozen different varieties of cheese.

They also sell raw milk, and they have customers that drive 100 miles to buy it. Thankfully, there's plenty left over to produce the cheeses that are served in restaurants statewide, sold in shops big and small, and enjoyed by urban and rural families alike.

Shiner Bock and Cheddar Cheese Soup with Jalapeños and Garlic Croutons

Shiner Bock beer is virtually an institution in Texas. When you see a person with his or her hand wrapped around one of those dark brown bottles with the familiar yellow-gold label, you know you're dealing with a serious beer-drinkin' Texan. It's a hearty, European-style beer produced by the Spoetzl Brewery in Shiner pretty much the same way it's been brewed for more than 100 years. Now, if you don't live in Texas, you can substitute another European-style bock beer in this soup, but please, don't use one of those limp tasting, *lite* beers in it, or you'll ruin a very tasty pot of soup.

SERVES 10 TO 12.

SOUP:

¼ cup canola oil

2 medium onions, chopped

3 carrots, peeled and sliced thin

3 celery stalks, chopped

4 baking potatoes, about
   2½ pounds total, peeled and
   cut into ½-inch dice

4 jalapeños, seeds and veins
   removed, minced

⅓ cup whole-grain mustard

1 longneck bottle (12 ounces) Shiner
   Bock beer, or substitute another
   European-style dark bock beer

2½ quarts chicken stock, preferably
   homemade

3½ cups (14 ounces) shredded
   Texas Cheddar cheese, such as
   Veldhuizen Family Farm's
   Redneck Cheddar

Kosher salt

1 cup whipping cream

GARLIC CROUTONS:

4 cups ½-inch-square French bread
   cubes

1½ cups (3 sticks) unsalted butter

2 tablespoons finely minced garlic

¼ teaspoon kosher salt

To make the soup, heat the canola oil in a heavy-bottomed 6-quart soup pot over medium-high heat. When the oil is hot, add the onions, carrots, celery, and diced potatoes. Cook, stirring occasionally, until the onions are wilted and transparent, about 8 minutes. Add the jalapeños, mustard, beer, and chicken stock. Stir to blend well, cover, and simmer for 30 minutes, or until the potatoes are very soft and have started to break apart. Puree the soup in batches in a high-speed blender until completely smooth. Return soup to a clean pot and stir in the cheese. Cook, stirring, just until the cheese has melted. Season to taste with salt. Do not allow the soup to boil once the cheese has been added. Stir in the whipping cream and cook just to heat the cream through. Set aside to keep warm while making the croutons. Preheat oven to 300°F. Cover a baking sheet with foil; set aside.

Place the French bread cubes in a medium-sized bowl. Combine the butter, garlic, and salt in a heavy-bottomed 2-quart saucepan over medium heat. Cook to melt the butter and lightly brown the garlic, but take care not to burn it. You should just begin to get a nice garlic aroma from the pan. Remove from heat and set aside for 15 minutes. Strain the butter through a fine-mesh strainer, pressing down on the garlic to extract every drop of juice. Pour the mixture evenly over the bread cubes, then toss rapidly to coat all bread cubes. Turn the buttered cubes out in a single layer on the prepared baking sheet. Bake in preheated oven until the bread cubes are lightly brown and very crisp, about 15 minutes. Scatter the croutons on a wire rack set over a baking sheet and cool completely before using. To store the croutons for later use, place them, totally cooled, in a storage container with a tight-fitting lid for up to 2 days.

Serve the soup hot, topped with a good scattering of the croutons.

Roasted Fresh Tomato and Basil Soup

I created this soup recipe, in which the fresh Roma tomatoes are oven roasted to concentrate their taste, then cooked into a simple but delicious soup using fresh basil from my summer herb garden. If you don't grow your own tomatoes, the farmers' markets have loads of them during the summer—along with fresh basil. The little swirl of homemade pesto puts the soup over the top in flavor. And, of course, what's better with a bowl of tomato soup than a grilled cheese sandwich, especially when it's made with artisan raw milk Gruyere cheese produced right up the road in Dublin at Veldhuizen Family Farm? (See recipe on pages 378–380.)

SERVES 6 TO 8.

16 ripe homegrown tomatoes, preferably San Marzano or heirloom Roma, cut in half lengthwise

Texas extra-virgin olive oil for drizzling over the tomatoes

Raw sugar

Kosher salt

9 large garlic cloves, minced

1 large yellow onion, coarsely chopped

⅓ cup firmly packed, roughly chopped fresh basil leaves

1½ quarts chicken stock, preferably homemade

¼ cup additional Texas extra-virgin olive oil

2 heaping tablespoons tomato paste

½ cup dry white Texas wine

2 cups whipping cream

¼ teaspoon cayenne

Kosher salt and freshly ground black pepper

½ cup grated Parmesan cheese

Basil Pesto, your favorite version, or see recipe for Chicken Breast Rolls Stuffed with Goat Cheese and Spinach (pages 221–222)

Preheat oven to 400°F. Line a baking sheet with parchment paper. Arrange the halved tomatoes on the prepared baking sheet. Lightly drizzle them with a bit of olive oil, then very lightly scatter them with raw sugar and salt. Roast the tomatoes in preheated oven until the edges begin to caramelize, about 45 minutes. Remove from oven and set aside to cool. Combine the onion, garlic, and basil in the container of a high-speed blender with a little of the chicken stock. Puree until very smooth. Transfer to a bowl and set aside.

Heat the ¼ cup olive oil in a heavy-bottomed 6-quart saucepan over medium-high heat. When the oil is hot, add the tomato paste. Cook, stirring constantly, until the sauce has darkened to almost a mahogany color, about 2 minutes. Do not allow it to burn. Add garlic, onion, and basil puree, stirring to blend into the tomato paste. Sauté, stirring often, until the puree is thickened, about 7 minutes. Puree the roasted tomatoes in the blender until smooth, adding a little more of the chicken stock as needed. Add the tomato puree to the pot; stir to blend well. Cook, stirring often, until thickened, about 5 minutes. Add the remaining chicken stock and wine, stirring to blend well. Cook for 10 minutes. Add the whipping cream and stir to incorporate. Stir in the cayenne and season to taste with salt and freshly ground black pepper. Lower heat to medium, cover the pan, and simmer the soup for 15 minutes. Whisk in the Parmesan cheese, cover, and cook an additional 15 minutes.

To serve, ladle a portion of the soup into individual bowls. Add a small dollop of the pesto to center of bowl and swirl it around the surface of the soup with a spoon. Serve hot.

Creamy Cilantro Soup with Chipotle Crema

There are many versions of this soup within the cuisine of interior Mexico, with different cooks adding their own special touch. It is a delicious soup with a delicate but complex and gratifying taste that can be enjoyed year-round. Leftover soup may be refrigerated for up to 3 days, then gently reheated.

SERVES 8 TO 10.

3 leeks, white portion only
¼ cup canola oil
2 medium-sized zucchini, sliced
5 large garlic cloves, minced
4 serrano chiles, seeds and veins removed, minced
3 russet potatoes, about 1½ pounds, peeled and cut into 1-inch dice
6 cups rich chicken stock
3 bunches cilantro leaves and tender top sprigs, roughly chopped
1½ cups heavy cream
Kosher salt

Thin (about ⅛-inch) julienne-cut strips of corn tortillas, fried until crisp
Chipotle Crema (see recipe below)

CHIPOTLE CREMA:
¾ cup sour cream
3 chipotle chiles in adobo sauce
1 tablespoon freshly squeezed lime juice
1 tablespoon adobo sauce from can of chiles
½ teaspoon kosher salt

Make the chipotle crema. Combine the sour cream, chipotle chiles, lime juice, adobo sauce, and salt in the work bowl of a food processor fitted with the steel blade. Process until smooth. Place the sour cream mixture in a wire strainer and, using the back of a spoon, stir the mixture through the strainer into a bowl. Keep stirring until nothing remains but seeds and pulp from the chiles. Discard pulp and seeds. Transfer the crema to a squeeze bottle and refrigerate until ready to use.

To make the soup, slice the root ends from the leeks, then slice the leeks in half lengthwise, and rinse under running water, spreading the layers out to remove all traces of grit and dirt. Slice the leeks thin; set aside.

Heat the canola oil in a heavy-bottomed 6-quart soup pot over medium heat. Add the leeks, zucchini, garlic, serrano chiles, and potatoes. Cook, stirring frequently, until leeks are wilted and transparent, about 10 minutes. Add the chicken stock, cover, and cook for 30 minutes, or until the potatoes are very soft. Stir in the cilantro and puree the soup in batches in a blender or food processor until smooth, then return to clean pot. Add the heavy cream and cook, stirring once or twice, for about 10 minutes to heat the cream through. Season to taste with salt.

To serve, pour hot soup into bowls or soup plates and squiggle some of the chipotle crema across the center of each bowl. Nest a little mound of the fried tortilla strips in the center of the bowl.

Corn Tortilla Soup

Tortilla soup is one of the best Mexican imports. No one knows for sure where it originated, although most culinary historians believe it originated in Mexico City and made its way north in the twentieth century. Diana Kennedy, the undisputed expert on interior Mexican cuisine, refers to tortilla soup as "Mexican soul food soup." It's a simple soup composed of chicken stock with a fried mixture of tomatoes and onions. Various versions of the soup add other seasonings and garnishes. This version adheres to the traditional method of preparation, and it's mighty tasty.

SERVES 6 TO 8.

6 white corn tortillas

½-inch canola oil for deep-pan-frying, heated to 350°F

2 tablespoons plus 2 teaspoons leaf lard* or solid shortening

1 large onion, roughly chopped

4 large garlic cloves, minced

4 ripe homegrown Roma tomatoes, blistered, peeled, and seeded

2 quarts chicken stock, preferably homemade

1 heaping teaspoon dark chili powder

1 heaping teaspoon toasted, then ground, coriander seeds

1½ cups fresh corn kernels

Kosher salt

5 dried pasilla chiles, seeded and deveined, snipped into very thin julienned strips

3 cups (12 ounces) shredded
    Mozzarella Company Cacciota
    cheese, or substitute Monterey
    Jack cheese

Lime wedges, one for each bowl
    of soup
2 Hass avocados, peeled, seeded,
    and cut into ¼-inch dice

Begin by frying the tortillas. If they are very fresh or very moist, dry them out for a few minutes in a single layer. Cut the tortillas in half, then slice the halves into ¼-inch wide strips. Fry the strips in the hot oil until they are crisp but not darkly browned. Drain well on absorbent paper towels set on a wire rack over a baking sheet. When completely cool, the strips can be stored in a tightly sealed container for up to 2 days until ready to use.

To make the soup, combine the onion, garlic, and tomatoes in a blender. Puree until mixture is smooth; set aside. Heat the lard or shortening in a heavy-bottomed 6-quart pot over medium heat. When the fat is hot, pour in the pureed tomato mixture and fry until the mixture becomes somewhat dry, about 20 minutes, stirring often.

Stir in the chicken stock, chili powder, coriander, and corn. Cover and simmer for 30 minutes on medium-low heat. Taste for seasoning, adding salt if needed.

While the soup is simmering, place the pasilla chile strips in a dry skillet over high heat until they begin to give off an aroma. Shake the pan and toss chiles constantly. Do not allow them to burn. Remove from skillet and set aside.

When ready to serve, divide the fried tortilla strips equally among the serving bowls. Top each with a portion of the cheese and toasted chile strips. Squeeze a lime wedge into each bowl. Ladle the hot broth over the top and garnish with a scattering of the diced avocado. Serve hot.

---

* Notes on using lard: Lard is a perfectly natural fat, although in recent years it has become a four-letter word to most home cooks. Freshly rendered (leaf) lard is not hydrogenated and therefore does not contain trans fats. Buy fresh lard from your farmers' market, an ethnic market (especially Mexican markets), or a charcuterie market that makes its own. Or you can make your own at home by slowly (4 to 5 hours) cooking pork fatback until it renders all of its fat, leaving only some nice brown cracklin's, which make a great addition to salads and to biscuits or cornbread. (Or you can just salt 'em and eat 'em.) Be sure to keep fresh lard refrigerated.

Lard actually contains less saturated fat than butter (40 percent; butter contains 60 percent). It's also much higher in monounsaturated fat, said to decrease the risk of heart disease, than butter and has three times as much of the beneficial polyunsaturated fats. It is a great source of vitamin D, protects the liver from toxins, and helps bones absorb calcium. Besides, it makes the flakiest, tastiest pie pastry and biscuits—the way your grandmother used to make them. So, embrace natural lard in moderation, as with all fats. But never, ever, buy the Armour lard in one-pound blocks from the supermarket. It is hydrogenated, and hydrogenated fats should never pass your lips!

Garlic, Sage, and Egg Soup on Rustic Bread

Ahh, easy comfort food. I love to make this soup in late spring and early summer when I can get fresh garlic at the farmers' market, or from my garden if I had time to plant it earlier. The soup is so easy to make, and eating it is like an elixir to the body. I use fresh eggs from "my girls" in the backyard and sage from the herb bed, along with homemade chicken stock, which I endeavor to always have on hand. So, in a flash, a simple and delicious dinner is on the table. Serve in shallow, rimmed soup plates.

SERVES 4.

- 2 large garlic heads
- ⅓ cup plus 3 tablespoons Texas extra-virgin olive oil, divided
- 1 tablespoon minced fresh sage
- 1½ quarts chicken stock, preferably homemade
- Kosher salt and freshly ground black pepper
- 4 eggs
- 4 slices toasted or grilled rustic-style bread
- 4 large sage leaves

Remove the individual cloves from the head of garlic, peel them, and cut each clove into thin slices. Heat the 3 tablespoons of olive oil in a deep-sided, heavy-bottomed 12-inch skillet over medium heat. When the oil is good and hot, add the garlic. It should create a nice sizzling sound when it hits the pan. Season the garlic with salt and toss in the sage. Cook just until the garlic is wilted and transparent, about 3 minutes. Don't let it brown.

Add the chicken stock and stir to scrape up any browned bits from bottom of pan. Season to taste with salt and pepper. Cook to heat the stock through. In a separate skillet large enough to accommodate the 4 eggs, heat the ⅓ cup olive oil until very hot, then add the eggs. They will immediately bubble and become lacy and crusty at the edges, Baste them with the oil as they cook until the whites are set and the yolks are cooked the way you like them. Place a slice of the toasted bread in each bowl. Using a slotted metal spatula, slide an egg onto each portion of the bread. Return the skillet to medium-high heat and fry the sage leaves for about 2 minutes, or until they are crisp. Spoon a portion of the garlicky broth, making sure to include lots of the garlic, over each serving and place one of the fried sage leaves on each egg. Serve at once.

BRENNAN VINEYARDS

D<small>R. PAT BRENNAN</small> and his wife, Trellise, purchased the historic McCrary House in Comanche in 1997. The purchase was followed by the acquisition of 33 acres adjacent to the McCrary property, and in 2002, they established a vineyard. The Wilkerson family of Comanche joined the Brennans, and the winery was completed in 2005. When Brennan Vineyards was formed in 2002, the commitment was to make world-class wine from Texas grapes. The founders coined a motto to describe their wines: "Sophisticated Wine with Texas Roots." In order to fully accomplish that goal, Brennan winemaker Todd Webster works with noted Texas winemaker Kim McPherson as a consultant.

Currently Brennan Vineyards has 37 acres of grapes and grows 12 varieties of *Vitis vinifera*, or "old-world" grapes. The varieties were chosen because of the Texas climate and its challenges. Brennan also purchases grapes from some of the top growers on the Texas High Plains.

Brennan Vineyards wines are marketed under both the Brennan Vineyards name and the Austin Street label. The two labels represent different wine styles, grape origins, and price points. Currently Brennan Vineyards has 10 different wines in the market, including their popular Buffalo Roam, a distinctive Rhone-style blend. Brennan wines have fared very well in competition. Their Viognier, Austin Street Comanche Red, and Brennan Cabernet Sauvignon have won many awards.

Pat Brennan likes to pair his excellent Viognier with the Chilled Yellow Squash and Poblano Chile Soup with Lime and Chile Crema (pages 56–57), as the fruit in the wine complements the spice in the soup. Try the Brennan Lily with August E's Oyster Stew (page 73). The wine's crisp acidity goes very well with the oysters. The rustic Garlic, Sage, and Egg Soup (pages 70–71) calls for a light red wine. The Brennan Buffalo Roam is a blend of syrah and mourvèdre that works well with poultry, as in the chicken stock and egg in the soup.

August E's Oyster Stew

Dawn and Leu Savanh opened August E's Restaurant in Fredericksburg, in the heart of the Texas Hill Country, in 2004. They describe their menu as "nouveau Texas cuisine," created from an innovative fusion of traditional Texas fare with the foods of Leu's Laos/Thai roots.

The menu changes throughout the year. This recipe, which is one of my favorites when I visit the restaurant during oyster season, showcases Leu's ability to create unique flavor pairings. Often when oysters are cooked into a soup or sauce, they're overcooked, but Leu adds the raw oysters to the soup base per order, just before it is served. Biting into one of the barely warmed oysters in Chef Leu's pristine, herb-infused broth is a transcendental moment for oyster lovers.

SERVES 10.

2 sheets of prepared puff pastry
(5 inches × 5 inches), thawed
if frozen

2 tablespoons unsalted butter

2 medium shallots, cut into small dice

1 large garlic clove, minced

¼ cup dry white Texas wine

2 quarts chicken stock, preferably
homemade

2 tablespoons sherry wine vinegar

1 tablespoon minced fresh thyme

1 tablespoon minced fresh sage

1 quart whipping cream

Kosher salt and freshly ground
black pepper

8 ounces raw oysters, drained

1 tablespoon minced flat-leaf parsley

Preheat oven to 425°F. Line a baking sheet with parchment paper. Cut the sheets of puff pastry into 1-inch squares. Place on the prepared baking sheet and bake until golden brown and puffed, about 7 to 10 minutes; set aside.

Melt the butter in a heavy-bottomed 6-quart pot over medium heat. Add the shallots and garlic; cook, stirring to prevent the garlic from browning, until shallots are translucent, about 4 minutes. Add wine, chicken stock, sherry wine vinegar, and fresh thyme and sage. Bring to a boil over medium-high heat. Add the heavy cream and continue to boil the soup, reducing and thickening it slightly, for 15 minutes. Transfer the soup to the container of a high-speed blender in half-container batches and puree until smooth. Begin at low speed to avoid a disastrous eruption, gradually shifting to high speed. Return the soup to the pot and season to taste with salt and pepper. Keep warm over low heat until ready to serve.

When you are ready to serve the soup, ladle equal portions of the broth into wide-rimmed shallow soup plates and add 3 to 4 raw oysters to the hot bisque. Garnish with minced parsley and float 2 of the puff pastry squares on the surface as garnish.

GOODE COMPANY

Houston's Goode Company family of restaurants is a local success story. Founder Jim Goode has always loved to cook. Jim grew up on the Texas coast in the small town of Clute and always considered having the Gulf of Mexico "in his backyard" as a precious resource. In the early part of his career he was a well-respected graphic design artist in Houston and often threw barbecues for clients. By the late 1970s, Jim was looking for a career change. He announced that he wanted to open either a barbecue restaurant or a bait camp. Fate made the decision in favor of barbecue.

Jim often dined at a barbecue place on Houston's Kirby Drive, owned by a husband-and-wife team. The husband died suddenly, and the wife didn't want to run the place by herself, so she asked Jim if he'd be interested in taking it over. Although he jumped at the chance, understand that this was a man who knew nothing about operating a restaurant. He just loved to barbecue. He took possession of the restaurant, which he named Goode Company Barbecue, on the Thursday before Labor Day in 1977 and opened for business the following Tuesday. Jim's uncle, Joe Dixie, knew a little about restaurant equipment, so he was a big help. Joe and Jim would spend entire nights at the place cooking the barbecue.

Jim was having the time of his life, and the business was flourishing. The man did make mean barbecue! Jim had also always loved Mexican food, having grown up eating it at his grandmother's table. In 1983, Jim added the Goode Company Taqueria across Kirby Drive from the barbecue restaurant, taking him away from home even more. In the mid-1980s, he and his wife divorced, and she moved to Louisiana with their son, Levi.

Jim spent a lot of time traveling to Louisiana. On those visits the father and son would fish and cook and eat at all of the great mom-and-pop diners on the back roads and bayous of South Louisiana. Jim fell in love with Cajun food and its bold, spicy seasonings, especially the seafood. In 1986, Jim opened the flagship Goode Company Seafood behind the Taqueria on Kirby. It was an instant success.

When Levi grew up, he returned to Texas to work with his dad at the Goode Company restaurants, which by then were firmly entrenched as iconic Houston dining spots. Today, Levi Goode is the president of Goode Company restaurants. He described the family's culinary heritage in this way: "The offerings at our restaurants aren't contrived but rather an expression of the family history. And we do have a piece of Texas history in these restaurants."

Goode Company Seafood Gumbo

The seafood gumbo at Goode Company Seafood is legendary. People drive from near and far to get it—and many stop by on their way home from work to pick up a quart or two to take home!

SERVES 12 TO 14.

½ cup canola oil

½ cup all-purpose flour

1 cup chopped celery

2 cups chopped onions

1 cup chopped green bell peppers

2 tablespoons minced fresh garlic

1½ teaspoons minced fresh thyme

4 dried bay leaves

½ cup tomato paste

½ teaspoon cayenne

3 quarts heated seafood stock

1 pound claw crab meat

1½ pounds small boiled and peeled shrimp

24 oysters, lightly sautéed in butter

Kosher salt

Gumbo filé, for garnish

Thinly sliced green onions, for garnish

Cooked white rice

Heat the canola oil in a heavy-bottomed 12-quart stockpot over medium-high heat until hot but not smoking. Gradually whisk in the flour. Cook, whisking constantly, for 20 minutes, or until the roux is the color of peanut butter. Add the celery, onion, and bell pepper. Cook, stirring constantly, for 20 minutes, or until the vegetables are very tender. The roux will cool slightly as the vegetables are added, and it will darken as the vegetables release their natural sugars. Stir in the garlic, thyme, bay leaves, tomato paste, and cayenne. Cook, stirring constantly, for 10 minutes, or until heated through and tomato paste has darkened slightly. Add the seafood stock and bring to a full boil, stirring occasionally. Reduce the heat to medium and simmer for 10 minutes, skimming the surface of any foam or fat that accumulates. Add the crabmeat, shrimp, and oysters. Season to taste with salt. Cook just to heat through. Discard the bay leaves. Serve the gumbo hot over white rice. Garnish each serving with a dusting of gumbo filé and scatter some green onions on top. Serve at once.

A TURTLE HUNT

TURTLE SOUP IS indeed one of the "grand old ladies" of classic Creole cuisine. Recipes for its preparation were closely guarded secrets written down in the "receipt books" of plantation households and passed down through the generations. I fell in love with its intoxicatingly rich, dark, complex flavor on my first taste many years ago and early in my career. I became a woman on a mission to learn how to make it in the authentic manner.

A dear friend and fellow food lover arranged for me to learn its preparation from the ground up—literally—with an elderly lady who was famous for her turtle soup. She called to tell me she was putting out some baited lines on her marshy pond and to arrive the next morning to see what the lines had for us. She told me to wear jeans and boots. When I arrived, she gathered a large burlap sack, a big thick stick, an axe, a set of wire cutters, and an oversized pair of pliers. Then, in the early-morning light, we trudged to a large pond or small lake that looked like a swamp to me. It was hard to tell where the pond actually began, as the shoreline was very soft and rimmed with high grasses.

Although there are many varieties of turtles, many of them endangered because of habitat loss and human exploitation, Tante T assured me that we were after the common diamond-backed terrapins, or "snapping" turtles, which can grow into gargantuan-sized critters. The bait lines, I discovered, were long pieces of wire staked to higher, dry ground with a large hook on the other end. She had baited the hooks with small fish or frogs and thrown them out into the water. As she tugged on the first line, the surface of the water shimmered violently and I could see the writhing coils of a rather large black and yellow reptile. "Water moccasin," Tante T said nonchalantly. I was staring into the cotton-white, open mouth of one of North America's most deadly creatures. I could see its fangs and Tante T's large hook protruding out of the bottom of its lower jaw. I will never forget the sight. She simply cut the wire with the wire cutters she had brought along, and the snake slithered away quickly, I'm sure to deal with the large hook in its mouth. I was relieved beyond measure that it decided not to deal with the ones who had caused its dilemma.

The second two lines yielded nothing, which was a good thing, as I was shaking so badly that the muscles in the back of my legs were quivering uncontrollably. Tante T said something had gotten away with the bait. I was thankful not to have to face the "somethings." As she pulled on the fourth line, a big smile broke across her face. "Oh yes, Mr. Turtle—and a nice, big one." She pulled it to the bank while it was trying to snap at everything in sight. She pulled the wire taut so that its head was exposed and poked the big stick at it. The turtle latched onto that stick with a death grip. Tante T pulled hard on the end of the stick; then, in a flash she dispatched its head with the axe. She pushed the turtle into the tow sack, and we trudged back to her house, dragging the sack. The turtle was about 14 inches in diameter. The two of us lifted it into a washtub. Then we brought several pots of water to a boil and poured them over the turtle to scald it and make the skin loose so it would be easier to remove the shell. First she peeled the body out of the heavy, armored top shell. It was not a pretty sight, and the smell was ghastly. Then she cut the meat into sections. As she did, she explained that there are seven types of meat on a turtle carcass and that each has a different taste and texture. I could see the different colors and grains of the meat. Then she boiled the meat, a step that she said was essential to tenderize it before making the soup.

Finally, we set about to making the masterpiece

pot of soup from her long list of bewitching aromatic herbs and spices. As it simmered and developed the aromas I associated with turtle soup, I was amazed to realize that I couldn't wait to get a bowl of that soup, even after the ordeal of the capture and cleaning.

In the ensuing years after moving back home to Texas, I've met a lot of coastal hunters and fishermen who hunt snapping turtles in the same marshy, snake-infested waters where I first encountered them. I've tasted their stews, often made with okra when it was in season, and braised turtle steaks with all sorts of added ingredients and seasonings, all of which I enjoyed. And because of my first experience with the turtle, I realize that eating wild foods really connects me with nature itself. I am grateful for having the opportunity to eat so many varieties of food that come to my table fresh from the uncontaminated places where they lived.

79

Turtle Soup with Madeira

When the Brennan family of New Orleans Commander's Palace (among others) restaurant fame decided to open Brennan's of Houston more than 40 years ago, their legendary turtle soup became a menu mainstay, bringing the venerable dish to Texas soil, where it developed legions of fans. The dish has been consistently rated as one of the top 100 dishes in Houston. Those fans were deprived of the heavenly brew when Brennan's of Houston was destroyed by fire in the ravages of Hurricane Ike in 2008. Thankfully, Brennan's and turtle soup rose from the ashes, reopening in the spring of 2010, so Houstonians can once again partake of the lusty soup. This is not the recipe from Brennan's but my own version developed over the years of tasting and tweaking since the day I first learned to make it on the banks of a marshy pond in Louisiana. It's rich and satisfying. Unless you're adept at hunting diamond-backed terrapins, you'll have to rely on a specialty market such as Louisiana Foods Seafood Market in Houston to order it for you. Or, if you know a chef well, you could ask the chef to order it for you. Be sure to specify that you want boneless meat, which saves the time-consuming step of removing hundreds of often tiny bones. Trust me, this soup is worth walking on fire, if required, to make it.

SERVES 8 TO 10.

5 pounds boneless turtle meat cut into 1-inch pieces
6 quarts beef stock, preferably homemade
½ cup unsalted butter
½ cup canola oil
1 cup all-purpose flour
½ pound artisan smoked ham, cut into ¼-inch dice
1 large onion, finely chopped
2 celery stalks, finely chopped, including leafy tops
2 tablespoons minced flat-leaf parsley
3 large garlic cloves, minced
1 teaspoon freshly ground black pepper

Dash of red (cayenne) pepper
2 fresh bay leaves, minced
2 teaspoons minced fresh thyme
½ teaspoon ground cloves
½ teaspoon ground allspice
¼ teaspoon ground mace
1 heaping tablespoon tomato paste
3 additional quarts beef stock, heated
1 tablespoon Worcestershire sauce
Kosher salt
3 tablespoons fresh lemon juice
Dry Madeira
2 or 3 hard-cooked eggs, chopped fine, for garnish

Combine turtle meat and 6 quarts beef stock in a heavy-bottomed 10-quart soup pot over medium heat. Simmer, covered, about 1½ hours, or until meat is very tender.

Drain meat and set aside to cool. Discard cooking stock. Using a sharp knife, chop the turtle meat finely; set aside. Combine butter and canola oil in a heavy-bottomed 6- to 8-quart soup pot over medium heat. When the fat is hot, add flour all at once and stir constantly to make a peanut butter–colored roux, about 25 minutes. Add the ham and turtle meat, vegetables, herbs, and spices. Cook, stirring constantly, until vegetables are very wilted, about 15 minutes. Add the tomato paste and stir to blend well. Cook, stirring constantly, until the tomato paste is darkened and thick, about 5 minutes. Heat the remaining 3 quarts of beef stock. Slowly add the hot stock, stirring to blend well. Stir in Worcestershire sauce, salt to taste, and lemon juice. Bring to a boil to thicken, then reduce heat, cover pan, and simmer 1 hour. To serve, spoon 2 tablespoons of Madeira, or to taste, into each soup plate and ladle 8 ounces of the soup over it; stir to blend. Garnish soup with some of the chopped egg and serve hot.

Deep in the Heart of Texas Chili

Chili. Now there's a subject that could get you in a lot of trouble in Texas. Kind of like gumbo in Louisiana. Texans are mighty opinionated about their chili. Battles have been fought over chili; friends have been made and lost over the dark and spicy brew. You see, each chili cooker thinks his or her method is the *only* way to make it. Then there's the long-fought controversy over beans, with equal forces lined up for and against adding beans to chili.

Chili is a truly Texan creation. From the 1860s to the 1930s, the famous Chili Queens of San Antonio would arrive around dusk at the various plazas around the city to set up their tables, pots, pans, and braziers to cook their fiery, chile-laden concoctions that became known simply as *chili*. They would cook until dawn, selling their thick stew to the businessmen, troubadours, cowboys, those out for a night of entertainment, and visitors to the city. The first Chili Queens graced Military Plaza until 1889, when the San Antonio City Hall was built there. It is generally believed that the Chili Queens were the inspiration for the creation of the whole Tex-Mex genre of cooking. And just to make it an unequivocal fact, the Texas legislature decreed chili the "Official State Dish" in 1977.

But you know what I think? I think the rivalry and the controversy make for dozens of equally fabulous bowls of chili. Just attend one of the many chili cook-offs in Texas and taste for yourself. The granddaddy of all chili cook-offs is held the first weekend of November in tiny Terlingua in Brewster County near Big Bend. It's an abandoned cinnabar-mining town that's mostly a ghost town the rest of the year, inhabited by a few intrepid souls. The cook-off is the official event of the Chili Appreciation Society founded by legendary chili aficionado Wick Fowler. The first Terlingua Chili Cook-Off was held in 1967, pitting Fowler against newspaper columnist and humorist H. Allen Smith from New York. Now, of course, you automatically know who the Texans were rooting for. It was a weekend that changed the status of chili forevermore. H. Allen Smith lost the cook-off and never got over it. In fact, he later moved to Alpine, became a Texan, and wrote a wonderfully funny book about the event, *The Great Chili Confrontation.*

I've added masa harina to this chili at the end of the cooking process as a thickener. (It also adds a nice little kick of corn flavor.) Masa harina is the flour from which tamale dough is made. It's available in supermarkets wherever there is a large Hispanic population. This recipe is also unique in that you're actually making your own chili powder rather than buying a "blended" chili powder. It's much tastier this way. This chili is a rich, thick, dark concoction that makes for one very serious "bowl o' red."

SERVES 8 TO 10.

12 ancho chiles, stems and seeds removed
7 pasilla chiles, seeds removed
2½ tablespoons toasted, then ground, cumin seeds
1 tablespoon toasted, then ground, whole coriander seeds
1½ tablespoons dried Mexican oregano
2 teaspoons unsweetened cocoa
1½ tablespoons sweet Hungarian paprika
½ teaspoon cayenne
2 teaspoons freshly ground black pepper
6 pounds beef chuck roast

⅓ cup fresh leaf lard, preferably, or solid shortening
2 large onions, chopped
15 garlic cloves, minced
⅔ cup tomato paste
1 can (15 ounces) tomato sauce
3 quarts chicken stock
4 cups cooked pinto beans
Kosher salt
½ cup masa harina whisked into ⅔ cup hot chicken stock

GARNISH:
Shredded Texas Cheddar cheese
Chopped white onions
Diced avocado

Heat a heavy-bottomed 12- to 14-inch skillet over medium-high heat. When the pan is hot, add a layer of the chiles. Cook, turning often, until a strong chile aroma emanates from the pan. The chiles will *not* be dry and crisp to the touch, and the aroma should not be one that is bitter and charred. The cooking time will vary, depending on how much moisture the chiles are holding, but about 3 to 4 minutes is a good average time. Do not allow the chiles to burn. Spread the chiles on a wire rack to cool and become moderately crisp. Repeat until all chiles have been toasted. Grind the chiles to a fine powder in a mortar and pestle, or make it easy on yourself and use an electric spice/coffee grinder. Shake the chile powder through a fine strainer after grinding to remove any large pieces. Combine the ground chiles with the cumin, coriander, Mexican oregano, cocoa, paprika, cayenne, and black pepper. Set the chile and spice mixture aside.

Trim the chuck roast well, removing all fat, gristle, and tendons. Chop the meat by hand into ½-inch dice; set aside. Melt the lard or shortening in a heavy-bottomed 8-quart Dutch oven over medium-high heat. When the fat is very hot, add the meat and sear until well browned on all sides, stirring often. Add the onions and garlic. Cook, stirring often, until onions are wilted and transparent, about 7 minutes. Add the tomato paste and stir to blend well. Cook, stirring, until the tomato paste is very thick and dark in color, about 5 minutes. Add the tomato sauce and ground chile and spice mixture. Stir to blend well, then add the chicken stock. Bring the mixture to a full boil, then lower heat to a simmer and cover. Cook, stirring occasionally, for about 1½ hours. Stir in the pinto beans, salt to taste, and masa mixture. Cook, uncovered, an additional 30 to 45 minutes on low-medium heat, or until the chili is thickened and the meat is fork tender. Stir often to prevent sticking. Taste and adjust seasonings as desired. Serve hot, topped with shredded Cheddar cheese, chopped onions, and diced avocado.

EASY TIGER BAKE SHOP & BEER GARDEN

A BAKERY AND BEER GARDEN were not part of the plan when the principals of Austin's ELM Restaurant Group went scouting for a location for a casual French food spot. But the street-level entry of the historic two-story building on East Sixth Street seemed ideal for a bake shop, while the speakeasy feel of the downstairs area, coupled with the expansive outdoor patio overlooking Waller Creek, was perfect for a beer garden. A German concept began to emerge, with fresh-baked pretzels and hearty loaves baked upstairs, complementing the craft beers and house-cured sausages served below.

Both chef Drew Curren and baker David Norman believe in classic, hands-on techniques. Everything at Easy Tiger is prepared from scratch, and much of the meat and produce is sourced locally. The lye-dipped pretzels, house-fermented sauerkraut, and house-made mustard are a nod to classic German flavors, as are the house-made link sausages, which are based on classics such as bratwurst, knockwurst, and knoblewurst. The corned beef, pastrami, and beef jerky are Drew's favorite companions for good beer. In addition to making pretzels, which have become the specialty of the house (and are divine when dipped in the house-made beer cheese), David and his team turn out artisanal baguettes, miche, rye, ciabatta, and laminated pastries such as croissant, pain au chocolat, and a house-spiced tiger claw.

The way David sees it, bread and beer are a natural pairing given the yeast and fermentation process used in both. "Fermentation is in a way the ultimate expression of local, because the microbial cultures involved in natural fermentation are unique to the particular environment where they are cultivated, " says David. "So my Waller Creek sourdough starter as well as Drew's sauerkraut and other fermented items are a unique expression of the terroir of this place."

David Norman's Easy Tiger Sourdough Bread

SOURDOUGH STARTER:

DAY 1:

¾ cup unbleached flour

¼ cup dark (whole)
   rye flour

⅓ cup water

Mix together to a stiff
dough, put in clear plastic
or glass container, and mark
the starting level with a
piece of tape. Cover and
let sit at room temperature
for 24 to 48 hours.

DAY 2 (OR 3):

Save about ⅓ of the starter
from above, discarding the
rest. Add the following to
it and knead until all flour
is moistened and a stiff
dough is formed.

¾ cup unbleached flour

¼ cup dark rye flour

⅓ cup water

Put in clear plastic or glass
container, and mark the
starting level with a piece of
tape. Let sit at room temperature for 24 hours.

DAYS 3–7:

Save about ⅓ of the starter
from above, discarding the
rest. Add the following to
it and knead until all flour
is moistened and a stiff
dough is formed.

1 cup unbleached flour

⅓ cup water

Put in clear plastic or glass container, and mark the starting level with a piece of tape. Let sit at room temperature for 8 hours. You should start to see an increase in the volume, indicating building yeast activity.

Now is the time to feed the starter every 8 hours. Follow the same procedure as above, reserving about ⅓ of the starter and feeding it with 1 cup flour and ⅓ cup water every 8 hours.

By day 4 or 5 you should see about a tripling in volume during the 8-hour fermentation. This means that you have good yeast activity and you could begin using the starter to make bread. However, to obtain a truly mature starter with the proper acidity and flavor, you will want to continue this same feeding process for a full 7 days.
When you are ready to make a batch of bread, feed the whole amount of the starter with the following ingredients.

   1½ cups unbleached flour
   ¼ cup water

Allow this to rise for 2 to 4 hours, then refrigerate overnight, or let rise for 6 hours and use then.

Make sure you save about ½ cup of the starter and feed it again with 1 cup flour and ⅓ cup water so you can keep your starter going. Use the rest of the starter in the following recipe or your favorite sourdough recipe.

You can keep feeding the starter if you are going to keep baking, or if not, you can hold it in the fridge. You should pull it out and feed it once a week if you want to keep it fresh and healthy. Let it sit at room temperature for 8 hours before returning it to the fridge. Remember to take the starter out of the fridge and feed at least 6 hours, or overnight, before you want to bake again.

SOURDOUGH BREAD:
MAKES 2 LOAVES.

The rest of the starter from above after reserving ½ cup to feed and keep going	4½ cups unbleached flour
	2½ teaspoons salt
	1½ to 1¾ cups water

Mix in a stand mixer to combine ingredients, adjusting water for a medium-wet dough. You don't want a dough that's too stiff, but not an extra-wet dough either, as the acids in the starter will soften the dough as it ferments.

Knead until the gluten is well developed. The dough will be very elastic and spring back when you make an indentation with your finger.

Form into a smooth ball and place in a large bowl. Cover with plastic wrap or a damp towel. Allow to rise for 1½ to 2 hours, turning it out and "punching" it down (give it gentle folds) and returning it to the bowl once after the first hour.

Preheat oven (preferably with a pizza stone on the middle rack) to 500°F.

Divide dough in two and form into 2 balls, stretching the gluten to start a tight surface. Allow to rest for 15 minutes, then tighten the balls further. Put them on a sheet tray or wooden board and cover with a damp towel; allow to almost double in volume.

If you have a pizza stone preheated, transfer the loaves one at a time to a wooden peel. Cut an X in the top of the loaf with a razor blade or serrated knife. Create some steam in your oven either by misting with a spray bottle or carefully pouring a small amount of water into a heavy-bottomed pan that has also been preheating. Slide the loaf onto the stone, and then quickly cut and add the second loaf. After about 5 minutes, reduce the heat to 450°F. Bake for 20 to 30 minutes or until the loaves sound hollow when rapped on the bottom.

If you don't have a pizza stone, the loaves can be cut and then baked right on the sheet pan.

Jack Allen's Kitchen Skillet Cornbread

Jack Gilmore serves up a mean little skillet of cornbread at his popular Austin restaurant, Jack Allen's Kitchen, on Highway 71, just past the traffic logjam known to locals as "the Oak Hill Y." The wonderful, slightly sweet bread with its crisp crust belies the simplicity of the recipe. Because the recipe makes two or four skillets, depending on how you wish to serve it, each time you make it, you'll always have some in reserve! The cornbread freezes very well for up to 2 months. It's great with fried fish, shrimp, or oysters. But for a double Texas treat, serve the cornbread with Deep in the Heart of Texas Chili (see recipe on pages 81–83).

MAKES TWO 10-INCH SKILLETS OR FOUR 6½-INCH SKILLETS.

1½ cups yellow cornmeal, preferably stone ground

1¼ cups unbleached all-purpose flour

⅓ cup plus 1 tablespoon sugar

1 tablespoon baking powder

1 tablespoon baking soda

1 cup plain yogurt

⅓ cup plus 1 tablespoon creamed corn

⅓ cup plus 1 tablespoon whole-kernel corn

1½ cups buttermilk (not low fat)

3 eggs

½ cup plus 1 tablespoon melted butter

¼ teaspoon kosher salt

Preheat oven to 400°F. Spray either four 6½-inch cast-iron skillets or two 10-inch cast-iron skillets with nonstick cooking spray and place them in the preheated oven while you make the batter.

Mix all dry ingredients together in a large bowl, blending well. In a separate bowl, whisk all wet ingredients together. Stir the wet ingredients into the dry ingredients just until all dry ingredients are moistened and no traces of unblended flour or cornmeal remain. Do not overmix.

Remove the skillets from the oven one at a time and fill with the batter. For the smaller skillets, use 1 cup plus 2 tablespoons of the batter for each skillet. For the larger skillets, use 3½ cups per skillet. The batter will sizzle in the hot pan, forming a nice crisp crust. Return pans to the hot oven and bake for 20 minutes, or until a toothpick inserted in the center of the cornbread comes out clean and the tops are golden brown.

Remove from oven and slice into wedges to serve. If not serving right away, turn the cornbread out of the skillets onto a cooling rack. Reheat to serve. If you freeze any of the cornbread, let it cool completely, then wrap in foil. To use, put the cornbread, still frozen in the foil, in a preheated 375°F oven for 15 minutes. Unwrap and cook for 5 minutes to recrisp the crust.

HOMESTEAD GRISTMILL

AFTER THE MODERN American Industrial Revolution in the late 1800s and early 1900s, the number of water-powered stone gristmills began to dwindle significantly. Small, locally supported mills used to fill the countryside in America. It is estimated that in the late 1800s there were 23,000 gristmills in America, with 350 in Texas alone.

The Homestead Gristmill is part of an agrarian community in Waco that strives to preserve many of the crafts, skills, and farming methods practiced for hundreds of years in America before the Industrial Revolution. The mill was built in central New Jersey in the eighteenth century. It closed in 1918 and stood abandoned for many years, until it was finally condemned to be demolished. The Homestead community's barn restoration operation found the mill, dismantled it, and brought it to Texas in 2000. It was carefully restored at its present location in Waco, opening for business on Labor Day of 2003.

Proprietor Shahar Yarden was born in Israel in 1964 and moved to the United States in 1985. He apprenticed as a miller in North Carolina at the Old Mill of Guilford. There he learned the craft of grinding grains with stone mills from Charles Parnel, an 86-year-old Scotsman who had been a miller his entire life. Shahar moved to Texas in 1990 to become the miller at Homestead Gristmill.

The mill operates much as it did when it was first built, grinding 13 different grains, including corn, wheat, and gluten-free grains. The mill also makes grain and flour blends into a variety of baking mixes, stone-ground grits, and granola. Chefs all over Texas use the mill's products, and it supplies the members of the local community with flour and cornmeal. There's a pleasant aroma of freshly ground grains permeating the mill. Makes you want to bake something!

Pecan Crescents

Since my daughter was very small, these delicious little crescent rolls, with their flaky sour cream pastry, were her favorite Sunday breakfast food. Even though she is grown and has a family of her own, I still make them for her whenever she comes to visit. They're really easy to make, and they freeze very well, so make a gigantic batch to store and enjoy for many Sundays to come.

MAKES 16 CRESCENTS.

PASTRY:

2 cups sifted all-purpose flour

¼ teaspoon salt

1 cup (2 sticks) frozen unsalted butter, cut into 1-inch cubes

1 egg yolk, beaten

¼ cup sour cream

PECAN FILLING:

½ cup granulated sugar

¼ cup firmly packed light brown sugar

1½ teaspoons ground cinnamon

¾ cup chopped pecans

Combine the flour, salt, and butter in the work bowl of a food processor fitted with the steel blade. Pulse on/off 4 to 5 times to break the butter into pea-sized bits. In a small bowl combine the egg yolk and sour cream; beat well and add to flour mixture. Process just until combined but still crumbly.

Turn the dough out onto a lightly floured work surface; gather into a ball and knead 3 to 4 times to form a cohesive dough. Divide the dough into 4 equal portions and pat each into a disk. Wrap each disk in plastic wrap and refrigerate for about 30 minutes to firm up the dough.

Prepare the filling by combining all ingredients in a small bowl and blending well; set aside. Preheat oven to 375°F and line a baking sheet with parchment paper; set aside. Remove one disk of the pastry at a time and roll out on a lightly floured work surface to a 12-inch round. Using a pizza cutter or sharp knife, cut the round into 4 wedges. Sprinkle a portion of the filling evenly over the dough, leaving a ½-inch border at the round edge of the wedges. Roll up each wedge, beginning at the outside edge. Place the crescents on the prepared baking sheet with the pointed ends underneath. Bend each crescent, curving the ends in toward each other. Repeat with remaining dough disks. Bake in preheated oven for 20 to 25 minutes, or until golden brown and crispy. Cool on wire rack. When completely cool, store in an airtight container or freeze.

Hill Country Cinnamon Rolls

Big, gooey cinnamon rolls dripping with icing and stuffed with pecans and raisins are among my favorite breakfast foods. I've worked with this recipe over the years and am proud to say that it produces sinfully rich and delicious cinnamon rolls. I try to always have them on hand when I have overnight guests. What better aroma to wake up to than homemade cinnamon rolls baking in the oven? You can bake the rolls ahead of time and freeze them unglazed. Thaw the rolls the evening before you wish to serve them and reheat in a medium oven just until they're heated through; then drizzle on the icing and serve hot.

MAKES 9 TO 10 LARGE ROLLS.

2 tablespoons instant-rise active
  dry yeast
1 cup warm water (105°F to 115°F)
⅓ cup plus 1 tablespoon granulated
  sugar, divided
4 cups unbleached bread flour
1 tablespoon vanilla extract
1 teaspoon kosher salt
2 eggs
½ stick (4 tablespoons) unsalted
  butter, softened
Additional 3 tablespoons unsalted
  butter, melted

FILLING:

6 ounces cream cheese, softened
  and cut into chunks
1 cup chopped Texas pecans
½ cup golden raisins
1 tablespoon ground cinnamon
½ cup granulated sugar
½ cup dark brown sugar

GLAZE:

⅓ cup unsalted butter, melted
2 cups powdered sugar
2 teaspoons vanilla extract
4 tablespoons half and half

To make the dough, combine the yeast, warm water, and 1 tablespoon of the sugar in a 2-cup Pyrex measuring cup. Stir gently to blend. Set aside until yeast has dissolved and the mixture is foamy, about 4 minutes.

Combine the remaining ⅓ cup sugar, flour, vanilla, salt, eggs, and softened butter in the work bowl of a food processor fitted with the steel blade. Process until all ingredients are well blended. Add the yeast mixture, scraping measuring cup to include all liquid. Process until the dough comes together and pulls away from the sides of the bowl, about 20 seconds. Check the consistency of the dough, adding additional flour, if needed, by the tablespoon. Process after each addition until the consistency is right. The dough should be cohesive and not sticky. Turn mixture out onto a lightly floured work surface and knead for about 3 minutes to form a smooth, elastic dough.

Coat a large mixing bowl with canola oil. Place the dough in the bowl, turning to coat all surfaces with the oil. Cover bowl with plastic wrap and set aside to rise until dough is doubled in bulk, about 45 minutes.

While dough is rising, combine the filling ingredients, except cream cheese, in a small bowl. Toss with a fork to blend well; set aside. Place the chunks of cream cheese in a clean processor bowl and process until smooth and creamy. Remove to a separate bowl.

When dough has doubled in bulk, punch it down and turn out onto a lightly floured work surface. Roll the dough out into a 12-inch square. Use a rubber spatula to spread the cream cheese evenly over the surface of the dough. Fold the dough into a rectangle as though you were folding a letter. Then fold one end of the dough to the middle and fold the other end over to cover it, making a small square.

Add a little more flour to the work surface and roll the dough out into a rectangle about 18 inches long and 12 inches wide. Brush the dough with the 3 tablespoons of melted butter, and then scatter the filling over the dough, leaving a 1-inch border at the long sides. Roll the dough, pinwheel-style, beginning at the long side closest to you. Be sure that the roll is evenly thick in diameter. Pinch the long seam to seal the dough and turn dough seam side down. Line a half-sheet baking sheet with parchment paper; set aside.

Using a thin, sharp knife, cut off the scraggly ends of the roll and discard. Cut the dough into slices 1½ to 2 inches thick, depending on how thick you want the rolls to be. Arrange the slices almost touching on the prepared baking sheet. Cover loosely with plastic wrap and set aside to rise for 30 minutes. Preheat oven to 350°F.

While the dough is rising, make the glaze. Combine the melted butter, powdered sugar, vanilla, and half and half in a bowl. Whisk to make a medium-stiff paste with no lumps of powdered sugar left; set aside.

When the rolls have risen, bake them in the preheated oven until they are lightly browned and sound hollow when thumped on the bottom, about 25 to 30 minutes. Transfer the rolls to a cooling rack set over a baking sheet. Spoon the glaze over the hot rolls, covering liberally and using all of the glaze. Allow rolls to cool slightly before serving.

If you wish to bake the rolls ahead of time, don't glaze them. Reheat them before serving, then spoon on the glaze and serve.

CONFITURAS

STEPHANIE MCCLENNY is a self-taught cook. While in college she worked as the caretaker for an elderly couple. One of her duties was to shop for, and cook, three meals a day. It was an excellent opportunity to hone her kitchen skills—and, she confesses, "I really got the cooking bug."

She later ran a small café in East Austin and then wrote a food blog called *The Cosmic Cowgirl*, but Stephanie really found her place in the food world when she began canning. Inspiration may have come from her family; although she doesn't have her own childhood memory of canning or "putting up" foods, her mother told her that when she and her siblings were small, their mother often had jelly bags hanging all over the house. Stephanie herself began canning summer tomatoes to have a delicious year-round supply of sunshine in a thin skin, then moved to pickling the bounty of Hill Country peaches and making jam using Celeste figs from a friend's tree. Friends and family requested more, and she obliged.

In 2010, Stephanie formed Confituras. She sources only Texas fruits, vegetables, herbs, and flowers for her award-winning jams, jellies, and other preserves. "It keeps me honest," says Stephanie, "and it keeps me experimenting with new, seasonal flavor pairings. When I find fresh blueberries and basil available to harvest at the same time in July, they end up in a jar together. Canning provides me with an endless source of culinary creativity, both in terms of what Mother Nature has to offer at any given time and what I can create from those offerings."

Simply the Best Buttermilk Biscuits

Next to Texas toast, the most important bread in Texas is biscuits. For a real cowboy breakfast, you gotta' have biscuits and gravy. You can have other stuff, too, but the biscuits and gravy had better be there. I'm always amazed at the number of people who are terrified of making biscuits. There's really nothing to it, once you get the hang of it. If there are any secrets to making great biscuits, they would be to use fresh leaf lard and to not over-work the dough, or the biscuits will be really tough and dense—kind of like hockey pucks. Just be gentle with the dough. When you roll it out, use gentle strokes, rolling only in one direction so that you don't get it all riled up and tough.

MAKES 12 (2½-INCH DIAMETER) BISCUITS.

---

3 cups all-purpose flour

¼ cup powdered milk

2 tablespoons baking powder

2 tablespoons sugar

1 teaspoon kosher salt

1 teaspoon cream of tartar

½ cup leaf lard, or substitute solid vegetable shortening if you absolutely must

1 stick unsalted butter, room temperature, cut into chunks

¾ cup plus 2 tablespoons buttermilk (not low fat)

Melted unsalted butter for brushing tops

Preheat oven to 400°F. Spray a 13 × 9-inch baking pan with nonstick vegetable spray; set aside. In a bowl, combine all ingredients except lard, butter, and buttermilk. Toss to blend well. Add the lard and butter. Using your hands or a pastry blender, work the fat into the dry mixture until the mixture resembles coarse oatmeal. Make a well in the center of the mixture and pour in the buttermilk. Using a large spoon, quickly, but gently, combine the ingredients, making sure all dry ingredients are well blended. But don't mess with it once the dry ingredients are blended!

Turn the dough out onto a well-floured work surface and, with floured hands, knead it 8 or 10 times to form a smooth and cohesive dough. Roll the dough out gently to ¾-inch thickness. Using a 2½-inch biscuit cutter, cut the dough into rounds. Be sure to use a straight, forceful, downward motion with the cutter and do not twist it, or you'll crimp the edges and the biscuits won't rise completely. Place biscuits in the prepared baking pan with the sides touching. Gently gather any dough scraps together and pat again to ¾-inch thickness. Cut remaining dough into rounds.

Bake in preheated oven for 15 to 18 minutes, or until light golden brown and cooked through. Remove pan from oven and brush the tops of the biscuits with the melted butter. Get the honey or your favorite preserves ready to spread on those hot biscuits!

Czech Cream Cheese and Peach Kolaches

Texas has a sizable Czech population, and many Czech foods have become an integral part of today's Texas cuisine—kolaches being one of the most popular examples. Czech immigrants from Moravia, Silesia, and Bohemia began to arrive in Texas in the early 1850s. The city of Caldwell remains a stronghold of Czech culture, having proclaimed itself the Kolache Capital of Texas, celebrating its status with an annual Kolache Festival in September. The city of West also boasts a large Czech population and vies for top honors in kolache competitions. The delectable little pastries, which derived their name from the Czech word *kolae*, meaning "cake," can be filled with a variety of ingredients, but the most traditional are made using fruits, jams, cheese, or poppy seeds. Sausage- and cheese-filled buns, sometimes called savory kolaches, are also of Czech origin but are more properly called *klobasnikis*.

MAKES 24.

DOUGH:

1 tablespoon instant-rise dry yeast

⅓ cup sugar, divided

¼ cup canola oil

1 teaspoon kosher salt

1 cup whole milk

4 to 4½ cups sifted all-purpose flour, plus additional for work surface, or more if needed

4 tablespoons unsalted butter, softened

2 eggs, beaten

6 tablespoons additional unsalted butter, melted and cooled

CREAM CHEESE AND PEACH FILLING:

8 ounces cream cheese, softened, cut into small chunks

1 egg yolk

¼ cup sugar

Grated zest of 1 large lemon

1 teaspoon vanilla

⅔ cup Texas peach preserves

STREUSEL TOPPING:

½ cup frozen unsalted butter, cut into ½-inch cubes

1 cup sugar

1 cup all-purpose flour

Begin by making the streusel topping. Combine all ingredients in the work bowl of a food processor fitted with the steel blade. Process, using on/off pulses, until the mixture resembles coarse meal. Do not overprocess. Turn mixture out into a zip-sealing bag and store in freezer while preparing the filling and dough.

Make the dough. Combine the yeast and 1 tablespoon of the sugar in a 2-cup Pyrex measuring cup. Heat the milk to approximately 110°F. Gently whisk half of the milk into the cup with the yeast and sugar. Set aside to proof, or until yeast has dissolved and mixture is bubbling and foamy. In the bowl of a stand mixer fitted with a dough hook, place remaining sugar, oil, salt, remaining ½ cup of milk, and 1 cup of the flour. Starting on low speed, beat the mixture until flour is incorporated, then increase to medium speed, and beat until blended. Add the yeast mixture, remaining flour, softened butter, and eggs. Begin again on low speed until the flour is incorporated, then increase speed to medium, and knead the dough until it is very smooth and elastic, about 6 minutes. The dough should not stick to the sides of the bowl. If it is too wet, add additional flour, 1 tablespoon at a time, beating to combine after each addition, until dough is the right consistency.

Turn dough out onto a work surface and knead 4 to 5 times by hand, or until the dough springs back when pulled. Lightly oil a large bowl and place the dough in the bowl, turning to coat all surfaces with the oil. Cover bowl with plastic wrap and set aside to rise in a draft-free spot until the dough is doubled in bulk, about 1 hour.

While the dough is rising, make the filling. Combine all ingredients except peach preserves in the work bowl of a food processor fitted with the steel blade. Process until smooth. Turn out into a bowl and set aside.

When the dough has doubled in bulk, punch it down and divide into 2-ounce balls. Line 2 baking sheets with parchment paper. Arrange 12 of the balls on each prepared baking sheet, placing them 3 across and 4 down. Flatten the balls with the palm of your hand. Using a pastry brush, baste each flattened piece with some of the melted butter, taking care not to drip butter on the parchment paper. Cover loosely with plastic wrap and allow to rise for 20 minutes.

Flatten the dough balls once more and make a deep indentation in the center of each. Spoon equal portions of the cheese filling in each indentation. Top the cheese on each kolache with 1 heaping teaspoonful of the peach preserves. Scatter a portion of the streusel topping over each. Cover loosely with plastic wrap and set aside to rise for 30 minutes. Preheat oven to 350°F.

When kolaches have risen, bake them in the preheated oven for 30 to 35 minutes, or until golden brown. The cheese should be lightly browned, and the peach preserves melty and lightly browned. Remove to a wire rack and cool slightly before serving. The kolaches can be cooled completely and frozen. Wrap tightly in plastic wrap and place in zip-sealing bags, squeezing out all the air from the bags. Freeze for up to 6 weeks.

Polish Sausage Klobasnikis with Cheese and Jalapeños

Most people in Texas know these traditional Czech pastries as kolaches. Often, they're called pigs in a blanket. But the real Czech word for the wonderful pastries filled with a sausage and often cheese and jalapeños, although the chiles are a strictly Texan addition, is *klobasniki*. There are also other variations of the pastry that are filled with Czech-style pan sausage and sauerkraut or cooked cabbage. If you don't get around to making your own, there's a Czech-owned bakery in Ellinger on that well-traveled road from Houston to Austin, by the name of Hruska's, that makes heavenly kolaches and klobasnikis, including the sausage and sauerkraut or cabbage ones. You'll know you're there because of the snarl of cars jockeying for a parking space in the small parking lot/gas pump area out front (and because the speed limit drops to 55 mph right before you get to the store). There are many meat markets in rural Texas towns that make great Polish-style sausage. One of my favorites is Dziuk's Meat Market in Castroville, a charming town that offers a bit of Alsace in Texas. The Kiolbassa Provision Company of San Antonio also crafts a quite tasty Polish-style sausage that does not contain MSG or nitrates and is available in mainstream supermarkets in Texas.

MAKES ABOUT 28 PASTRIES.

8 ounces solid vegetable shortening

1 cup sugar

1 teaspoon kosher salt

1 cup boiling water

1 tablespoon plus 1½ teaspoons instant-rise, active dry yeast

2 eggs, slightly beaten

1 cup warm (105°F to 155°F) water

6½ cups bread flour

3½ pounds Texas Cheddar cheese, shredded

Sliced, pickled nacho-sliced jalapeños

14 good-quality Polish sausage links, cut into about 3-inch lengths

In the bowl of a stand mixer, cream the shortening and sugar until light and fluffy, using the mixer's beater blade, about 5 minutes. Add the salt, then the boiling water. Mix on low speed until the shortening is completely melted and mixture has cooled to between 105°F and 115°F. Add the yeast, beating just to blend. Add the eggs and warm water; beat until well mixed. Replace the paddle blade on the mixer with the dough hook. Add the bread flour and mix with the dough hook, beginning on low speed and increasing to medium as the flour is incorporated, stopping to scrape down sides of bowl as needed, until a smooth dough is obtained. Knead the dough with the hook for about 5 minutes.

Place the dough in a large, oiled bowl, turning to coat all sides of the dough; cover tightly with plastic wrap and refrigerate overnight, or for at least 4 hours.

In the morning, line 3 baking sheets with parchment paper; set aside. Separate the dough into 2 equal pieces by weight. Roll each portion of the dough into a rectangle about 28 inches wide and 1/8-inch thick. Beginning at the long side of the dough, roll the rectangles, pinwheel-style, into tight rolls. Be sure the roll is uniform in thickness its entire length. Cut each roll of dough into 14 slices, each about 2 inches. Roll each piece out into a round about ¼-inch thick. Roll the dough using gentle strokes in one direction to avoid activating the gluten protein in the flour, which will make it very elastic and hard to roll. If the dough becomes springy and elastic while you're trying to roll it out, simply cover it loosely with a clean kitchen towel and let it rest for about 10 minutes.

Scatter each dough round with ½ cup of the cheese, leaving a 1-inch border at the edge, and place desired number of jalapeño slices on the cheese. Place a piece of the sausage in the center of the cheese. Fold the sides of the dough tightly over the sausage and cheese, aligning the edges in a straight line; then roll the dough, starting at the edge closest to you, around the sausage tightly. Place the klobasnikis, seam sides down, on prepared baking sheets, allowing about 3 inches between each pastry. Set aside to rise, covered loosely with plastic wrap, for about 45 minutes. Preheat oven to 350°F.

Bake the klobasnikis for about 30 to 35 minutes, or until dough is golden brown and firm to the touch. Cheese should be completely melted inside the dough. Cool on wire racks to almost room temperature before serving. The sausages inside will retain heat longer than the pastry.

Pan de Campo

Pan de campo is a rustic camp bread that was prepared by chuckwagon cooks in Dutch ovens over open fires during the early days of Texas ranching and cattle drives. In 2005, Governor Rick Perry signed into law a bill that designated pan de campo as the official State Bread of Texas. Today the bread is generally cooked on a flat grill or comal set over hot burners on the stovetop. Pan de campo is a multipurpose bread. It can be used as a "wrap" for stewlike dishes such as carne guisado or spread with butter and home-made jam, or molasses, for breakfast. Or it can just be served as a side bread with a meal, where it's often used to sop up refried beans or other scoopable sides. Recipes for pan de campo vary from cook to cook—some call for baking powder and others for yeast. I adapted this version from a recipe used by Don Strange of Texas, one of Texas's most beloved and well-known caterers. Don's version is yeast based, and I love its soft, foldable texture and delicate but compelling flavor. The recipe makes a lot of pan de campo, but it freezes well. I love to have it on hand when I need a bread for dinner.

1½ tablespoons instant-rise yeast

1 cup warm water (105°F to 115°F)

2 tablespoons sugar, divided

5¼ cups all-purpose flour

1 tablespoon kosher salt

¾ teaspoon baking soda

¾ teaspoon baking powder

1½ cups buttermilk

⅔ cup canola oil

Stir the yeast into the warm water in a 2-cup Pyrex measuring cup to blend. Gently whisk in 1 tablespoon of the sugar. Set aside until the yeast has dissolved and the mixture is foamy. Combine the flour, salt, baking soda, baking powder, and remaining tablespoon of sugar in the work bowl of a food processor fitted with the steel blade. Pulse 3 to 4 times to blend dry ingredients well. Add the yeast mixture, buttermilk, and canola oil. Process until the dough forms a ball. The dough should not be sticky. Add additional flour, 1 tablespoon at a time, as needed to form a soft, nonsticky dough. Process to blend after each addition. Turn dough out onto a work surface and knead 4 to 5 times to form a smooth dough. Place the dough in a large, lightly oiled bowl and turn to coat all surfaces. Cover the bowl tightly with plastic wrap and set aside in a warm, draft-free spot to rise until doubled in bulk, about 1 hour.

Punch the dough down until no air remains. Divide the dough into 36 portions, about 2½ ounces each. Roll each portion out into a ball. (The balls should be about the size of a golf ball.) Using a rolling pin, roll each ball into a 6-inch disk. Refrigerate while heating grill.

Heat a flat griddle on the stovetop or on a char-grill. When the grill is medium hot, place as many of the dough rounds as will fit on the grill in a single layer, not touching. Cook the breads until lightly browned and puffed on both sides, about 1½ minutes per side, or until small bubbles appear on the top surface of the dough. Turn once with a metal spatula. Serve hot.

You can freeze any pan de campo that you will not need for up to 1 month. As soon as the breads are completely cool, wrap them singly in foil and freeze in a large zip-sealing freezer bag. Simply reheat the frozen bread(s) without unwrapping, in a 350°F preheated oven for 15 minutes. They will taste remarkably just like they were freshly baked.

Texas Toast

There are a few stories on the origin of the classic Texas toast, but the one that seems to be the most plausible places its origin in Beaumont. The Pig Stand restaurant chain, a Texas institution for many, many years, was founded in Dallas in 1921. A young man by the name of Royce Hailey started as a carhop with the chain in 1930 and worked his way up to become the president in 1955. In 1941, he was working at the Calder Avenue Pig Stand in Beaumont, when he asked the Rainbo Bakery, which supplied the bread for the restaurant, to slice it thicker, as he thought the thin slices looked a bit stingy on the plate. When the bread arrived, it was *so* thick that it wouldn't fit in the toasters. One of the cooks in the kitchen suggested that they butter both sides of the bread and toast it on the oven racks. They did, and customers loved the gigantic, crispy, buttery slabs. Hailey named it Texas toast, and a Texas tradition was born.

The thick-sliced, butter-basted, white bread is a required accompaniment to chicken-fried steak or a nice grilled rib eye. Unless you bake your own white bread in the big pullman-loaf pans, you'll have to get it at your favorite bakery. You can substitute good-quality rounded-top white bread sliced thick. It just won't look the same as the square Texas toast at your favorite steakhouse. But good bread slathered with butter and toasted until crisp would never taste bad, whatever the shape. The recipe will make a lot of Texas toast, depending on the size of the loaf of pullman bread. When I make it, I make the entire loaf into Texas toast, using what I need at the time. Then I wrap the leftover slices tightly in foil in batches of 2 or 4 slices and freeze them in zip-sealing plastic bags. Reheat in the foil in a 350°F oven for 15 minutes. Open the foil and lay the toasts directly on the oven rack; recrisp for 5 minutes, then serve hot.

Unsliced white pullman bread loaves
Melted unsalted butter

Cut the bread into slices about 1-inch thick, using a serrated bread knife, or ask if the bakery will slice it thick for you. Heat a flat griddle or a large skillet until medium hot. Using a pastry brush, baste both sides of the bread slices with melted butter. Be sure to brush all the way to the edges.

Lay the buttered slices on the hot griddle or in the skillet and cook until golden brown on both sides, turning once. Don't allow the bread to actually brown. It should be light golden colored and slightly crisp. Cut the slices in half diagonally and serve hot.

3

SALADS FROM TEXAS GARDENS, ORCHARDS, *and* WATERWAYS

★

★

A well-made salad can be a work of art, a beautiful thing that's visually appealing and also delicious. But salads are only as good as the ingredients used to compose them. Buying a variety of fresh greens rather than the "salad mixes" sold in sealed bags at the supermarket will give you two legs up on making a very good salad.

There are so many kinds of greens being grown in Texas in the spring. In the winter months we can enjoy the heartier greens like spinach, Swiss chard, and kale. I love to just stroll through the farmers' markets and look at them—the colors, the textures, the shape of the leaves, and of course, the extremely varied tastes: watercress with its subtle peppery nip; arugula with its distinctive bite that ranges somewhere between the taste of horseradish and mustard; radicchio, from the chicory family, with its brilliant ruby leaves and fresh, subtly bitter taste, which is a nice counterpoint when combined with sweeter greens; butterhead with an almost creamy texture to its delicate, light green

---

leaves; iceberg with its wonderful crunch. I could go on and on. Then there are the salad "fixin's" as I call them—those fruits, vegetables, mushrooms, and herbs that add flavor and texture to tossed greens or become the base for salads when greens are not available. Texas is blessed with year-round options—strawberries, citrus fruits (especially grapefruit), radishes, beets, and onions shine in cool months. I also love to include fresh fennel with its licorice-like flavor notes, sliced thin, in some salads—and throw in some of the delicate ferny fronds from the top of the stalks for yet another textural addition. One salad in particular that I love to serve with holiday meals is composed of fresh spinach, apples, slivered red onion, and sliced fennel. It's a nice wintery combination that I dress with a Raspberry Poppyseed Dressing (see the recipe on page 129).

In warmer months, we turn to watermelon, eggplant, cucumbers, peppers, and of course, homegrown tomatoes. Sometimes I make a salad of just some sliced heirloom tomatoes from my garden or the farmers' market, with a little salt and pepper, a drizzle of nice Texas olive oil and aged balsamic vinegar, and perhaps a couple of julienned basil leaves.

A good salad can set the pace for a great meal to follow. It can be a good side dish—especially for a slaw lover like myself. Or salad can be a great meal by itself. There are endless varieties of shellfish salads. Or you can top a green salad with cheese, nuts, beans, eggs (especially little quail eggs), or another protein to transform it into a healthy meal. (Please go beyond grilled chicken breasts, as delicious as they may be!) Nest a couple of succulent grilled quail in the greens, or top a salad of crisp greens like romaine with a couple of crispy fried oysters, a grilled fish fillet, or some thinly sliced grilled beef. Scatter some smoked trout or boiled blue crabmeat over a salad. Salads are limited only by your imagination, and I encourage you to experiment beyond what I've included here.

Get in the habit of making your own salad dressings, too. A simple vinaigrette takes mere minutes to whisk together—and one bowl—but it can be worlds tastier than a bottled dressing because it's fresh. A word on dressing salads is in order here. Don't drown the salad in dressing. The best way to dress a salad is to drizzle the dressing over the surface of the salad in a "Z" pattern. Then either toss it or, if it is a plated individual salad, just serve it. If you are adding garnishes to your salad, always add the dressing first, and then place the garnishes (or meats, etc.) on top.

And don't forget yet another way to add flavor to salads—croutons and bread. Make your own croutons from the array of rustic breads available at the rising number of artisan bakeries around Texas. You can easily make them from all kinds of bread. Just brush slices of bread with butter or olive oil and cut into desired-size cubes. Toast on a baking sheet in a 350°F oven until crisp and golden brown. Or you can simply brush a small slice of rustic bread with olive oil and grill it or toast it. Lay the bread across a salad for a different presentation. But always remember that whenever you serve a chilled salad, the plates should be well chilled in the freezer before plating the salads. Nice addition to chill the salad forks, too, adding them to the side of the plate when you serve the salads!

THE TEXAS OLIVE INDUSTRY

TEXAS'S NEWEST OIL BOOM

SINCE THE FIRST big oil strike at Spindletop dome in 1901 in Beaumont, entrepreneurs, adventurers, speculators, con men, and ladies' bridge clubs have all chased the often elusive dream of getting rich on the black gold. Today, a new breed of wildcatters pursues a different oil—the green gold: delectable extra-virgin olive oil produced from olives grown in the Texas terroir. Although olive trees were brought to Texas by the Spanish, who planted them at the missions they established along the Camino Real, a real industry didn't grow up around olives at that time, as it did in California. In the 1970s and 1980s, Texas A&M scientists experimented with growing a few varieties of olives, mostly Italian. They had no luck so declared that growing olives on a commercial basis in Texas was not possible.

But then one of those stubborn Texans, a man named Jim Henry, came along and asked, "Why not?" He asked to see the research and discovered that the experts had not conducted any broad, long-term studies across multiple varieties of olives in multiple climates and soil types in Texas. So Jim and a few other stalwart Texans started their own trials and kept after them on the premise that parts of Texas look so much like Spain and Italy that it was simply a matter of finding the right combination of tree, soil, water, and climate that would work. It was much the same story as that of the pioneers of the Texas wine industry.

Jim began his experimenting in 1992 in Marble Falls, but his orchard of Italian varieties froze to death the first two winters. He abandoned the orchard but not the dream, setting his sights on land farther south. Around 1994, Henry discovered a handful of annually fruiting 60-year-old olive trees in a residential backyard in Asherton, south of Carrizo Springs, and declared he had found the perfect place to grow olives. By 1997, he had planted another experimental orchard with 10 varieties he thought would do well in the harsh South Texas heat. Another grower, Jerry Farrell, put in 2,500 trees in a high-density orchard in Artesia Wells with help from the USDA Agriculture Station, which started to take an interest in this new agricultural opportunity. Henry was now convinced that Spanish varieties and the new high-density technology were the key to success. He bought land near Asherton and planted 40,000 trees, and the Texas Olive Ranch was born.

Growers still battle freezes, heat waves, and hurricanes, but today there are more than 60 olive orchards in Texas, scattered from the Hill Country to the Rio Grande Valley to the Gulf Coast. Olive trees grow in rocky limestone; in sandy, hurricane-flooded soil along the coast; and in dry mesquite scrubland where rattlesnakes, coyotes, and mountain lions still roam. Spanish varietals arbequina and arbosa, and the Greek olive known as koroneiki, have proven to be the most successful fruit.

Harvests of Texas olives, like all Texas crops, have their ups and downs, but the quality of Texas olive oil just gets better and better. In 2012, Texas Olive Ranch entered the Los Angeles International Olive Oil Competition and, against stiff competition from 416 other producers from around the Northern Hemisphere, won a silver medal for outstanding taste, character, and complexity with their Arbequina ExtraVirgin oil, as well as a bronze medal for their Koroneiki ExtraVirgin oil.

The Texas Olive Council expects the number of olive growers to double in the coming years. At farmers' markets across Texas every week, people experience the taste of truly fresh, unadulterated olive oil that was produced in Texas. Look for other olive products—soaps, brined olives, and from Sandy Oaks' Olive Orchard in Elmendorf, an innovative olive leaf jelly, which is delicious when piled on Texas goat cheese and served with crackers.

Watermelon and Basil Salad with Goat Feta Cheese

This is a unique summertime salad, especially when the Hempstead watermelons are at their ripe and flavorful best. It's such a simple, easy-to-make salad, but the combination of flavors and textures is the real essence of a Texas summer.

SERVES 4 TO 6.

6 cups 1-inch cubes of seedless Texas watermelon, grown in Hempstead if possible

10 ounces crumbled Texas goat feta cheese

½ small red onion, sliced paper thin

1 cup fresh basil, cut in julienned strips

Texas extra-virgin olive oil

Kosher salt

Combine the watermelon chunks, goat feta, and red onion in a bowl and toss to blend. Just before serving, cut the basil leaves and add to the salad. Add just enough olive oil to moisten the ingredients and salt to taste. Toss to blend in the basil and salt. Serve at once before the basil strips turn dark.

Spinach and Strawberry Salad with Basil-Raspberry Vinaigrette

Each year when early spring rolls around, I can't wait for my little strawberry patch to produce berries. We eat these berries fresh, usually for breakfast, or use them to make a nice strawberry shortcake. The patch is small but right outside our kitchen door, and the berries are so sweet. I also use the homegrown berries in this very tasty salad. My spinach is nice and crispy with the still-cool weather, and the basil is getting a good start toward reaching the giant bush status it will attain by fall. If I need more than my patio patch can provide, I visit Gary Marburger at Fredericksburg's Marburger Farms. Another great spot for fresh, in-season strawberries is Poteet, the Strawberry Capital of Texas, about 30 miles south of San Antonio.

SERVES 4 TO 6.

20 ounces (approximately) small fresh spinach leaves, well washed and dried
½ small red onion, halved lengthwise, then sliced thin
4 ounces crumbled goat feta cheese
2 cups sliced strawberries
½ cup dried cranberries
⅓ cup toasted, sliced, skin-on almonds
Basil-Raspberry Vinaigrette (recipe follows)

BASIL-RASPBERRY VINAIGRETTE:
1 cup chopped fresh basil
½ cup raspberry vinegar
2 medium garlic cloves, minced
1 tightly packed tablespoon light brown sugar
2 teaspoons Dijon mustard
½ teaspoon crushed red pepper flakes
½ teaspoon kosher salt
1 cup Texas extra-virgin olive oil

Begin by making the basil-raspberry vinaigrette. Combine all ingredients except olive oil in the work bowl of a food processor fitted with the steel blade. Process until smooth. With the processor running, add the olive oil in a slow, steady stream through the feed tube until all has been added. Process an additional 15 seconds or so to form a good emulsion. Refrigerate in a tightly sealed container until ready to use. Note that this is an all-natural dressing, so it will separate. Simply shake well before using.

To serve the salad, arrange a bed of the spinach on each chilled serving plate. Drizzle desired portion of the dressing over each salad. Scatter red onion slivers, cheese, strawberries, cranberries, and almonds over the salads and serve at once.

Mixed Green Salad with Cilantro Dressing

This is the "House Dressing" at my house. We get rave reviews and many requests for the recipe from dinner guests. It's a refreshingly different salad dressing, with a really zesty, in-your-face taste. The dressing will keep, refrigerated, for about 5 days, or 2 days if using homemade mayonnaise.

Lots of cooks get confused about the term lemon or lime "zest." The zest is the very thin, colored outer portion of the citrus rind. Use a grater or a special kitchen tool called a microplane to remove only the colored portion, never cutting into the white pith, which would impart a bitter taste. Be sure to use fresh jalapeños in this recipe. The pickled ones would change the taste structure of the dressing. The dressing also makes a great dip for veggie crudités.

SERVES 6 TO 8.

SALAD:

Mixed greens, including field greens, if available
Very thinly sliced red onion
Cherry tomatoes, sliced in half
Cucumber rounds
Avocado slices
Optional, but yummy other ingredients: sunflower and/or radish sprouts, roasted corn kernels

CILANTRO DRESSING:
MAKES ABOUT 2 CUPS.

4 large garlic cloves, peeled and trimmed
2 cups tightly packed cilantro sprigs, leaves, and stems
2 medium jalapeños, seeds and veins removed, minced
2 tablespoons champagne vinegar
¼ teaspoon kosher salt
1 teaspoon real maple syrup
1 tablespoon freshly squeezed lime juice
¾ teaspoon minced lime zest
1 cup real mayonnaise, preferably homemade

Make the cilantro dressing. Place the steel blade in the work bowl of a food processor. With processor running, drop the garlic cloves through the feed tube to mince. Scrape down sides of bowl. Combine all remaining ingredients in the work bowl. Process until smooth. Refrigerate, covered, for about 4 hours before using to allow time for the flavors to meld.

Arrange the mixed greens on individual salad plates and pour desired amount of dressing over the top. Garnish the salad with slivered red onions, cherry tomato halves, cucumber rounds, and avocado slices.

Rio Grande Valley Citrus Salad with Agave-Chipotle Dressing

This is a salad with a lot of zing. It's great to serve with Mexican entrées with which it shares a lot of flavor affinity. The combination of citrus and chipotle chiles is a really good pairing, as the citrus tends to tame the chiles' heat a bit, leaving a nice little glow of subtle spice. The agave nectar adds just a hint of sweetness that complements the citrus and evens out the grapefruit's puckery attributes. It's a very good salad for winter when the Rio Star grapefruits from the Rio Grande Valley are at the peak of their season.

SERVES 4 TO 6.

Mixed tender and crisp greens, such as Bibb lettuce, arugula, radicchio, and romaine hearts, washed, patted dry, and torn into bite-size pieces
3 large oranges, segmented
2 Rio Star grapefruits, segmented
½ small red onion, sliced very thin
Thin-sliced watermelon radishes
Agave-Chipotle Dressing (recipe follows)

AGAVE-CHIPOTLE DRESSING:
MAKES ABOUT 1¼ CUPS.
⅓ cup champagne vinegar
2 heaping tablespoons frozen orange juice concentrate
4 green onions, roughly chopped
2½ tablespoons minced cilantro
1 or 2 chipotle chiles in adobo sauce, depending on your heat preference
2 heaping teaspoons lemon zest
2 heaping teaspoons orange zest
2 tablespoons agave nectar
½ teaspoon kosher salt
⅔ cup Texas extra-virgin olive oil

Begin by making the dressing. Combine all ingredients except olive oil in the work bowl of a food processor fitted with the steel blade. Process until smooth and well blended. With the processor running, pour the olive oil through the feed tube in a slow, steady stream until all has been added. Process for about 15 seconds to form a strong emulsion. Place in squeeze bottle and refrigerate until ready to use.

To assemble the salad, place a portion of the mixed greens on chilled salad plates. Arrange the orange and grapefruit segments, sliced onion, and radish slices as desired on each salad. Drizzle desired portion of dressing on each salad and serve.

FAIN'S HONEY

EVERYONE LOVES HONEY. It's one of those things we take for granted, like salt and pepper. But honey has a fascinating story. Honeybees collect the nectar of up to 2 million flowers in the production of just one pound of honey, traveling nearly 55,000 miles between flowers in the process. The bees deposit their nectar in beeswax cells in the hives. It is very thin, having little sugar content. Then they furiously fan their wings over the cells, evaporating the excess water until the nectar is transformed into the viscous, golden liquid we know as honey.

Fain's Honey was established in 1926 by H. E. Fain, present owner Keith Fain's grandfather. Desperate to earn money, H. E. robbed the hives on his land and sold the honey himself on the town square in Gatesville. The honey was pristine, and he made more money from it than he did farming. He soon established a reputation as a supplier of top-quality honey. During the Depression years, he kept his family fed by selling honey. Sugar was an expensive luxury most folks couldn't afford, so there was a ready market for honey.

In 1935, H. E. Fain moved his entire operation to the Rio Grande Valley, a beekeeper's paradise where honey can be produced 11 months of the year with enormous yields. But brush clearing, cotton defoliation, and the use of insecticides by the citrus industry wiped out most of his colonies, and he relocated to the Texas Hill Country with his remaining hives. He had done research, which indicated that Llano was a very good area for honey production. One plant in particular was of interest to him—white brush (called bee brush by locals). It produces tiny white, incredibly sweet-smelling flowers after each rain. The honey it produces is considered to be one of the most delicious, tasting just like the flower smells. Today

Fain's Raw Natural Honey is composed primarily of bee brush nectar and mesquite flower nectar. It's pure Texas terroir in a jar.

"Honey production today is a risky livelihood," Keith relates. "The bees are subject to mites, fire ants, pesticides. Heavy rains affect production, as do droughts, and bees are getting more aggressive all the time." Today Keith has about 1,000 bee colonies, but the products are made in a small-scale, hands-on operation. He doesn't "mess with Mother Nature" by feeding his bees any substances to lengthen the production season.

Arugula and Bibb Lettuce Salad with Figs, Goat Cheese, and Texas Honey and Lemon Vinaigrette

Much of Texas is blessed with two growing seasons—one in the spring and another in the fall—so we can enjoy fresh lettuces and homegrown tomatoes in both seasons, unless there's an unseasonably early freeze in the fall or a drought that extends into the spring. Arugula is at its peppery best when the nights get a bit chilly. I like to combine the zesty arugula with tender and delicate Bibb lettuce for both the textural and taste contrasts. The honey and lemon dressing also plays off the bite of the arugula with a hit of citrusy tang from the lemon and a little melody of deep, musky sweetness that only honey can provide.

SERVES 4.

SALAD:
Equal portions of fresh, peppery
    arugula and Bibb lettuce for 4
    portions, torn into bite-size pieces
12 fresh figs, halved, or quartered if
    figs are large
1 cup crumbled semi-hard Texas goat
    cheese
Toasted pecan pieces

TEXAS HONEY AND LEMON VINAIGRETTE:
MAKES ABOUT 1 CUP.
1 teaspoon minced lemon zest
¼ cup freshly squeezed lemon juice
¼ teaspoon kosher salt
2 tablespoons Texas honey
3 tablespoons chopped fresh chives
½ cup Texas extra-virgin olive oil
Freshly ground black pepper

Begin by making the dressing. (Dressing can be made a day ahead and refrigerated.) Combine all ingredients except olive oil and pepper in the work bowl of a food processor fitted with the steel blade. Process until well blended. With the processor running, add the olive oil in a slow, steady stream through the feed tube until all has been added. Add freshly ground black pepper to taste and process for about 15 seconds longer. Transfer to storage container and refrigerate until ready to serve.

To assemble the salad, toss the arugula and Bibb lettuce together. Place equal portions of the mixed greens on individual salad plates. Arrange some of the figs on each salad. Drizzle desired portion of dressing over the salads, then scatter ¼ cup of the crumbled goat cheese over each, and garnish with a few pecan pieces.

Green Salad with Avocado Dressing and Tortilla Strips

With its subtle "south-of-the-border" flavor notes, this salad is a good one to serve with simple grilled meats or a Mexican entrée. You can top the salad with crabmeat, grilled shrimp, or chicken and turn it into an entrée. The dressing is a perfect taste-mate to the seafood or chicken.

SERVES 6 TO 8.

SALAD:

6 cups torn iceberg lettuce
3 cups sliced romaine lettuce
3 ripe tomatoes, preferably
    homegrown, cut into wedges
½ cup sliced ripe olives
Thinly sliced watermelon radishes
½ small red onion, sliced very thin
3 tablespoons chopped cilantro
Tortilla Strips (see recipe below)
2 ounces Cotija cheese, crumbled

TORTILLA STRIPS:

6 white corn tortillas
Canola oil for deep-frying,
    heated to 350°F

AVOCADO DRESSING:

¾ teaspoon whole cumin seeds
¾ teaspoon whole coriander seeds
1 large avocado, peeled, pitted, and
    roughly chopped
⅔ cup sour cream
½ teaspoon minced lime zest
2 teaspoons freshly squeezed
    lime juice
2 garlic cloves, minced
½ teaspoon kosher salt or fine sea salt
½ teaspoon cayenne
2 tablespoons canola oil

Begin by making the tortilla strips. (These can be made up to a day ahead of time.) Place the tortillas on a cutting board in a stack. Cut in half, then cut each half into strips ½ inch wide. Deep-fry the strips in batches in the preheated canola oil, just until crisp. Drain on a wire rack set over a baking sheet. When completely cool, store in an airtight container.

Make the dressing. Combine the whole cumin and coriander seeds in a small, heavy-bottomed skillet over medium-high heat. Toast the seeds, shaking the pan often, until they become aromatic, about 3 to 5 minutes. Take care that you don't burn the seeds. Grind the toasted seeds in a spice grinder or mortar and pestle into a powder; set aside.

Combine the remaining dressing ingredients in the work bowl of a food processor fitted with the steel blade. Add the cumin and coriander and process until the dressing is smooth. Transfer to a covered container and refrigerate until ready to use.

To serve the salad, toss the greens together and divide among individual salad plates, preferably chilled. Top each salad with desired portion of the dressing, then garnish each salad with some of the tomato wedges; sliced olives, radishes, and red onion; and chopped cilantro. Scatter some of the fried tortilla strips and Cotija cheese over each salad and serve at once.

FULL QUIVER FARMS

FULL QUIVER FARMS is a family-owned and -operated dairy farm in Central Texas, about 60 miles south of Dallas. Mike and Debbie Sams, the owners, sell their raw cow's milk, hand-made cheeses, grass-fed meats, and free-range eggs from their store on the farm. Their cheeses are also marketed through Whole Foods, Central Market, Austin's Wheatsville Co-op, and some farmers' markets.

The Sams' story began in 1993 when they started a dairy herd and began to milk cows, shipping their milk through a commercial distributor. Although their pockets were empty, the pair had high hopes for the future, dreaming of working together as a family and eventually passing the farm on to their children. But with milk prices fluctuating wildly and a heavy debt load, they soon became very discouraged.

The Sams struggled to make ends meet for 10 years, getting deeper and deeper into debt, their hopes dashed. They realized that they would have to do something different or be forced to sell their farm. They decided to try their luck at making cheese. Why not? They had the milk, and children at home to help, so they made cheese!

They began to have success at farmers' markets, and as their financial situation improved, the pair found that they enjoyed their work on the farm more than ever. The family was working together, as they had envisioned, rather than living scattered around the country. Their entire operation uses organic practices. The cows graze on fresh grass in the pasture. The chickens scratch for bugs and cackle happily while they lay their eggs, and the farm's pigs squeal with delight when they're fed the whey left over from the cheesemaking process.

The family motto is a good one: "It's more than good food—it's a way of life!"

Roasted Beet Salad with Peppered Bacon and Goat Cheese

This salad was an instant hit with diners the first time I served it. The earthy tastes of both the beets and the goat cheese topped with the vinaigrette, which is made from the richly flavored broth in which the beets are roasted, blend to make a unique combination of flavors. A scattering of crumbled peppered bacon provides yet another earthy touch and adds a meaty dimension to the salad.

SERVES 4 TO 6.

Mixed romaine, radicchio, butter
　　lettuce, and arugula
Roasted Beet Vinaigrette
　　(recipe follows)
Roasted Beets (recipe follows)
8 ounces plain, mild Texas goat
　　cheese, shaped into small rounds
　　using a melon baller
5 slices artisan peppered bacon,
　　cooked until crisp, then drained
　　and crumbled

ROASTED BEETS:

Texas extra-virgin olive oil
5 medium-sized red beets
5 medium-sized golden beets
4 large shallots, roughly chopped
3 arbol chiles
1½-inch section of fresh ginger root,
　　sliced thin and crushed
1 cup soy sauce
¼ cup real maple syrup
2 quarts chicken stock, preferably
　　homemade
⅓ cup light brown sugar
½ cup dry sherry

ROASTED BEET VINAIGRETTE:

⅓ cup red wine vinegar

¾ teaspoon kosher salt

1 teaspoon freshly ground black pepper

1½ teaspoons minced fresh thyme

1½ teaspoons snipped fresh chives

1½ teaspoons minced flat-leaf parsley

1½ tablespoons Dijon mustard

⅔ cup roasting liquid from cooked beets

1½ cups Texas extra-virgin olive oil

Begin by roasting the beets. Preheat oven to 375°F. Heat a glaze of the olive oil in a braising pan over medium-high heat. Sauté the beets, shallots, chiles, and sliced ginger root until ginger is browned, about 5 minutes. Add remaining beet ingredients and bring to a boil. Remove from heat, cover pan, and roast in preheated oven until beets are soft, about 45 minutes to 1 hour. Set aside until cool. When the beets are cool enough to handle, drain them, reserving ⅔ cup of the roasting liquid. Strain the liquid and set aside. Peel the beets and cut them into bite-size pieces; refrigerate until chilled.

Make the vinaigrette. Combine all ingredients except olive oil in the work bowl of a high-speed blender. Blend until very smooth. With the blender running, add the olive oil in a slow, steady stream through the top until all has been added. Blend an additional 15 to 20 seconds to form a strong emulsion. Cover and refrigerate until ready to use. Shake vigorously before using.

To assemble the salad, combine the greens, tossing to blend well. Arrange a portion of the greens on individual, chilled salad plates. Drizzle desired portion of the vinaigrette over the salad. Arrange some of the pieces of roasted beets over each salad. Place several balls of the goat cheese around the salads and scatter the crumbled bacon on top. Serve at once.

Grilled Romaine Salad with Caesar Vinaigrette

For a unique take on Caesar salad, try grilling romaine hearts on a gas grill or the ridged side of a comal grill on your stovetop. The slight nuance of char from the grill marks adds a really nice flavor to the salad. You can make the dressing, a variation on the classic Caesar dressing, and the croutons a couple of days ahead of time, but you must wait until just before serving to grill the lettuce.

SERVES 6.

SALAD:

6 fresh hearts of romaine, cut in half
    lengthwise
Texas extra-virgin olive oil
Caesar Vinaigrette (recipe follows)
Thin-sliced red onion rings
Shaved Pecorino Romano cheese
Garlic Croutons (see recipe below)
Halved grape tomatoes

GARLIC CROUTONS:

2 cups ½-inch-square cubes of day-
    old French bread
½ cup fruity Texas extra-virgin olive oil
1½ teaspoons granulated garlic
1 teaspoon kosher salt

CAESAR VINAIGRETTE:

3 large garlic cloves, peeled
1 large shallot, roughly chopped
¾ teaspoon dry mustard
¾ teaspoon freshly ground
    black pepper
4 anchovy filets
1 egg
1 slice white onion, ½-inch thick
2 teaspoons sugar
⅓ cup red wine vinegar
1½ cups Texas koronecki extra-virgin
    olive oil

Make the croutons. Preheat oven to 275°F. Line a baking sheet with parchment paper; set aside. Place the bread cubes in a large bowl; set aside. In a separate bowl, combine olive oil, granulated garlic, and salt; whisk to blend well. Pour the olive oil mixture over the bread cubes and toss to moisten all cubes. Turn out onto prepared baking sheet in a single layer. Bake for 15 to 20 minutes in preheated oven, or until the bread cubes turn golden brown and become crisp. Turn out onto a wire rack set over a baking sheet to cool. Cool completely and store in an airtight container until ready to use.

Make the vinaigrette. Place the steel blade in the work bowl of a food processor. With processor running, drop the garlic cloves and roughly chopped shallot through the feed tube to mince. Stop the machine and scrape down sides of bowl. Add all remaining dressing ingredients except olive oil. Process until smooth. With the processor running, add the olive oil in a slow, steady stream through the feed tube until all has been added. Process an additional 15 seconds to form a strong emulsion. Store dressing in a tightly sealed squeeze bottle until ready to use.

To assemble and serve the salads: Brush cut sides of romaine hearts lightly with olive oil. Grill, cut side down, on comal or gas char-grill until slight grill marks appear. Place on serving plates, cut side up, and drizzle desired amount of dressing over the lettuce from the squeeze bottle. Toss a few red onion rings over each salad, followed by some of the shaved Romano, and scatter some of the croutons and grape tomato halves on each salad and around the plate. Serve at once.

HOUSTON DAIRYMAIDS

OUSTON DAIRYMAIDS BEGAN on October 28, 2006, at a stall at a Houston farmers' market. To prepare for the market, owner Lindsey Schechter made visits to Texas farms and dairies, collecting an exciting array of handmade Texas cheeses for customers to sample and purchase. She made a display of all of her finds: fresh goat cheeses from the Hill Country, Gruyere and extra-aged Cheddar from Dublin, golden-yellow butter from outside Dallas. While waiting for the market to officially open, she wondered if she would sell anything. Eight o'clock opening time came, and her stall was suddenly swamped. There was a continuous crowd throughout the day.

Houston Dairymaids continues to prosper, having forged close relationships with 11 Texas cheesemakers. Lindsey has been a great boon to Texas cheesemakers. Most are small operations on their farms, and they lack the resources and facilities to

ship their cheeses, although the cheeses are in high demand by both the public and chefs from all over the state. And many of them are not adept at marketing. Houston Dairymaids delivers to wholesale customers in Houston and ships cheeses to chefs throughout the state. When Lindsey first opened, it was rare to find a cheese plate on a Houston menu, much less one that included Texas cheeses. Now she sells cheese to more than 200 restaurants, hotels, caterers, country clubs, and bars. In March 2012, she opened Houston's first retail cheese shop in the popular Heights neighborhood.

Lindsey has succeeded because she selects the very best cheeses, cares for them properly, and teaches her retail customers what makes each cheese special. So the cheesemakers can stay busy on their farms and dairies, caring for their animals and perfecting their craft, while Lindsey's job is singing their praises and selling their cheeses.

Iceberg Wedge Salad with Pecans and Buttermilk, Blue Cheese, and Texas Tarragon Dressing

The "iceberg wedge" is a salad that was served in the halcyon days of the Texas oil boom at the Shamrock Hilton Hotel in Houston, a flagship of Nicky Hilton's hotel empire. I remember that when I was a child, my mother, who loved blue cheese, would always order the iceberg wedge salad at the old Trader Vic's Restaurant located in the Shamrock when we dined there. It always looked so regal—a pristinely cut, towering wedge of crisp green lettuce with a drape of the blue-mottled dressing across the middle. The Shamrock is long gone, its former location now the epicenter of Houston's sprawling Medical Center, but the iceberg wedge salad is a hot "new" trend in the salad arena, which proves that good foods never fade too far beneath the surface of trendiness.

SERVES 4 TO 6.

1 head iceberg lettuce, core removed,
    sliced into 4 to 6 wedges,
    depending on size, and well chilled
6 slices peppered bacon, cooked until
    crisp, drained, and crumbled
Sweet and Spicy Pecans
    (see recipe below)

SWEET AND SPICY PECANS:
MAKES 1½ CUPS.
3 tablespoons agave nectar
1½ tablespoons sugar
¾ teaspoon kosher salt or fine sea salt
¼ teaspoon ground cinnamon
⅛ teaspoon cayenne
½ teaspoon ground cumin
1½ cups pecan halves

DRESSING:
MAKES ABOUT 1¼ CUPS.
½ cup homemade aioli
3 tablespoons whole buttermilk
    (not low fat)
¼ cup crème fraîche
2 small green onions, roughly
    chopped, including green tops
1 medium garlic clove, minced
¾ teaspoon Meyer lemon juice, or
    substitute regular lemon juice
1 teaspoon Tabasco
¾ teaspoon minced fresh Mexican
    mint marigold, also known as
    "Texas tarragon"
¾ teaspoon minced flat-leaf parsley
1 teaspoon minced fresh mint
1 teaspoon celery salt
⅛ teaspoon freshly ground black pepper
Kosher salt
1 cup (4 ounces) crumbled Texas
    blue cheese, such as Veldhuizen
    Bosque Blue or Pure Luck Texas
    Hopelessly Bleu

To make the pecans, preheat oven to 325°F. Line a baking sheet with parchment paper and set aside. Combine the agave nectar with remaining ingredients except pecans in a large bowl. Whisk to blend well. Add the pecans and stir to coat them well. Spread out on the prepared baking sheet. Bake the pecans for 5 minutes. Cover a second baking sheet with foil; set aside. Using a fork, stir the pecans to coat again with the melted syrup and spice mixture. Continue to bake for another 10 minutes, or until pecans are golden and bubbly. Turn out onto the foil-covered baking sheet and quickly separate the nuts with a fork, spreading them in a single layer. Set aside until cool. The pecans can be made up to 2 days ahead of time and stored in a tightly covered container at room temperature.

To make the dressing, combine all ingredients except salt and blue cheese in the work bowl of a food processor fitted with the steel blade. Process until mixture is very smooth. Season to taste with salt; pulse to blend. Add the blue cheese crumbles and pulse to slightly blend the cheese into the dressing. There should still be visible chunks of cheese, so don't overprocess after adding the cheese.

Turn dressing out into a storage container with a tight-fitting lid and refrigerate until ready to serve. The flavor develops nicely if the dressing is allowed a 24-hour rest in the refrigerator before serving.

To serve, place an iceberg wedge in the center of each chilled salad plate. Drizzle a portion of the dressing across the center of each wedge. Scatter some of the crumbled bacon and pecans around the plates and serve.

Grilled Mushroom and Goat Cheese Salad with Fresh Tomato Dressing

This is a must-do summer salad. I make it only in the summer when I can get fresh, fresh tomatoes right off the vines outside my back door or at the farmers' market. I love to use heirloom Brandywine tomatoes. They have a remarkable flavor, like that of the tomatoes that my grandfather used to grow. The mushrooms can be marinated, grilled, and stuffed ahead of time, and the dressing can be prepared up to a day before serving. Serve this salad as a prelude to a light meal or as a light meal on its own.

SERVES 4.

8 large Kitchen Pride white mushrooms, about 2 inches in diameter, stems removed
4 bamboo skewers, soaked in water for 1 hour
Mixed torn Bibb lettuce leaves and baby arugula

MUSHROOM MARINADE:
1 cup Texas extra-virgin olive oil
4 large garlic cloves, minced
1 teaspoon crushed red pepper flakes
1 tablespoon minced flat-leaf parsley
1 tablespoon minced cilantro
½ teaspoon kosher salt
½ teaspoon freshly ground black pepper
1½ teaspoons sugar

MUSHROOM STUFFING:
4 large garlic cloves, peeled and trimmed
8 ounces plain Texas goat cheese
½ teaspoon kosher salt
2 teaspoons minced fresh basil
3 green onions, roughly chopped, including green tops

FRESH TOMATO DRESSING:
4 large heirloom tomatoes, or 6 homegrown Roma tomatoes, such as San Marzano, roughly chopped
3 shallots, minced
¼ cup sherry wine vinegar
¼ cup tomato juice
½ teaspoon lime zest
Juice of 1 large lime
1 teaspoon Cholula Hot Sauce
2 tablespoons minced flat-leaf parsley
2 tablespoons minced fresh cilantro
½ teaspoon sugar
½ teaspoon kosher salt
¼ teaspoon freshly ground black pepper
⅓ cup Texas extra-virgin olive oil

Begin by making the mushroom marinade. Combine all ingredients in a nonaluminum bowl and whisk to blend well. Add the mushrooms and toss to coat well, inside and out. Set aside to marinate at room temperature for 2 hours, tossing occasionally to keep the mushrooms coated with the marinade.

To make the stuffing, place the steel blade in the work bowl of a food processor. With processor running, drop the garlic cloves through the feed tube to mince. Stop the processor and scrape down the bowl. Add the remaining ingredients and process until fairly smooth, leaving a little texture on the green onions. Refrigerate until ready to use.

To make the dressing, combine all ingredients except olive oil in the work bowl of a high-speed blender. Process until smooth. With the blender running, add the olive oil in a slow, steady stream through the top, until all has been added. Blend an additional 20 seconds to form a smooth emulsion. Refrigerate until ready to use. Shake well before using.

Heat a gas char-grill or a stovetop cast-iron grill or comal to medium-high heat. Remove the mushrooms from the marinade and thread them onto the skewers. Grill for about 2 to 3 minutes per side, turning once, or until they are well marked and ever so slightly softened. Take care that you don't overcook them, or they will collapse. Set aside to cool. Refrigerate if not using within an hour.

When you are ready to serve the salad, arrange mixed greens on chilled plates. Drizzle desired portion of the dressing over each salad. Stuff each mushroom with a portion of the cheese mixture and nestle 2 mushrooms into the greens on each plate. Serve at once.

EL CAMINO DE LAS CABRAS DAIRY

AN INTERESTING SIDE NOTE to the writing of this book was that it was like a small study in what motivates people from diverse backgrounds to change the paths of their lives to become creators of handcrafted food and beverage products. The cheesemakers were an especially fascinating group of folks. Some grew up on industrial dairy farms, with knowledge of the industry, but had shunned the practices of the industrialized production of milk. Others entered the craft from a lifelong love of animals, with cheesemaking being an end result of raising those animals. Still others were traditional farmers starting small, family-owned farms with an array of animals. Making goat cheese was a natural adjunct to the overall income of the farm. A few merely loved cheese and the whole process of making it.

Candace Hinkle Conn, who has a PhD in biology from Louisiana State University, started keeping goats in 1999. Before she knew it, she was covered up in goats. She had so much milk that her family couldn't drink it all. She started making goat milk cheese and goat milk soaps, but that didn't use up much of the milk either.

Then Candace found Pure Luck Dairy in Dripping Springs and attended one of its three-day seminars on making goat cheese. When the seminar was over, Candace told her husband that now she knew exactly what she wanted: to buy a ranch, raise dairy goats, and make cheese. In 2009, the family moved from Beaumont, where Candace taught biology at Lamar University and worked as a microbiologist in the laboratory of Christus St. Elizabeth Hospital, to their new ranch outside San Angelo. And she started making cheese.

Most of the goats on the ranch now are Nubian or Nubian crosses. The Nubians give less milk than other goats, but it is very creamy and makes excellent cheese. Candace names her goats and

bottle-raises the babies so they won't be afraid of her. All of the cheesemakers I've met have told me that happy goats make great cheese, so it's easy to see why Candace's El Camino de las Cabras cheeses are so darned good.

LOVE CREEK ORCHARDS

BAXTER AND CAROL ADAMS, founders of the Love Creek Orchards, are special folks who have given Texas a couple of real treasures. In 1981, they purchased 1,863 acres along Love Creek in the Bandera Canyonlands west of Medina. The land had been overgrazed and neglected, but the pair fell in love with its rugged beauty. Over the years, they lovingly restored the land and the native grasses. They called their jewel-in-the-rough the Lost Creek Ranch.

The couple began to experiment with growing dwarf apple trees, which produce regular-sized fruit that ripens in July, earlier than apples from full-sized trees. The dwarf trees were successful, and in the mid-1990s, the Adamses planted a second apple orchard right in the middle of Medina. As the trees began to produce, the Adamses needed a place to sell their apples, so they purchased a lovely old rock house just down the road from the orchard. Soon the store was much more than an apple market, as they added local arts and crafts along with homemade jams, jellies, breads, sauces, butters, homemade apple bread, and their now-legendary, washtub-sized apple pies made from the orchard's Pink Lady apples. The store became a tourist destination, and soon the Adamses added the Patio Café, serving home-style foods and some really good barbecue when they have time to make it.

Although they have sold the store to new owners, the Adamses continue to operate the Love Creek Orchard, where you can still pick your own apples, blackberries, and peaches in season. You can also purchase bigtooth "lost" maple trees, which Baxter Adams brought back from the brink of extinction in Texas on the Love Creek Ranch. The Adamses' second gift to Texas came in 2000, when they sold 1,400 acres of the original Love Creek Ranch to the Nature Conservancy to create the Love Creek Preserve. The land is held in a trust so that Texans will be able to enjoy its beauty for generations to come.

Spinach, Apple, and Fennel Salad with Red Onion and Raspberry-Poppyseed Vinaigrette

I love this salad. It just makes me feel good when I eat it. The flavors are so crisp and clean. The crunch comes from fennel, an often overlooked vegetable with a marvelously refreshing, licorice-like flavor. The vegetable, which is also known as finocchio, has a broad, bulbous base, which resembles celery, and thin upper stems with fernlike fronds. I like to use the whole thing, including some of the ferny fronds. Fennel grows well in Texas, and I always like to have a bulb or two of it in my spring garden.

SERVES 4.

SALAD:
8 cups fresh baby spinach
½ small head fennel, thinly sliced, feathery tops reserved
2 medium Pink Lady apples, peeled, cored, and sliced into wedges ¼-inch thick
½ small red onion, halved lengthwise, thinly sliced

RASPBERRY-POPPYSEED VINAIGRETTE:
MAKES ABOUT 1¼ CUPS.
½ cup sugar
½ teaspoon dry mustard
½ teaspoon kosher salt
¼ cup raspberry-flavored vinegar
1 slice medium onion, ½-inch thick, roughly chopped
½ cup canola oil
1½ teaspoons poppy seeds

Prepare the dressing. Combine sugar, mustard, salt, vinegar, and onion in the work bowl of a food processor fitted with the steel blade. Process until smooth. With the processor running, pour the canola oil in a thin, steady stream through the feed tube until all has been added. Add the poppy seeds and pulse just to blend. Transfer dressing to a storage container and refrigerate until ready to serve.

To assemble the salad, combine the spinach, sliced fennel, sliced apple, and onion in a salad bowl. Drizzle with desired amount of dressing and toss to moisten all ingredients. Garnish with some of the reserved ferny fennel tops and serve.

Iceberg and Watercress Slaw

People who know me well know that I love slaw. In fact, I have made a study of slaw, tasting countless varieties made from myriad collections of ingredients. My husband really doesn't like slaw in its traditional preparation, so I'm always on a relentless search to find styles of slaw that he likes. I'm happy to say that this was one I created that he really likes. It's a great match to fried, grilled, or broiled fish and shellfish and my favorite topping for soft-shell crab po'boys. The shredded iceberg, along with the crispy almonds and crushed noodles, gives a nice crunch. The watercress adds its characteristic peppery note, and the dressing really enhances the flavor of fish and shellfish. It's perfect to serve with your next batch of fried catfish.

SERVES 4.

½ cup canola oil

1 cup skin-on sliced almonds

2 packages (2.1 ounces each) ramen noodles, crushed with a rolling pin into small bits

4 cups thinly shredded iceberg lettuce

2 cups roughly chopped watercress leaves and tender top stems

2 tablespoons toasted sesame seeds

6 green onions, sliced thin

⅓ cup chopped pickled jalapeño slices

DRESSING:

¼ cup soy sauce

2 teaspoons Sriracha Hot Chili Sauce

2 tablespoons Texas wildflower honey

¼ cup unseasoned rice vinegar

2 tablespoons balsamic vinegar

1 tablespoon dark sesame oil

½ teaspoon kosher salt

½ teaspoon freshly ground black pepper

⅓ cup canola oil

Heat the ½ cup canola oil in a heavy-bottomed 10-inch skillet over medium-high heat. When the oil is hot, add the almonds. Cook, stirring, just until they brown lightly, about 2 minutes. Remove them with a flat mesh skimmer and drain on a paper towel–lined wire rack set over a baking sheet. Reheat the oil and add the crushed ramen noodles. Cook, stirring constantly, just until they are lightly browned, about 1 minute. Remove with the flat skimmer to the paper towel–lined rack. Allow both almonds and noodles to cool.

In a large bowl, combine the shredded lettuce, chopped watercress, fried almonds and noodle bits, toasted sesame seeds, green onions, and chopped jalapeño slices. Set aside while making the dressing.

Combine all dressing ingredients, except the canola oil, in the work bowl of a food processor fitted with the steel blade. Process until smooth and well blended. With the processor running, add the canola oil in a slow, steady stream through the feed tube until all has been added. Continue to process for about 15 seconds to form a strong emulsion. Pour the dressing over the iceberg mix in the bowl and toss to coat and mix all ingredients. Serve at room temperature.

Jicama Slaw

Even if the homely jicama tuber doesn't qualify as an up-to-the-minute trendsetter, it has long been used in Mexican cooking. In fact, the primary commercial source for jicama is Mexico. It's a tasty tuber with a nice crunch, and it can be served raw as a snack when sliced into strips and tossed with fresh lime juice, salt, and chili powder, or it can be used in salads and slaws or cooked. Jicama doesn't turn brown, and it keeps its crunch, even when cooked. When buying jicama, opt for the smallest ones, indicating they are young. Larger, older jicama can be tough and dry, with stringy and starchy texture, instead of crisp and slightly sweet. Opt for jicama that are smooth and unblemished, never wrinkled. Nick the tuber with your fingernail to be sure that the skin is thin and the flesh juicy.

This decidedly sassy, bold-flavored slaw gets a thumbs-up for jicama at any meal built around slow-smoked meats dripping with great barbecue sauce. The rich, smoky meat and spicy seasonings are offset by the cool, crunchy mouth feel of the jicama. The slaw is also good with seafood—fried or grilled—and your best backyard burger.

SERVES 6 TO 8.

1 small jicama, peeled and cut into matchstick strips
1 package prepared coleslaw mix
1 small yellow bell pepper, blistered, peeled, and chopped
1 small red bell pepper, blistered, peeled, and chopped
1 large homegrown tomato, seeded and finely diced
1 large tomatillo, husk removed, well washed, and finely diced
2 green onions, chopped, including green tops
1 ear of fresh corn, roasted until lightly browned, kernels removed from cob

1 heaping tablespoon minced cilantro
2 jalapeños, seeds and veins removed, minced
¼ cup mayonnaise
2 tablespoons sugar
1 tablespoon red picante sauce
1 large garlic clove, minced
2 teaspoons bold chili powder
1 teaspoon toasted, then ground, cumin seeds
1 teaspoon Cholula Hot Sauce
1 teaspoon minced lime zest
Kosher salt, to taste
1 tablespoon freshly squeezed lime juice

Combine the first nine ingredients in a large bowl and toss to blend well. Combine the remaining ingredients in a separate bowl and whisk until smooth and well blended. Add the dressing to the slaw and fold to blend. Refrigerate, covered, until ready to serve.

White Bean and Veggie Salad

This easy-to-prepare salad has Texas summer written all over it. Pick up the fresh herbs and veggies at the farmers' market and toss them together for your weekend dinner on the patio. Great with grilled chicken, burgers, deli sandwiches, or as part of an alfresco chilled meat and salad buffet. It's also good for taking to bring-a-dish suppers. The white kidney bean, known in Italy as the cannellini bean, is the signature bean of Tuscan cooking and is used in soups, such as the classic minestrone, and other dishes. Interestingly, however, the cannellini bean originated in the Andes region of Peru. You can substitute black beans in this dish if you wish.

SERVES 8.

¼ cup freshly squeezed lime juice

½ cup roughly chopped flat-leaf parsley

1 cup chopped cilantro, divided

2 heaping teaspoons toasted, then ground, cumin seeds

1 tablespoon agave nectar

1 cup Texas extra-virgin olive oil

6 cups cooked white kidney beans (cannellini beans), or black beans, well drained

8 green onions, sliced thin, including green tops

2 large red bell peppers, blistered, peeled, seeded, and finely chopped

2 cups quartered homegrown grape tomatoes

1 cucumber, seeded and finely chopped

2 large avocados, peeled and cut into bite-size pieces

3 large jalapeños, seeds and veins removed, minced

Fresh arugula

Kosher salt and freshly ground black pepper

In the work bowl of a food processor fitted with the steel blade, combine the lime juice, parsley, ½ cup of the cilantro, cumin, and agave nectar. Process until smooth. With the processor running, add the olive oil in a slow, steady stream until all has been added and dressing is well blended. Turn out into a medium-sized bowl.

Add the drained beans, green onions, bell pepper, tomatoes, cucumber, avocado, and jalapeño. Scatter the remaining ½ cup of cilantro on top and toss to coat all ingredients with the dressing. Fold in desired amount of fresh arugula. Season to taste with salt and pepper. Set aside at room temperature for at least 1 hour, or refrigerate overnight so that the flavors meld together nicely. Serve cold or at room temperature.

DUCHMAN FAMILY WINERY

"I GREW UP ON a farm in Iowa," recounts Stan Duchman, "and I've always yearned to somehow return to my family's agricultural roots. My wife, Lisa, and I wanted to work with the great food-friendly grapes of Italy." They partnered with two of the most respected names in the Texas wine industry, viticulturist Bobby Cox and grape grower Cliff Bingham, whose Texas High Plains AVA (American Viticultural Area) estate is widely considered one of the top vineyards in Texas today.

The next piece of the puzzle was finding the right winemaker. Texas wine legend Mark Penna, now dearly missed after succumbing to a long battle with cancer in late 2011, embraced the challenge, and in 2005 the team—with the help of Mark's apprentice Dave Reilly—had their first vintage in the cellar. Dave took over winemaking responsibilities in 2009 and continues to serve as the chief winemaker.

An early success came when the Duchmans presented their 2008 Vermentino—from a white grape grown traditionally on the Italian rivers and the island of Sardinia—at a blind tasting at the 2009 Aspen Food and Wine Festival, where Texas wine prodigy and master sommelier Paul Roberts famously refused to believe that the wine had been made from grapes grown in the Lone Star State. "That was a proud, proud moment," remembers Stan fondly. Subsequent awards for their Montepulciano solidified Stan's belief that Italian varieties—because of their versatility and generally high levels of acidity—were ideally suited for the emerging Texas terroir.

The Duchman Dolcetto is a nice pairing with the Roasted Beet Salad with Peppered Bacon and Goat Cheese (pages 119–120), because of the good match with the earthiness of the beets and the smoke and pepper of the bacon. For the White Bean and Veggie Salad (page 132), try the Duchman Trebbiano, which matches the refreshing quality of the salad and has enough acid to stand up to the creaminess of the avocado.

Duchman Viognier works with the fresh clean flavors of the tomatillo and cucumber in the Gazpacho Salad with Crabmeat San Luis (pages 134–136). The acid in the wine stands up to the richness of the crabmeat and the heat in the dish. Duchman Family Winery's signature white, Vermentino, is a great pairing with the Chicken Breast Rolls Stuffed with Goat Cheese and Spinach (pages 221–222). The Mediterranean flavor profile of the pesto in the dish is a natural with the Italian varietal.

Gazpacho Salad with Crabmeat San Luis

In the 1950s, the small coastal villages anywhere from 30 to 60 miles southwest of Houston were dotted with family-owned restaurants that specialized in the freshest seafood you could find. Many of them were owned by Greek families who also owned fishing fleets and/or were seafood wholesalers. Those places were weekend meccas for Houstonians, and a few of them stand out in my childhood memory. One in particular was located near Shore Acres. Although it is gone and I have long forgotten its name, I do remember that it was a Greek surname. I know that the dining rooms were part of a grand old home with huge windows overlooking Galveston Bay. My father's business partner lived in Shore Acres, and we would often spend weekends in his family's home. Those weekends always included at least one meal at this restaurant.

I remember platters of whole red snapper dripping with buttery sauces; shrimp cocktails, along with shrimp cooked in a variety of dishes; oysters on the half shell, which my mother and I would devour in huge numbers;

and a plethora of Gulf blue crabmeat dishes. There were platters of chilled whole boiled crabs, chilled cracked crab claws served with cocktail sauce, fried crab "fingers," stuffed crabs, crabmeat au gratin, and a jelled salad piled with luscious lumps of crabmeat folded into a sauce that my young palate considered to be quite exotic. The memory of that dish has lingered on my "mind's tongue" for all these years, and I finally decided to try to re-create it. Writing the recipe from memories of the textures and major flavor perceptions of the palate—sweet, sour, salty, bitter, and certainly savory umami, even though it didn't have a name back then—was a challenge, but the result pleased my memory of weekends on the Texas Gulf Coast, so I will share this in the hopes that others like it, too.

SERVES 8.

SALAD:

10 firm tomatillos

3 ripe Roma tomatoes, seeded and coarsely chopped

1 small red onion, coarsely chopped

2 medium garlic cloves, minced

2 medium cucumbers, peeled and seeded, then roughly chopped

2 serrano chiles, seeds and veins removed, minced

10 large cilantro sprigs, leaves and tender top sprigs only

½ cup freshly squeezed lime juice

1½ teaspoons kosher salt

1 cup club soda, or Topo Chico sparkling water

4 packages (¼ ounce each) unflavored gelatin, stirred into ¼ cup water in a small metal bowl

Green leaf lettuce leaves, washed and patted dry

Avocado slices as garnish

CRABMEAT SAN LUIS:

8 ounces fresh regular lump Texas blue crabmeat

¼ cup real mayonnaise

2 tablespoons sour cream

2 tablespoons bottled chili sauce

1 tablespoon Texas extra-virgin olive oil

1 tablespoon sherry vinegar

1 tablespoon prepared horseradish

2 teaspoons Creole mustard, or other whole-grain mustard

2 teaspoons freshly squeezed lemon juice

1½ teaspoons minced flat-leaf parsley

1 green onion, roughly chopped

½ teaspoon kosher salt

1 tablespoon drained capers

Spray eight 4-ounce decorative molds with nonstick spray and place them on a baking sheet; set aside. Remove the husks from the tomatillos and wash them well to remove all stickiness. Chop coarsely. Combine the tomatillos, tomatoes, onion, garlic, cucumber, chiles, cilantro, lime juice, and salt in blender; process until smooth. You will need to puree the vegetables in batches, turning each batch out into a large bowl. When all have been pureed, stir in the club soda or sparkling water. Heat about 1 inch of water in a skillet until very hot. Set the bowl of gelatin in the water and stir until gelatin is completely dissolved. Whisk into the vegetable mixture, blending well. Divide the mixture among the prepared molds and refrigerate until completely set, at least 6 hours.

To make the crabmeat San Luis, use your fingers to pick through the crabmeat to remove any bits of shell or cartilage, taking care not to break up the lumps of meat. Set aside. Combine remaining ingredients, except capers, in the work bowl of a food processor fitted with the steel blade. Process until smooth. Transfer to a bowl and stir in the capers and reserved crabmeat; refrigerate, covered, until ready to use.

To serve, place a lettuce leaf on each serving plate. Invert a molded gazpacho salad in the center of each leaf to release the salad. If the salads do not release easily, dip the bottom of the molds very briefly—just a couple of seconds—in a bowl of hot water. Top each salad with a portion of the crabmeat and garnish plates with an avocado slice. Serve immediately.

MAIYA'S RESTAURANT

Saarin's Salad

Maiya Keck, owner of Maiya's Restaurant in Marfa, an isolated burg of 2,000 souls near Texas's Big Bend region, is a pioneer in bringing fine dining to West Texas. When Maiya opened her restaurant in 2002, her philosophy was to cook what she knew and loved. She calls it "the Roman sensibility": simple, fresh, and seasonal grilled or roasted meats and vegetables. This salad, which she named after her sister Saarin, because it's one of her favorite flavor combinations, is a work of art and a true homage to Maiya's philosophy. The combination of bold and understated flavors with contrasting textures and colors, topped with a dash of delicious handmade horseradish, is one you'll want to savor often. The dish would make a noteworthy first course or luncheon entrée, with a nice glass of Texas Viognier.

SERVES 4.

16 large (16 to 20 count) shrimp, peeled and deveined, with tail sections left intact

3 average-sized fresh red beets, about 1¾ pounds

2 ripe, but not mushy, avocados, peeled and sliced into wedges

3 ounces fresh horseradish root

⅓ cup water

⅓ cup white wine vinegar

½ teaspoon kosher salt

Mixed salad greens

Texas extra-virgin olive oil

Additional white wine vinegar

Additional kosher salt or fine sea salt

Chopped flat-leaf parsley

Drop the shrimp into a generous pot of salted, boiling water. Cook just until they turn pink and the flesh turns from translucent to opaque. The texture should be soft, with a bit of crispness. Drain the shrimp and drop them into a salted ice-water bath to stop the cooking. When the shrimp are completely cool, drain them and refrigerate until ready to assemble the salad.

Make the horseradish. Peel the outside of the root using a vegetable peeler or paring knife. Cut the white root in small to medium-sized dice. Put the root in the work bowl of a food processor fitted with the steel blade and pulse, adding the water, white wine vinegar, and the ½ teaspoon salt. Process until the horseradish is smooth and pureed. Store in refrigerator for up to 1 month. You can use store-bought horseradish if you must, but the flavor will be severely compromised.

Preheat oven to 400°F. Cook the beets. Wash the beets and put them in a large, deep baking dish; add water to cover and cover dish with foil. Cook in the preheated oven until they are soft enough that you can poke them through with a skewer, about 1½ hours. Drain and let the beets cool, then peel off the skin, and trim off the ends. The skin should slip off easily if the beets are done. Cut the beets into about 10 to 12 wedges each. Refrigerate until ready to assemble the salad.

To assemble the salad, place a small pile of mixed greens on each individual salad plate. Line up the ingredients across the middle of the plate, 1 wedge of beet, then

1 shrimp, and 1 slice of avocado; repeat 3 more times, ending with a beet wedge on each plate. Drizzle the salads with olive oil and white wine vinegar; add a pinch of salt. Spoon desired amount of the fresh horseradish over the top, but don't be stingy—it adds an amazing zing of flavor. Scatter some of the chopped parsley over the top and serve.

THUNDER HEART BISON: RANCH TO TRAILER

Asian Bison Steak Salad with Sesame Lime Vinaigrette

This bison-meat-only food trailer was the brainchild of Patrick Fitzsimons, son of Thunder Heart Bison founders Hugh and Sarah Fitzsimons. Chef Cat New weaves her culinary artistry to create mouthwatering dishes with buffalo meat, ranging from salads to spring rolls to bison short ribs, tacos, and more. Bison is a leaner alternative to beef, and it's really getting a lot of attention thanks to Cat's innovative dishes using the flavorful meat, such as this delightfully fresh salad. The combination of having a healthy red meat choice and Cat's magic in the kitchen has made the bison trailer a very popular spot, wherever it roams.

SERVES 4.

SALAD:
1½ pounds bison rib eye or sirloin
1 tablespoon sesame oil
1 tablespoon coarsely ground black pepper
Pinch of sea salt
1 pound organic spring mix
¼ cup shredded or julienned carrots
¼ cup shredded or julienned beets
¼ cup very thinly sliced radishes, preferably watermelon radishes
1 cucumber, seeded and sliced
1 cup shredded, fried wontons

2 tablespoons toasted white and black sesame seeds

DRESSING:
⅓ cup rice wine vinegar
¼ cup rice wine
Juice and zest from 1 lime
2 tablespoons tamari
2 tablespoons toasted sesame oil
¼ cup regular sesame oil
1 to 2 tablespoons honey
Sea salt and fresh cracked black pepper

Trim the steak of excess fat and tendons; set aside. Combine the sesame oil, salt, and pepper, blending well. Rub the mixture into the meat on all sides; set aside while assembling the salad.

Make the dressing. Combine the vinegar, rice wine, lime juice and zest, and tamari in blender; blend until smooth. With the blender running, slowly add the oils in a small stream through the top until well blended. Add the honey, salt, and pepper to taste; blend just to combine. Set aside.

Sear the steak to desired degree of doneness, although rare to medium rare is recommended for bison, in a cast-iron skillet or grill over flames just before serving. Let the steak rest for about 5 minutes before slicing thinly. Arrange an equal portion of the steak slices, slightly overlapping on one side of each serving plate.

To plate the salad, place the greens and veggies in an aesthetically pleasing manner around the steak slices. Drizzle a portion of the dressing over steak and greens. Scatter some of the fried wonton strips and toasted sesame seeds over each salad. Serve at once.

4

FRESH FROM *the* WATERS

★

★

Texas's reputation as a dry place is somewhat misleading. There are more than 80,000 miles of rivers, 367 miles of coastline, and countless lakes. We have a thriving seafood industry and have become a popular destination for anglers whether their preference is freshwater, inland bays, or deep-sea fishing.

One of the most interesting commercial fishing villages is Palacios, a sleepy little town on the Texas Gulf Coast about 100 miles southwest of Houston. Many Texans have never even heard of it. The bay was named after José Félix Trespalacios, who was the Mexican governor of the region when Stephen F. Austin brought 300 families to the Texas coast to settle on a Spanish land grant in 1821. Eventually the city was named simply Palacios, and the pronunciation was Americanized to "Puh-LASH-us," rather than the proper Spanish "Pa-LA-see-ohs." Today it's known mainly for the 100-plus-year-old Luther Hotel, which offers a front-row view of the bay, and its port, which covers 600 acres and is home to a fleet of some 300 commercial shrimp boats, earning it the designation "Shrimp Capital of Texas." Much of the shrimp and blue crabmeat wholesaled from the Texas coast comes from Palacios. The local Texas Gulf brown shrimp, in particular, is amazing. It has a greater depth of flavor than shrimp from any other region of the United States. It's briny and vibrant; the heads and shells make righteous-tasting stock.

Actually, two types of shrimp are harvested in the Texas Gulf waters—brown shrimp and white shrimp. Brown shrimp is a nocturnal species and the most abundant of the Gulf shrimp species, averaging 60 to 70 percent of the total Gulf production. Most brown shrimp are harvested offshore by large trawlers in deep waters. White shrimp are milder tasting and are harvested during the day close to shore in the bays, mostly by smaller, shallow-draft boats.

There's a season during which shrimpers are allowed to harvest brown shrimp, because shrimp are an annual renewable resource. The life cycle of the shrimp ends within 12 to 18 months, so the Gulf is closed to shrimping for two months each year beginning on May 15 to allow the juvenile inshore spring production to grow to a larger, more marketable, commercial size.

The Gulf of Mexico is the largest remaining natural (wild) oyster-producing region in the world. Hurricanes, droughts, and water politics (oysters need fresh water from rivers that supply drinking water to cities upstream) have combined to create some hard years for oystermen, but a new initiative to sell oysters by appellation (as they were a century ago) is an encouraging change in the tide. Oysters are harvested and sold all year, but they are usually at their tastiest in late January.

Always try to source fish fresh from a reputable seafood market. A seafood market that specializes in fresh fish should not smell fishy. That smell comes from fish and shellfish that are definitely over the hill. I call the aroma in a good fish market "faintly marine." When you buy fresh fish, buy whole fish whenever possible and have the market clean and fillet your purchase to your specifications. That way you can look the fish in the eyes. Seriously, the eyes tell it all about the freshness of the fish. They should never be sunken or cloudy but rounded and clear, like eyes are supposed to be. And the flesh should be moist but never slimy, another indicator of advancing decomposition. When you press a finger into the flesh, it should spring back and not leave an indentation. The gills of the fish should be bright red in color, not brownish, and like the market itself, the fish should not smell fishy. If it smells fishy, trust me, it will only get fishier when you cook it. We anglers are the lucky ones because we know that the fish we catch is fresh. And we're not limited to the varieties of fish available at a seafood market. I love to cook everything that we catch on weekends of fishing and have discovered some delicious specimens among the fish that other anglers throw back.

The good news is that a number of chefs are discovering the wonderful tastes of many species of "trashfish," or "bycatch." Popular fish like red snapper, for instance, are being fished to extinction, so we all need to get familiar with triggerfish and lesser-known species of grouper, both of which I'd put up against a red snapper any day. Foodways Texas, a nonprofit organization dedicated to documenting the historical food cultures of Texas, has held several seminars on sustainable seafood practices and featured meals prepared by top Texas chefs from bycatch fish. So next time you decide to cook fish, buy a variety you've never cooked before. Most good fish markets can guide you on the best ways to cook them. You might discover a new favorite!

GALVESTON BAY OYSTER APPELLATIONS

A N *APPELLATION* IS a name given to wines and foods that describes their point of origin. It has long been the custom in the Pacific Northwest and on the East Coast to list the appellation of the oysters, or the specific reef from which they were taken. Just as you and I do, they have names. Well, perhaps not Terry or Mike, but monikers like Blackberry Pointe, Conway Cup, or Cedar Creek, or they are Malpeques from Prince Edward Island, Blue Pointes from Connecticut, Wellfleets from Massachusetts, or Westcott Bay from the San Juan Islands off the coast of Washington State.

Texas Gulf oysters from Galveston Bay used to be known by appellations until the early 1900s. There were (and still are) 31 appellations in Texas that have been around since the late 1800s, when Galveston was a bustling city and one of the most important ports in the United States. But the appellations were slowly lost when the Chesapeake Bay oysters became overharvested and the bay waters

stressed, paving the way for oyster-killing parasites. There simply weren't enough East Coast oysters to meet the demand, so oysters began to be sourced from the Gulf Coast. The appellations gradually slipped away until oysters harvested from Texas to Florida became known simply as "Gulf Coast oysters."

In 2010, a movement to restore appellations to Galveston Bay oysters began, pioneered by Jeri's Seafood, a Smith Point oyster distributor in Anahuac. Jeri's Seafood began to hand-sort the oysters from various reefs for size and shell thickness (the thicker the shell, the less brittle it is, making it easier to shuck). Then Foodways Texas, a nonprofit organization dedicated to preserving Texas food culture, hosted an appellation tasting at its annual conference, and the movement gained momentum. Soon a few Houston-area seafood restaurants began to serve Galveston Bay appellation oysters during the oyster season.

Of course, appellation oysters are not for mass

distribution to huge oyster bars that serve thousands of oysters per week, and they are, by virtue of the increased labor and time involved, more expensive than the generic Gulf Coast oysters. Jim Gossen of Louisiana Foods, a Houston seafood supplier, notes that oysters from different reefs have decidedly different tastes and even different appearances. He describes the difference between hand-selected appellation oysters and oysters harvested by the traditional oyster shovel method as one of quality. In a 50-pound sack of oysters there might be four or five oysters that are of top quality, but all of the hand-selected appellation oysters are the same size and the best representatives of the particular reef. A distributor might examine 1,000 oysters to select fewer than 100 that will bear the appellation's name. I think of it like wine: There are many Tempranillos in Texas, and each, because of the particular terroir in which the grapes were grown and the skill of the winemaker, is different. In the oyster appellations, a Ladies' Pass oyster, from a reef halfway between Smith Point and the western end of Bolivar Peninsula, has a delicate taste with a high level of salinity; whereas an Elm Grove oyster, from an eastern Galveston Bay reef, has a high degree of minerality; and Whitehead Reef oysters are very salty with a rich, creamy mouthfeel. Oysters from Trinity Bay on the far northern end of Galveston Bay get a lot of plankton-rich fresh water that flows into the bay from the Trinity and San Jacinto Rivers, so the oysters are bigger, fatter, and sweeter with less salinity than those from the eastern regions of Galveston Bay.

Oystering is a hard life, as subject to the vagaries of Mother Nature as farming. The movement toward selling oysters by appellation, however, just might allow the oystermen to earn a better living.

Oysters Shrimphooley

Any serious oyster lover in the state of Texas knows about Gilhooley's Raw Bar in the little coastal fishing town of San Leon. It's not the most compelling place and has often been referred to as a "biker bar," but I beg to differ. There are at least as many pickup trucks as motorcycles in the parking lot at any given time! And when oysters are sweet and salty in peak season, Gilhooley's seems to get the best of the haul, perhaps because it's the favorite haunt of Misho Ivic, a local oyster producer. Rustic or not, it's my oyster haven of choice. There are tables inside and outside, loud music, and cold longnecks. On weekends, you can't get near the place.

Oysters Shrimphooley is a dish for when oysters are *not* in season and at their sweet best. They're served up on well-seasoned old trays fresh off the pecan wood-fired grill, and you just can't find a better oyster half shell dish, even in the fanciest of restaurants. You can cook them on a gas grill, but they lose something without the pecan smoke. Or you can even broil them in the oven, but they really aren't the same.

MAKES 12 HALF SHELL SERVINGS.

8 tablespoons (1 stick) unsalted butter, softened and cut into small cubes	1½ teaspoons Tabasco
	12 oysters, shucked, on the half shell
1 tablespoon Worcestershire sauce	12 small shrimp (36 to 40 count) peeled, deveined, and boiled
1 tablespoon finely minced garlic	½ cup finely grated Parmesan cheese
½ teaspoon kosher salt	Lemon wedges for serving

Build a fire in the barbecue grill using pecan hardwood charcoal, and let it burn down to the point where the coals are glowing red, covered by a layer of white ash. Combine the softened butter, Worcestershire, garlic, and Tabasco in the work bowl of a food processor fitted with the steel blade. Process until smooth. Scrape out into a bowl.

Select an old baking sheet and cover it with foil. Arrange the oysters in their shells on the prepared sheet, taking care not to spill the flavorful clear oyster juice, called oyster liquor. Put a shrimp on top of each oyster, then add a portion of the butter mixture over the shrimp. Scatter the Parmesan cheese over the top of the oysters. When the fire is right, use chef's tongs to place oysters on the rack over the hot fire and cook just until the oysters curl at the edges, the butter is melted, the cheese is browned, and the shell is nice and blackened by the fire, about 6 to 7 minutes. Place them back on the baking sheet and serve hot with lemon wedges.

Oyster Pan Roast

Oyster pan roast is way at the top of my favorite ways to prepare oysters in those chilly months whose names begin with an *r*, when oysters are at their salty best. It's hearty enough to serve as a main dish, perhaps with an added salad, and oh, so satisfying to oyster lovers. After you've eaten the oysters, the purpose of the slice of toasted French bread on the top is to sop up the rich sauce remaining in the dish. It's almost as good as the oysters themselves!

When buying shucked oysters in their liquor, make sure they're fresh. Look at the oysters. They should be plump and have a pearly, translucent look, and they should be light tannish in color, not dull and whitish. The liquor should be clear and viscous. If it is cloudy and thin, then the oysters are not fresh.

SERVES 6.

36 shucked Gulf oysters and their liquor
¼ cup melted unsalted butter
1 cup dried bread crumbs
½ cup grated Parmesan cheese
Kosher salt
Additional 4 tablespoons (½ stick) unsalted butter
2 large shallots, chopped fine
4 green onions, sliced thin, including green tops
2 tablespoons minced flat-leaf parsley
1 heaping tablespoon minced fresh sage
½ teaspoon minced fresh rosemary

1 teaspoon crushed red pepper flakes
½ teaspoon freshly ground black pepper
1½ quarts whipping cream blended with the liquor from the oysters
2 tablespoons Herbsaint, or other anise-based liqueur
1 tablespoon Worcestershire sauce
Kosher salt

TOAST GARNISH:
6 slices French bread, cut on the bias 1-inch thick
Melted unsalted butter
Kosher salt

Preheat oven to 450°F. Arrange 6 individual gratin dishes on baking sheets; set aside. Drain the oysters in a fine-mesh strainer, capturing the liquor in a bowl below. Set oysters and liquor aside. In a small bowl, combine the ¼ cup melted butter, bread crumbs, and Parmesan cheese, tossing to blend well; season to taste with salt. Set aside.

Melt the additional 4 tablespoons of butter in a heavy-bottomed, deep-sided 12-inch skillet over medium heat. When the butter has melted, add the shallots, green onions, parsley, sage, rosemary, red pepper flakes, and pepper. Cook, stirring often, until shallots and green onions are wilted and transparent, about 7 minutes. Add the whipping cream/oyster liquor mixture, Herbsaint, Worcestershire, and salt to taste. Cook, stirring frequently, until the mixture reduces and thickens, about 10 minutes.

While the sauce is reducing, place 6 of the oysters in each of the gratin dishes. Make the toast garnish. Butter one side of each French bread slice and salt lightly. Grill the bread slices on a comal or grill until light golden brown and crisp, with nice grill marks.

Pour a portion of the sauce over the oysters in each dish. Top with a scattering of the bread crumb/Parmesan mixture, covering the entire surface of the dish. Place the baking sheets in preheated oven and bake for 7 to 10 minutes, or just until the oysters begin to curl at the edges and the topping is browned and bubbly. Do not overcook the oysters! They should still be quite liquidy.

Remove from oven and place a toasted bread slice on top of each serving. Place the dishes on underliner plates and serve hot.

Curry-Fried Oysters with Texas Peach Remoulade Sauce and Pico de Gallo

Anyone who knows me well knows that I love oysters just about any way you can prepare them—or not prepare them. I love them raw on the half shell most of all. This dish was created for the reception for 400 at the grand opening of a Texas winery. Even the oyster haters in the crowd loved the dish. The sauce has a nice kick to it—what I like to call "a fiesta for your mouth"—that pairs beautifully with the hint of curry in the oyster batter. The secret to the success of the dish is that the oysters must be cooked just until the moment a crust forms; then get them out of the fryer onto a draining rack. They should have that nice, paper-thin crust from the batter but still be almost liquid inside. The tasty remoulade can be prepared a couple of days ahead of time and held in a tightly sealed container in the refrigerator—and it's also great on other shellfish.

SERVES 4 TO 6.

TEXAS PEACH REMOULADE SAUCE:
2 cups real mayonnaise, preferably homemade
¼ cup whole-grain mustard
3 green onions, minced, including green tops
1½ tablespoons minced flat-leaf parsley
1 large chipotle chile in adobo sauce, minced

1 tablespoon freshly squeezed lemon juice
1 tablespoon Worcestershire Sauce
12 large garlic cloves, minced
½ teaspoon red (cayenne) pepper
½ teaspoon kosher salt
Pinch of finely ground black pepper
7 tablespoons Texas peach preserves*

OYSTERS:

36 medium-sized shucked oysters

3 eggs beaten into 6 cups milk

4 cups unseasoned corn flour
seasoned with 1½ teaspoons salt,
1½ teaspoons finely ground black
pepper, 1 teaspoon granulated
garlic, and 2 tablespoons
curry powder

Canola oil for deep-frying, heated
to 350°F

PICO DE GALLO:

5 large homegrown Roma tomatoes,
cut into tiny (¼-inch) dice

1 small white onion, cut into tiny dice

3 serrano chiles, seeds and veins
removed, minced

1 bunch cilantro leaves and tender
stems, minced

Juice of ½ large lime, or to taste

Kosher salt

Begin by making the remoulade sauce. Combine all ingredients in the work bowl of a food processor fitted with the steel blade and process until smooth. Transfer to a storage container with tight-fitting lid and refrigerate until ready to use. Serve at room temperature.

Make the pico de gallo by combining all ingredients in a nonreactive bowl. Toss to blend well. Taste to determine if enough salt has been added. Salt is the ingredient in a good pico de gallo that creates harmony among the ingredients and makes them do a little tango in your mouth. If you are making the pico more than 2 hours in advance of serving, however, do not add the salt, as it will make the tomatoes "weep" and water down the pico. When making it ahead of time, add the salt just before serving.

To prepare the oysters, pat them very dry on absorbent paper towels. Dip each oyster in the egg wash, coating well. Press them into the curry-seasoned corn flour, coating well. Shake off all excess. Deep-fry the oysters in small batches, taking care not to crowd the oil. Fry them just until a golden crust forms. They should have a delicate, crisp crust yet still be soft inside. Turn the oysters out on a wire rack set over a baking sheet to drain. Repeat with remaining oysters.

To serve, spoon some of the remoulade sauce on each serving plate. Nest desired number of fried oysters in the sauce and spoon some of the pico de gallo next to the edge of the sauce. Serve quickly while the oysters are crisp and hot.

----

* I developed this recipe using Fischer & Wieser Homemade Peach Preserves. They're made right in my backyard in Fredericksburg, from the original recipe of company founder Mark Wieser's aunt Estelle.

McPHERSON CELLARS

THE MCPHERSONS ARE one of the pioneering families in Texas grape growing and winemaking. The patriarch, Dr. Clinton "Doc" McPherson, is known as the father of modern Texas wine. In partnership with fellow Texas Tech professor Bob Reed, Doc, who was a chemistry professor, founded the Llano Estacado Winery in 1976. It was the first winery to be built in Texas since the repeal of Prohibition. He remains one of the state's prime grape growers. Doc was the first in Texas to plant sangiovese grapes in his original Sagmor Vineyard. He so named the vineyard because the original trellises on which the vines climbed were rustic and tended to "sag."

Doc's son, Kim, graduated from Texas Tech with a degree in food nutrition science and then completed the enology and viticulture program at the University of California at Davis. After working in Napa Valley, he returned to Texas in 1979 to become the winemaker at Llano Estacado. In 1990, he became the winemaker at CapRock Winery, a position that he held until 2007, when he established his own winery. It was during his years at CapRock that he began producing his own McPherson Cellars wines, which he named to honor his father. Kim converted the 1930s-era Coca-Cola bottling plant in Lubbock's historic Depot District into a modern and efficient winery facility and, in the fall of 2008, opened McPherson Cellars.

Kim has long been known for his philosophy of "planting to the land." His focus has always been on Rhone, Italian, and Spanish varietals that thrive on the Texas High Plains. Under the McPherson Cellars label he produces a long lineup of wines from Texas High Plains–grown grapes, including some from Doc's original Sagmor Vineyard. McPherson Cellars offers a range of interesting reds, whites, a sherry, a rosé, and a sparkling wine.

Kim's Texas wines have won more than 450 medals in state, national, and international wine competitions, including two Double Gold Medals at the prestigious San Francisco Wine Fair. He remains one of the key players in the evolution of the wine industry in Texas.

McPherson produces a number of wines that go well with seafood. My favorite wine with denizens of the deep is Albariño, a Spanish varietal that originated in northwestern Spain, where, appropriately, seafood is a staple. Pair the McPherson Albariño with the Oyster Pan Roast (pages 148–149). Kim also produces a stellar Roussanne that is dry and exceptionally aromatic and flavorful with loads of citrus and herbaceous tealike aromas and the subtle, delicious lemon candy characteristics of the grape. I love to have it with the Eggplant Steaks with Seafood Dressing (pages 178–179).

When you serve the Crawfish Dauphine (pages 154–155), one of my personal favorites, pair it with either the McPherson Viognier or dry Chenin Blanc, which is an excellent wine to pair with seafood dishes in general. For the Shrimp Mac 'n Cheese with Hatch Chiles (pages 159–160), serve Kim's Vin Gris Rosé, a complex dry rosé. Kim tells folks to pair his rosé with foods that are a little bit spicy, but I think it is an excellent match for almost anything!

Crawfish Dauphine

Texans have developed a love for "mudbugs," a favorite nickname for crawfish. There are many crawfish farms in the eastern coastal regions of the state where local rice farmers flood their fields after harvesting the rice crop, turning their land into crawfish ponds as an adjunct income, and a delicious one at that. This easy recipe features the humble crawfish as the flavor base for a delicious dish with multidimensional flavors. When you buy peeled crawfish tails, insist on local Texas or Louisiana ones. Avoid crawfish tails from China, as they have a very musky to downright unpleasant taste. And don't ever wash the peeled crawfish tails. The orange substance spread on the tails is the delicious fat from the heads of the crawfish, and it adds an important flavor element to the dish in which the tails will be used. The tasty fat is the reason that real crawfish lovers suck the heads of fresh boiled crawfish!

SERVES 6.

¼ pound (1 stick) butter

2 tablespoons canola oil

1 pound tiny button mushrooms, whole, or regular mushrooms cut into quarters

3 shallots, chopped fine

2 roasted, peeled, and seeded red bell peppers, cut into ½-inch dice

1 large celery stalk, cut into ½-inch dice

2 tablespoons minced flat-leaf parsley

1 teaspoon minced fresh thyme

1 teaspoon cayenne

3 cups seafood stock, or stock made from Knorr brand shrimp bouillon cubes

1 quart whipping cream

2 pounds cooked and peeled crawfish tails with fat

2 tablespoons Pernod, or anisette

Kosher salt and freshly ground black pepper

Beurre manié made from 1 stick softened unsalted butter blended in food processor with ½ cup all-purpose flour until no unblended traces of flour remain

1½ pounds penne rigate pasta, cooked al dente and drained

Minced flat-leaf parsley as garnish

Melt butter in a heavy-bottomed, deep-sided 12-inch skillet over medium heat. Add the canola oil and heat. When the oil mixture is hot, add the mushrooms and shallots. Cook until mushroom liquid has evaporated, about 10 minutes, and mushrooms are lightly browned. Add the red bell peppers, celery, parsley, thyme, and cayenne, stirring to blend well. Cook, stirring often, until celery is wilted, about 5 minutes. Add the stock, stirring to scrape up any browned bits from bottom of pan. Cook to reduce the liquid by one-half. Stir in the whipping cream, crawfish tails, and Pernod. Season to taste with salt and pepper. Simmer for about 15 minutes, then bring to a boil. Begin to stir in small bits of the beurre manié, whisking until it is totally incorporated before adding more, until desired thickness is attained. It should be slightly thickened but still very pourable, like a cream soup.

To serve, place a portion of the pasta in individual pasta bowls and ladle a portion of the crawfish mixture over the top. Garnish with a scattering of the minced parsley and serve hot.

Richard Loper's Astounding Annual Crawfish Boil

Richard Loper first learned to love crawfish when he was 15 and his family moved to New Orleans. He and some of his native Louisiana friends would go into the swamps just west of the city on weekends and set out a few crawfish nets. They would usually catch just enough for a good mess o' crawfish, and his friend's mother would boil them up in a spicy court bouillon for the boys to eat. When he left for college in Ohio, he sorely missed those boiled crawfish.

Richard settled in the Lower Montrose community of Houston. Twice a year the Westheimer Street Organization held a street festival that attracted an eclectic mix of characters. His house was literally 30 feet from the festival and became a natural base for friends attending the party. It struck him that he could boil up some crawfish and make it a real party. For the spring festival he boiled crawfish, and in the fall it was shrimp.

As the years passed, the boils became bigger and bigger, finally reaching the point where Richard was literally boiling crawfish into the dark of the night and into the early-morning hours in his lone beer-keg cooker. One year as he was beginning to prepare for the annual event, he saw a homeless man pushing a grocery cart down the street. In the cart were two empty beer kegs. A swift transaction of cash for kegs, and the help of a good friend and his plasma cutter (a special type of flame-driven cutter), and Richard could again handle the growing load of crawfish. The invitation-only boil continues. Richard says his compulsion to do the boil year after year is his desire to bring all of these old friends together for one night, to catch up with friends he hasn't seen since the boil the year before, to relive stories from boils of the past, but most important of all—to share some good crawfish with his Texas extended family.

FOR THE BOIL:

3 pounds small red new potatoes

2 large onions, sliced

1 head celery, chopped into
    2-inch pieces

4 heads garlic, sliced in half
    horizontally

2 large lemons, quartered

1 pound smoked sausage, cut into
    2-inch pieces

8 ounces white mushrooms

1 artichoke

12 eggs

12 half ears fresh or frozen corn

2 pounds fresh green beans

35 pounds live crawfish

SPICE MIX:

8 ounces each: ground black pepper,
    cayenne, chili powder, and
    kosher salt

4 ounces granulated garlic

COCKTAIL SAUCE:

1 bottle corn syrup–free ketchup

1 bottle Heinz chili sauce

Juice of 1 large lemon

Worcestershire sauce, to taste

Tabasco, to taste

Fresh grated horseradish, the hotter
    the better, and lots of it!

Make the cocktail sauce. Combine all ingredients in a bowl and whisk to blend well. Refrigerate until ready to use.

Fill a 15-gallon beer keg set on a butane burner half full of water and add the spice mix. Turn on the burner.

Rinse the crawfish in a cooler with fresh water. Fill and drain the cooler several times until the water runs clear. Set crawfish aside.

When the water begins to simmer, add the first 8 boil ingredients. Cover the pot and bring the water to a full, rolling boil. Steam will be coming out from beneath the lid.

Add the eggs, corn, and green beans. Cover and bring back to a rolling boil.

When the pot is really boiling, add the crawfish. Cover and bring back to a boil. Boil for 5 minutes. Turn off the heat and throw in a 10-pound bag of ice. This stops the cooking and starts the crawfish and veggies soaking up all those good spices. Let the keg sit for 20 minutes.

Cover a large table with plastic and paper. Drain the crawfish and veggies and pour them all out onto the table. Serve with bowls of the cocktail sauce and several rolls of paper towels. Dig in!

Creamy Shrimp 'n Mac with Hatch Chiles

Mac 'n cheese is a quintessential American comfort food. It's one of those foods that brings a smile to the face and a memory to the forefront no matter how old you are. This adaptation, made with our fresh and flavorful Texas Gulf shrimp and the inimitable Hatch chiles from Hatch, New Mexico, serves as a main course. Toss together a green salad, warm a crusty baguette, and you have a fine meal in no time at all. I've included a step in this recipe that helps give the dish an extra boost of shrimp flavor—cooking the shrimp shells in the milk that will be used to make the béchamel sauce, the base for the cheesy sauce in all mac 'n cheese dishes. The best thing about this dish is that you can make up several individual servings in gratin dishes and freeze them for those times when you need a tasty, hot meal but just don't have the time to prepare one.

MAKES 8 SERVINGS.

1¼ pounds small-to-medium (36 to 40 count) shrimp

2½ cups whole milk

1½ cups elbow macaroni

3 tablespoons unsalted butter

1 small leek, white and light green portion only, halved and sliced thin

3 green onions, sliced thin, including green tops

4 ounces sliced crimini or baby bella mushrooms

2 blistered, peeled, and seeded Hatch chiles,* cut into ½-inch dice

½ teaspoon cayenne

1 teaspoon kosher salt

3 tablespoons all-purpose flour

½ cup whipping cream

1 teaspoon Worcestershire sauce

1 teaspoon Dijon mustard

4 ounces (1 cup) shredded sharp provolone cheese

4 ounces (1 cup) shredded sharp Texas Cheddar cheese

4 ounces (1 cup) shredded Texas Gouda cheese

3 tablespoons melted butter

½ teaspoon kosher salt

⅔ cup panko bread crumbs

⅓ cup grated Parmesan cheese

Begin by peeling and deveining the shrimp. Set shrimp aside at room temperature and place the shells in a 2-quart saucepan. Add the milk and cook, stirring often, over medium heat until milk is hot. Set aside, leaving the shells in the pan with the milk. Preheat oven to 350°F. Cook the macaroni in a large pot of salted, boiling water for about 7 minutes, leaving it slightly al dente, or a tiny bit underdone. Drain well, shaking the colander to remove all traces of water, and transfer to a large bowl; set aside.

Melt the 3 tablespoons of butter in a heavy-bottomed 3-quart saucepan over medium heat. When foam subsides, add the leeks, green onions, mushrooms, Hatch chiles, cayenne, and salt. Sauté, stirring often, until onions are wilted and mushrooms are lightly browned, about 5 minutes. Add the flour all at once and stir quickly to form a smooth paste, blending in all the flour so that no traces of flour remain. Continue to cook, stirring constantly, for a minute or so to cook away the starchy taste. Strain the milk through a fine strainer into a bowl. The milk may appear to be curdled, but that's natural. Discard shells and add the warmed milk, whipping cream, Worcestershire sauce, and mustard to the butter roux, mixing well; bring to a boil, stirring, until the mixture thickens.

Reduce heat to medium low and add the cheeses. Stir until cheese is melted and the sauce is smooth. If your shrimp are longer than 2 inches, cut them in half. Stir the cheese sauce and shrimp into the cooked macaroni and divide among individual 6- to 8-ounce gratin dishes, or turn out into a 9 × 13-inch baking dish. Place the dishes on 2 large baking sheets. (If you're using one baking dish, it doesn't need to be placed on a baking sheet.) Toss the melted butter with the panko bread crumbs and salt, moistening all crumbs, then add the Parmesan cheese, blending well. Top each serving with some of the crumb mixture or, if using the baking dish, scatter evenly over the top. Bake in pre-heated oven for about 30 minutes, or until golden brown on top and bubbly. Serve hot.

----

* Hatch chiles, reputed to be the great-grandfather of California's Anaheim chili, are grown in the region of Hatch, New Mexico. Texans have fallen madly in love with our neighbor's special chile, whose taste can't be duplicated when grown in Texas. The chile will grow, and is cultivated in other states along the Rio Grande, and even in towns near Hatch, but the unique taste is said to result from a combination of the 4,000-foot elevation and hot days and cool nights in Hatch. Our homegrown Texas grocery chain H-E-B sets up chile roasters in front of its stores during Hatch chile season each year, roasting thousands of pounds of the chiles so customers can purchase them and stock up the freezer. They are only available fresh during August and early September each year. The frozen chiles can be ordered year-round online.

JACK ALLEN'S KITCHEN

Jack Gilmore's Shrimp and Cheesy Grits

Austin chef Jack Gilmore is one of those larger-than-life kind of guys. His boundless energy and creativity have given Texans and food lovers across the country lots of good vittles over the years. He was the chef who developed the Z'Tejas Southwestern Grill chain of restaurants and spent 20 years shaping the Tex-Mex menus of the chain. But Jack is a free-spirited person who likes to make work fun—and he's all about sourcing foods locally. The program at Z'Tejas became too corporate for Jack's personality, and there was little opportunity for local sourcing. On the anniversary of his twentieth year, he quit.

Gilmore and Z'Tejas regional operations manager, Tom Kamm, started talking to local farmers and livestock producers, knowing that if they were loyal to the farmers, the farmers would take good care of them, too. The menu at Jack Allen's Kitchen in Austin is eclectic, but purely Texas, inspired by the best those local farms can deliver.

Naturally, all of the seafood used in the restaurant comes from the Gulf. Jack's shrimp and grits isn't on the regular menu but appears occasionally as a special. If it's available, don't miss it.

SERVES 4.

----

3 cups water

1 cup whipping cream

Kosher salt and freshly ground black pepper

1 cup stone-ground grits

3 tablespoons butter

1 cup (4 ounces) shredded sharp Texas Cheddar cheese

1 cup (4 ounces) crumbled Veldhuizen Family Farm Bosque Blue cheese, or substitute another Texas blue cheese, such as Mozzarella Company's Deep Ellum Blue

1 pound large (16 to 20 count) shrimp, peeled and deveined, tail section left intact

Spicy Cajun-style seafood seasoning

6 smoked bacon slices, chopped into ½-inch dice

1 medium onion, cut into ½-inch dice

1 large garlic clove, minced

4 teaspoons freshly squeezed lemon juice

1 cup peeled, seeded, and chopped homegrown Roma tomatoes

2 tablespoons minced flat-leaf parsley

1 cup thinly sliced green onions, including green tops

Combine the water and cream in a heavy-bottomed 4-quart pan over medium-high heat. Add salt and pepper to taste and bring to a full, rolling boil. Add the grits and whisk vigorously until the water is absorbed, about 20 to 25 minutes; don't let them burn. The grits should be smooth and creamy. Remove pan from the heat and whisk in the butter and cheeses, making sure they are well incorporated. Set aside to keep warm.

Rinse the shrimp and pat them completely dry. Toss with enough of the seafood seasoning to coat the shrimp heavily; set aside. Fry the diced bacon in a heavy-bottomed 12-inch skillet, preferably cast iron, over medium-high heat until browned and crisp. Using a slotted spoon, remove the bacon pieces and set aside to drain. Add the onion to the pan and cook just until onion is wilted and transparent, about 5 minutes. Toss in the garlic and shrimp and cook, stirring often, just until the shrimp turn pink and are opaque throughout. Add the lemon juice, chopped tomatoes, parsley, green onions, and reserved bacon. Sauté for 3 minutes.

Spoon a portion of the hot grits into individual rimmed bowls. Spoon equal portions of the shrimp mixture over each serving and serve immediately.

Monica Pope's Grilled Shrimp, Broccoli Rapini, Shell Peas, and Red Pepper Vinaigrette

Monica Pope is an iconic Houston chef, having created four of the city's most popular restaurants over a span of 20 years. The newest venture, Sparrow Bar + Cookshop, has the most eclectic personality of any of her restaurants—to date, because I'm sure she's not done yet. The food is simple, made from the freshest local ingredients, but infused with international influences. Houston is one of the most culturally diverse cities in the South, so both the ingredients and the diversity of the menu are perfectly in keeping with Monica's longtime mantra to "eat where your food lives."

Pope learned to cook, and more important, to love cooking, from her Czech grandmother. "My food journey started because I wanted to find out who I was, who my family was, where we came from, how we cooked," she said. "Really, I wanted to hear stories. Food is the language of family, and stories are the salt. And you have to have salt—it's the ingredient that makes food taste like what it is supposed to taste like; salt brings food alive. There is nothing worse than eating something that you can *almost* taste."

This recipe is typically simple to prepare, but it abounds with flavor. "It's a great summertime dish when there are many varieties of fresh shell beans and peas available," Pope said, "along with lots of summer veggies."

SERVES 4 TO 6.

---

24 shrimp (16 to 20 count), peeled, and deveined, with tail section left intact

Kosher salt or fine sea salt, cayenne, paprika, fresh minced dill, rosemary, or thyme

RED PEPPER VINAIGRETTE:

1½ whole red bell peppers, roasted, peeled, seeded, and roughly chopped

1 medium garlic clove, minced

1½ teaspoons champagne vinegar

1 tablespoon grapeseed oil

1 tablespoon Texas extra-virgin olive oil

Kosher salt and freshly ground black pepper

BROCCOLI RAPINI:

3 heads broccoli rapini, stems
   sliced and florets chopped
Grapeseed oil for sautéing
1 red onion, chopped
1 large garlic clove, minced
2 cups dry white wine, or substitute
   homemade chicken stock
Kosher salt and freshly ground
   black pepper

PEAS:

1 cup fresh shell peas, such as
   zipper cream peas

Place the peeled shrimp in a bowl. Make a blend of the spices and herbs as desired and add to the shrimp. Toss to coat shrimp well.

Slice the stems of the broccoli rapini ⅛-inch thick and separate from the florets. Heat a glaze of the grapeseed oil in a heavy-bottomed sauté pan. Add the red onion and garlic; sauté for 2 to 3 minutes. Add the broccoli rapini stems and sauté for 5 minutes, then add the florets and white wine or stock. Cover and steam for another 5 minutes. Season to taste with salt and pepper. Set aside to keep warm.

Make the vinaigrette. Combine the roasted red pepper, garlic, and vinegar in the container of a high-speed blender. Puree until smooth. With the blender running, pour the combined oils through the top of the container and blend until smooth and well emulsified. Season to taste with salt and pepper. Refrigerate until ready to use.

Boil the peas in salted water until tender, about 30 minutes, if fresh. Do not overcook. Drain and set aside.

Place the shrimp on a hot grill and cook for 2 to 3 minutes. Turn and cook on the other side for about 1 minute.

To assemble and serve: Spoon a pool of the vinaigrette in the center of each plate, using all of the dressing. Using chef's tongs, pile a portion of the greens in the vinaigrette on each plate. Arrange the grilled shrimp as desired on the greens. Scatter some of the peas over each plate and serve at once.

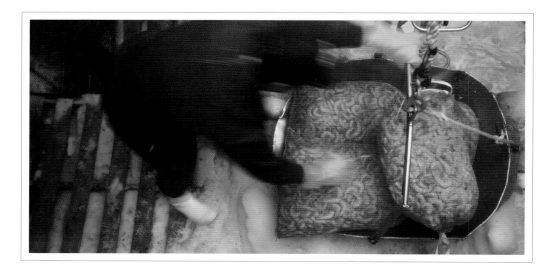

PHILLY SEAFOOD

T HE PORT OF Palacios is home to Philly Seafood, one of the largest privately owned shrimping groups in the United States. Antonia and Edward Garcia Sr. grew up in Palacios and have lived in the city their entire lives. Edward actually started working as an oysterman before venturing into shrimp. The couple bought their first shrimp boat in 1952, a wooden hull trawler named *Texas 18*. The *Texas 18* was the first shrimp boat owned by a Hispanic in the waters of Matagorda Bay. Shortly after Edward set up his operation, the boat was destroyed in an explosion. It was believed to be an act of ethnic violence, although the incident was never positively proven to be arson. Edward simply went back to work as an oysterman and within six months purchased his second boat, *Texas 1*.

The family business began to grow in the mid-1980s even as many other shrimpers were selling their boats. The Garcias' four sons and their sons began to expand the company, becoming boat owners themselves. In addition to the four sons, two daughters, four nephews, and many grandsons became actively involved in the business.

In 2002, the family reorganized into Philly Seafood, believing it was no longer enough just to sell shrimp; they had to develop a brand that represented their values, hard work, and dedication to sustainable practices.

Today Philly Seafood has 30 boats under its umbrella. The boats, large steel-hull trawlers, shrimp the deep Gulf waters for 30 to 60 days at a time. The average harvest per boat, per trip, is 40,000 to 70,000 pounds, but shrimping is a risky and costly business. "Each time a boat leaves the dock, they are carrying $75,000 worth of fuel before netting the first shrimp," said Regina Peña, Edward's daughter and president of the company.

Philly Seafood treats its catch as gently as possible to help maintain its delicious wild flavor. "Shrimp," Regina reflected, "are caught in a hostile environment. They are dragged by nets on the bottom of the Gulf in 80-degree water. When they reach the deck, it's 100 degrees or higher." The shrimp are quickly washed with seawater, headed, then stored in tanks with a safe bisulfite to prevent the development of melanosis bacteria. Agitators in the tanks gently stir the water to keep the shrimp moving.

The company processes 98 percent of its shrimp in Port Lavaca, a short 23 miles from where the boats dock. They directly employ 130 to 140 people and indirectly support local net makers, fuel providers, and engine mechanics, as well as 100 people at the processing plant. Philly Seafood is now a recognized brand in the retail seafood landscape across the United States. The company's two biggest wholesale accounts are the San Antonio–based H-E-B grocery chain and Ben E. Keith Food Service.

As consumers become more educated about their food supply, they are beginning to select more domestically produced fish and shellfish. In doing so, they are choosing products whose origins are local and regulated, as opposed to those imported from unknown waters and processed by methods that may not be safe. The extended Garcia family thinks of themselves as family farmers: their farm is the Gulf of Mexico, and their crop is shrimp. They have good years and bad years. But shrimping is a Texas family tradition, and like so many farmers in this book, the Garcias care deeply about the environment that sustains them. They need and deserve our support.

Not Really "Barbecued" Barbecued Shrimp in Soppin' Broth

This is one of my favorite foods to serve for informal dinners. I say informal because the shrimp are cooked in their shells, with heads on, and eaten with the fingers. It's one of those "roll up your sleeves" dishes. When we serve the dish at home, we give each diner a hand towel. The shrimp are spicy and buttery and addictive. Serve with some good French bread for "sopping up" the spicy sauce. And lots of napkins!

SERVES 6 TO 8.

1 cup olive oil

2 pounds unsalted butter

1½ cups fish or shrimp stock*

8 large garlic cloves, minced

5 fresh bay leaves, minced

1 tablespoon minced fresh rosemary

1 heaping teaspoon minced fresh basil

1 teaspoon dried leaf Mexican oregano

¾ teaspoon red (cayenne) pepper

1½ teaspoons freshly grated nutmeg

1 tablespoon Hungarian paprika

⅓ cup finely ground black pepper

⅓ cup freshly squeezed lemon juice

1½ teaspoons kosher salt

5 pounds head-on unpeeled Texas Gulf brown shrimp (16 to 20 count)

Heat the olive oil in a heavy-bottomed 8-quart Dutch oven over medium heat. Add the butter and cook to melt it. Pour in all remaining ingredients except shrimp. Cook, stirring occasionally, for 25 minutes, to brown the butter slightly. Stir in the shrimp and blend them into the buttery sauce. Cook, stirring often, until shrimp are done and have turned a rich coral-pink, about 25 minutes. Do not overcook.

To serve, divide the shrimp among individual serving bowls. Ladle an ample portion of the buttery sauce into each bowl.

---

* If you don't have access to homemade fish stock, you can make a perfectly good stock from Knorr brand shrimp bouillon cubes. They are available at most large H-E-B stores in Texas. Simply follow the directions on the box. Or you can also save shrimp shells and heads, which are especially flavorful, in the freezer. When you've accumulated a good batch of them, you can make a decent stock from them. Or you can use bottled clam broth.

HAAK WINERY

FOR RAYMOND HAAK, what began as a seemingly innocent planting of two grapevines given to him by his wife, Gladys, as a gift in 1969 developed into a passionate love affair with growing wine grapes and creating fine wines. Raymond and Gladys planted their vineyard in Santa Fe. People scoffed, saying that wine grapes can't grow 15 miles from Galveston Bay! But Raymond had done his homework and found the grape varieties that not only grew but thrived. The winery opened in 2000. The Haaks weren't sure how much traffic to expect at the winery, since Santa Fe isn't exactly a hot destination, but they got a little help with the public response.

A few short weeks after the opening of the winery, Michael Lonsford—then the popular wine writer for the *Houston Chronicle*—wrote a glowing review of two of Raymond's wines made from the blanc du bois grape—a dry and an off-dry, and shared his amazement at finding a real winery with state-of-the-art equipment located less than 20 minutes from the Gulf of Mexico. The article sent local wine lovers flocking to the winery, and the good word about Haak wines soon spread far beyond Santa Fe.

Raymond then produced a port-style wine from the Lenoir grape. Upon sampling the wine, noted wine expert D. C. Flynt remarked that it reminded him of an old Madeira, prompting the Haaks—who had always loved to travel—to make a trip to the island of Madeira to research. There, they discovered the rich history of the wine, which dates back to the sixteenth century when Portuguese winemakers shipped their product around the world via the port of Madeira. The long sea voyage changed the wines—in a good way—and the altered taste was eventually linked to the barrels being inadvertently exposed to very high temperatures in the ships' holds during the voyage. The Portuguese began to age the wine at temperatures as high as 140°F for a period of time, following a two-year barrel aging at cellar temperature. They called the resulting wine Madeira, and it became a favorite throughout Europe. To their surprise, the Haaks also discovered that many of the Madeiras produced on the island are crafted from the very Lenoir grape that they had been growing in their own vineyards in Santa Fe.

When they returned home, the Haaks built an *estufa*—a large, room-sized oven chamber in which the port is heat-fermented in barrels for six months at 105°F, after being barrel-aged in the cellar for two years. After the heat fermentation, the wine is left in the barrels until the need arises to bottle another vintage, as the quality of the wine continues to improve in the barrel, but aging stops once it is bottled. Many Madeiras are barrel-aged for 10 years or longer before bottling. Interestingly, the label on a bottle of Madeira shows the date it was bottled (noted as *engaltafada* or "bottle" on the label) as well as the actual vintage date—or the date on which the wine was placed in the barrels. Once a Madeira is bottled, it will retain its taste quality for years, even after being opened.

The first release of the Haaks' 2003 Jacquez (Lenoir/black Spanish) Madeira has garnered 14 medals—including three gold—and a silver at the prestigious San Francisco International Wine Competition. It was the first (and the only to date) Madeira to be produced in the United States and will be the only one ever allowed to be called Madeira. Raymond's label was approved mere days before the 2006 agreement between the US government and the European Union that banned the use of the titles "Port," "Sherry," "Madeira," and others of similar European-styled wines went into effect.

In 2006, Raymond produced a Madeira from the blanc du bois grape. The wine won instant acclaim and numerous medals. The Haaks make several other interesting (dry) wines from blanc du bois.

For some great pairings with seafood, try these Haak wines: Haak Dry Blanc du Bois with Monica Pope's Grilled Shrimp, Broccoli Rapini, Shell Peas, and Red Pepper Vinaigrette (pages 163–164). The wine exhibits citrus flavors with a crisp grapefruit finish that is palate cleansing and a refreshing complement to the spice- and herb-seasoned shrimp.

Haak Reserve Blanc du Bois with Not Really "Barbecued" Barbecued Shrimp in Soppin' Broth (page 167). The rich hint of butter and soft grapefruit finish will blend and complement the spicy butter and lemon sauce.

Haak Semi-Sweet Blanc du Bois with Shellfish Cheesecake with Garlic and Lemon Butter Sauce (pages 180–181). This nicely balanced wine is finished with a slight residual sweetness of 1.5 percent sugar. This little hint of sweetness brings forth a bright array of tropical fruit flavor of papaya, mango, and pineapple to complement the seafood, spice, garlic, and butter in the recipe.

Summer Corn and Shrimp on Wilted Spinach with Chipotle-Garlic Cream

I never get enough of the sweet, briny Texas Gulf brown shrimp. When they're in season, I buy as many as I can logically fit into my freezer, portioning them in 1-pound batches. This simple dish was adapted from one that I had years ago at Houston's iconic Ruffles restaurant, created for a summer menu by chef/owner Bruce Molzan. Although the dish has several moving parts, it's easy to make and is loaded with fresh Texas flavors, right down to the subtle spicy sauce. I especially like this dish because it's a complete meal all by itself. Serve with a loaf of rustic bread and a crisp white Texas wine or summery dry rosé, and you've got yourself one fine meal!

SERVES 4.

Lemon twists and cilantro sprigs as garnish

SUMMER CORN:
3 large ears of fresh corn, shucked, silk removed
1 tablespoon Texas extra-virgin olive oil
½ teaspoon kosher salt
⅔ cup whipping cream
½ stick (4 tablespoons) unsalted butter, cut into small chunks
1 large red bell pepper, blistered and peeled, cut into tiny dice

SHRIMP:
¼ cup Texas extra-virgin olive oil
1½ pounds Texas Gulf brown shrimp (16 to 20 count), peeled and deveined, with tail sections left intact
½ teaspoon kosher salt
½ teaspoon freshly ground black pepper
4 large garlic cloves, minced

SPINACH:
3 tablespoons Texas extra-virgin olive oil
4 large garlic cloves, peeled and sliced in thin slivers
20 ounces baby spinach leaves, stems removed
Kosher salt

CHIPOTLE-GARLIC CREAM:
10 large roasted garlic cloves
1 cup seafood stock, or substitute stock made from Knorr brand shrimp bouillon cubes, or bottled clam broth
2 chipotle chiles in adobo sauce, minced
2 teaspoons adobo sauce from canned chipotle chiles
2 cups whipping cream
Kosher salt
2 tablespoons minced cilantro

Bring a large saucepan of water to a full, rolling boil and add the cleaned ears of corn. Boil until corn is tender, about 10 to 15 minutes. Remove from heat and set aside. When corn is cool, use a sharp knife to cut the kernels from the cob into a bowl. Scrape the cobs over the bowl a second time to get all of the milky juice that you can; set aside; discard cobs.

Heat the 1 tablespoon olive oil for the corn in a heavy-bottomed 12-inch skillet over medium heat. Add the corn kernels, also scraping in all of the milky juice, and salt. Sauté for about 2 minutes, stirring often, until kernels are slightly browned. Add the whipping cream and cook until cream is thickened. Remove from heat and set aside.

Make the chipotle-garlic cream. Remove the roasted garlic cloves from the skins. Combine the garlic, seafood stock, minced chiles, adobo sauce, and whipping cream in a heavy-bottomed, deep-sided 10-inch skillet over medium-high heat. Cook at a brisk simmer about 10 to 15 minutes, or until garlic has become very soft and liquid has thickened to a sauce consistency. Remove from heat and puree the sauce in a high-speed blender. Add salt to taste and return to a saucepan to keep warm while finishing the meal.

Heat the olive oil for the shrimp in a heavy-bottomed 12-inch skillet over medium-high heat. Place all the shrimp in a bowl and toss with the salt and pepper to season. When oil is very hot, add the shrimp to the skillet and sear for 1 minute, tossing often. Add the garlic and stir to blend well. Cook, tossing constantly, until shrimp are completely opaque, about 2 minutes. Set aside to keep warm.

Return the corn to medium heat. When the corn mixture is hot, quickly stir in the butter chunks. Stirring constantly, cook just until butter has melted. Stir in the diced roasted red bell pepper and remove from heat. Set aside to keep warm.

Heat the olive oil for the spinach in a heavy-bottomed 12-inch skillet over medium heat. Toss in the slivered garlic and cook, stirring, just until garlic is slightly transparent, about 2 minutes. Add the spinach, tossing with tongs, and cook just until spinach is slightly wilted. Add salt to taste. While spinach is cooking, reheat the chipotle-garlic cream and stir in the minced cilantro; remove from heat at once.

Remove the spinach from the skillet directly to serving plates, using chef's tongs. Drizzle a large spoon of the corn mixture over the spinach. Place desired number of shrimp and pour a portion of the chipotle-garlic cream over the top. Garnish plate with a small clump of cilantro and a lemon twist, if desired.

Soft-Shell Crab Po'boys

It's mighty hard to beat the taste of a freshly fried soft-shell crab. Many people don't understand the whole dynamics of *soft-shell* crabs. They're the same blue crabs from which sweet lump crabmeat is picked after the crabs are boiled. As the crabs grow, their shells don't, so they periodically must shed their shells and grow new ones. This process takes only a matter of a day or so, during which time the crabs are completely vulnerable. Crab fishermen recognize when crabs are about to "bust," or shed their shells, and they rush them to the market before the new shells form. But they're only good when they're pristinely fresh, and yes, you eat the whole thing! I do my best to eat my weight in fried soft-shells when I visit the coast and find them on the menu at my favorite restaurants. Perhaps best of all is a fried soft-shell po'boy. To me, it's the very essence of the Gulf. Every place that serves them has its own way of frying them, and the toppings are limitless. I created this version with a tasty slaw-type concoction made with iceberg lettuce and watercress, which adds its little peppery nip. The flavors in the slaw and its dressing pair fabulously with the lusciously sweet meat of the crab.

MAKES 4 PO'BOYS.

4 large soft-shell crabs
1 cup all-purpose flour
1 cup yellow cornmeal, preferably stone ground
½ teaspoon cayenne
1 teaspoon paprika
1 teaspoon granulated garlic
1½ teaspoons kosher salt
1 teaspoon finely ground black pepper

4 eggs whisked into 2 cups whole milk
Canola oil for deep-frying
½ stick (4 tablespoons) unsalted butter, melted
4 slices of good French bread, 6-inch sections
Iceberg and Watercress Slaw (see recipe on page 130)

First clean the crabs. Place the crabs dark shell side up and lift up the "aprons" on each side by the soft tips. You will see spongy, gill-like appendages covering both sides. Remove them from each of the crabs, then pat the shell back in place. Using kitchen shears, snip off the eyes and the feelers, which are in the middle of the shell on the front of the crabs; discard. Set crabs aside. In a large bowl, whisk together the dry ingredients, blending well; set aside. Place the egg and milk wash in a separate bowl. Whisk until all traces of egg are blended.

Pour enough of the canola oil into a heavy-bottomed, deep-sided 12-inch skillet to reach 2 inches in depth. Heat the oil over medium-high heat to 350°F, using a deep-fry thermometer to maintain an even temperature. Use absorbent paper towels to pat the crabs very dry. First dredge them in the cornmeal and flour mixture, coating well all over; shake off excess. Next dip them in the egg and milk wash, coating well and shaking off excess. Finally, dredge them once again in the cornmeal and flour mixture, coating well and shaking off excess. Lower the crabs into the hot oil and fry, turning once, until golden brown and crisp on both sides, about 3 to 4 minutes total. Transfer to a paper towel–lined wire rack set over a baking sheet. Season on both sides with salt and black pepper.

Using a serrated bread knife, slice the French bread pieces almost in half, leaving a "hinge" on one side. Brush the inside of the bread pieces with the melted butter and toast on a hot, flat, cast-iron grill or in a hot oven until light golden brown. Place a crab on each toasted bun and top with a portion of the slaw. Serve at once.

BUDDY ALFREY, TEXAS CRABBER/ COMMERCIAL FISHERMAN

"I LOVE THE WATER. Been on it most of my life. My daddy was a commercial crabber and fisherman his whole life, too. You couldn't do this if you didn't love the water and what the water gives to us. It's hot out there in the summer, and it's mighty cold in the winter when the blue northers blow in, and that cold north wind is whipping up the water something fierce. Makes you cold all the way to your bones. Then there's the Texas rains, and floods, and storms, and hurricanes. Can't work when one of them comes along. And afterward, a lot of times you go back to the water and the bays have changed. Cuts have been silted over by shifting sands. If you're lucky, you got all of your crab traps out before it hit. Otherwise, they're gone."

Buddy Alfrey is Texas grit personified, like many of the independent crabbers, oystermen, and fishermen along the Texas Gulf Coast. Buddy's small boats ply the waters around Galveston and Matagorda Bays, as well as the nearby rivers, where he catches bait for his crab traps.

Buddy makes his living from Texas Gulf crabs, or "blue" crabs. Chefs and consumers alike pay top dollar for the sweet succulent meat from the crabs. When the crabs "bust," or lose their shells as they do often as they grow, there's a short window of time—about 12 hours—before the new shells harden. In this short interim, the crabs are known as "soft-shells." Crabbers know how to tell when a crab is about to shed its shell. The "busters" are separated from the rest of the catch and kept in the water until they lose the shell, then sold to the markets at a premium price.

Buddy sells most of his catch to a large crab-picking house in Port Arthur and a few small markets. "Catches fluctuate, so there's no steady income. And the going price on any given day is what you get paid. I'm a sole independent fisherman. I have a family, and we live on my income. My wife keeps track of the books, and we're well and happy. And we have good fish and crabs to eat. Can't ask for much more."

Grilled Spicy Gulf Crabs

This is a great dish to make for a crowd at the beach house. Have the marinade prepared and ready to use before you purchase the crabs. Or for even more fun, catch your own crabs, either by setting out a few crab traps or the old-fashioned way, with a chicken neck tied on a long string. As you catch the crabs (or when you buy them), drop them into an ice chest about half full of iced water. This will stun them and make them totally inactive. Gulf blue crabs are sweet and succulent, and the spicy marinade in this recipe lights up their flavor even more. Serve with good cold Texas craft beers.

SERVES 6.

18–24 large live blue Gulf crabs, held in an ice bath until stunned and completely inactive

MARINADE:
12 cups grapeseed oil
20 dried arbol chiles, roughly chopped
1 cup minced pickled (sushi-style) ginger
1 large head of garlic, cloves peeled and minced
1 tablespoon kosher salt
3 tablespoons chopped cilantro

Prepare the marinade the day before you will buy or catch the crabs. Combine all ingredients except the cilantro in an 8-quart soup pot over medium heat. Cook, stirring occasionally, for about 30 minutes, or until the garlic is completely soft and the oil is very aromatic. Remove oil from heat and allow it to stand overnight. It should be reddish and very spicy. Strain the oil, discarding solids, and stir in the cilantro. Cover and set aside at room temperature.

To prepare the crabs, remove them, one at a time, from the ice-water bath. Working quickly, before they get warm and frisky, remove the top shell from the crab and rinse under running water to remove all fat and intestines. Remove the gills (dead man's fingers) on each side of the open cavity. Then break the crabs in half at the middle. Repeat with remaining crabs. Place the crabs in a single layer in large, shallow baking dishes. Pour the marinade over the crabs and turn them over several times to coat well. Cover with plastic wrap and refrigerate for 2 hours.

Preheat a gas grill to medium-high heat. Remove crabs from marinade and grill, turning them often with chef's tongs. Cook for about 8 to 10 minutes, or until the meat is white and opaque and the shells are bright orange and lightly charred. The grill will flare when the oil from the marinade drips onto the flame, so take caution with loose clothing and bare hands. Do not squirt the flames with water!

Serve the crabs hot with crab-cracking tools or small wooden mallets. And lots of napkins.

HAIRSTON CREEK FARM

GARY ROWLAND, co-owner of Hairston Creek Farm, was no stranger to growing things when he and his wife, Sarah, purchased their 36-acre farm in 1990. Gary grew up in the melon fields of East Texas. After receiving a degree in horticulture from Texas A&M, he worked at one of the Texas A&M Agricultural Experimental Stations, experimenting with vegetables. Eventually, he landed a contract job as an agronomist for the government of Bermuda. It was there that he met Sarah.

When his contract with the Bermuda government ended, Gary and Sarah moved back to the United States and established Hairston Creek Farm, a small sustainable family farm in central Burnet County between Marble Falls and Burnet, specializing in organic vegetables, herbs, and fruit. The family maintains a small apiary (bee hives) to improve pollination on the vegetables, with the honey being a delicious by-product. The couple's two children are beekeepers and bottle their own honey for sale at the farmers' markets along with their produce, jams, jellies, and "yard" eggs.

Sadly, Sarah lost a long battle with breast cancer in 2012, but I'll never forget what she once told me: "Most people tend to think of food as they do water and electricity—it's just *there*. They have no idea where it comes from, and they're passing that attitude on to their children!" Gary later expanded on that thought and summed up why the farm goes through the rigors of maintaining its organic certification year after year: "It just makes sense to grow organically—on a family level, community level, national level, and on a global level. With every acre of organically grown vegetables and livestock, there's an acre that's free of chemical fertilizers, insecticides, and herbicides. We just need more of those organic acres to clean up the world!"

Sarah Rowland is missed by all who knew her.

Eggplant Steaks with Seafood Dressing

I've always loved this dish. To me, it's comfort food that can just as well double as the starring dish at an upscale dinner party. It's loaded with flavors that kind of ping around the palate with each bite. When I discovered the wonderful taste and texture of the beautiful Sicilian eggplants that Gary Rowland grows at his Hairston Creek Farm, I started using them exclusively for the "steaks" in this recipe.

SERVES 4 TO 6.

3 Sicilian eggplants, about 8 ounces each, or regular globe eggplants

12 shucked oysters, optional

1 pound lump Gulf crabmeat

1½ pounds medium shrimp (26 to 30 count), peeled and deveined

Paul Prudhomme's Seafood Magic seasoning

½ cup canola oil

1 onion, cut into ½-inch dice

1 green bell pepper, cut into ½-inch dice

1 red bell pepper, roasted, peeled, seeded, and cut into ½-inch dice

1 celery stalk, cut into ½-inch dice

¾ teaspoon minced fresh thyme

1½ teaspoons minced fresh basil

½ teaspoon cayenne

½ teaspoon freshly ground black pepper

1 teaspoon kosher salt

¼ cup all-purpose flour

1½ cups seafood stock, or shrimp stock made from Knorr brand shrimp bouillon cubes, slightly warmed

2 cups whipping cream

Juice and zest of 1 large lemon

4 green onions, sliced thin, including green tops

¼ cup minced flat-leaf parsley

Canola oil for deep-pan-frying, heated to 350°F

2 eggs thoroughly beaten with 2 cups milk

2 cups stone-ground cornmeal, blended in a baking dish with 1 cup all-purpose flour, 1 tablespoon kosher salt, 1 tablespoon finely ground black pepper, 2 teaspoons smoked paprika, 2 teaspoons cayenne, and 1 tablespoon granulated garlic

1 cup canola oil for pan-frying, heated to 350°F

Peel one of the eggplants and cut it into small cubes. Place the cubes in a 2-quart saucepan and add water to cover. Simmer over medium heat until the eggplant is very tender, about 7 minutes. Drain thoroughly through a fine wire strainer; set the strainer over a bowl and set aside. Slice the remaining 2 eggplants into lengthwise slices about ⅝-inch thick; set aside.

Drain the oysters, if using them, and set them aside in a bowl. Pick through the crabmeat to remove any bits of shell or cartilage, taking care not to break up the lumps of meat any more than necessary. Set aside. Season the shrimp liberally with the Cajun seafood seasoning. Heat the canola oil in a heavy-bottomed, deep-sided 12-inch skillet over medium-high heat. When the oil is very hot, add the shrimp and quickly sauté, stirring often, just until the shrimp are beginning to brown, about 3 minutes. Remove with a slotted spoon and set aside, reserving the hot oil in the skillet.

Add the vegetables, cooked eggplant, and seasonings to the skillet. Cook, stirring occasionally, until the onion is wilted and transparent, about 7 minutes. Stir in the flour, blending well. Cook, stirring, for 3 to 4 minutes, then add the warmed seafood stock. Stir to blend the stock into the roux and cook for about 5 minutes to thicken. Stir in the whipping cream along with the lemon juice and zest, blending well. Lower heat to medium and allow the cream to thicken slightly for about 10 minutes. Taste for seasonings, adjusting as desired. Keep warm over low heat.

Dip the eggplant slices in the egg and milk wash, shaking off excess; then dredge them in the seasoned cornmeal/flour, coating well on both sides and shaking off excess breading. Begin to fry the eggplant in the hot oil a few slices at a time. Don't crowd the skillet or the temperature of the oil will plummet and they won't fry crisply. Fry until both sides are golden brown, about 4 minutes per side, turning once. Drain on a wire rack set over a baking sheet. Repeat until all of the slices have been cooked.

Add the seared shrimp, crabmeat, and oysters, if using them, to the sauce in the skillet. Cook just to heat the seafood through and until the oysters curl at the edges. Stir in the green onions and parsley.

To serve, place 1 or 2 eggplant steaks on each serving plate and spoon a portion of the seafood mixture over the top. Serve hot.

Shellfish Cheesecake with Garlic and Lemon Butter Sauce

There are many versions of this rich and delicious creation around Texas. A slice makes a nice entrée serving, along with a good salad and some stellar bread, and is a perfect match for a chilled glass of Texas Albariño.

SERVES 12.

1 cup (4 ounces) grated Pecorino Romano cheese

1 cup dry bread crumbs

1 stick (½ cup) unsalted butter, melted

3 tablespoons Texas extra-virgin olive oil

1 medium onion, chopped into ¼-inch dice

1 red bell pepper, blistered, peeled, and chopped into ¼-inch dice

½ teaspoon kosher salt

2 teaspoons Paul Prudhomme's Seafood Magic seasoning

1 tablespoon minced flat-leaf parsley

2 teaspoons minced fresh lemon thyme

28 ounces cream cheese, softened

4 eggs, well beaten

2 teaspoons Texas Pete Hot Sauce

½ cup whipping cream

1 cup (4 ounces) shredded Mozzarella Company Cacciota cheese, or substitute Monterey Jack cheese

6 ounces Texas or Louisiana crawfish tails, cooked, peeled, and chopped

6 ounces boiled Texas Gulf shrimp, peeled, deveined, and chopped

6 ounces regular lump blue crabmeat, gently picked through to remove any bits of shell or cartilage

Garlic and Lemon Butter Sauce (see recipe below)

GARLIC AND LEMON BUTTER SAUCE:

2 large garlic cloves, peeled and trimmed

2 tablespoons freshly squeezed lemon juice

1 tablespoon minced flat-leaf parsley

2 tablespoons grated Pecorino Romano cheese

¼ teaspoon kosher salt

¼ teaspoon cayenne

1 stick (½ cup) unsalted butter, melted and hot

Make the cheesecake first. Preheat oven to 350°F. Combine the Pecorino Romano cheese, bread crumbs, and melted butter in a small bowl. Toss to moisten dry ingredients well. Turn the mixture out into a 9-inch springform pan and press into bottom and up the sides of the pan. Refrigerate while making the filling.

Heat the olive oil in a heavy-bottomed 12-inch skillet over medium-high heat. When the oil is hot, add the onion, red bell pepper, salt, Seafood Magic seasoning, parsley, and lemon thyme. Sauté, stirring often, until onion is wilted and transparent, about 5 minutes. Set aside.

Beat the cream cheese in the bowl of a stand mixer on medium high until creamy. Add the beaten eggs, hot sauce, whipping cream, and shredded cheese. Beat at medium high until well blended. Add the reserved onion and seasoning mixture from the skillet and beat just to blend. Turn mixture out into a large bowl. Add the crawfish, shrimp, and crabmeat. Fold gently but thoroughly into the cream cheese mixture, taking care not to break up the lumps of crabmeat.

Turn the mixture out into the prepared springform pan. Place the pan in a larger pan and add boiling water to come halfway up the side of the springform pan. Bake the cheesecake in preheated oven for 1¼ to 1½ hours, or until firm and golden brown on top. Turn oven off and leave the cheesecake in the closed oven for 45 minutes.

Make the garlic and lemon butter sauce. Combine all ingredients except butter in the work bowl of a food processor fitted with the steel blade. Process until well blended. With the processor running, pour the hot butter through the feed tube in a slow, steady stream until all has been added. Continue to process another 15 to 20 seconds. Turn out into a bowl and keep hot.

Remove the cake from the oven and carefully remove the ring from the springform pan. Using a sharp, thin-bladed knife, cut the cheesecake into slices and place on individual plates. Drizzle a portion of the sauce over the slices and serve at once.

Crispy Seafood Cakes with Chile, Cilantro, and Lime Cream

I positively adore any kind of pan-sautéed seafood cakes, including crab cakes. The quality of crab cakes relies primarily on the quality of the crab meat and the amount of it used in the cakes relative to the amount of breading. I decided to try a version adding tasty crawfish. It worked quite nicely, and they became a menu favorite at the lodge where I was chef. The cakes can be made in the morning if you're serving them for dinner, refrigerated on a parchment-lined baking sheet, and covered with a second sheet of parchment until you're ready to cook them.

MAKES 12 CAKES.

6 ounces medium-sized Texas Gulf shrimp, boiled, peeled, and deveined, chopped into ½-inch dice

6 ounces regular lump blue crabmeat, picked through gently to remove any bits of shell and cartilage

6 ounces Texas or Louisiana crawfish tails, boiled and peeled, chopped into ½-inch dice

2 cups soft, fresh bread crumbs

⅔ cup real mayonnaise, preferably homemade

2 medium garlic cloves, minced

3 green onions, sliced very thin, including green tops

1 red bell pepper, blistered, peeled, and cut into ¼-inch dice

1 tablespoon freshly squeezed
    lemon juice
1 teaspoon Paul Prudhomme's
    Seafood Magic seasoning
1 tablespoon Worcestershire sauce
1 teaspoon Tabasco
½ teaspoon kosher salt
¼ teaspoon cayenne
1 egg, well beaten
2 cups panko bread crumbs
¼ cup canola oil
Chile, Cilantro, and Lime Cream
    (recipe follows)

CHILE, CILANTRO, AND LIME CREAM:
⅔ cup Mexican crema
1 serrano chile, seeds and veins
    removed, roughly chopped
⅓ cup packed cilantro leaves and
    tender top stems
1½ tablespoons freshly squeezed
    lime juice
2 teaspoons medium-hot chili powder
½ teaspoon kosher salt

Begin by making the chile, cilantro, and lime cream. Combine all ingredients in the work bowl of a food processor fitted with the steel blade. Process just long enough to blend well. Turn out into a bowl and refrigerate, tightly covered, until ready to use.

To make the seafood cakes, line a baking sheet with parchment paper; set aside. Combine the shrimp, crab, crawfish, and fresh bread crumbs in a large bowl. Toss to blend well, taking care not to break up the lumps of crabmeat; set aside. In a separate bowl, combine the mayonnaise, garlic, green onions, red bell pepper, lemon juice, Seafood Magic seasoning, Worcestershire sauce, Tabasco, salt, cayenne, and beaten egg. Whisk to blend thoroughly. Add to the seafood mixture and fold in, making sure all the shellfish and bread crumbs are moistened well. Shape the mixture into 12 cakes, patting them together firmly. Pour the panko bread crumbs into a shallow dish and press both sides and the edges of each seafood cake into the crumbs, coating well. Shake off any loose crumbs. Place the cakes on the prepared baking sheet, cover with a second sheet of parchment paper, and refrigerate for 1 hour to firm them up.

Heat the canola oil in a heavy-bottomed 12- to 14-inch skillet over medium-high heat. When the oil is hot, add a single layer of the cakes and cook until golden brown, about 2 minutes on each side, turning once. Remove to a wire rack set over a baking sheet. Repeat with remaining cakes, adding and heating additional canola oil if needed. Serve hot with the chile, cilantro, and lime cream.

Mustard-Fried Catfish with Olive and Caper Tartar Sauce

This is an old recipe from Texas fishing camps, which are the true man caves of real Texas fishermen. They're usually quite rustic, but they always have a rudimentary kitchen, a barbecue grill, and a butane fryer. After a day of fishing, the fishermen return to the camp with the day's catch, which they clean and turn into a supper fit for a king, to be washed down with the requisite washtub of iced longnecks.

6 skinned catfish fillets
   (5 to 6 ounces each)
Canola oil for deep frying, heated
   to 350°F
2 cups prepared yellow,
   "ballpark-style" mustard
3 eggs, well beaten
1 tablespoon Tabasco
1 cup corn masa flour (flour
   used for making tortillas)
1 cup yellow cornmeal
1 cup all-purpose flour
1 cup Italian-seasoned bread crumbs
2 teaspoons kosher salt
1 teaspoon granulated garlic
1 teaspoon sweet Hungarian paprika
Lemon wedges and whole trimmed
   green onions as garnish

Olive and Caper Tartar Sauce
   (see recipe below)

OLIVE AND CAPER TARTAR SAUCE:
1¼ cups real mayonnaise, preferably
   homemade
⅓ cup dill relish
¼ cup finely chopped pimiento-
   stuffed olives
1 heaping tablespoon chopped capers
1 tablespoon minced flat-leaf parsley
½ small yellow onion, chopped fine
   (about 2 tablespoons)
1 tablespoon fresh lemon juice
1 teaspoon dry mustard
½ teaspoon kosher salt
½ teaspoon freshly ground
   black pepper

Begin by making the tartar sauce. Combine all ingredients in a small bowl and whisk to blend well. Cover with plastic wrap and refrigerate until ready to serve, or up to 3 days.

Use absorbent paper towels to pat the fish fillets dry; set aside. Heat the canola oil to 350°F, preferably in a deep fryer with a thermostat, or use a candy thermometer to maintain an even temperature while frying the fish.

In a medium-sized bowl, combine the mustard, eggs, and Tabasco, whisking to blend well so that no traces of unblended egg remain. Turn the mustard mixture out into a baking dish; set aside. In a separate bowl, combine all remaining ingredients except garnishes and tartar sauce. Toss with a whisk to blend well. Pour into a separate baking dish.

Dredge the fish fillets first in the mustard mixture, turning to coat all surfaces. Let excess batter drip off. Next, dip the fish in the cornmeal mixture, turning to coat well and leaving no bare spots of mustard. Shake off excess breading. Gently place the fish in the hot oil 2 or 3 pieces at a time. Don't crowd the pan, or the temperature will drop, resulting in a soggy crust. Fry until golden brown and crispy, about 5 to 6 minutes, turning once. Drain on a paper towel-lined wire rack set over a baking sheet. Keep hot in a warm oven while frying the remaining fillets.

Serve hot with lemon wedges and trimmed, whole green onions. Pass tartar sauce separately.

THE TRASHFISH MARKET

THE WORD *TRASHFISH* is not an appealing moniker for anything one might consider eating. But it's all about economics. Commercial fishermen target specific types of fish when they take their boats out in the Gulf. Whatever else winds up on their decks is bycatch and is generally thrown back. Most of it will die. The fishermen bring to market what the consumers and the majority of restaurants demand—recognizable, familiar species of fish like red snapper, swordfish, flounder, and tuna. These are the fish consumers want to purchase at seafood markets and what they expect on the menus at their favorite seafood restaurants. The result is that many of the popular species of fish are being seriously overfished, and their long-term existence is being threatened. This is what happened to the Gulf redfish during the heyday of blackened redfish. The ideal-sized redfish fillet for blackening was about 6 ounces, and, of course, came from the younger fish, known to chefs and fishermen as "rat reds." The demand for the young fish almost decimated the Gulf redfish population, resulting in a total moratorium on commercial fishing of the species and strict size limits of 20 to 28 inches in length for anglers. Redfish available on the commercial market today is farmed, and personally, I think the taste of the fish has been greatly diminished.

However, a few wholesale purveyors, such as Airline Seafood and Louisiana Foods, both based in Houston, have begun creating a market for bycatch. Airline handles what Vice President of Operations Mark Musatto refers to as a "Toys'R'Us" selection of crabs, fish, shellfish, and mollusks, as well as more than 20 species of snapper, super deep-water fish like golden tile fish, long-tailed bass (saltwater version), barrel fish, and 20 or more varieties of grouper (including gag, scamp, calico, strawberry, Kitty Mitchell—named after a brothel madam in Galveston—Warsaw, snowy, and cloudy).

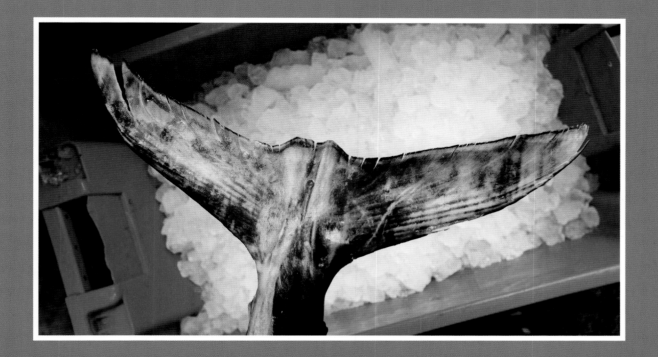

They also sell scorpion fish, triggerfish, bar jacks, amberjack, cobia, Gulf of Mexico kampache (a.k.a. almaco jack), wahoo, and most every tuna in the sea, including blue fin, which spawn in the warm waters of the Gulf of Mexico. Mark was adamant to point out that all of the local fish sold at Airline Seafood are hook-and-line or hand-line caught. They do not buy from trawlers.

The variety of fish and shellfish that Airline handles creates opportunities for educating its clients about the bounty, beauty, and diversity that the Gulf holds. But Mike doesn't like the term "bycatch" because it implies unprofitable or inedible catch; he calls today's offerings "complete catch."

Louisiana Foods takes a similar approach and even used a similar term for its short-lived retail bycatch market. The Total Catch Market that formerly was held at Louisiana Foods in Houston every Saturday morning was created by Jim

Gossen, co-owner of Louisiana Foods, because he wanted to introduce more species to the public. He gave P. J. Stoops, one of his longtime and very knowledgeable fishmongers, the job of opening the market. Stoops was especially adept at explaining to customers the best way to prepare the various fish and to show them how to fillet the sometimes unusual specimens. It was a very exciting turn for lovers of really fresh fish. For me, just knowing that the fish is local makes me want to try it. As avid anglers, my husband and I have been catching many of the underutilized species for years, and we've discovered some really tasty fish. Some of our favorites are sheephead, triggerfish, golden gulf croaker, tilefish, and scorpion fish. I've even cooked sting ray wings!

Sadly, Jim had to close the Saturday market even though it had been very successful. Consumers flocked to the market to learn about the many species of fish, but there was an even greater interest from area chefs who were ordering bycatch fish from the wholesale branch of Louisiana Foods. Soon there simply weren't enough trashfish to meet the demands of both the chefs and the Saturday Total Catch Market.

When I contacted Jim Gossen about the closing of the market, here's what he told me: "Certainly, we are still selling the bycatch, but only to restaurants. The problem was we were holding bycatch for the Saturday market, and chefs were ordering on Friday, but we couldn't fill all of their orders because we were holding so much of the fish for the market. This caused a conflict within our wholesale business, which is our focus and main business. I guess that's a good problem. I only wish we could supply everyone who wants bycatch. Maybe in the future we will see more bycatch brought in by our boats. A few years ago all of this fish was simply being thrown back. Now it is going to the dining public."

Here's hoping the Total Catch Market is back in business soon.

Bryan Caswell's Grouper with Braised Collards and Pecan-Shallot Cracklin'

Although he's cooked all over the world for some truly elite chefs (Jean-George Vongerichten, Charlie Palmer, Jose Muneisa), Bryan Caswell was destined to be at the helm of a restaurant like Reef. He spent most of his childhood on the Gulf Coast waters, where he honed his skills as an angler. And in doing so, he soaked up a lot of knowledge about the denizens of the waters, along with a lot of sunshine. At Reef, Caswell is free to express his love and knowledge of fish in a seafood-based menu unlike that of any other Houston eatery. He often features bycatch, claiming, "The most important thing is that it's fresh." The menu reflects the chef's globetrotting past, fusing elements from many regions—the Gulf Coast, Louisiana, Mexico, and, in this case, Thailand. Caswell loves the balance of hot and cold items often on the plate in Thai cuisine. In this simple, yet innovative dish he combines hot collard greens with grilled fish and a cool topping.

SERVES 4.

COLLARDS:

2 bunches fresh collard greens, about 26 ounces, thick midribs removed
1 tablespoon Texas extra-virgin olive oil
10 bacon slices, cut into small dice
1 large onion, halved, then sliced thin
6 large garlic cloves, minced
2 cups dry white Texas wine, such as Chardonnay
Kosher salt and freshly ground black pepper
2 quarts chicken stock

PECAN-SHALLOT CRACKLIN':

⅔ cup Texas extra-virgin olive oil
10 large shallots, cut into ¼-inch dice
½ cup finely chopped Texas pecans
¾ teaspoon minced lemon zest
¾ teaspoon minced fresh tarragon
1¾ teaspoons minced flat-leaf parsley
2 teaspoons finely chopped chives

GROUPER:

1 pound scamp grouper fillet, cut into 4-ounce pieces
1 teaspoon fine sea salt
½ teaspoon cayenne
3 tablespoons Texas extra-virgin olive oil
2 small portobello mushrooms, stems removed, wiped clean with a damp paper towel

Chop the collard greens into bite-size pieces; set aside. Heat 1 tablespoon olive oil in a deep braising pan over medium-high heat. When the oil is hot, add the diced bacon and cook until crispy. Lower heat to medium and add the onion and garlic; sweat until onion is wilted and transparent, about 5 minutes. Remove all solids from pan and set aside; retain fat in pan. Turn heat to high. When the fat starts to smoke, add the collards and allow them to sauté, stirring often and allowing the liquid that is produced to reduce until evaporated. Add back the onion, bacon, and garlic mixture and deglaze the pan with the wine, scraping up all browned bits from bottom of pan. Reduce by half, then add the chicken stock. Simmer for 1½ to 2 hours, or until collards are very tender. Keep warm.

Make the pecan-shallot cracklin'. Heat the oil over medium-high heat and add the shallots. Cook, stirring often, until they are brown and crispy, about 18 to 19 minutes. Watch them very closely, as they go from perfectly done to critically burned in a nanosecond. Remove quickly, using a flat, metal, fine-mesh skimmer. Combine with the pecans, lemon zest, and herbs in a medium bowl; set aside until cool. If you are making the cracklin' ahead of time, refrigerate after cooling. Bring to room temperature to use.

To cook the grouper and mushrooms, use absorbent paper towels to pat the fish dry. Season the fish pieces with salt and cayenne; set aside. Heat the olive oil in a 12-inch cast-iron skillet until it is very hot, almost smoking. Add the fish pieces and cook 2 to 3 minutes per side (just until it turns opaque throughout), turning once, until browned on both sides. Set aside to keep warm. Repeat with remaining pieces of fish, taking care not to crowd the pan. And don't overcook the fish, or it will be as tough as a tennis shoe.

Add the portobello mushrooms to the pan and cook quickly, turning once, until they are crisp, about 5 minutes total.

To assemble and serve the dish, spoon a portion of the greens, along with enough of the pot likker to make them float, into individual deep-rimmed bowls. Slice the portobellos into slices on the bias. Lay 3 slices on top of the greens in each bowl. Top with a piece of the fish and garnish with a liberal amount of the cracklin'. Serve at once.

Flounder in Parchment Paper with Crabmeat and Tequila and Chipotle Butter Sauce

Fish baked in parchment paper is a time-honored dish that never goes out of style. There's nothing like the aroma when the parchment is slit open at the table. It actually makes me salivate, and I can't wait to tear into the perfectly cooked treasure inside once the sauce has been added. Select a nonoily, delicately flavored, white-fleshed fish like flounder to prepare the dish. The flavor of oily-fleshed fish tends to concentrate when cooked in parchment, often resulting in the "fishy" flavor that makes a lot of people not like fish. Those fish are great on the grill, where the oiliness of the flesh pairs beautifully with the smoke and char.

SERVES 4.

FLOUNDER:

5 parchment paper hearts (see instructions below)

⅔ cup plus 2 tablespoons unsalted butter, divided

4 fresh Gulf flounder fillets, 5 to 6 ounces each, or if the fillets are larger, cut them into 5- to 6-ounce pieces

8 ounces lump blue crabmeat

Fine sea salt and freshly ground black pepper

4 lime wedges

20 mixed red and yellow small cherry tomatoes, halved

Kosher salt and freshly ground black pepper

Fresh chive sprigs, sliced into ¼-inch segments

3 egg whites, beaten until frothy

TEQUILA AND CHIPOTLE BUTTER SAUCE:

4 tablespoons (½ stick) unsalted butter

2 tablespoons minced shallots

½ teaspoon minced garlic

½ teaspoon dried Mexican oregano

2 teaspoons toasted, then ground, coriander seeds

⅛ teaspoon freshly ground black pepper

2 canned chipotle chiles in adobo sauce, roughly chopped

1 cup plus 2 tablespoons seafood stock, preferably homemade

⅓ cup Republic Tequila Reposada

1 cup whipping cream

1½ tablespoons cornstarch mixed into 2 tablespoons cold seafood stock

1 tablespoon freshly squeezed lime juice

1 tablespoon Asian sweet chili sauce

1 tablespoon minced cilantro

Kosher salt

Begin by making the parchment paper hearts. Fold four 12 × 16½-inch parchment paper sheets (known as "half sheets" at restaurant supply stores) in half from the long side to make 8¼ × 12-inch rectangles. Using a pencil, sketch a half-heart outline beginning at the tip of the closed edge of the paper, and ending back at the closed edge at the bottom of the paper. Repeat with remaining folded parchment sheets. Cut the hearts out with scissors; set aside. Preheat oven to 375°F.

Use absorbent paper towels to pat the flounder fillets dry. Remove any small bones. Place the parchment hearts on a work surface so that they open to the left, like a book. Melt ⅔ cup of the butter. Using a pastry brush, butter the right-hand portion of the hearts with some of the butter to within 2 inches of the outside edge. Lay one of the fillets on each buttered side of the hearts, placing it about 1 inch from the center. Carefully pick through the crabmeat to remove any bits of shell or cartilage, taking care not to break up the beautiful lumps of meat. Brush the fillets with some of the butter, then top each with 2 ounces of the crabmeat. Season to taste with salt and pepper. Drizzle remaining melted butter over the crabmeat.

Melt the remaining 2 tablespoons of butter in a heavy-bottomed 10-inch skillet over medium-high heat. When the butter is melted, sauté the halved cherry tomatoes, stirring often and seasoning to taste with salt and freshly ground black pepper, for about 2 minutes. Using a slotted spoon, arrange a few of the tomatoes over and around each portion of fish, squeeze a lime wedge over each serving, and scatter some of the sliced chives over the top.

Use a pastry brush to brush 2 inches of the open edges of the hearts with the beaten egg whites. Fold the left-hand sides of the hearts over the fish, matching them up with the outside edge. Press into the egg white to seal. Now brush the outside 2 inches of the sealed heart with more of the egg white and begin to fold the edge, starting at the center of the folded side of the heart, into pleats. When you reach the bottom of the heart, brush the pleats with more egg white and repeat the pleating. When you reach the bottom this time, twist the tip 4 to 5 times to seal. Brush the sealed pleats again with the egg whites. Place the hearts on 2 baking sheets and set aside while making the sauce.

To make the tequila and chipotle butter sauce, melt the butter in a heavy-bottomed 10-inch skillet over medium heat. When the foam subsides, stir in the shallots, garlic, oregano, ground coriander, and black pepper. Sauté until shallots are wilted and transparent, about 3 minutes.

While the shallots are cooking, combine the chipotle chiles and the seafood stock in a high-speed blender. Add the shallot mixture to the blender and puree until silky smooth. Pour the puree into a clean skillet and add the tequila. Cook to reduce by about half. Add the whipping cream; bring to a boil, stirring. Whisk in the cornstarch mixture and cook until thickened, about 3 minutes. Stir in the lime juice, sweet chili sauce, and cilantro. Season to taste with salt. Keep warm while baking the fish.

Place the baking sheets in preheated oven. Bake for 15 minutes, or until the parchment paper is golden brown and the hearts are puffed up. If you are using two shelves in the oven, switch the baking sheets halfway through the cooking time. Remove from oven and quickly place on individual serving plates. Customarily, the plates are carried to the table with the hearts unopened. The sauce is carried in a sauce boat or small pitcher. In front of the diners, the parchment is slit open down the middle using a small, very sharp paring knife or scissors. The aroma that wafts up to the diner when the heart is opened is quite compelling. Pull the parchment paper aside from the middle of the slit and spoon or pour a portion of the sauce into the heart. Enjoy.

Grilled Triggerfish with Hoja Santa and Tomatillo Sauce

Even among those who love fish, the homely gray Gulf triggerfish is mostly unknown. Among anglers, the fish, which is a bottom feeder that inhabits the same areas as the popular, but seriously overfished red snapper, has long been considered a "trashfish" and is generally thrown back. The fish has a large head, so the percentage of edible meat is lower than that of other fish, and its skin is very tough and difficult to remove by traditional methods. However, the fish is making its way up the food chain, most believe, due to the overfishing of more popular species. Often called "poor man's lobster," triggerfish has firm, pure white flesh, similar to that of the grouper, but the taste is more like that of red snapper, which is the reason that it's beginning to show up on restaurant menus. The fish can be prepared by just about any method: grilling, pan searing, broiling. Triggerfish also freezes better than just about any other fish—for up to six months, without becoming "fishy."

This recipe pairs the tasty fish with a unique sauce made from the flavorful herb hoja santa, which is used often in Mexican cooking. The herb has a great affinity for fish. The heart-shaped leaves of the plant, which can reach a foot in diameter, are also used as wraps, usually with fish. The flavor of the herb is hard to describe but has been likened to everything from root beer (it contains the same oils as the sassafras plant) to eucalyptus, tarragon, and mint. Hoja santa has recently been discovered by chefs at upscale restaurants in the Northeast, and herb growers in the region now charge up to $1.50 per leaf! In Texas it grows like wildfire and will take over a garden in short order. I grow mine in pots because I don't have room in my herb beds for the gigantic, invasive plant. The plant dies back in the winter but is one of the first signs of spring when it bounces back, larger each year, as soon as we have a couple of weeks with no frost.

SERVES 4.

GRILLED FISH:

4 triggerfish fillets, 6 ounces each, unskinned

Texas extra-virgin olive oil

Fine sea salt and freshly ground black pepper

HOJA SANTA AND TOMATILLO SAUCE:

MAKES ABOUT 3½ TO 4 CUPS.

1 cup loosely packed torn hoja santa leaves, with stems and thick veins removed

1½ cups chicken stock, preferably homemade

4 large garlic cloves, peeled, trimmed, and roughly chopped

1 medium white onion, peeled and roughly chopped

3 serrano chiles, seeds and veins removed, roughly chopped

1 blistered, peeled, and seeded poblano chile, roughly chopped

2 medium tomatillos, husks removed, roughly chopped

3 tablespoons Texas extra-virgin olive oil

Kosher salt and freshly ground black pepper

1 heaping tablespoon minced cilantro

Lemon wedges

Begin by making the hoja santa and tomatillo sauce. Combine all ingredients except olive oil, salt and pepper, and cilantro, in the container of a high-speed blender. Puree until very smooth. Set aside.

Heat the olive oil in a heavy-bottomed, deep-sided 10-inch skillet over medium-high heat. When the oil is hot, pour in the hoja santa puree. Stir vigorously and bring to a full boil. Reduce heat quickly and simmer for about 15 minutes. Season to taste with salt and pepper, and stir in the cilantro, blending well. Keep warm over low heat while grilling the fish.

Heat a gas char-grill to medium high. Spray the grilling rack with high-heat nonstick spray. Remove any small bones from the sides and top portion of the fish, using tweezers or needle-nose pliers. Glaze the fillets on both sides with olive oil and season with salt and pepper. Place the fish on the hot grill, skin side down, and cook for about 4 minutes, or until well marked by the grill. Flip the fish and cook for an additional 4 to 5 minutes, or until the fish turns opaque throughout. The fillets should still be firm in texture with no signs of the fleshy flakes beginning to separate. Do not overcook the fish.

To serve, place a grilled fillet on each serving plate and spoon a portion of the sauce across the center, allowing it to pool on the plate on either side of the fish. Serve hot with lemon wedges.

Pan-Seared Black Drum with Shrimp Essence and Capers

Black drum, cousin to the prized redfish, is one of the underutilized species of southern saltwater fish. I love to fish for drum on the bottom of the bays near the shore because they're real fighters—and so tasty. The best time to snare them in the Texas Gulf is in the fall and winter months when the water is cold. The drum is a silver fish with large black stripes when young and resembles the sheephead, another underutilized fish. It's not a particularly glamorous specimen, but the fish is very meaty, with pure white large flakes, and versatile for many methods of cooking. The fish can grow to up to 100 pounds, but the large ones are not very tasty and should be released alive, after you take a quick picture, of course! The best size for cooking is between 1 and 4 pounds.

The shrimp essence is so delicious that it's well worth dealing with the shrimp heads and shells. The shells are so flavorful that I would never throw them away! I collect them in freezer bags until I have enough to make a good pot of shrimp stock, and/or this sauce. Always try to purchase head-on shrimp, as the heads make such tasty stock. If you deal with a serious seafood seller, perhaps you can ask to have some saved for you. The sauce can be served on any simply seared or broiled fish fillet. I love to serve the dish on lightly seared greens.

Seared Boggy Creek Farm Spinach
with Shiitake Mushrooms and Garlic
(see recipe on page 369)
Lemon wedges as garnish

DRUM:

6 black drum fillets, 5 to 6 ounces
each, skinned
Texas extra-virgin olive oil
Fine sea salt and freshly ground
black pepper
All-purpose flour

SHRIMP ESSENCE:

¼ cup plus 2 tablespoons Texas extra-
virgin olive oil, divided
2 pounds shrimp heads and shells
3 large garlic cloves, minced
1 small yellow onion, chopped
½ teaspoon cayenne
6 large flat-leaf parsley sprigs
4 large basil leaves, roughly chopped
2 tablespoons tomato paste
2 cups fish or shrimp stock, preferably
homemade, or substitute stock
made from Knorr brand shrimp
bouillon cubes
2 large shallots, minced
⅔ cup whipping cream
Kosher salt and freshly ground
black pepper
4 tablespoons (½ stick) unsalted
butter, cut into ½-inch cubes
2 tablespoons capers, well drained

Begin by preparing the shrimp essence. Heat the ¼ cup of olive oil in a heavy-bottomed 12-inch skillet over medium-high heat. When the oil is hot, add the shrimp heads and shells. Cook, stirring often, until the shells are beginning to brown, about 7 to 8 minutes, and a nice shrimp aroma emanates from the pan. Add the garlic, onion, cayenne, parsley, and basil. Cook, stirring frequently, until onions are wilted and transparent, about 5 minutes. Add the tomato paste and stir to blend well. Cook, stirring constantly, until the paste is darkened and thick, about 5 minutes. Add the stock and stir well, scraping up all browned bits from the bottom of the pan. Cook to reduce the liquid by about one-third, around 10 minutes. Remove the pan from the heat and strain the juices from the pan, reserving both juice and solids.

Transfer the solids to the work bowl of a food processor fitted with the steel blade. Add about half of the broth from the pan. Process until the shrimp heads and shells are as smooth as possible. Using a fine-mesh wire strainer, strain the shrimp mixture into the remaining broth, stirring the solids with the back of a big spoon to extract every possible drop of liquid from the shell mixture. Discard head and shell puree. Set broth aside.

Heat the remaining 2 tablespoons of olive oil in a heavy-bottomed 10-inch skillet over medium heat. When the oil is hot, add the shallots and cook, stirring often, just until they are wilted and transparent, about 4 minutes. Pour in the reserved shrimp stock and the whipping cream. Whisk to blend well. Cook for about 7 minutes, or until the sauce is thickened and season to taste with salt and pepper. Set aside to keep warm while cooking the fish.

To prepare the fish, turn the fillets skin side down and cut out the dark blood line from each fillet and discard. Heat a shallow glaze of olive oil in a heavy-bottomed skillet over medium-high heat. Season both sides of the fillets with salt and pepper, then lightly dredge the fillets in the flour, shaking off excess. When the oil is hot, add the fillets, skin sides down, to the pan. Cook for 4 minutes to form a golden crust, then turn and cook an additional 3 minutes on the other side. Set aside to keep warm.

Return the sauce to medium heat and cook until hot. Add the cubes of butter all at once and whisk vigorously to incorporate until all butter is blended and the sauce is smooth and creamy. Stir in the capers and remove from heat.

Prepare the spinach and mushrooms.

To serve, place a portion of the spinach in the center of each plate and place a seared drum fillet in the center. Spoon a portion of the shrimp essence over the fish and serve hot, garnished with a lemon wedge.

5

IF IT
FLIES

★

★

Poultry has long been a mainstay of the Texas diet. However, over the years, the poultry we buy at the supermarket has changed dramatically. Huge chicken-raising operations evolved to meet demand in growing cities, which had previously been supplied by smaller, regional farms (or even a friend or family's backyard flock). In the new industry, thousands of chickens are enclosed inside huge buildings with almost no room to move, much less peck around in an open yard or pasture. Their feed includes genetically modified ingredients, antibiotics, and growth hormones to shorten the length of time it takes them to reach market weight and to keep them well during their short life span. Then they're crammed into cages and shipped to giant processing plants where they are killed and processed by the thousands. Egg factories house caged chickens by the thousands in large, brightly lit buildings with no windows so that they lay eggs without stopping, as chickens normally do when the sun goes down. They're fed the same engineered feed but containing only pharmaceuticals designed to increase their egg production. These chickens are, quite literally, egg factories, and they don't live very long.

But there are more and more alternatives every day. Dozens of farms have reverted to raising pastured, free-range chickens, turkeys, and in some cases, even ducks. These are happy birds that are allowed to peck and scratch in the dirt and eat green things and bugs as nature intended. They get better feed and are allowed to grow at Mother Nature's pace. Their eggs are tastier, too. Sure, you have to go to the farmers' market, and the eggs are more expensive than supermarket eggs and chickens. They're grown by folks trying to make a living with 100 chickens, not 10,000. And the natural, non-GMO, no-soy feed can cost three times as much as "hen scratch" feed, not to mention the fees the farmers must pay to have their small processing plants certified by the USDA. I still think it's worth it for the taste alone, but certainly for the peace of mind.

Then there are quail—delicious and meaty little birds. There are two major quail farms in Texas, Bandera Quail in Bandera and Texas Quail Farm in Lockhart, that produce all-natural birds. Chefs from around the state purchase quail from these farms to serve in their restaurants. Most of our pastured-chicken farms also raise all-natural turkeys for the holiday season, although they must be ordered ahead from your favorite grower at the farmers' market.

Naturally raised birds have smaller breasts than the supermarket chickens that are bred to produce huge breasts. The natural, free-range birds also tend to be somewhat tougher because they get a lot of exercise and stay slim. Keep in mind, however, that meat muscles in livestock that receive a lot of exercise are tastier than those that do not. It's an easy task, however, to overcome the toughness of free-range birds. Brining is especially effective with such poultry. The art of brining poultry (and pork) was once a closely guarded "chef" procedure that has finally become popular with home cooks. It adds several hours to the process of cooking poultry, but it's easy to brine a bird the night or morning before it will be cooked. Brining is a simple technique: Cook the brine and chill it, then immerse the meat in the brine, and keep it refrigerated for anywhere from 6 to 24 hours before cooking it by your traditional method. The difference, however, is amazing. The bird is juicier, and the meat has more flavor.

BENDING BRANCH WINERY

BENDING BRANCH WINERY, located outside Comfort, was founded by Bob Young, a retired physician, and his wife, Brenda. Bob, who earned a certificate in enology at University of California at Davis, is the winemaker, and his daughter Alison and son-in-law John Rivenburgh also work in the business. Bob likes to point out that great wines begin with great fruit. "It's that simple," he said. "With sleek labels, marketing campaigns, logo placement, and endless choices in bottling, it's very easy to forget that wine is at its heart an agricultural product."

Bending Branch is one of the state's newer wineries; the first vines were planted in 2009. In deciding what to plant, Bob and John considered many factors: the grapes' native home; whether they can withstand, or develop resistance to, the limitations posed by the terroir; and whether the rootstock would likely thrive in their dry caliche soil.

Of the varietals they planted, they have found the most success with Mediterranean grapes, but two in particular have become their "signature" grapes. Tannat, a southwestern French varietal, gets its name from the word *tannin* and has a reputation as a tannic powerhouse. Bob was also intrigued by the "healthy characteristics" of the tannat grape, which is naturally high in procyanidins, the most active of the polyphenol compounds that have been linked to lower risks of heart disease and cancer. And the tannat requires less water—another plus for a drought-prone climate. Picpoul, loosely translated as "lip stinger," a white varietal, hails from the Languedoc region, also in southwestern France. Named for its notoriously high natural acidity, this grape maintains its bright acid through the hot days and equally warm nights of the Texas Hill Country. The unique flavor profile and complexity make this wine a great parallel for adventurous palates looking for food-friendly wines "off the beaten path." The Bending Branch Texas Tannat is a brilliant match for the Seared and Roasted Duck Breasts with Balsamic Glaze (pages 204–205).

Two wines in the Bending Branch portfolio pair excellently with Leslie Horne's Bandera Quail Paella (pages 231–232). The Estate Grown Picpoul Blanc is ideal because its naturally high acidity acts as a neutralizer for dishes that are high in salt and acidic components like tomato. The Bending Branch Newsom Vineyard Tempranillo is a classic match for paella. It is seldom a coincidence that regional cuisines pair well with wines from the region. Tempranillo, a Spanish native (as is paella), is a wine that offers great versatility when pairing with food. While highly tannic wines can be "combustible" with spicy foods, the Tempranillo is structured, with moderate tannins and acidity, and can marry successfully with the paella.

Seared and Roasted Duck Breasts with Balsamic Glaze and Sweet Potato Tarts

This is a really, really delicious entrée that also happens to be easy to prepare. The secret to success with the dish lies in not overcooking the duck breasts. They should be served slightly on the rare side of medium. The sweet potato tarts with their crunchy pecan topping are the perfect side dish—lots of earthy flavors on one plate. Sautéed greens, such as Boggy Creek Seared Spinach with Shiitake Mushrooms and Garlic (see recipe on page 369), are another welcome companion on the plate.

SERVES 4.

DUCK:

3 ounces aged balsamic vinegar

1½ teaspoons Dijon mustard

1 tablespoon raspberry liqueur

¼ teaspoon finely minced fresh thyme

2 tablespoons firmly packed
   light brown sugar

4 skin-on boneless duck breasts,
   about 6 to 8 ounces each

SWEET POTATO TARTS:
PASTRY:

1 cup all-purpose flour

¼ pound (1 stick) very cold unsalted
   butter, cut into ½-inch bits

1 teaspoon sugar

¼ teaspoon kosher salt

¼ teaspoon ground cinnamon

1½ teaspoons finely minced
   orange zest

3 to 4 tablespoons ice water

SWEET POTATO FILLING:

2 medium sweet potatoes, about
   18 ounces total

4 tablespoons unsalted butter,
   cut into ½-inch bits

3 tablespoons firmly packed light
   brown sugar

¼ teaspoon ground cinnamon

SUGARED PECANS:

4 tablespoons unsalted butter

3 tablespoons light brown sugar

½ teaspoon ground cinnamon

3 cups chopped pecans

Begin by making the tart pastries. Combine all ingredients except ice water in the work bowl of a food processor fitted with the steel blade. Process until butter is broken up and the mixture resembles raw oatmeal. With the processor running, add the ice water through the feed tube. Stop and check the dough before it forms a ball. The dough should hold together when you squeeze a portion of it in your palm. Add another tablespoon of water if needed and process very briefly.

Roll the dough out on a lightly floured work surface. Cut the dough into 4 portions and fit each portion into a 4-inch-diameter, removable-bottom tart tin. Do not stretch the pastry; instead, lift the edges and allow the pastry to slide into the tin. Pat pastry into bottom and sides of tins and cut off excess simply by rolling the rolling pin across the top of the tin. Prick the pastry all over with the tines of a fork and place on a small baking sheet. Preheat oven to 350°F. Freeze the pastries for 30 minutes, and then bake in preheated oven for about 10 to 15 minutes, or until light golden brown. Remove pastry from tins and cool on wire rack while preparing filling and nuts.

To make the sugared pecans, melt the butter in a heavy-bottomed 10-inch skillet over medium heat. Add the brown sugar and cinnamon, blending well. Cook until sugar has dissolved. Stir in pecans and turn to coat well. Lightly toast them, about 5 minutes. Remove pecans with a slotted spoon, spreading them out on a small baking sheet. Set aside to cool. Leave the oven on to cook the duck breasts.

Peel the sweet potatoes and cut them into small chunks. Place potatoes in a heavy-bottomed 3-quart saucepan, add cold water to cover by 2 inches, and bring to a boil. Continue to boil the potatoes until they are very soft, about 25 minutes. Drain the potatoes and transfer to a medium-sized bowl. Add the butter bits, brown sugar, and cinnamon. Mash the potatoes until smooth, blending in the butter and sugar well. Set aside to keep warm.

Prepare the duck breasts. Begin by preparing the glaze. Combine all ingredients except duck breasts in a medium-sized bowl. Whisk to blend well and turn out into a heavy-bottomed 10-inch sauté pan. Cook to reduce to a syrupy consistency over medium heat, whisking often, about 8 to 10 minutes. Remove from heat and set aside to cool. When glaze has cooled, pour it into a plastic squeeze bottle; set aside at room temperature.

Place the duck breasts, skin side down, in a heavy-bottomed 12-inch, ovenproof skillet over medium-high heat. Sear the skin for 2 minutes without turning. Turn the breasts skin side up and transfer the pan to the hot oven. Roast the breasts for 10 to 12 minutes, or 8 minutes if using a convection oven. The breasts should be cooked to the slightly rare side of medium. Do not overcook or they will be very tough and not very flavorful. Set them aside in the skillet for 5 minutes to rest; then place the breasts, skin side up, on a cutting board.

Slice the duck breasts on the bias, against the grain, into thin slices. Fan the slices out on serving plates and drizzle a portion of the balsamic glaze over each breast. Fill the tart shells with the sweet potato filling and scatter a portion of the pecans over the top of each tart. Set one tart on each serving plate. Serve hot.

Chicken Enchiladas with Salsa Verde Cocida

Enchiladas are invariably one of the most popular dishes on Tex-Mex menus. Places like Matt's El Rancho in Austin, founded by the late Matt Martinez in 1952; Molinas in Houston, founded in 1941; Joe T. Garcia's in Fort Worth, founded in 1935; Mi Tierra in San Antonio, founded by the Cortez family in 1941; and El Fenix in Dallas, founded in 1918, established the benchmark dishes (and flavors) that we think of as Tex-Mex food today. Enchiladas can be filled with a variety of cheeses or meats and are topped with many different sauces. I especially like these enchiladas filled with poached chicken and topped with a sauce made from tomatillos and chiles.

SERVES 6 TO 8.

ENCHILADAS:

1 free-range chicken, about 3 pounds
1 tablespoon whole black
    peppercorns
1 large onion, roughly chopped
4 large garlic cloves, smashed with
    side of chef's knife
⅓ cup fresh leaf lard
18 white corn tortillas
6 ounces shredded Monterey Jack
    cheese
Salsa Verde Cocida (recipe follows)
Sour cream and small-dice white
    onion as topping

SALSA VERDE COCIDA:

3 pounds tomatillos, husks removed
    and discarded
¼ cup fresh leaf lard
2 large garlic cloves, minced
1 medium white onion, roughly
    chopped
3 serrano chiles, blistered, peeled,
    seeded, and roughly chopped
2 teaspoons sugar
½ teaspoon kosher salt
2 tablespoons minced cilantro

Prepare the chicken. Place chicken in a large soup pot with the black peppercorns, roughly chopped onion, and garlic cloves. Add cold water to cover and bring to a boil over high heat. Lower heat to a simmer and cook until the meat is very tender, about 1 hour. Remove the pot from the heat and allow the chicken to cool in the cooking broth. When it is cool enough to handle comfortably, remove all meat from the bones. Reserve 1 cup of the cooking broth. Discard bones, fat, and skin.

Shred the meat, using your fingers to pull it apart. Place meat in a shallow baking dish and add the reserved cooking broth; set aside. Preheat oven to 350°F.

Make the salsa verde cocida. Wash the tomatillos thoroughly to remove the sticky residue from their skin. Place tomatillos in a heavy-bottomed 4-quart saucepan and add cold water to cover. Bring to a boil over high heat and cook for 5 minutes, or until the tomatillos appear about ready to crack open. Remove pan from heat and drain into a colander. Roughly chop the tomatillos and place in the work bowl of a food processor with garlic, onion, and serrano chiles. Process until smooth; turn out into a bowl and set aside. In a heavy-bottomed 12-inch skillet over medium-high heat, melt the ¼ cup of lard. When the lard is quite hot, add the tomatillo puree, sugar, and salt. Cook over medium-high heat, stirring constantly, for 5 minutes or until slightly thickened. Taste for salt, adjusting as you wish. Remove from heat and stir in the cilantro; set aside, covered, to stay hot.

To assemble the enchiladas: Heat the ⅓ cup lard in a heavy-bottomed 10-inch skillet over medium heat. When the fat is hot, begin frying the tortillas, one at a time, using chef's tongs, just until they become softened and pliable, about 15 seconds. Dip the tortilla in the salsa to lightly glaze. Transfer to a plate and repeat with remaining tortillas.

Place a portion of the shredded chicken down the center of each tortilla and top with a heaping tablespoon of the Monterey Jack cheese. Fold the tortilla over the chicken from both sides and place seam side down in a baking dish. Repeat with remaining tortillas, placing them side by side in the baking dish. Bake in preheated oven about 25 minutes, or until cheese is melted and enchiladas are bubbly.

Place 2 or 3 enchiladas on each serving plate and spoon a portion of the salsa over them. Garnish with a dollop or squiggle (from a squeeze bottle) of sour cream and a scattering of white onions. Serve hot.

Armenta's Amazing Chicken Enchiladas Suizas

Armenta's Café on San Angelo's South Oakes Street is an institution in the city and is open seven days a week for breakfast, lunch, and dinner. Everyone eats here, from shirt-and-tie businesspeople to laborers, to tourists, so there's always a line at this otherwise nondescript little place. The small, colorful dining room, where every inch of wall space is covered with Mexican folk objects, is a cacophony of clattering plates and utensils, conversation, and scooting tables and chairs as the staff scramble to arrange seating for large parties of diners. A constant stream of trays filled with chips and salsa flows from the kitchen. The aromas are heavenly. In short, this is Tex-Mex nirvana. Chicken enchiladas suizas is one of the café's most popular dishes. It's a perfect dish to make for a crowd.

MAKES 12 ENCHILADAS.

2 skinless chicken breasts, 8 ounces each

3 cups water

2 cups chicken broth

2 large garlic cloves

2 bay leaves

5 fresh cilantro sprigs

Kosher salt

2 pounds Roma tomatoes

2 serrano chiles, stems removed

½ cup plus 2 tablespoons canola oil, divided

¾ cup chopped onion

12 corn tortillas

½ cup sour cream

¾ cup crumbled queso fresco cheese

Begin by cooking the chicken. Place the breasts in a heavy-bottomed 4-quart saucepan. Add 3 cups water, chicken broth, garlic, bay leaves, and cilantro sprigs. Season to taste with salt. Bring to a boil and cook for about 35 minutes, or until chicken is very tender and cooked through. Set pan aside and allow chicken to cool in the cooking broth. When the chicken is cool enough to handle, remove from pan. Reserve the garlic cloves; discard cooking water. Pull the chicken meat from the bones and shred it using your fingers; set aside to keep warm.

Preheat broiler and place oven rack 6 inches below heat source. Put the tomatoes and serrano chiles on a baking sheet and place under the broiler. Broil, turning often, until chiles and tomatoes are charred all over. Peel the chiles and transfer to a blender with the unpeeled tomatoes and any collected juices from the baking sheet. Add the reserved garlic from the chicken broth. Puree until very smooth; set aside.

Heat the 2 tablespoons of canola oil in a heavy-bottomed 12-inch skillet over medium heat. When the oil is hot, add the diced onions and cook until light golden brown, about

7 minutes. Add the blended tomato and chile mixture, stirring to blend well. Cook, stirring often, until the sauce is thick, about 15 minutes. Keep warm.

Heat the ½ cup of canola oil in a deep-sided skillet over medium heat. When the oil is hot, working with one tortilla at a time, hold the tortilla with chef's tongs and submerge it in the hot oil for about 15 seconds, or just until pliable. Place on a plate and repeat with remaining tortillas.

Working quickly, place a portion of the shredded chicken meat in the center of each tortilla. Roll the tortillas tightly around the chicken and place them, seam side down, on individual plates. Spoon a portion of the tomato and chile sauce over the enchiladas, top with a dollop of sour cream, and scatter some of the crumbled queso fresco over the top. Serve at once. Traditionally, Armenta's serves the enchiladas with refried beans and Mexican rice.

Chicken Thigh Chalupas with Pickled Red Onions

Chalupas are a delightful Tex-Mex dish, and they're also quite versatile. You can serve platters of them as party finger food by cutting the tortillas into small rounds with a biscuit cutter to make mini chalupas, or they can be a first course to a casual meal or the entrée of a light meal. I especially love this version with chicken thighs, which I consider to be the tastiest meat on a chicken. The thigh meat has the best of both worlds, with a richer, deeper taste than the breast meat and the juiciness of the leg meat. However, you can put any topping on a chalupa that you like, and the tortillas can be corn or flour. As I said, it's a very versatile dish!

MAKES 12 CHALUPAS.

3 tablespoons canola oil

1½ pounds bone-in, skinless pastured-chicken thighs

Kosher salt and freshly ground black pepper

1 medium white onion, halved stem to root, peeled, and sliced thin

1 teaspoon toasted, then ground, cumin seeds

2 canned chipotle chiles in adobo sauce, with 1 tablespoon of the sauce from the can, roughly chopped

4 large garlic cloves, minced

1 can (15 ounces) Ro-Tel diced tomatoes and their liquid

⅔ cup chicken stock, preferably homemade

Kosher salt and freshly ground black pepper

12 flour tortillas, each 6 inches in diameter, shallow pan-fried until crisp and light golden brown

Shredded iceberg lettuce

Pickled Red Onions (see recipe on page 21)

Crumbled Cotija cheese

1 cup roughly chopped cilantro leaves

Thinly sliced fresh jalapeño chiles, optional

Heat the canola oil in a heavy-bottomed cast-iron skillet over medium-high heat. Season the chicken thighs with salt and pepper. When the oil is hot, place the thighs, skinned side down, in the skillet and cook to brown. Turn the chicken and brown the other side, about 12 minutes total. Using tongs, remove the chicken and set aside.

Add the onion, cumin, and chipotles with their sauce to the skillet. Cook, stirring often, until the onions are browned, about 8 minutes. Add the garlic and stir to blend. Cook for about 2 minutes. Add the tomatoes and liquid and chicken stock; bring to a boil. Reduce heat and simmer, stirring often, until the sauce is thickened and somewhat reduced, about 25 minutes. Remove from heat and set aside to cool slightly.

Preheat oven to 350°F. Puree the sauce from the skillet in a high-speed blender until very smooth. Take care not to fill the blender container too full of the hot liquid and always start on low speed to prevent volcanic-like eruptions of hot liquid. When the sauce is pureed, season to taste with salt and freshly ground black pepper.

Wipe out the skillet and place the reserved chicken thighs in it. Pour the pureed sauce over the chicken and transfer the skillet to preheated oven. Roast for 45 minutes, or until the meat is tender and cooked through. The sauce should be quite thick and dark around the edges of the pan. Remove pan from heat. Remove the chicken thighs and pull the meat from the bones into shreds. Discard the bones and stir the chicken back into the sauce, blending well.

To serve the chalupas, place 2 of the fried tortillas on each serving plate and top with a scattering of the shredded iceberg lettuce. Top each chalupa with a portion of the chicken and sauce, some of the pickled red onions, crumbled Cotija cheese, chopped cilantro, and thin-sliced jalapeños, if desired. Serve at once.

Frito Pie with Guajillo Chiles

The mention of Frito pie brings back memories from my childhood in that era when going out to eat Tex-Mex food at Houston's El Fenix restaurant was an exciting family outing. Tex-Mex foods like enchiladas and tamales and guacamole, which at the time seemed quite exotic, paired with refried beans and Mexican rice on the #1 Combination Plate were the most treasured comfort foods in Texas. And they were purely Texas creations, along with chili.

Right at the top of the Tex-Mex comfort food list was Frito pie. The origin of the dish is hotly disputed, with Santa Fe, New Mexico, also claiming the honor, but any Texan knows that the dish was created by the mother of Texan Elmer Doolin, who, in 1932, began to produce and market the corn chips that his mother, Daisy Dean Doolin, had created. He called them *fritos*, and the rest, as they say, is history. Daisy wanted to help her son market the chips, so she created the Frito pie as a way to lure customers by showcasing a quick and tasty use for Elmer's corn chips.

On the days when the school cafeteria served Frito pie, nobody brought lunches from home. Mother would occasionally treat us to her version, which was much like the original. She would heat canned, store-bought chili and pour it over the corn chips right in their little bags, slitting the bags open on one side, and kind of "poofing" the bags into bowl shapes. Then she'd top it all with shredded Cheddar cheese and chopped onions.

Today I make a version in which the chili is made from scratch with chicken. Just remember that you're eating some Texas history here.

1 medium-sized bag Fritos, the
 original small, thin ones
Chile Sauce (see recipe below)
Meat Mix (see recipe below)

2 cups (8 ounces) shredded Texas
 Cheddar cheese
6 green onions, sliced thin, including
 green tops

CHILE SAUCE:

8 guajillo chiles, stems and seeds
 removed
1 large onion, roughly chopped
3 ripe heirloom tomatoes, roughly
 chopped
2 tablespoons tomato paste

1½ teaspoons ground cumin
1 teaspoon kosher salt
½ teaspoon freshly ground black
 pepper
3 cups chicken stock, preferably
 homemade

MEAT MIX:

3 tablespoons canola oil
1 onion, cut into ½-inch dice
1 can (15 ounces) cooked black
 beans, drained

1 can (15 ounces) cooked pinto
 beans, drained
1½ pounds cooked free-range chicken
 meat, torn into bite-size shreds

Prepare the chile sauce. Place the seeded chiles in a bowl and add boiling water to cover them. Set a plate on top of the chiles to keep them submerged. Set aside for about 30 minutes, or until the chiles are very soft and pliable. Drain the chiles, reserving ½ cup of the soaking liquid, and tear them into rough pieces. Add the torn chiles and all remaining sauce ingredients to the container of a high-speed blender. Add the reserved chile soaking broth. Puree until the mixture is very smooth. Turn out into a bowl and set aside.

Heat the oil in a heavy-bottomed, deep-sided 5-quart braising pan over medium-high heat. When the oil is hot, add the onion and cook, stirring occasionally, until wilted and transparent, about 5 minutes. Add the beans and chicken meat, stirring to blend well. Cook until chicken is hot, about 5 minutes. Pour in the chile sauce, incorporating well, and cook until the mixture is quite thick, about 20 minutes; stir often to prevent sticking. Preheat the broiler and place oven rack 6 inches under heat source.

Place desired portion of Fritos (usually about 1½ to 2 cups) in the bottom of 6 oven-proof soup bowls. Place the bowls on a large baking sheet. Pour a portion of the chile mix over each serving. Top each serving with some of the grated cheese and scatter some of the sliced green onions over the tops. Place the baking sheet under the preheated broiler and broil for about 1 minute, or just until the cheese is melted and nice and bubbly. Place the bowls on underliner plates and serve hot. Be sure to warn that the bowls are very hot!

Homemade Chicken Pot Pies

Few would dispute the comfort evoked by a hot chicken pot pie on the table on a cold winter evening. Made-from-scratch chicken pot pie does require an investment of time, but the component parts can be made ahead as time permits, and the pies assembled when you're ready to bake and serve them. The dish is especially good if you use pastured chicken that has been poached and cooled in the cooking broth. Marjoram adds a spicy, fragrant undertone to this recipe. One of my favorite herbs, marjoram is often over-looked, which is a shame because it can add an amazing flavor note to many meat dishes, and it also has a special affinity for beans and peas. The herb, native to the dry, sunny, rocky hills of the Mediterranean, is a relative of oregano but has a sweeter, more delicate flavor. It is easy to grow, too, but if you can't find it, you may use dried marjoram, which is more pungent in flavor because drying concentrates the essential oils, so use just one-third the amount called for in the recipe.

MAKES 4 PIES.

PASTRY:

3 cups unbleached all-purpose flour

1 teaspoon baking powder

1¾ teaspoons kosher salt

½ cup leaf lard, chilled and chopped into small chunks

1 stick (¼ pound) unsalted butter, cut into ½-inch dice and chilled

½ to ⅔ cup ice water

1 egg beaten with 1 tablespoon water for egg wash

Kosher salt and freshly ground black pepper

FILLING:

1½ sticks unsalted butter

2 large celery stalks, cut into ¼-inch dice

3 medium-sized carrots, peeled and cut into ¼-inch dice

1 large yellow onion, cut into ¼-inch dice

1 tablespoon minced fresh marjoram

3 tablespoons minced flat-leaf parsley

½ teaspoon freshly ground black pepper

⅔ cup all-purpose flour

5 cups chicken stock, preferably homemade

2 heaping teaspoons MSG-free chicken base paste

¼ cup whipping cream

4 cups cooked whole chicken (about one 3½-pound hen), skinned and boned, cut into bite-size pieces

2 cups frozen green peas, thawed

Kosher salt

Begin by making the pastry. Combine the flour, salt, and baking powder in the work bowl of a food processor fitted with the steel blade. Pulse 3 to 4 times to blend the ingredients. Add the lard and butter. Using the pulse feature again, process to break the fats into small bits so that the mixture in the bowl resembles coarse meal. With the processor running, add ½ cup of the ice water through the feed tube. Stop the machine and check the consistency of the pastry. When you squeeze a portion of it in your hand, it should form a cohesive ball. If it is too crumbly, add additional water with the processor running until the consistency is right. Do not process long enough for the dough to form a ball in the bowl. It should still be loose and crumbly.

Turn the pastry out onto a work surface and gather it together with your hands, gently kneading and forming it into a firm, not crumbly, ball, but don't mess with it too much or the fats will melt and the pastry will be tough and impossible to roll out. Divide the dough into 6 equal portions, preferably using a scale, and pat each portion into a disk. Wrap each portion in plastic wrap and refrigerate while making the filling. Preheat oven to 375°F. Line a heavy-duty baking sheet with foil; set aside.

To make the filling, melt the butter in a heavy-bottomed Dutch oven over medium-high heat. When the foam subsides, add the celery, carrots, onion, marjoram, parsley, and black pepper. Cook, stirring often, until onion is wilted and transparent, about 7 minutes. Add the flour all at once, stirring rapidly to blend, until no traces of flour remain. Simmer, stirring, 3 to 4 minutes to cook out the starchy taste. Add the chicken broth and chicken base. Stir to blend the stock into the vegetable mixture, then bring to a rolling boil to thicken. Lower heat to a simmer and cook for about 5 minutes. Stir in the cream and cook just to heat through. Remove pan from the heat and stir in the chicken pieces and the peas, blending well. Season to taste with salt.

Divide the filling among six 12-ounce ovenproof bowls; set aside. Remove the pastry disks from the refrigerator one at a time. Roll the first disk into an 8-inch round on a lightly floured work surface. Using a pastry brush, brush the upper 1½ inches of the filled bowl with some of the egg wash. Place the pastry on top of the bowl and cut the edges so that about 1½ inches of pastry hangs over the side of the bowl. Crimp and pleat the pastry, sticking it to the egg wash. Scatter some of the flaky salt and freshly ground black pepper over the top of the pie and cut 2 parallel rows of diagonal steam vents in the top of the pastry. Place on the prepared baking sheet. Repeat with the remaining pies. Bake for about 45 to 50 minutes, or until the pastry is crisp and golden brown and the filling is bubbly. Serve hot.

FALL CREEK VINEYARDS

In 1973, Austin attorney/businessman/rancher Ed Auler and his wife, Susan, went to France to look at cattle but wound up spending more time at wineries than ranches. Ed noted how similar the soil, terrain, and climate in the French wine country were to those at their ranch in Tow, at the tip of Lake Buchanan, some 80 miles northwest of Austin. The observation stuck in Ed's mind long after the couple came home.

When the Aulers decided to try growing grapes, they called in the late Andre Tchelistcheff, one of the great California winemakers, to look at their soil. Tchelistcheff firmly believed they could grow *Vitis vinifera* (old-world European) grapes on the ranch.

The couple established Fall Creek Vineyards in 1975, one of the first wineries in the state and the first in the Hill Country. A winery facility and tasting room opened in 1983. Soon the long, tree-lined entrance to Fall Creek became a destination for wine lovers from Austin and, eventually, the state and beyond. The current tasting room was built in 1990.

Over the years, Ed Auler has helped pass legislation that paved the way for the Texas wine industry's remarkable expansion. Susan Auler founded the now internationally known Texas Hill Country Wine and Food Festival in 1986. The couple also helped establish the Texas Wine and Grape Growers Association (TWGGA), which unites winemakers and grape growers to further education within the industry and act as a link to the Texas legislature. In short, the Aulers are pioneers of the Texas wine industry in every sense of the word.

Chad Auler, Ed and Susan's son, has assumed the winery's sales and marketing operations, taking Fall Creek Vineyards into its second generation as a family business and sixth generation as stewards of this land.

Fall Creek has a large portfolio of wines. My particular favorite pairing is Fall Creek Caché, a blend of chardonnay, muscat canelli, and sauvignon blanc, with the Chicken Breast Rolls Stuffed with Goat Cheese and Spinach (pages 221–222). Caché is also a very good match with the Crispy Seafood Cakes with Chile, Cilantro, and Lime Cream (pages 181–182). The creamy body of the wine complements the crispy texture of the cakes, and the honeyed muscat notes balance the piquant sauce. To achieve the full effect of the muscat canelli component of the wine, serve it chilled to just below room temperature.

Fall Creek's Sauvignon Blanc, with its edgy, citrus flavor, connects perfectly with the acidity of the tomato cream sauce and is punctuated by the capers in the Pan-Seared Black Drum with Shrimp Essence and Capers (pages 195–197). Bryan Caswell's Grouper with Braised Collards and Pecan-Shallot Cracklin' (pages 187–188) is just right for Fall Creek Vineyard's crisp, dry, un-oaked Chardonnay.

Fall Creek's unctuous Chenin Blanc has the right amount of residual sugar, redolent of peach and pear aromas, to beautifully complement the rich flavors of the Chicken Thigh Chalupas with Pickled Red Onions (pages 210–211).

A number of Fall Creek wines are great for red meats. Its well-defined Tempranillo, with elegant berry scents and earthy, spicy flavors, is a textural and flavor balance to the Braised Shoulder of Lamb with Aromatics and Rosemary Demi-Glace (pages 275–277). The lean flavors of the Grilled Broken Arrow Ranch Rack of Venison with Shallot–Black Cherry Compote (pages 294–296) beg for a strong partner, and Fall Creek's top-tier Meritage, Meritus, "dances" toe to toe with the dish. Meritus is also an excellent match for the Grilled Bison Tenderloin with Balsamic-Horseradish Aioli (pages 286–288).

NEWSOM VINEYARDS

Neal and Janice Newsom began farming in northern Yoakum County, just 15 miles east of the New Mexico state line, in 1979. The farm sits on a plateau about 3,700 feet above sea level and is part of the Texas High Plains. The area is known for long, hot days and cool nights, flat fields with endless skies, and world-class sunsets. Neal's family has been farming for at least four generations, although he doesn't remember what his great-great-grandfather grew in East Texas before the Civil War. They've been on the Texas High Plains for more than 100 years.

The Newsoms started by raising watermelons, pumpkins, soybeans, peanuts, and cotton, which was their main crop. In the mid-1980s, when they decided to diversify their plantings, Neal remembered that one of his professors at Texas Tech, Dr. Roy Mitchell, in 1973 compared the High Plains with wine-growing regions in other parts of the world. Furthermore, grapes require less water than cotton and are a perennial crop. (Cotton can be fragile when it emerges from the ground, and

Neal recalls planting it as many as three times in one spring.) Grapes provide the same economic return with less land and like the desert environment in the High Plains; they have very deep root systems.

Further research revealed that the High Plains soil consists of red, sandy loam overlying a caliche limestone, which is well drained and well suited for growing wine grapes. The caliche provides a complex chalky minerality that adds a distinctive flavor to the fruit. The climate is also good— semi-arid, little rain, and plenty of sunshine. The abundant sunshine makes the red grapes dark and inky. And those hot days and cool nights with low humidity help the grapes mature slowly while developing needed acid and structure. But according to Neal, "The magic bullet is our altitude. You can't buy altitude just anywhere; you have to go where it is, the High Plains of Texas. No trees, no birds, no bugs, no bears or deer, or other mammalian varmints. Who would've thought that having no trees would be an advantage? The grapes here

are happy grapes. Besides, folks just love to talk about grapes and wine. Nobody ever cared what variety of cotton I planted."

The couple planted their first three acres with cabernet sauvignon grapes in 1986. Today the Newsoms grow 10 varieties of wine grapes on well over 100 acres, which they sell to about 12 wineries. They grow mainly *Vinis vinifera* grapes, the classic European wine grapes like cabernet, merlot, syrah, tempranillo, and sangiovese that produce the most popular wines worldwide and yield about three tons of grapes per acre.

Wines made from Newsom grapes have won more than 100 awards, including the Qualia Award in 2012 from the Texas Wine and Grape Growers Association, and have been featured on PBS, NPR, and in numerous publications. Newsom grapes/wines make up many wineries' most prized bottles. "Every region of Texas has or will find some style of wine they can do very well," says Neal. "We can and have grown wines that score with the best in the world, and we have nothing to fear from the new or old world. We have done the French, California, Chilean, and Argentinean thing. Now it's Texas's turn!"

Growing wine grapes is a challenge even for an experienced farmer like Neal Newsom, even in the relatively favorable terroir of the High Plains, so I asked him to lead me through the growing season in more detail. In late fall, elbon rye is planted as a cover crop between the rows to reduce erosion and cool the soil in the spring to delay bud break for as long as possible. The rye is plowed under after the last freeze date so that it does not compete with the vines for moisture during the growing season. The High Plains has minimal disease and insect pressure because of the semi-arid climate, but hard freezes after bud break, hail, and high winds can be devastating.

Pruning begins in the early spring. Then comes bud break, and the little clusters emerge as the most fragrant tiny flowers imaginable. If you ever have the opportunity, walk through a vineyard during "bloom time." The bouquet is intoxicating!

Then comes the tying, or training the vines, and removing new growth from the trunks. The roots need to grow deep in order to reach moisture. Grapes require 18 to 20 inches of water annually. Since the rainfall total in the High Plains is low, only 16 inches in a good year, and 4 or less in a not-so-good year, underground drip-irrigation systems are put in place when the vines are planted. The irrigation water comes from the Ogallala Aquifer.

In April, new plantings are made. The Newsoms use mostly own-rooted vines because they do best on the High Plains. By July, the grapes are beginning to turn color, an occurrence called *verasion*. When the sunlight shines just right on the berries of the red varieties, they look like rubies. As harvest nears, it's "tasting time." The different varieties have different tastes and colors as fresh fruit. Each one ripens at a different time, so harvest begins in August and continues until October, when the last varieties ripen. Samples are pulled, and the juice is extracted and measured on a refractometer to determine the *brix* (sugar) level of the fruit. At around 25 brix, the grapes are ready to harvest, and the growers pray for no rain, which would dilute the flavor of the grapes.

At the end of the summer, as the hot sun finally sets, the Newsoms head to the vineyard to harvest at night because the grapes are cooler and more flavorful. They own their mechanical harvesters, which are driven over the vines to shake the grapes loose so they fall onto a conveyer belt and travel to the large bins the tractors are pulling behind them one row over.

As dawn is breaking, Janice has the last of the bins weighed, then loaded onto refrigerated trucks, which haul the grapes to the waiting wineries. The wineries then crush the fruit and turn it into award-winning wines for us all to enjoy with a fine dinner or just to sip on the patio under a Texas sky full of stars.

Chicken Breast Rolls Stuffed with Goat Cheese and Spinach Served on Pasta with Basil Pesto

These little gems are one of my favorite go-to recipes when I need a stunning dish that doesn't require hours to prepare. I grow huge amounts of basil in the spring and summer, so I try to keep it trimmed by making mountains of pesto, which I freeze in half-cup batches for future use—perfect for making a quick pizza or flatbread or a simple pasta dish.

SERVES 4.

4 baked Chicken Breast Rolls
  (see recipe below)
1 pound penne rigate pasta, cooked
  al dente and drained
Basil Pesto (recipe follows)
Grated Asiago cheese, such as Mill-
  King Market and Creamery's Asiago

CHICKEN ROLLS:

4 boneless, skinless free-range chicken
  breasts, 6 to 8 ounces each
8 ounces mild-flavored Texas artisan
  goat cheese
1½ cups chopped, blanched fresh
  spinach
2 green onions, sliced thin, including
  green tops
4 large garlic cloves, minced
⅓ cup toasted pine nuts
1 teaspoon minced fresh rosemary
½ teaspoon kosher salt
½ teaspoon freshly ground black
  pepper
2 tablespoons plus ¼ cup Texas extra-
  virgin olive oil

BASIL PESTO:
MAKES ABOUT 1¼ CUPS.
2 large garlic cloves, peeled
3 tablespoons raw pine nuts
¼ teaspoon kosher salt
3 cups gently packed fresh
  basil leaves
¼ cup flat-leaf parsley leaves
½ cup plus 2 tablespoons Texas
  extra-virgin olive oil
½ cup grated Parmesan cheese

Begin by making the pesto. Place the steel blade in the work bowl of a food processor. With processor running, drop the garlic cloves through the feed tube to mince. Scrape down sides of the bowl and add the pine nuts and salt. Process until finely ground.

Add basil and parsley leaves. Pulse on/off just to break up the leaves. With the processor running, pour the olive oil through the feed tube in a steady stream. When all has been added, stop the machine and scrape down sides of bowl. Process an additional 15 seconds. Add the Parmesan cheese and pulse just until well blended. Turn out into a bowl and set aside.

Pat the chicken breasts very dry, using absorbent paper towels. Trim off any fat or stray pieces of meat. Place the breasts, skinned side down, on a cutting board. Using a veal pounder or rolling pin, pound the breasts thin, taking care not to tear holes in the meat. Set aside.

Combine the remaining chicken ingredients, except the ¼ cup olive oil, in a small bowl and whisk to blend well. Divide the mixture among the chicken breasts, placing an equal amount in the center of each breast. Fold the top and bottom edges of the breasts 1 inch toward the center. Now fold the right edges of the breasts toward the center, covering the filling. Next, fold the left edges toward the center to completely cover the filling and overlap the right edges as far as possible, forming a tight cylindrical bundle. Secure the roll with a toothpick intertwined through the meat. Preheat oven to 375°F.

Heat the ¼ cup olive oil in a heavy-bottomed cast-iron skillet over medium-high heat. When the oil is hot, place the chicken rolls, seam side up, in the hot oil. Cook quickly just to brown and sear the meat. Turn and repeat on the other side. Transfer the rolls to a baking dish and bake in preheated oven for about 35 minutes, or until cooked through. Set aside to keep warm.

To serve, toss the hot pasta with pesto, blending well. Place a portion of the pasta in each pasta bowl. Remove the toothpicks from the chicken rolls. Using a sharp, thin-bladed knife, slice the rolls into ½-inch rounds and arrange them, slightly overlapping, down the center of the pasta. Scatter some of the Asiago cheese over the dish and serve hot.

Chicken Thighs with Pumpkin Seed and Tomatillo Sauce

The cuisine of interior Mexico, which uses a wider scope of ingredients than our Tex-Mex dishes, becomes more and more established in Texas every year. Austin's Fonda San Miguel has long been a bastion of delicious, authentic interior Mexican foods, but dozens of new restaurants and chefs are introducing us to exciting new ingredients and flavor combinations.

Variations of this sauce are popular in many regions of Mexico, from the Yucatán to Puebla, where the herb hoja santa is often added. I love this sauce, which is called *pipian verde* in Spanish, with chicken, but it's equally good with shrimp.

SERVES 4.

POACHING CHICKEN THIGHS:

6 bone-in, skin-on pastured-chicken thighs

Kosher salt and freshly ground black pepper

1 onion, quartered

5 cups chicken stock, preferably homemade

PUMPKIN SEED AND TOMATILLO SAUCE:

5 ounces (about 1 cup) raw, hulled pumpkin seeds

1 teaspoon sesame seeds

1 white onion, peeled and sliced

1 large garlic clove, peeled

3 serrano chiles, chopped, including seeds

6 ounces tomatillos (about 4 average size), husked and rinsed well, roughly chopped

½ teaspoon dried Mexican oregano

¾ cup shelled pistachios, chopped

½ cup chopped cilantro

1 fresh hoja santa leaf, thick stem discarded, roughly torn

Kosher salt and freshly ground black pepper

Begin by poaching the chicken thighs. Season the thighs with salt and pepper and place them in a large, heavy-bottomed, deep skillet. Add the onion and chicken stock. Cover the skillet and bring to a simmer over medium heat. Poach the chicken pieces, turning once, until the juices run clear, about 20 minutes. Remove the thighs and set aside. Strain the poaching liquid, discarding onion, and reserve.

Make the sauce. Heat a cast-iron skillet over medium heat and toast the pumpkin seeds, stirring and tossing often, until they puff and brown lightly. Take care not to burn them. Remove from skillet and set aside to cool. Place the sesame seeds in the same skillet and toast them just until they are golden, about 2 to 3 minutes. Stir often and take care not to burn the seeds. Turn out into a bowl and set aside to cool. When the seeds have cooled, combine the pumpkin and sesame seeds in a spice/coffee grinder and grind to a smooth paste; set aside.

Return the skillet with the poaching liquid to medium heat and add the onion, garlic, chiles, tomatillos, oregano, and half the pistachio nuts. Cook until the vegetables are wilted and tender, about 15 minutes.

Using a slotted spoon, transfer the vegetables from the skillet to the container of a high-speed blender with 2 cups of the chicken stock. Fill the container no more than half full. Place the lid firmly on the blender and cover it with a towel, holding your hand on the top. Begin on low speed to avoid a messy and possibly painful overflow. Gradually increase the speed to high and puree until smooth. Repeat with remaining vegetables, if needed. Return pureed vegetables to the skillet over low heat. Whisk the pumpkin seed/sesame paste into the sauce. Cook, adding additional chicken stock if needed to make a velvety sauce. Partially cover the pan and simmer for 20 minutes. The sauce should coat the back of a wooden spoon, but not be gloppy thick. Thin with stock, if needed.

Pour 1 cup of the sauce in the blender container and add the cilantro and hoja santa leaf. Puree until smooth and stir into the sauce in the skillet. Season to taste with salt and black pepper. Return the chicken thighs to the skillet and bring the sauce to a boil. Cook just to heat the chicken through, about 15 minutes.

To serve, place 1 or more thighs on each serving plate and spoon the sauce over the top. Garnish each plate with a scattering of the remaining pistachios.

PEELER FARMS

IN 2007, MARIANNA PEELER decided to raise a few free-range hens as a hobby on her farm outside Floresville. She soon found, however, that her family couldn't eat all the eggs that her flock produced, so she began giving them away to grateful friends. Eventually she realized that with the combined cost of the supplemental feed she uses, which is organic, non-GMO, and soy-free, plus the amount of time required to care for the flock, she couldn't afford to keep giving away the eggs. So she started selling them. The demand for her eggs grew, and then people began to ask if she raised chickens for meat.

Similarly, Marianna and her husband, Jason, decided to raise a few turkeys for Thanksgiving, which they gave away as gifts. The lucky recipients raved about the taste of the birds. That was enough to convince Marianna she was on to something. She set up a USDA-inspected production facility on the farm and began to harvest and process chickens. Each fall she also takes orders at the farmers' markets in Austin, San Antonio, and Fredericksburg for Thanksgiving turkeys.

The Peelers seek out breeds that both thrive in the environment of the farm and produce quality eggs and meat. There's quite a mélange of colors and feather patterns in their flock of Aracaunas, Rhode Island Reds, Blue Cochins, Americanas, Naked Neck Turkens, Buff Orpingtons, White Leghorns, Dominiques, Barred Rocks, Speckled Sussex, and others. Several Freedom Rangers, or Poulet Rouge, a heritage breed that does extremely well on pasture, were recently added. Marianna says they are great grass foragers and more instinctive about predators than other breeds.

Peeler also raises Jumbo Cornish Rock X as meat birds—"they produce very tender meat and are consistent in their growth"—and ducks, a mix of Khaki Campbell and Pekin hens. While most people think of the Pekin as a meat duck, it also produces good eggs.

Despite these expansions, Marianna wants to keep her flocks as a relatively small operation, producing quality, free-range organic eggs and birds, and her farm now serves some of Texas's top chefs.

But along with the good, there's an ugly side to farming. Farmers are at the mercy of Mother Nature, and she's not always kind. Chickens have many natural predators—among them are hawks, owls, skunks, and raccoons. Although Marianna has pretty much solved the ground predator problem with electric fencing, there's nothing she can do about the hawks and owls. While the chickens have a mobile coop under which they can retreat, sometimes a hawk or owl will swoop down too quickly for the chickens to make it to the coop and safety.

Then there's the weather. Chickens, like people, sometimes can't survive the torrid summer heat of south-central Texas, despite the shade and sprinklers that Marianna provides in the pasture. Sometimes they can't survive the cold of a Texas blue norther. Summer thunderstorms will rip across the land with little warning—violent winds, torrential rains, and lightning that looks as though it is slitting the very heavens asunder. In the summer of 2010, Marianna lost 103 chickens in one night to just that sort of storm. She recalls being awakened in the middle of the night by the fury of the storm. Her first impulse was to race to the farm to protect the chickens. But her husband convinced her to stay indoors, away from unremitting lightning strikes and the chicken coops made of metal. She realized there was nothing she could do but listen to the storm rage. The Peelers are farmers, and painful though it is, Mother Nature calls the shots.

Brined and Roasted Free-Range Chicken with Herbs and Olives

A perfectly roasted chicken is a work of culinary art. Success starts with a young, free-range bird, weighing absolutely no more than 2½ pounds. Ask your pastured-chicken provider to pick out a small one and save it for you. The next step is to brine the bird. The problem with perfectly roasting a chicken is that you are dealing with two types of meat—the lean breast meat, which tends to dry out more quickly, and the more fatty and dense thighs and legs. Brining the bird helps to add moisture (and flavor) to the breast meat. You'll be amazed at the moistness and heightened flavor of a brined chicken. Roast the chicken for 20 minutes per pound and turn every 15 minutes to provide an evenly crisp, golden crust on the bird.

SERVES 4.

BRINE:

1½ gallons water, divided

1 cup plus 2 tablespoons kosher salt

1 cup plus 2 tablespoons brown sugar

1 large onion, quartered

1 tablespoon whole black peppercorns

4 large fresh thyme sprigs

CHICKEN:

2½-pound free-range chicken

½ cup Texas extra-virgin olive oil

1 tablespoon minced fresh basil

2 teaspoons minced fresh rosemary

1 teaspoon kosher salt

½ teaspoon freshly ground black pepper

1 medium yellow onion, peeled and halved from stem to root, then sliced thin

2 large garlic cloves, peeled and sliced thin

1 quart chicken stock, preferably homemade

3 large fresh thyme sprigs

Additional kosher salt

1 cup pitted kalamata olives, halved

1 stick (¼ pound) unsalted butter, cut into ½-inch cubes

Begin by brining the chicken. Place 3 quarts of the water in the refrigerator to chill. You will need a 10- to 12-quart storage container with a tight-fitting lid and a space in your refrigerator large enough to store it, or a cooler and lots of ice. In a heavy-bottomed 6-quart soup pot, combine the remaining 3 quarts of water and remaining brine ingredients. Bring the mixture to a boil over medium-high heat, then reduce heat to a simmer. Cook the brine mixture for about 15 minutes, or until aromatic and the salt and sugar have dissolved. Set aside to cool completely. When the cooked mixture has cooled, pour it into the storage container. Place the chicken in the brine, than add the 3 quarts of chilled water. Fill the container with ice cubes, cover, and refrigerate for 24 hours. If you don't have room in your refrigerator for the large container, put a layer of ice cubes in the bottom of a cooler, then set the container in the cooler. Add ice to come completely up to the top of the covered container. Cover the cooler and set aside in a cool place for 24 hours, maintaining the level of ice.

After 24 hours, remove the chicken from the brine; discard brine. Preheat oven to 400°F. Pat the chicken very dry all over, using absorbent paper towels, including inside the body cavity. In a small bowl, combine the olive oil, basil, rosemary, salt, and pepper, whisking to blend well; set aside. Place the chicken on a cutting board. Using your fingers, very carefully separate the skin from the meat of the breast, taking care not to rip holes in the skin. (It helps to take off any rings you may be wearing.) Continue down the sides of the bird and all the way back to the thigh joints. Using a pastry brush, baste the meat under the skin with some of the olive oil mixture, stirring it often to keep the seasonings blended. Pat the skin down and brush the skin of the chicken all over with the oil blend. Using kitchen twine, tie the legs together. Reserve leftover oil.

Heat 1 tablespoon of the reserved oil in a heavy-bottomed 8- to 10-quart roasting pan over medium-high heat. When the oil is hot, add the onion; cook for about 5 minutes, or until onion is wilted and transparent and just beginning to brown. Add the garlic and cook an additional minute. Pour in the chicken stock and toss in the thyme sprigs. Place a roasting rack in the pan and set the chicken, breast side down, on the rack. Roast the chicken in preheated oven 20 minutes per pound, turning ¼ turn every 15 minutes and basting each time with the remaining oil after you have whisked it to blend the seasonings. (Chicken should be breast side up when done.) To check for doneness, pierce the chicken in the thickest part of the thigh. The juices should run clear. Or you can insert an instant-read meat thermometer in the thickest part of the thigh; it should register 160°F when the chicken is done. Remove chicken to a cutting board and cover with foil to keep warm while it rests for 10 minutes.

Remove the roasting rack from the pan and discard thyme sprigs. Skim the fat from the broth, then transfer the roasting pan to the stovetop over medium-high heat. Stir in the olives and cook to reduce the liquid by half, stirring often to release any browned bits of meat and vegetable glaze from the bottom of the pan. Turn heat to low and quickly add the butter cubes all at once, whisking furiously until the butter is blended. Quickly remove from heat and season to taste with salt and freshly ground black pepper. Set aside to keep warm. The sauce cannot be held over heat or reheated, or it will separate.

Carve the chicken into desired serving pieces, using a sharp knife so you don't tear up the crispy skin, and pile onto a platter. Pass the sauce separately.

BECKER VINEYARDS

Becker Vineyards, on the Highway 290 wine corridor between Stonewall and Fredericksburg, was founded by Dr. Richard Becker, a San Antonio endocrinologist, and his wife, Bunny. "We were looking for a log cabin to restore," began Bunny. "But the cabin came with a much larger piece of property than we were looking for."

The couple purchased their property in 1990 and decided they would grow grapes. They began planting in 1992. The first harvest was in 1995. New vineyard properties were acquired in subsequent years, and the Beckers now grow more than a dozen varietals.

Becker was the first Texas winery to introduce albariño, a white varietal from Galicia in northern Spain. The grapes seem to be thriving in Texas, which is a good thing for those of us who love seafood; they are natural partners.

The winery facilities built by the Beckers—in a nod to their original log cabin perhaps—are reproductions of nineteenth-century structures from the area. Also planted on the property behind the winery is a three-acre lavender field. "We had been to Provence, and the countryside was just purple with lavender. We knew that the terrain and climate were similar to the Hill Country," explained Richard. Each spring, the winery hosts a weekend-long Lavender Festival, featuring a luncheon in which the courses are created using culinary lavender. Over the years Becker wines have garnered countless medals and earned a prominent place in Texas as one of the largest wineries, and its wines are among the most widely distributed.

Serve the Becker Vineyards Provençal, a great French-style rosé made from mourvèdre, grenache, and syrah, with the Brined and Roasted Free-Range Chicken with Herbs and Olives (pages 227–228). I think of this as a summer dish, and a nice rosé is always a good match for summer dishes. Becker also produces a number of wines that pair well with dessert. One of my favorites is the Clementine, a late-harvest viognier, with the Mexican Fresh Apple Cake with Leche Quemada (pages 391–392).

BANDERA QUAIL

THE DIAMOND H RANCH, home of Bandera Quail, was originally founded by Tom and Polly Harrington in 1991 when they moved to Bandera to retire. Tom discovered, however, that he wasn't too good at being retired and began to look around for a hobby. An avid hunter, he noticed that the wild quail population seemed to be dwindling. He began to raise a few bobwhite quail to sell to ranchers. Eventually he began raising quail for meat and found a demand from restaurants. But since it is illegal to raise and sell native animal species, such as bobwhite quail, for meat, Tom had to find another breed that would satisfy the tastes of the dining public.

A poultry science professor at Texas A&M University introduced Tom to the Coturnix quail, which is native to eastern Asia, where it has been domesticated for more than 1,000 years, was selectively bred to produce heavier quail better suited for meat production, and offers good egg production. Tom worked further with the A&M team to produce a Coturnix with white meat, like the bobwhites Texans love. The White Texas A&M Coturnix Quail are raised at Bandera Quail. About 85 percent of the quail at Bandera are raised for meat. These quail are harvested at seven weeks of age, with a new batch harvested each week of the year.

Well into his 80s, Tom decided to retire in 2008, for good this time, and closed the Diamond H Ranch. It was a great loss to chefs all over the state. In 2010, Chris Hughes, owner of Broken Arrow Ranch, purveyors of wild game meats, bought the Diamond H Ranch from Tom and revived the quail farm, marketing the birds under the brand Bandera Quail, ensuring they are once again on the menu at restaurants across the state.

Leslie Horne's Bandera Quail Paella

My good friend Leslie Horne is one of Texas's premier producers of artisan charcuterie. She is the genius behind Aurelia's Spanish-Style Chorizo, an authentic air-cured Spanish-style chorizo, produced in Austin but lauded by chefs around the country.

Leslie fell in love with paella while studying chorizo making in Spain. Back in her Texas kitchen she began to experiment with traditional paella recipes, and she is now officially known as our own "Paella Queen." She has toted her giant paella pans to festivals and events around the state, making paella for up to 200 hungry fans at a time! One of my favorites is this paella, which she created using her incredible chorizo and plump, flavorful Texas quail from the Diamond H Ranch in Bandera.

SERVES 6.

6 semi-boneless Bandera quail

3 tablespoons Spice Rub
(recipe follows)

6 cups chicken broth

¼ teaspoon crumbled saffron threads

¼ cup Texas extra-virgin olive oil

1 large onion, cut into ¼-inch dice

1 red bell pepper, cut into ½-inch dice

2 teaspoons sweet smoked Spanish
paprika

3 links Aurelia's Spanish-Style Chorizo,
sliced into rounds ½-inch thick

12 ounces medium-sized white
mushrooms, sliced in half

1 medium tomato, preferably
homegrown or heirloom, peeled
and grated

6 medium garlic cloves, minced

4 tablespoons minced flat-leaf parsley

3 cups short-grain rice

2 cups fresh or frozen green peas

Blistered and peeled red bell pepper
strips as garnish

SPICE RUB:
MAKES ABOUT ¾ CUP.

¼ cup whole cumin seeds

2 tablespoons whole coriander seeds

1½ teaspoons whole Tellicherry black
peppercorns

1 tablespoon paprika

2 tablespoons Spanish smoked
paprika

1 teaspoon cayenne

2 tablespoons kosher salt

¼ cup Texas extra-virgin olive oil

Pat the quail very dry, using absorbent paper towels; set aside. Make the spice rub. Toast the cumin and coriander seeds and whole peppercorns in a dry skillet over medium-high heat until there is a nice aroma emanating from the pan. Shake the pan while cooking, and be sure you don't burn the spices. Remove pan from heat and grind the spices to a fine powder, using a mortar and pestle or spice/coffee grinder. Combine with the remaining spices and olive oil, stirring to make a smooth paste. Rub the mixture over all sides of the quail, coating them well. Place in a single layer on a platter or baking sheet. Refrigerate for 1 hour.

Combine the chicken broth and saffron in a heavy-bottomed 4-quart pot over medium heat. Bring the mixture almost to a boil, but don't let it begin to boil, or too much of the broth will evaporate. Remove from heat and set aside to stay hot.

Place a 15-inch paella pan over two burners over medium-high heat, and add the olive oil. When the oil is hot, brown the quail quickly on all sides. Remove from pan and set aside.

Add the onion and bell pepper to the pan, cooking until onion is wilted and transparent. Stir in the smoked paprika, chorizo, and mushrooms; cook for 2 minutes. Add grated tomato, garlic, and parsley. Continue to cook, stirring frequently, until mushrooms are soft and garlic becomes aromatic. Add the rice; stir just to coat well with the pan drippings.

Carefully add the hot saffron chicken broth. Taste and add salt, if needed. Bring the mixture to a boil; cook for 10 minutes, without stirring, rotating the pan over the two burners for even cooking. Add the quail, arranging them evenly in a ring around the pan. Scatter the green peas evenly over the entire pan, but again, don't stir. Garnish the top of the paella with strips of roasted red peppers. Cook for an additional 10 minutes, without stirring. The liquid should be absorbed and the rice should be browning lightly on the bottom of the pan. Taste. The rice should have a slight firmness. Turn the heat off and cover the pan loosely with a clean towel or foil. Let rest for 10 minutes so that the rice will finish cooking.

Serve hot, making sure that each serving includes a quail.

MESSINA HOF WINERY AND RESORT

PAUL AND MERRILL BONARRIGO were part of the group of agricultural pioneers who believed, even back in the 1970s, that quality wine grapes could grow in Texas. Paul grew up in the Bronx, New York, but his extended family in Messina, Sicily, has been making wine since the 1800s. Merrill was born and raised in Bryan, where she graduated with one of the first classes of women at Texas A&M University in 1975 (her ancestors emigrated from Hof, Germany).

In 1983, Messina Hof's first year of commercial production, they made 1,300 gallons of Papa Paulo Port, which is still one of their most popular wines. All of the grapes grown on the winery's 100-acre estate are Lenoir, or "black Spanish," a native American grape, and are used to produce the port, among other estate wines. By 2012, the Bonarrigos had vineyards in several regions of the state, including the High Plains, where they grow different varietals. According to Paul, the winery controls around 25 percent of the grapes grown in Texas. In 2012, Messina Hof produced 265,000 gallons of wine from more than 18 varietals. Messina Hof has received the highest number of awards in national and international competition of any winery in Texas, and its wines are among the most widely distributed in the state. In 2012, Messina Hof opened a state-of-the-art tasting room on the 290 wine corridor near Fredericksburg.

For my Thanksgiving Texas Style (pages 235–236), I went to Messina Hof. The menu contains many flavors. Paul and Merrill Bonarrigo created the meal from my recipes, and their wine selections included the Messina Hof Cedar Crest Cabernet Franc, Chardonnay from Merrill's Vineyard, and Beau, a light red blend of shiraz and moscato. For the red wine lovers, the bacon on the brined turkey gave it enough weight to handle the Cabernet Franc; the Chardonnay went impressively well with the roasted turkey with oyster dressing, and the Beau was great with Sue Heatly's cranberry chutney on the menu.

To pair with the amazingly complex flavor of the Smoked Wild Boar Leg with Blackberry Mustard Sauce on pages 302–304, Paul and Merrill chose two wines. The Cedar Crest Cabernet Franc has enough fruit and smoke to balance nicely with the boar leg, and the Beau, a sweeter red, was a great match to the heat of the dish.

Thanksgiving Texas Style

I was not raised by a mother who loved to cook; therefore, she never taught me to cook. So I will always remember the first time I prepared Thanksgiving for my new in-laws. I guess that I had learned just enough about cooking to make me brave enough to invite them to our apartment in Austin for our first Thanksgiving dinner.

I got out my trusty *McCall's Cook Book*, a wedding gift from my mother, and plotted my dinner. I don't remember much about the dinner except the turkey. I do know that I didn't know what giblets were, so I skipped the gravy. The turkey looked so regal reposing on the platter. I had cooked it just like the recipe instructed. It was nicely browned and wiggled in the places that the recipe said it should wiggle when done. I carried it to the table proudly and asked my father-in-law to do the honors of carving—mainly because I didn't have a clue how to do so. As he began to carve the turkey, this disgusting pile of something fell out of the cavity of the bird onto my mother's gifted damask tablecloth. I was horrified. Gracious lady that she was, my mother-in-law scooped it onto her bread plate and dispatched it to the kitchen. When she returned, she said quietly: "It was just the giblets, dear. You forgot to take them out." I missed her terribly when I divorced her son!

Thanksgiving dinner is one of my now-husband's favorite meals. Being country born and bred, he likes the traditional dishes and delights in seeing the table fitted with all of its leaves, and every inch covered with platters, tureens, and bowls of his favorite foods—and at least two kinds of pies for dessert waiting on the sideboard. I always cook a big turkey, because my favorite part of Thanksgiving dinner is cold turkey sandwiches the next day.

THE MENU:

AUGUST E'S OYSTER STEW (SEE RECIPE ON PAGES 73–74)

BRINED AND ROASTED FREE-RANGE TURKEY WITH GIBLET GRAVY
(SEE RECIPE ON PAGES 236–239)

COUNTRY CORNBREAD DRESSING (SEE RECIPE ON PAGE 239)

OYSTER DRESSING (SEE RECIPE ON PAGE 240)

THOMPSON FAMILY THANKSGIVING SWEET POTATO CASSEROLE
(SEE RECIPE ON PAGE 347)

SPINACH, APPLE, AND FENNEL SALAD WITH RED ONION AND
RASPBERRY-POPPYSEED VINAIGRETTE (SEE RECIPE ON PAGE 129)

TEXAS GOAT CHEESE AND CILANTRO MASHED POTATOES
(SEE RECIPE ON PAGE 248)

SUE HEATLY'S CRANBERRY CHUTNEY (SEE RECIPE ON PAGE 241)

FRENCH GREEN BEANS WITH GARLIC AND PEPPERED BACON
(SEE RECIPE ON PAGE 362)

YOUR FAVORITE BREADS AND DINNER ROLLS

SAN SABA TEXAS PECAN PIE (SEE RECIPE ON PAGE 432)

COCONUT BUTTERMILK PIE WITH SOUR CREAM PASTRY
(SEE RECIPE ON PAGES 438–439)

- -

SERVES 8 TO 10.

- -

Brined and Roasted Free-Range Turkey with Giblet Gravy

Brining poultry before roasting it was once one of those secret tricks used by chefs to make the birds more delicious than you knew how to make them. But thanks to the Food Network and foodie magazines, the secret is out, and home cooks are learning that this simple maneuver will assure an incredibly moist, tender, and amazingly tasty bird. The method also works very well for chicken and all cuts of pork.

- -

SERVES 10 TO 12.

- -

18- to 20-pound fresh free-range
turkey, with giblets and neck

BRINE:

6 quarts water, divided

¾ cup kosher salt

2 teaspoons whole allspice berries

1 tablespoon whole peppercorns

4 fresh sage sprigs

3 fresh marjoram sprigs

4 thyme sprigs

1 large onion, sliced

¼ cup plus 2 tablespoons sugar

FOR ROASTING THE BIRD:

Melted unsalted butter

6 sprigs fresh thyme

Kosher salt and freshly ground
black pepper

8 slices applewood-smoked bacon

1 quart rich chicken stock, preferably
homemade

GIBLET GRAVY:

Giblets and neck from turkey

1 quart rich chicken stock, preferably
    homemade

½ cup pan drippings from turkey

1 large celery stalk, finely chopped

1 small onion, finely chopped

1 teaspoon minced fresh thyme

1 teaspoon minced fresh sage

Kosher salt and freshly ground
    black pepper

½ cup all-purpose flour

1 hard-cooked egg, chopped

Prepare the brine first. Combine 1½ quarts of the water and all remaining brine ingredients in a heavy-bottomed saucepan over medium-high heat. Chill the remaining 4½ quarts of water. Bring to a boil to dissolve the salt and sugar. Cook for 10 minutes, then remove from heat, cover, and set aside for 1 hour to cool.

Remove the giblets and neck from the turkey, reserving them for the gravy. Rinse the turkey well and drain.

Stand turkey in a 20-quart, nonmetal storage container. (A squeaky-clean 5-gallon bucket will work.) Combine the cooled brine syrup with the 4½ quarts of ice water and pour over the turkey. Add enough ice cubes to make the water level cover the turkey. Cover and refrigerate for 24 hours. If you do not have a giant refrigerator to hold this very large bucket, stand the container in an ice chest almost as deep as the bucket. Surround the bucket completely with ice and keep well iced for 24 hours.

When you are ready to roast the bird, remove it from the bucket and discard the brine. Rinse the turkey thoroughly, inside and out. Pat dry with paper towels. Preheat oven to 375°F. Place the turkey in a roasting pan large enough that the flesh does not touch the sides or ends of the pan. Baste the turkey all over with a liberal amount of melted butter. Place 2 of the thyme sprigs inside the turkey cavity. Season with salt and pepper. Arrange the remaining thyme sprigs over the breast area and lay the bacon slices, slightly overlapping, over the breast. Tie the turkey legs together. Pour the chicken broth into the bottom of the pan, cover, and place in preheated oven, legs first.

Roast the turkey for 3½ hours, or until the leg joint near the backbone wiggles easily and the juices run clear when the turkey is pricked with a skewer in the thick part of the thigh where it joins the body. Baste with the pan drippings every 20 minutes. Uncover the bird for the last 20 minutes of cooking to brown the skin.

While the turkey is roasting, simmer the giblets and necks in the chicken stock, covered, for 1 hour. Drain, reserving the broth for the gravy. Cool the giblets and chop finely. Pull the meat from the neck and chop it also. Set meats aside.

Remove turkey from roasting pan and allow it to rest, covered loosely with foil, for 20 minutes before carving. After the bird has been removed from the roasting pan, pour ½ cup of the fat from the pan into a heavy-bottomed 10-inch skillet; set aside. Skim any remaining fat from the roasting pan. Pour the reserved stock from giblets into the roasting pan. Place pan over high heat and scrape up any browned bits from bottom of pan. Strain through a fine strainer and set aside.

Heat the fat in the skillet over medium heat. Add the celery, onions, thyme, and sage; cook until vegetables are limp, about 10 minutes. Add salt and pepper to taste and stir in the flour all at once. Cook, stirring, for 3 to 4 minutes. Pour in the strained broth in a slow, steady stream while stirring. Bring to a boil to thicken. Add the chopped giblets, neck meat, and hard-cooked egg.

Carve the turkey and arrange the meat and drumsticks on a large platter. Pour the giblet gravy into a gravy bowl and pass separately with the turkey.

Country Cornbread Dressing

"To stuff, or not to stuff?" The two terms can refer to the same ingredients. The choice becomes whether to bake them alone, in which case the dish is generally referred to as "dressing," or to stuff the mixture inside the bird before roasting, thus making it "stuffing." If you choose to stuff the dressing inside the turkey, be sure that both the turkey and the stuffing have been well chilled before you stuff the turkey, and bake it in a moderately hot oven. If you are cooking the mixture as "dressing" with a turkey, take advantage of the turkey drippings to add extra flavor and moistness to the dressing as it cooks.

SERVES 10 TO 12.

½ cup unsalted butter
1 large onion, chopped
1 large green bell pepper, chopped
2 large celery stalks, chopped
5 smoked bacon slices, diced
1 tablespoon minced fresh sage
1 tablespoon minced fresh thyme
1 tablespoon minced fresh rosemary
1 teaspoon dried Mexican oregano
1 teaspoon kosher salt

½ teaspoon freshly ground
   black pepper
¼ pound smoked ham, coarsely
   ground
4 cups crumbled cornbread
6 cups French bread cubes
3 eggs, beaten
About 1¼ cups chicken or turkey
   stock, or more as needed

Preheat oven to 350°F. Melt the butter in a heavy-bottomed 12-inch skillet over medium heat. Add onion, bell pepper, celery, bacon, seasonings, and ham. Sauté, stirring often, until vegetables are wilted and bacon is cooked but not browned, about 10 to 15 minutes. Place cornbread and French bread in a large bowl. Pour the vegetable mixture over the bread; toss to combine. Stir in beaten eggs. Add enough stock or broth to make a moist dressing, stirring to break up the cornbread and French bread. Turn the dressing out into a large baking dish or casserole and bake in preheated oven for 1 hour. Add additional stock as needed to keep the dressing moist. Or even better, if you are cooking the dressing with a turkey, add some of the turkey drippings while the dressing is cooking. Serve hot.

Oyster Dressing

I learned to adore oysters during the years I lived in Louisiana. Oyster dressing is always present on any Creole Thanksgiving table. When I moved back to my home state of Texas, I didn't even think about not making oyster dressing, as my family had gotten used to it being part of our Turkey Day meal. Then I began to discover that Texans like oyster dressing, too—stands to reason, with our abundant supply of great Gulf oysters. If you like oysters, you'll love this dressing.

SERVES 10 TO 12.

9 cups French bread cubes, lightly packed, about 12 ounces
¼ cup unsalted butter
Heart, gizzard, and liver from 1 chicken, minced
1 onion, cut into small dice
1 green bell pepper, cut into small dice
1 celery stalk, cut into small dice
4 green onions, sliced thin, including green tops
3 garlic cloves, minced
¼ cup minced flat-leaf parsley
2 teaspoons minced fresh thyme
3 fresh bay leaves, minced
2 teaspoons minced fresh sage
¾ teaspoon minced fresh marjoram
½ teaspoon cayenne
1 teaspoon kosher salt
14 small to medium oysters (about 1 pint) and their liquor
2 eggs, beaten
1 cup chicken stock, or more as needed, preferably homemade

Preheat oven to 350°F. Spread the French bread cubes on a baking sheet. Dry them in the preheated oven for 10 minutes. Place the dried bread cubes in a large bowl; set aside. Melt the butter in a heavy-bottomed 12-inch skillet over medium-high heat. Add the giblets, onions, bell pepper, celery, green onions, garlic, parsley, and seasonings. Sauté until onion is wilted and transparent and giblets are browned, about 7 minutes. Pour the cooked vegetables and giblets over the bread cubes; toss to combine. Add the oysters and their liquor and the eggs. Stir until blended. Add enough stock to make a moist dressing, stirring to break up the cubes of bread. Bake in preheated oven for about 1 hour, or until golden brown and firm. Add additional stock as needed to keep the dressing moist as it cooks. Serve hot.

Sue Heatly's Cranberry Chutney

My sister, Sandy, has been making this delicious chutney for years. It is a deliciously different alternative to most cranberry presentations at the Thanksgiving table. The recipe was shared with her by her friend Sue Heatly, who created the recipe and who is also quite an accomplished cook. The chutney is perfect with turkey, but for the rest of the year, try it with pork or chicken, which are equally delicious pairings.

SERVES 10 TO 12.

1 cup water

1½ cups sugar

1 large orange, unpeeled, seeded, and cut into small dice

1 (2-inch) slice of fresh ginger root, peeled and sliced

2 cups fresh cranberries, stems removed

½ teaspoon ground cinnamon

¼ teaspoon ground cloves

½ cup golden raisins

Combine the water and sugar in a heavy-bottomed 4-quart saucepan over medium-high heat. Bring to a boil, stirring to dissolve sugar. Add the orange and ginger, reduce heat, and simmer, uncovered, for 20 minutes to form a flavorful court bouillon. Add the cranberries, cinnamon, and cloves. Cook, uncovered, until the cranberries pop and disintegrate into a pulpy mass and the chutney thickens, about 15 to 20 minutes. Stir in the raisins and cook until the chutney is quite thick and bubbly, about 7 minutes. Serve at room temperature or chilled.

There are many options for serving Thanksgiving dinner. If your dining table is large enough, it looks grand to arrange all of the dishes on the table, with a platter of the sliced turkey in the center. If you're serving a crowd that will be seated at more than one table, I would place the dishes on a sideboard, buffet style, so that guests can fill their plates before being seated.

6

ON FOUR LEGS

★

★

Texans take their meat seriously. Cattle were first introduced to Texas by the Spanish, who brought them to provide meat for the missions they established in the western
and southwestern areas of the state. As the missions were
eventually abandoned, the cattle became feral, foraging on
the native grasses that covered the wild prairies. They were
tough, those early ancestors of the iconic longhorn cattle
for which Texas is famous today, and they thrived in the
rugged terrain. In the later part of the nineteenth century,
as the frontier pushed farther west, entrepreneurial Texans
began to round up the feral cattle by the thousands to establish huge, multi-million-acre ranches. The land's vegetation
was sparse, and raising cattle was not an issue of how many

cattle could be run per acre but rather how many acres it took to run a cow. Then began the legendary cattle drives to the markets in Fort Worth and the Midwest.

With the discovery of oil around the turn of the twentieth century, Texas became well established in the minds of anybody from somewhere else as the land of cattle and oil. Eventually, the two mingled, when oil was discovered on many of the large ranches, creating an entirely new genre of Texans—the cattle and oil barons. Steak was the meal of choice.

But further into the twentieth century, the face of the cattle industry began to change. In the quest for ever more marbling in the meat of the cattle, which meant higher prices for the prime grade, the feedlot system was established. Cattle were confined to corrals where they had no room to move around like cattle are meant to do. They were fed corn to fatten them up and add more marbling to the meat. But Mother Nature never intended that cows should eat grains. They were designed to eat grass, but the feedlot cattle had no access to grass. They become sick when they eat grain, so they have to be fed antibiotics to keep them well enough to get them up to maximum weight for slaughter. As the practice grew, so did the amount of antibiotics being ingested indirectly by humans who ate the meat. The waste from the feedlots began to seep into the groundwater and run off into rivers and streams. So now we also have to worry about *E. coli* bacteria in supermarket spinach grown downstream from these feedlot operations.

In addition, as pointed out by Dr. David L. Katz in his landmark book *The Way to Eat*, omega-3 fatty acids, an essential nutrient, are almost completely absent in domestic, grain-fed beef. Domestication has removed the omega-3 fatty acids from the flesh of livestock by changing their food supply.

I'm often asked about the differences in grass-fed versus grain-fed (feedlot) beef. The most obvious difference stems from a nutritional standpoint. A 3-ounce serving of traditional (feedlot) beef rib eye contains 222 calories, 15 grams of fat, 6 grams of saturated fat, 105 milligrams of cholesterol, and 21 grams of protein. Grass-fed and finished beef is leaner and lower in fat. It's also higher in omega-3 fatty acids, vitamin E, and conjugated linoleic acid, or CLA. Omega-3 fats cannot be made by the body and must be obtained from the diet. A 3-ounce serving of grass-fed beef rib eye contains 174 calories, 5 grams of total fat, 1.5 grams of saturated fat, 60 milligrams of cholesterol, and 25 grams of protein.

From the standpoint of taste, most people describe the taste of grass-fed beef as being richer, or *beefier*, than that of grain-fed beef. Grass-fed beef has a darker texture and a finer grain, which actually tends to make it more tender. However, because of the fine grain, and the fact that the fat in grass-fed beef has a lower melting temperature, it is very easy to overcook it. I feel that often this is the root of the complaint that grass-fed beef is tough. (And, being a chef, I know that the ideal way to cook a good steak is no more than medium rare.) The bottom line is, you should lower the cooking time for grass-fed rib eyes. The breed of cattle and type of grasses on which they graze can also affect the taste and texture of the meat. As a consumer, you should try grass-fed beef from several producers until you find one that meets your taste and texture criteria.

The folks who grew hogs watched the feedlot system with interest, and soon huge industrial hog farms were established, where thousands of hogs are confined in massive buildings, often with concrete floors. From birth in these compounds, the hogs spend their lives being fed antibiotic-laced feed on a diet designed to produce "lean pork." Flavor and tenderness have been literally bred out of pork. Hogs raised in such an environment have no place to exhibit their inherent "pig-ness" by wallowing in mud and foraging on native grass supplemented by natural feed. Waste from these hog operations, too, filters far beyond the compounds.

Well, you get the picture. It's become a completely unsustainable food system. But luckily, albeit very slowly, there are farmers who are giving up industrial methods of raising livestock. These intrepid souls are returning to raising grass-fed beef and pastured hogs on small family farms, free of pharmaceuticals and chemicals. These farmers are repairing land that has been overgrazed and not maintained, returning the pastures to native grasses, where happy cows and pigs can spend their lives as they were meant to. Most of these farmers sell their meats through farmers' markets, or they take orders online for pickup at the markets.

Pioneers like Steve Hughes, who founded the Broken Arrow Ranch, purveyors of wild-harvested venison, antelope, and wild boar, have given consumers an alternative to beef. These meats are totally natural and low in fat, not to mention delicious. These animals once provided a majority of the meat consumed by pioneer Texans. Eating game meat goes hand in hand with today's focus on health and wellness. Free-range venison and antelope average one-third fewer calories than beef and one-eighth the fat (about 2 percent). They're also lower in cholesterol than a skinless chicken breast and contain significant proportions of natural omega-3 fatty acids. Of course, the free-range game meats have no hormone or steroid injections and, for the most part, are not exposed to pesticides.

There are two producers in Texas raising bison, which once provided vast amounts of meat to the Native Americans. Bison's flavor is often described as a richer version of beef, with just a hint of sweetness. It's not gamey tasting at all, but the meat has a deeper red color (because of the lack of fat) and a coarser grain than that of beef. Bison are free-ranging animals, which means they feed on grasses and not grains, making their meat much healthier than conventional grain-fed beef. Remember that bison are basically wild creatures—majestically large ones. They thrive without human intervention. Therefore, bison meat is also free of hormones and antibiotics, so you can feel good about eating it! The primary health benefits of bison are its low fat content (less than a third as much fat as similar cuts of beef, pork, and even chicken), lower cholesterol (less than skinless chicken), and a high amount of iron. This makes it an ideal red meat choice for those of us who want to make sustainable, healthy choices in the meats we eat.

In Floresville, Grassland Oasis Farm raises meat goats, which they harvest into several cuts and sell through farmers' markets. Goat meat is another nutritious, low-fat choice for meat eaters. It is a very lean meat and contains significant amounts of calcium, magnesium, potassium, copper, and iron. Goats are incredibly intrepid creatures—rugged and hardy, able to survive with little water in the harsh desert climate of South Texas, where other animals would perish. Perhaps I like to imagine that by eating goat meat I will acquire some of that rugged tenacity!

And rabbit, once a staple meat on pioneer tables, is making a resurgence, with several farms raising them naturally and adventurous chefs featuring tasty dishes of rabbit on their menus.

The bottom line on our love affair with meat is that sustainable choices must be made. To turn the tide of dangerous, unsustainable practices in the livestock industry, we must support the small farmers out there doing hard physical labor to provide us with better-quality, safe meats. Is it more expensive? Yes, but is there a price that can be attached to the health and future well-being of you and your family, and certainly future generations? I think not. And put in perspective, it's fairly relative. For the price of a decked-out meal for a family of four at the Golden Arches, one could buy enough grass-fed ground beef and vegetables at the farmers' market to prepare the meal at home—and feel secure in knowing where it all came from.

The recipes in this chapter use a variety of the meats being produced in Texas today and offer a tantalizing array of flavors and textures. On your next trip to the farmers' market, select a meat you've never tried before, or at least a cut that you've never used. The farmer can usually guide you in the best ways to prepare each cut or type of meat. It's very rewarding to be in command of a variety of meats and many cooking methods by which to prepare them.

When you buy grass-fed, natural meats at the farmers' market, they will be frozen. The producers wrap, label, and freeze the various cuts as soon as the animal is processed to ensure that the meat doesn't develop any potentially harmful pathogens before you purchase it. When you buy frozen meats, return them to your freezer as soon as you get home if you don't intend to cook them right away. Thaw frozen meats in the refrigerator to prevent the development of any harmful pathogens that might sprout at room temperature. And don't freeze meats for longer than three months. Red meats lose flavor the longer they are frozen (as opposed to fish, which gets *fishier* with prolonged time in the freezer). Avoid thawing and then refreezing meats. When meat is frozen, the cells in the meat expand, and eventually the cell walls will break. When the meat is thawed, those broken cells release much of the meat juices, which are the essence of its flavor. So, if you refreeze meat once it has been thawed, then it will lose even more of its juices and its firm texture.

Iliana de la Vega's Mole Coloradito with Roasted Pork Tenderloin

I first met Iliana de la Vega many years ago when she and her husband, Ernesto Torrealba, ran the restaurant El Naranjo in Oaxaca, Mexico. The restaurant received worldwide acclaim for Iliana's reinterpretation of traditional Oaxacan cuisine. After closing the restaurant in 2006, Iliana began an extended culinary research mission throughout Latin America, interviewing and cooking with chefs and home cooks as well as culinary historians, anthropologists, farmers, and food producers. This led to her first assignment as a Latin American specialist at the Culinary Institute of America (CIA) in San Antonio, where she was a founding member of that institution's Latin American Advisory Council. In 2012, Iliana resigned from the CIA to focus once again on El Naranjo—now located in Austin!

Although Iliana is considered one of the most knowledgeable authorities on the cuisines of all of Latin America, she is so dedicated to authentic Mexican food that she prefers not to adulterate the menu at El Naranjo with foods or influences from other countries.

This sinfully delicious dish is so complex and flavorful that it's worth every minute of cooking time. If you're looking for a dish that will be forever remembered by anyone to whom you serve it, look no further.

SERVES 4 TO 6.

Mole Coloradito (recipe follows)
Roasted Pork Tenderloin
   (see recipe below)
3 tablespoons toasted sesame seeds
White Rice (see recipe below)
Warmed corn tortillas

ROASTED PORK TENDERLOIN:
2 pork tenderloins, about 1¾ pounds
   total, trimmed of silverskin
Canola oil
Kosher salt and freshly ground
   black pepper

WHITE RICE:
3 tablespoons canola oil
2 cups long-grain white rice
3½ cups water
Kosher salt

MOLE COLORADITO:
10 ancho chiles
2 pasilla chiles
4 large Roma tomatoes
4 medium garlic cloves, unpeeled
6 tablespoons canola oil, divided
2 slices day-old rustic white bread
15 whole blanched almonds
2 tablespoons pepitas
   (raw pumpkin seeds)
½ cup white sesame seeds
3 whole cloves
1 tablespoon dried Mexican oregano
10 whole black peppercorns
1 piece Mexican canela (stick of
   cinnamon), about 2 inches long,
   cut into ½-inch pieces
1 quart chicken stock, preferably
   homemade
Kosher salt
3 tablespoons sugar

To make the mole coloradito, wipe the chiles clean with a damp paper towel. Discard the seeds and stems. Toast the chiles in a hot cast-iron skillet just until they give off a pleasant aroma. Do not burn the chiles. Place the chiles in a medium-sized bowl and add boiling water to cover them and a plate or pan lid directly on the chiles to keep them submerged; set aside for about 20 minutes, or until chiles are softened and pliable. Remove chiles and set aside, reserving the water in which they were softened.

Dry-roast the tomatoes and the unpeeled garlic cloves in a hot cast-iron skillet until charred on all sides. Remove from skillet and set aside.

Add 3 tablespoons of the canola oil to a cast-iron skillet and fry the bread slices until they are pale gold. Add the blanched almonds, pepitas, sesame seeds, cloves, oregano, and black peppercorns. Cook, stirring, until just fragrant, about 1 minute; turn out into a bowl and reserve.

In a heavy-bottomed Dutch oven, heat the remaining 3 tablespoons of canola oil. Place the chiles in a blender with just enough of the soaking water to make them blend. Blend until smooth. When the oil is hot, add the chile puree to the pan and let it fry for about 8 to 10 minutes, stirring occasionally. Meanwhile, combine the reserved bread, nuts, seeds, and spices in the blender along with blistered tomatoes and garlic with just enough water to blend. Blend until smooth and add to the pot, stirring to blend well. Place the canela in the blender with a couple tablespoons of water and blend until smooth. Pour the blended cinnamon through a fine strainer into the pot. Simmer the mole until it is thickened, about 20 minutes, stirring often.

Add the chicken stock and bring to a boil. Cook for 15 minutes, then add salt to taste and the sugar. Cook to dissolve sugar. The mole should be thick enough to coat the back of a spoon. Keep warm while roasting the pork.

Preheat oven to 350°F. Lightly baste the tenderloins with canola oil and season them with salt and freshly ground black pepper. Heat a glaze of canola oil in a heavy-bottomed, ovenproof 12-inch skillet, preferably cast iron, over medium-high heat. When the oil is very hot, add the tenderloins and cook to sear and brown them all over. Transfer the skillet to preheated oven and roast for about 25 to 30 minutes, or until the tenderloins register 145°F on an instant-read meat thermometer. Remove from oven and cover loosely with foil. Set aside to keep warm.

While the pork is roasting, make the rice. Heat the canola oil in a heavy-bottomed Dutch oven over medium-high heat. When the oil is hot, add the raw rice and stir quickly to coat with the oil. Cook the rice, stirring often to prevent sticking, until it is golden brown. Be sure not to scorch the rice. Add the water and salt to taste. Stir to release browned bits from bottom of pan. Cover the pan and lower the heat to a bare simmer. Cook until the rice has absorbed all of the water, about 20 minutes. Fluff rice with a fork to serve.

Cut the tenderloins, on the bias, into slices ½ inch thick.

Place a serving of the rice on each plate and top with 3 or 4 slices of the pork, then a portion of the mole sauce. Scatter some of the toasted sesame seeds over the mole and serve hot with warmed corn tortillas.

Heritage Pork Carnitas

Pork carnitas is a classic Mexican dish made from slow-braised pork shoulder. Cooking the carnitas is a time-consuming process, but it's time well invested as the end result is so flavorful and tender. The quality of the pork will greatly affect the taste of the dish, so be sure to seek out pastured, heritage pork that has enough fat to make authentic carnitas. Lean, commercially bred and raised pork just won't do. When I make carnitas, I serve it with simple side dishes like a green salad or guacamole, rice, and refried beans to keep the spotlight on the pork. It's so tasty that I don't even add a salsa.

SERVES 4 TO 6.

4 pounds boneless heritage pork shoulder, cut into 3-inch chunks, trimmed of some fat, but only if the meat is extremely fatty, as the fat is an essential part of the flavor and tenderness of the finished dish

2 teaspoons kosher salt

¼ cup canola oil

1 onion, roughly chopped

1 cup freshly squeezed orange juice

1 bottle (12 ounces) of your favorite Mexican beer

Water

6 garlic cloves, peeled and sliced thin

1 orange, quartered

1 stick Mexican canela (cinnamon), about 3 inches long

1 teaspoon ancho chile powder

4 fresh bay leaves

½ teaspoon ground cumin

Begin by cooking the carnitas. Rub the pork cubes all over with the 2 teaspoons of salt. Place on a platter and set aside at room temperature for 1 hour.

Heat the canola oil in a heavy-bottomed roasting pan large enough to hold all of the pork in a single layer, not touching, over medium-high heat. If you do not have a large enough pan to do this, then sear the meat in batches. When the oil is hot, add the pork cubes and cook until they are well browned on all sides. The browning adds a major flavor dimension to the finished carnitas, so be sure that the meat is well seared to a deep brown on all sides. Remove pork and set aside. Add the onion to the pan and cook until lightly browned. Add the orange juice and stir to scrape up the flavorful browned bits from the bottom of the pan. Remove pan from heat.

Preheat oven to 350°F. Add the pork back to the pan and pour in the beer. Add all remaining ingredients, stirring to blend well. Add enough water so that the pork is almost covered. Place the roasting pan in the preheated oven, uncovered, and braise for about 3½ hours, or until the pork is very, very tender. Turn pork pieces 3 or 4 times while cooking. Remove pan from the oven, then remove the pork pieces; set aside. Strain the remaining pan juices through a fine strainer, pressing down on the solids to remove all of the intensely flavored liquid; discard the solids. Return the juices to the roasting pan; set aside.

Once the pork is cool enough to handle, cut it into bite-size pieces. The pork will literally be falling-apart tender. Discard any large pieces of fat. Return the pork pieces to the pan with the strained cooking broth and return pan to oven. Cook the pork until the liquid has evaporated completely and the meat is simmering in its own fat. Cook until pork is very crispy and caramelized, about 50 minutes. Remove pan from the oven and set the pork pieces aside to rest for 5 minutes before serving.

MAKIN' BACON

REVIVAL MARKET'S HOUSE-CURED AND SMOKED BACON

REVIVAL MARKET FOUNDERS Morgan Weber and Ryan Pera grew up in families that, directly and indirectly, nurtured their passion for old-fashioned, handcrafted food—especially meats. Weber grew up in the small Central Texas town of Yoakum where his grandparents owned a ranching operation. He ate fine family meals sourced from the surrounding fields. After studying music at Baylor University and doing a stint as a real estate developer in Houston, Morgan's family roots began to tug on his mind. In 2009, he visited the Stone Barns Center for Food and Agriculture in Westchester County, New York, and was so inspired by the full-circle, sustainable farm/retail operation that he decided to return to those roots with the mission of healing the family land that had been abused and overgrazed since his grandfather's death. He wanted to raise heritage breeds of hogs because their meat tastes better, they're hardier, and they're literally living (food) history. The newly named Revival Farms started with about 75 hogs on seven reclaimed acres. The breeds—Mangalista, Red Wattle, Gloucestershire, Old Spots, Ossabaw, and Mulefoot—were chosen for the particular qualities of meat and fat each provides. In addition to providing the meats for Revival Market, the farm has one of the best breeding herds of heirloom pork and lamb.

As a child, Ryan Pera learned to make artisan vinegars, pickles, and wine from his father. Although he had worked in New York for some of the Big Apple's leading chefs, it was his interest in salumi (Italian dry-cured meats made predominantly from pork) and charcuterie that led him to Morgan Weber. Today, Pera's creations are made from the meats produced at Weber's Revival

Farms and featured at Revival Market. It is one of the few markets in the country that actually raises the livestock from which it produces its products.

In addition to the charcuterie, salumi, and deli items, the market offers house-made stocks, seasonally inspired prepared foods, vinegars, pickles, demi-glace, and jams. The market also serves as a showcase for other artisan foods derived from the work of regional farmers and bakers.

Revival Market Bacon

A 5-pound pork belly makes a lot of bacon. Although it will last in the refrigerator for a couple of weeks since it's a cured product, its flavor is best if used within a week. So, after you slice the finished bacon, divide it into the portion size that you normally use, wrap the portions individually in plastic wrap, and freeze them in zip-sealing plastic bags. The bacon will retain its flavor for about 3 months frozen.

MAKES 5 POUNDS.

5-pound slab of heritage breed
  pork belly
¼ cup kosher salt

2 teaspoons curing salt #1
1 cup pure sorghum syrup, or 100%
  pure cane syrup, such as Steen's

Remove the rind from the pork belly if it has not been removed. Place the belly in a non-reactive pan large enough to accommodate it with a little space left over. Mix together the salt, curing salt, and sorghum or cane syrup, blending well. Rub the mixture over all sides of the belly. Cover tightly with plastic wrap and refrigerate. Rub the belly every day with just a couple pinches of kosher salt, turning it each day, for a full week. After the curing is completed, rinse the belly under cold running water, removing all of the rub. Now hang the pork belly or place it on a baking rack over a baking sheet, for about 6 to 12 hours to dry the belly and form the *pellicle*, a slightly tacky, hardened surface.

In a hardwood smoker, smoke the belly at 200°F until an instant-read meat thermometer registers 150°F. This will take about 3 hours, if the consistency of the 200-degree temperature is maintained. Ryan generally uses hickory for smoking his bacon, but oak, pecan, apple, and mesquite are other good choices. It just depends on your personal preference. Remove from the smoker and allow the belly to cool on a wire rack, then refrigerate overnight to firm up the meat before slicing. If you own an electric slicer, it's easy to slice your bacon to the thickness you wish. Alternatively, slice to desired thickness using a sharp butcher's knife. Refrigerate or freeze.

Roasted Pork Tenderloin with Port Wine Glaze, Grilled Sweet Potato Planks, and Port-Glazed Pecans

Pork has long been thought of as winter meat because that's when the hogs were butchered on the family farm or ranch. I find that pecans, also harvested in the fall, pair very well with pork. These port-glazed pecans, created by my friend and wine aficionado Paul Gingrich, are especially heavenly (and they also make great hostess gifts for holiday parties when packed into attractive tins lined with colorful tissue paper).

The rich, dark flavors of this dish are comforting on a blustery cold Texas evening. The rub for this pork imparts a smoky taste, while the sauce brings a hint of sweetness and the warming essence of a good Texas port wine. The grilled sweet potatoes, with their simple baste, are a perfect match to the sweet/spicy/aromatic flavors of the pork. A simple side dish of spinach pan-seared in olive oil with a bit of minced garlic and salt makes this a very satisfying meal.

SERVES 6 TO 8.

2 pieces pork tenderloin, about
  2¼ pounds total
Rub (see recipe below)
¼ cup canola oil
Port Wine Glaze (recipe follows)
Grilled Sweet Potato Planks
  (recipe follows)
Port-Glazed Pecans (recipe follows)

RUB:

1 tablespoon plus 1 teaspoon
  kosher salt
1 tablespoon plus 1 teaspoon
  dark brown sugar
1 tablespoon plus 1 teaspoon
  smoked paprika
2 teaspoons freshly ground
  black pepper
2 teaspoons dry mustard
1 teaspoon granulated garlic

PORT WINE GLAZE:

¼ pound (1 stick) unsalted butter,
  cut into small bits
2 large garlic cloves, minced
½ cup Texas ruby port wine
½ cup dark brown sugar
¼ cup whole-grain mustard
1 teaspoon ground cinnamon
½ teaspoon ground cloves
Kosher salt and freshly ground
  black pepper

GRILLED SWEET POTATO PLANKS:

2 medium sweet potatoes, peeled and
  sliced on the bias ⅜-inch thick
1½ cups Texas extra-virgin olive oil
2 tablespoons brown sugar
½ teaspoon granulated garlic
¼ teaspoon cayenne

PORT-GLAZED PECANS:
MAKES 2 CUPS.
1 cup sugar
½ cup Texas ruby port wine
2 cups pecan halves

Begin by preparing the pecans. Line a heavy-duty baking sheet with parchment paper; set aside. Combine the sugar and port wine in a heavy-bottomed 14-inch skillet over medium-high heat. Stir the mixture constantly. When the sugar has dissolved and the syrupy mixture begins to boil, quickly stir in the pecans. Continue to stir, turning the pecans to prevent burning. Cook for about 5 to 6 minutes, or until the mixture has thickened and the syrup has turned a deep caramel color. Remove pan from heat and turn the pecans out onto the prepared baking sheet. Quickly separate the pecans into a single layer with a wooden spoon. (Take care not to touch the pecans as they are hot as blazes!) Allow pecans to cool for about 30 minutes, or until they are totally hardened. Store in a moisture-proof container for up to 5 days.

Trim any fat and silverskin from the tenderloins and place meat on a baking sheet. Make the rub by combining all ingredients and tossing with a fork to blend well. Rub the mixture into the meat, massaging it in with your fingers and using all of the rub on the 2 pieces of pork. Place in refrigerator for at least 2 hours, or preferably overnight.

To make the glaze, melt the butter in a heavy-bottomed 1-quart saucepan over medium heat. Add the garlic and cook for 1 minute. Do not brown the garlic. Add the port wine, sugar, mustard, cinnamon, and cloves. Simmer the mixture over medium-high heat, whisking vigorously, until thick and syrupy, about 2 to 4 minutes. Remove pan from heat and season to taste with salt and pepper. Mixture should be highly seasoned. Pour half of the glaze into a small bowl; set aside. Preheat oven to 375°F.

Heat the canola oil in a heavy-bottomed 12-inch skillet over medium-high heat. When the oil is hot, add the pork tenderloins and sear on all sides until well browned. Transfer the tenderloins to an open roasting pan and baste with some of the glaze in the small bowl. Cook for 25 minutes, or until the pork reaches an internal temperature of 145°F. It should be medium, with a little pink showing in the center. Don't overcook or the meat will be tough and on the dry side. Baste the tenderloins with more of the glaze in the bowl as they cook. When done, remove from the oven and let tenderloins rest, loosely covered with foil, for 5 minutes before slicing ½-inch thick on the bias.

While the pork is roasting, prepare the sweet potato planks. Combine olive oil, brown sugar, granulated garlic, and cayenne; whisk to blend well. Brush potato slices on both sides with the oil and grill on a char-grill, comal, or stovetop grill until tender, lightly marked, and tender-crisp. Keep warm.

To serve, arrange 1 or 2 of the sweet potato planks on each serving plate. Arrange slices of the pork, slightly overlapping, on the potatoes. Spoon the remaining port wine glaze over the meat and serve hot. Garnish each serving with 5 to 6 port-glazed pecans.

Grill-Seared and Roasted Stuffed Heritage Pork Chops

This is a dish for the ardent pork lover—a thick, meaty pork chop stuffed with pork sausage! I was inspired by the Large Black hogs raised by Mark and Kelly Escobedo at South Texas Heritage Pork. The pork is melt-in-your-mouth tender, and the chops have that nice ring of fat around the edge that tenderizes the meat as it melts during cooking. Thank goodness real pork is returning to the market through the hard work of small producers like the Escobedos. I stuff the chops with Home-Style Polska Kielbasa produced by the Kiolbassa family in San Antonio. For a different, but also traditional, Texas flavor, stop by Dziuk's Meat Market in Castroville and purchase some of the handmade Alsatian-style fresh sausage. Follow the same procedure as if using the kielbasa.

SERVES 4.

----

4 bone-in, center-cut heritage pork chops, each 1½ inches thick

Brine (see recipe below)

12 ounces Polish kielbasa sausage, casings removed

½ small yellow onion, finely chopped

⅓ cup finely chopped green bell pepper

3 garlic cloves, minced

1 cup dried plain bread crumbs

½ cup beef broth

Texas extra-virgin olive oil

Pork Chop Rub (see recipe below)

BRINE:

1 gallon water, divided

1 cup kosher salt

4 fresh bay leaves

1 tablespoon whole coriander seeds, toasted

1 tablespoon whole black peppercorns

½ cup fresh thyme sprigs

1 cup brown sugar

2 oranges, quartered

1 large white onion, cut into thick slices

4 garlic cloves, crushed

PORK CHOP RUB:

½ cup medium-hot chili powder

1 tablespoon light brown sugar

¼ cup toasted, then ground, cumin seeds

2½ tablespoons dried Mexican oregano

2½ tablespoons granulated garlic

2 tablespoons kosher salt

2½ teaspoons grated lime zest

Begin by making the brine. Combine 4 cups of the water and remaining brine ingredients in a heavy-bottomed 3-quart saucepan over medium-high heat. Bring to a boil, stirring often, until the salt and sugar have dissolved. Reduce heat to a simmer, cover, and cook for 10 minutes. Remove from heat and stir in the remaining 3 quarts of water. Turn out into an 8-quart container and refrigerate until well chilled. When the brine is very cold, add the pork chops and brine. Refrigerate for 24 hours.

Make the stuffing. Break the sausage into small bits and place in the work bowl of a food processor fitted with the steel blade. Use the pulse feature to break up the sausage into small crumbles. Turn the meat out into a bowl and mix with the onions, bell pepper, garlic, bread crumbs, and beef broth. Stir to blend thoroughly; set aside.

Make the rub by mixing all ingredients together in a small bowl. Toss with a fork or small whisk to blend thoroughly and evenly. Store in a tightly covered container.

Remove the chops from the brine, discarding the brine. Pat the chops very dry, using absorbent paper towels. Using a small, sharp knife, make an incision about 2 inches wide into the meaty part of the side of each chop. Work the knife around in the small incision to make a pocket all the way to the bone of the chops and to within ½ inch of each side, taking care not to puncture the chop. Stuff each chop with one-fourth of the sausage mixture, packing it tightly. Press the small incision closed, using a toothpick if needed to hold it together.

Heat a gas char-grill to medium heat or spray a heavy-duty stovetop grill with non-stick spray and heat it over medium-high heat until very hot. Preheat oven to 350°F.

Baste the chops lightly on both sides with olive oil. Coat the chops very liberally on both sides with the rub. Grill the chops over medium-high heat for about 5 minutes, turning once to sear and brown both sides. Transfer the chops to an oiled baking dish and place on middle rack of preheated oven. Bake for about 35 to 40 minutes, or until an instant-read thermometer inserted in the center of the stuffing registers 150°F. Allow the chops to rest 5 minutes, loosely covered with foil, before serving.

RICHARDSON FARMS

In 2000, Jim and Kay Richardson bought a 200-acre farm in Rockdale. All of the buildings, including the old farmhouse, had been vacant for more than 20 years and were in total disrepair. Both of the Richardsons had full-time jobs, so they worked weekends with their whole family—their three children and their spouses, plus Jim's parents—to make the farmhouse livable.

After unfulfilling attempts at tree farming and vegetable raising, the Richardsons turned to livestock. They had already been raising hogs and cattle for their own consumption. It was also a natural transition for Jim, who is a veterinarian. As they increased their livestock, they started taking one hog to the processor every other week and one steer each month. They began to sell the pork chops, bacon, steaks, and roasts, one cut at a time. Before long they had several steady customers and

chefs asking for special cuts and larger quantities. In May 2006, they began to sell their meats at farmers' markets in Austin.

The couple raises their own forage crops for the animals—corn, wheat, oats, barley, and sorghum. The grains are grown, harvested, and stored on the farm to be ground for feed. The cattle are raised strictly on grass—alfalfa, brown mid-rib sorghum, and winter wheat and oats.

Now the family has ventured into raising broiler chickens, layers, turkeys, ducks, and a few guineas, buying the babies, only hours old, from a nearby hatchery. In 2011, the Richardsons built their own state-approved poultry-processing facility. By processing their own poultry, they are in complete control of the poultry from just after it hatches through its processing.

ALAMOSA WINE CELLARS

AFTER A CAREER in the oil patch in Houston, Jim Johnson decided to pursue his interest in wine, so he headed to California, where he attended the University of California, Davis, graduating with honors and a degree in enology and viticulture. He then worked at wineries in California before becoming the winemaker at a new venture near Austin. Jim was hesitant to leave a flourishing wine industry for the viticultural frontier of Texas but finally decided he wanted the challenge, and he did miss Texas. The morning that he packed up his truck to head out, he turned on the radio. The first song that came on was Asleep at the Wheel's "Boogey Back to Texas," and he knew he had made the right decision!

Still, Jim longed to have his own winery. During a conversation with his wife, Karen, he moaned that if he were to begin the process, he would be 60 years old before his arms cradled the first bottle of his own wine. Karen replied, "Well, Jim, you're going to be 60 anyway, so why not have a winery to show for it?" The pair founded Alamosa Wine Cellars in 1999 in the northernmost corner of the Texas Hill Country appellation, near the small town of Bend. Karen, a businesswoman in Austin, has split her time to assist Jim with the creation of the vineyard and winery. A tasting room was added in 2004.

Jim's distinctive portfolio of wines has received praise from around the country. *Wine Spectator* cited Jim Johnson as "the future of Texas wine" for his pioneering dedication to promoting Mediterranean varietals in Texas. His list includes a number of award-winning blends, including his signature El Guapo, a tempranillo blend.

Jim and Karen paired one of their signature reds, Texacaia, a sangiovese/tannat blend, with the Jaeger Schnitzel with Mushroom and Riesling Sauce (pages 260-261). With the Bin 555 South Texas Heritage Pork Roulade (pages 261-264), they recommend their legendary El Guapo. Alamosa was one of the first to produce a Viognier in Texas, and it is exceptional. I love to pair it with the Avocado Cream Soup with Crispy Tortilla Strips and Shrimp Pico de Gallo (pages 52-54).

Jaeger Schnitzel with Mushroom and Riesling Sauce

Jaeger schnitzel is a classic among the German schnitzels. The name means "hunter's cutlet" and was one of the dishes brought to Texas by the original German immigrants, who found plentiful deer and wild hogs in the Hill Country where they settled. Today the dish is most often prepared using pork, but you can still substitute venison or wild boar. The traditional side dish for schnitzel is spaetzle (see recipe for Herbed Spaetzle on page 349).

SERVES 6 TO 8.

2 pork tenderloins, about 2 pounds total, trimmed

4 bacon slices, cut into ½-inch dice

Additional bacon drippings as needed to make ⅓ cup

3 cups all-purpose flour seasoned with kosher salt and freshly ground black pepper

8 ounces small white mushrooms, sliced

1 small onion, cut into ¼-inch dice

1 tablespoon minced flat-leaf parsley

2 teaspoons minced fresh sage leaves

2 tablespoons additional all-purpose flour

½ cup dry Texas Riesling

2 cups beef stock

2 tablespoons sour cream

Kosher salt and freshly ground black pepper

Slice the pork tenderloins in half lengthwise and slice each half into 4 pieces. Place each piece between two sheets of plastic wrap or parchment paper on a cutting board and pound to about ¼-inch thick using a veal pounder preferably, or a meat mallet or dowel-type rolling pin. Take care not to take all your frustrations out on the meat to the point that you tear it. It should be evenly thick. Repeat with all pieces of pork; set aside.

Place the diced bacon in a heavy-bottomed 12-inch skillet over medium heat. Cook until the bacon cubes are crisp and have rendered their fat. Remove with a slotted spoon and drain on absorbent paper towels, retaining the drippings in the pan. Add additional bacon drippings as needed to make ⅓ cup.

Heat the drippings over medium heat. When the fat is hot, dredge the pounded pork cutlets in the seasoned flour, coating both sides well and shaking off excess flour. Working in batches, fry the meat in the bacon drippings until golden brown and crisp on both sides, turning once. Transfer meat to a wire rack set over a baking sheet and keep warm in a low (about 175°F) oven while cooking the remaining pieces. Reserve pan drippings.

Add the mushrooms to the hot drippings over medium heat. Cook, stirring often, until they are lightly browned and all of their liquid has evaporated. Add the onions, parsley, and sage; stir to blend. Cook until onions are wilted and transparent, about 5 minutes. Stir in the additional 2 tablespoons of flour, blending well. Cook, stirring, for about 2 to 3 minutes. Add the Riesling and cook, stirring constantly, scraping up the browned bits from the bottom of the pan, until the mixture thickens. Add the beef stock and stir to incorporate. Bring to a boil and then lower heat and simmer for 5 minutes. Stir in the sour cream, blending well, and season to taste with salt and freshly ground black pepper.

Serve the cutlets topped with a portion of the hot mushroom sauce and a side of herbed spaetzle.

BIN 555 RESTAURANT AND WINE BAR

South Texas Heritage Pork Roulade with Sweet Corn Pudding, Texas 1015 Onions, Beer, and Herbs

Bin 555 Restaurant and Wine Bar is one of several San Antonio restaurants owned by native Texan chef Jason Dady. Dady comes from a hospitality background. His paternal grandparents owned a local tavern for nearly 40 years and taught their young grandson the value of customer relations. His maternal grandfather was an old-time butcher who was much loved by the customers with whom he shared his expertise in meat.

When Dady began his own career, he saw in San Antonio the opportunity to grow as a chef. He sources as many of his ingredients for his various ventures as locally as possible, and all of his meats. The pork for this visually appealing and delicious dish was sourced, as are all of his pork cuts, from South Heritage Pork in Floresville.

SERVES 6 TO 8.

Fresh herbs of your choice as garnish, such as micro greens and edible flowers

PORK ROULADE:
1 tablespoon Texas extra-virgin olive oil
½ cup small-dice shallots
2 pounds pork shoulder

¼ cup Texas pecans
Kosher salt and freshly ground black pepper
1 tablespoon dried milk powder
20 bacon or, preferably, guanciale, slices
5 pounds boneless pork loin, well trimmed
1 additional tablespoon each kosher salt and freshly ground black pepper

CORN PUDDING:

6 ears fresh corn, shucked and
    silk removed

¼ cup water

2 tablespoons instant polenta

1 tablespoon butter

1 tablespoon kosher salt

TEXAS 1015 ONIONS:

2 large Texas 1015 sweet onions

1 tablespoon Texas extra-virgin
    olive oil

1 tablespoon chicken stock, preferably
    homemade

1 tablespoon each kosher salt and
    freshly ground black pepper

BEER AND PORK JUS:

1 tablespoon Texas extra-virgin
    olive oil

2 large yellow onions, peeled
    and sliced thin

3 celery stalks, cut into ½-inch dice

1 fennel bulb, roughly chopped

2 bottles Real Ale Brewing Company
    Coffee Porter

1 gallon roasted pork stock

1 bunch fresh thyme

Begin by making the roulade. Heat the olive oil in a heavy-bottomed 10-inch skillet over medium heat. Add the shallots and sweat (do not brown) just until they are translucent, about 4 minutes. Remove from pan and set aside to cool.

Dice the pork shoulder into 1-inch cubes and remove any thick pieces of fat. If you don't have a meat grinder, use fairly lean ground pork. Grind the pork shoulder with the pecans and shallots through a small die in a meat grinder. Season with salt and pepper. Once the pork mixture is ground, fold in the dry milk powder, which helps to bind the sausage. Set aside.

Lay down a large piece of plastic wrap. Lay the bacon or guanciale slices in the center of the plastic wrap, overlapping each piece so there are no gaps between slices. Spread a ¾-inch-thick layer of the sausage over the bottom half of the bacon or guanciale slices. Now lay the cleaned pork loin on top of the sausage-covered bacon or guanciale. Season with salt and pepper to taste. Roll tightly, using the plastic wrap to get it as tight as possible. Tie the ends of the plastic wrap in knots and place on a baking sheet. Refrigerate overnight.

When ready to roast the loin, preheat oven to 300°F. Remove the plastic wrap. Season the meat all over with the 1 tablespoon each of salt and pepper. Place the meat on a rack in a large roasting pan and roast in preheated oven for about 3 hours, or until the internal temperature of the pork registers 145°F on an instant-read meat thermometer. Set aside, covered loosely with foil, for 15 minutes before slicing.

While the pork is roasting, make the beer and pork jus. Heat the oil in a heavy-bottomed 5-quart braising pan over medium heat. Add the onions, celery, and fennel; sweat until vegetables are almost caramelized, about 10 minutes. Stir in the beer, scraping up any browned bits from the bottom of the pan. Reduce the liquid by three-fourths, then stir in the pork stock and thyme. Cook to reduce by half, or until *nape* consistency (the jus will coat the back of a metal spoon heavily enough that when you run your finger down the middle of the spoon, the mark will remain). Strain the jus through a fine strainer and set aside to keep warm.

Prepare the Texas 1015 onions. Preheat oven to 325°F. Peel the onions and cut in half lengthwise. Lay the flat surface on the cutting board and slice ½-inch thick diagonally, forming petals. Place in a roasting pan and add the oil, chicken stock, salt, and pepper. Cook in preheated oven until tender, about 30 minutes. Set aside to keep warm.

Make the corn pudding. Using a sharp chef's knife and working over a bowl, remove all kernels from the corn cobs. After kernels are removed, scrape the cobs again into the bowl with the back of the knife, to remove all of the *milk* from the cobs.

Place the corn and milk in a high-speed blender with the water and blend until very smooth. Pass the mixture through a fine-mesh strainer into a heavy-bottomed 4-quart saucepan, stirring with the back of a spoon to remove as much of the puree as possible, leaving any solids in the strainer. Place the pan over low heat and bring the mixture to a simmer, stirring constantly. It will begin to thicken.

Once the corn mixture has simmered for about 1 minute, slowly pour in the polenta. Continue to stir for another 2 minutes, or until mixture has thickened. Remove from heat and whisk in the butter and salt. Set aside to keep warm.

To assemble and serve the dish, use a rubber spatula to spread a layer of the corn pudding along the side of large serving plates. Slice the pork into 1-inch slices and place 1 slice at the edge of the corn pudding. Spoon on the onions, stacking them as you go.

Drizzle the beer and pork jus over the meat and garnish with herbs, greens, and edible flowers as desired.

SOUTH TEXAS HERITAGE PORK

MARK AND KELLY ESCOBEDO moved to Floresville in 2002 and started a locksmith business. In 2007, Mark changed the locks on a vacant farmhouse that was for lease just outside the city. The house was situated on 122 acres. He was impressed with the land and the house, so he and Kelly leased the entire property. After much research, the couple decided to raise heritage hogs rather than farm the land. They picked two rare breeds—the English Large Black and the Tamworth.

The English Large Black hog originated from the Old English Hog, established in the sixteenth and seventeenth centuries. Large Blacks have long, deep bodies, which produce excellent bacon. Their solid black coloring makes them hardy in extreme temperatures and protects them from sunburn. Large Blacks were born to graze.

The Tamworth, a red-colored hog, is one of the oldest breeds. It is the most direct descendant of the native pig stock of Europe that, in turn, descended from wild boars. The breed originated in the Midlands of England, taking its name from the town of Tamworth in Staffordshire. Tamworths are disease resistant and tolerant of extreme temperatures. The breed declined because they are born grazers and are not suitable for industrial confined-rearing methods. In grazing operations the hog is highly adaptable and produces both quality pork and bacon.

The Escobedos truly love and respect their animals. South Texas Heritage Pork was the first Animal Welfare Approved pork farm in Texas. This certification is the gold standard for both producers and consumers. Among other criteria, the certification requires that animals be allowed to range free and have access to pasture at all times. It guarantees consumers that the meat they are buying has been both humanely raised and harvested. Mark told me that he becomes emotional when he selects animals for processing. "I look these pigs in the eye for 18 months, up to the minute I push them off the back of the trailer at the processor. I want to be sure those chefs understand the connection we have with these hogs." As we admired the baby hogs trailing along behind their mothers, Kelly commented, "Happy, healthy hogs produce exceptional pork."

Open-Face Cheese and Chorizo Chiles Rellenos

Chiles rellenos is a typical Mexican dish that is generally made using roasted and peeled poblano chiles, or their dried version, ancho chiles, which are rehydrated in hot water and then stuffed. The dish is on the menu, in one form or another, at any Tex-Mex restaurant worth its chips and salsa. Chiles rellenos can be stuffed with a wide variety of fillings from various cheeses, or combinations of cheeses, to meat picadillos, ground meat mixtures similar to hash. Often, the stuffed chiles are battered, fried, and served with a sauce. This version is made using poblano chiles freshly blistered and stuffed with a cheese and chorizo mixture, then baked rather than fried, and topped with fresh pico de gallo. I like to serve them on a bed of Rosa's Mex-Mex Rice (see recipe on page 346), with a side of guacamole on shredded lettuce. It makes a really colorful and inviting plate—and with the rich combination of flavors, a delicious one.

12 ounces bulk-style Mexican chorizo

6 poblano chiles, roasted and peeled

8 ounces shredded quesadilla cheese

6 ounces plain Water Oak Farm
    goat cheese

Pico de Gallo (recipe follows)

PICO DE GALLO:

3 large Roma tomatoes, cut into
    ¼-inch dice

⅓ cup red onion, cut into tiny dice

2 serrano chiles, seeds and veins
    removed, minced

2 to 3 heaping tablespoons
    minced cilantro

2 tablespoons fresh lime juice

Kosher salt

Make the pico de gallo. Combine all ingredients in a non-aluminum bowl and stir to blend. Refrigerate, covered, until ready to use. *Note:* If you wish to make the pico de gallo ahead of time—up to 1 day—simply omit the salt, which causes the tomatoes to weep and the pico to become watery. Add salt to taste just before serving.

To make the chiles rellenos, brown the chorizo in a heavy-bottomed 10-inch skillet over medium heat. Press down on the sausage with the back of a large spoon as it cooks to break up any clumps and stir often. You're looking for little bitty crumbles of sausage here. When the chorizo is completely browned, strain into a fine-mesh strainer and press down on the meat with the back of a large spoon to press out all of the fat. Set aside to cool. Preheat oven to 375°F.

Using a sharp paring knife, slit the peeled chiles from the stem to the bottom. Carefully remove the seeds and veins, taking care not to tear the chiles (but it's not the end of the world if you do make a small tear). Set aside. When the chorizo is cool, combine it with the two cheeses, blending well. Divide the chorizo and cheese mixture between the chiles, stuffing equal portions into each chile. Pat the slit edges of the chiles over the cheese mixture and pat down any torn spots, leaving an open gap of about 2 inches in the center. Set the chiles, open sides up, on a rimmed baking sheet lined with parchment paper and bake in preheated oven for 15 minutes, or until the cheese is melted and gooey.

To serve, place a chile on each serving plate and top each with an equal portion of the pico de gallo. If you are serving the chiles with the Mex-Mex rice and guacamole, as I do, place a serving of the rice slightly to one side of the middle of each plate and nest a chile in it, then top with pico de gallo. Make a little pile of shredded lettuce on the opposite side of the plates and scoop some of the guacamole onto it. Serve at once.

Franklin Barbecue's Pulled Pork Sandwich

Although beef is foremost in the minds of Texans when you mention barbecue, the pulled pork sandwich served at Austin's wildly popular Franklin Barbecue is so fabulous it is worth the long wait usually required to get one. Adored by everyone from local bloggers to the *New York Times* and *Bon Appetit*, Franklin Barbecue has a line outside its door every single day, and very few complain about waiting three hours or more to get their barbecue. The sandwiches are great to prepare for a crowd, each of whom will love you, especially because they didn't have to stand in line.

MAKES 10 TO 15 SANDWICHES.

1 bone-in pork shoulder butt
   (Boston butt), about 3 to 4 pounds
¼ cup yellow "ballpark-style" mustard
Dry Rub (see recipe below)
Sweet Vinegar Sauce (recipe follows)
Good-quality white burger buns
Melted butter
Your favorite creamy-style coleslaw

DRY RUB:
1 cup coarsely ground black pepper
½ cup kosher salt
½ cup turbinado (raw) sugar

SWEET VINEGAR SAUCE:
2 cups distilled white vinegar
8 ounces ketchup (made without
   high-fructose corn syrup)
¼ cup light brown sugar
2½ tablespoons Worcestershire sauce
¾ teaspoon kosher salt
¼ teaspoon paprika
1 teaspoon Louisiana-style hot sauce
1 teaspoon coarsely ground black
   pepper

Make the dry rub by combining all ingredients in a small bowl and tossing with a fork to blend well; set aside until needed.

Make the sweet vinegar sauce by combining all ingredients in a heavy-bottomed 2-quart saucepan over medium heat. Whisk to blend well and cook just until the brown sugar has dissolved, about 4 minutes. Reheat when needed.

Build a hardwood fire, preferably oak or hickory, in a pit with an indirect firebox. Let the temperature settle at 275°F to 295°F. Meanwhile, place the pork butt on a cutting board and slather all over with the yellow mustard, then scatter the dry rub generously over the pork. When the temperature in the smoking chamber of the pit is right, place the pork butt on the grilling rack, uncovered, and cook until the bark is a toasty brown color, about 30 minutes, turning often.

Wrap the butt in foil and return it to the smoker for another 6 to 8 hours. Periodically check the meat for tenderness by unwrapping and tugging on the bone. When the bone

slides out easily, the meat is done. Remove meat from the pit, still wrapped in the foil, transfer it to a heavy baking sheet, and set aside for 30 minutes.

Unwrap the meat and pull it into shreds, using your fingers. Discard any gristle or tendons. Lightly baste the cut sides of the buns with a little of the melted butter and toast them in a skillet or on a flat grill until light golden brown and slightly crisp. Pile the meat onto the buns and drizzle generously with some of the sweet vinegar sauce. Top with a bit of coleslaw and serve at once.

Low- and Slow-Smoked Baby Back Ribs with Texas Peaches and Whiskey Barbecue Sauce

Pork baby back ribs are a favorite on the Texas barbecue circuit. And there's a definite art to cooking them. For the ultimate tenderness and juiciness, brine them before cooking. Baby backs are best cooked in a pit with a separate firebox so that they cook by indirect heat. They're actually cooked by hot smoke rather than hot coals—low and slow. The Texas Peaches and Whiskey Barbecue Sauce is one I adapted from a friend and fellow cookbook author Rick Rodgers. I added the chipotles for some Texas heat and because they pair so beautifully with our Hill Country peaches.

When I cook baby back ribs, I usually throw some links of good Texas sausage on the pit about 45 minutes before the ribs are done. It makes a great accompaniment, and you can slice up a few links and set them out on a plate to keep the backyard beer drinkers from getting too hungry while the ribs cook.

SERVES 6 TO 8.

BABY BACK RIBS:

2 racks meaty pork baby back ribs, about 4 pounds total

Brine (see recipe on pages 256–257)

Pork Rub (see recipe on pages 302–304)

Texas Peaches and Whiskey Barbecue Sauce (see recipe below)

TEXAS PEACHES AND WHISKEY BARBECUE SAUCE:

4 tablespoons canola oil

2 medium yellow onions, finely chopped

4 garlic cloves, minced

2½ cups ketchup (made without high-fructose corn syrup)

3 canned chipotle chiles in adobo sauce, minced

1½ cups peach preserves*
3 medium Hill Country peaches,
about 24 ounces total, peeled,
pitted, and finely chopped

⅔ cup Texas whiskey
½ cup apple cider vinegar
¼ cup whole-grain mustard

Begin by brining the rib racks. Place the ribs in a large, deep-sided baking dish in a single layer. Make the brine according to the recipe and pour over the ribs. Cover tightly and refrigerate overnight, or up to 24 hours.

Make the sauce. Heat the canola oil in a heavy-bottomed 4-quart saucepan over medium heat. Add the onion and cook, stirring often, until golden brown, about 10 minutes. Add the garlic and cook just until aromatic, about 1 or 2 minutes. Stir in the remaining ingredients, blending well. Bring to a boil, then reduce heat to low. Simmer uncovered, stirring often, until slightly thickened, about 30 minutes. Remove from heat and allow the sauce to cool. When sauce is completely cool, puree it in a high-speed blender until very smooth. Refrigerate in a tightly covered container until ready to serve. Reheat to serve.

To smoke the ribs, build a hardwood oak or hickory fire in the firebox of a smoker. You can add a few mesquite chips for a good hit of Texas smoke. The temperature inside the pit should be between 220°F and 250°F. Remove the ribs from the brine and pat dry with absorbent paper towels. Rub a liberal amount of the pork rub on all sides of the meat, then place the ribs on the cooking rack of the smoker. Cook the ribs, turning often, for about 2 hours, or just until the meat starts to crack between the bones when you bend the rack. Wrap the ribs in heavy-duty foil and return to the pit for another 30 minutes, placing them as far away from the firebox as possible.

To serve the ribs, remove them from the pit and allow them to rest in the foil for 20 minutes. Slice between the individual rib bones and pile them high on a big platter. Serve with chef's tongs for grabbing, and pass the barbecue sauce separately.

---

* I use Fischer & Wieser's Old Fashioned Peach Preserves in the recipe. They are made from an old recipe from the founder of the company Mark Wieser's aunt Estelle, and I think they are the best commercially produced peach preserves in Texas.

SANDSTONE CELLARS WINERY

WHEN ROBERT PARKER, one of the country's most respected wine writers, released the seventh edition of *Parker's Wine Buyer's Guide*, he added a new chapter, "East of the West Coast," to cover wineries from states other than Washington, Oregon, and California. Parker featured six Texas wineries, a huge boost of credibility to the industry. Sandstone Cellars, then only in its fourth year of production and having released only three wines, was one of the six.

Sandstone began, like so many other Texas wineries, when its founders were looking to simplify their lives. Scott Haupert, a Yale-educated concert and studio violist, and Manny Silerio, a high-profile merchandiser for Gap Inc.—close friends since their undergrad days in San Antonio—moved to Manny's hometown, Mason, in 2000. The friends, along with Manny's mother, Santos, opened a taqueria. They also bought a ranch a few miles outside Mason, across the road from a vineyard owned by Harvard-educated, former venture capitalist Don Pullum.

Don liked the Hickory Sand soils, sweet-water aquifer, hot days, and cool nights of Mason County. He planted the first vines at his Akashic Vineyard in 1998, focusing on warm-weather varieties like grenache, mourvèdre, primitivo, sangiovese, and syrah.

Scott and Manny began to hear more and more about the growing wine industry in Texas, so their interest in starting a winery also grew. "Don helped us formulate a plan, and after two years of paperwork, the winery became a reality." In 2004, Sandstone Cellars opened its doors on the square in downtown Mason.

Don, Scott, and Manny craft their wines using only grapes from the growing number of Mason County vineyards. Don calls their wines "fusion wines" because, like a chef who fuses elements from different cuisines into one dish, they blend varieties native to different parts of the Mediterranean into a single wine. Each wine is simply assigned a Roman numeral. However, the Sandstone Cellars VII, recommended by Texas master sommelier Drew Hendricks in *Food and Wine* magazine, was 100 percent touriga. Don found the touriga vintage that year to be too perfect to blend. The Sandstone VII touriga was also featured in *Saveur* magazine as one of "37 Great American Wines."

Sandstone's spirit was well expressed by noted San Diego wine blogger Chris Pratt, when he wrote about the Sandstone Cellars III: "And when I come across something like this wine, I really do get excited at the possibility that someone, a pioneer,

may be discovering (crafting?) something new, something specifically Texan, something that a hundred years from now will be as well known as, say, California Zinfandel." Sandstone has become one of the state's most popular boutique wineries.

The Braised Shoulder of Lamb with Aromatics and Rosemary Demi-Glace (pages 275–277) is a rich and complex dish. Pair it with the Sandstone Cellars VI, a full-bodied blend of touriga nacional, barbera, primitivo, and zinfandel. Pair the Grilled Double Lamb Chops with Garlic and Cilantro Pesto with Jalapeño, a medium-bodied dish (pages 277–278), with Sandstone Cellars XI, a medium-bodied wine produced from syrah, mourvèdre, touriga nacional, and viognier.

A rich mole sauce can render wine into dumb simplicity, but Iliana de la Vega's Mole Coloradito with Roasted Pork Tenderloin (pages 248–250) has found its match with the Sandstone Cellars VII. This particular mole is rich and complex, but the body is tempered by its pairing with pork tenderloin. This dish does not have simple umami; it has uuuuuumami!, as does the Sandstone Cellars VII, with its savory, earthy bouquet and flavor.

TWIN COUNTY LAMB

THE WENDEL FAMILY RANCH sits in the heart of the Texas Hill Country near Harper. Following a career with the US Department of Agriculture, Lloyd Wendel retired to his family's ranch and planned to pursue his hobby of woodworking. However, the pull of the land was stronger than his desire to retire.

Lloyd's wife, Isabelle Lauzierre, was born in West Africa, where sheep are raised for their wool as well as their meat, and mutton is more common than lamb, but she was not fond of the flavor. In 2004, Isabelle and Lloyd were at a family gathering where the main course was grilled Dorper lamb. For Isabelle, it was a revelation. "This is what lamb should taste like! Everybody needs to discover this fantastic meat!" she proclaimed to the table.

Isabelle soon discovered that the Dorper was developed in South Africa by breeders seeking to improve the quality of lamb meat. In fact, Dorpers shed their wool, requiring no shearing. Isabelle says that most of the birds' nests on and around their farm are quite cozy, as they're made with twigs and the naturally shed wool!

A few months following their fateful dinner, Lloyd and Isabelle purchased eight Dorper ewes. A year later, they got their first ram. Their animals are fed an all-natural, all-vegetarian diet, supplemented only when native grasses are in short supply. Supplemental hay for the lambs is produced from sorghum and oats grown at the ranch, so the taste of the meat is totally Texas terroir, whether the animals graze on the natural grasses or eat the supplemental hay.

While beef remains the king of meats in Texas, the tide is turning as Texans expand their culinary paradigms. A great many have learned that lamb, carefully raised and properly prepared, can be an incredible dining experience. Twin County Lamb is now featured on the menus of numerous restaurants in the Austin and Hill Country region.

Braised Shoulder of Lamb with Aromatics and Rosemary Demi-Glace

The most popular cuts of lamb are the rack and double-cut rib chops (if you're grilling), or the leg (if roasting). No doubt about it, those are mighty fine meats. But there are other equally delicious cuts that deserve recognition. One of my favorites is lamb shoulder. Because the shoulder is a cut that gets lots of exercise, it's very flavorful but also very tough, so it requires a moist-heat cooking method like braising. Here the meat is first pan-seared to give it a great-flavored crust, then slowly braised in lamb stock on top of a full-bodied collection of aromatic herbs and vegetables, and finally quickly broiled with a hint of Marsala wine. The crowning glory is a little douse of rosemary demi-glace accented with a hit of deep-flavored, meaty Texas Syrah. I like to serve the dish with Fresh Greens and Goat Cheese Gratin (see recipe on page 356) and simple oven-roasted potatoes.

SERVES 4 TO 6.

LAMB:

1 Twin County boneless shoulder of lamb (3 pounds)

Kosher salt and freshly ground black pepper

Texas extra-virgin olive oil for searing

1 small fennel bulb, root end removed, stalks and leafy tops cut into 2-inch sections

2 sweet Texas 1015 onions, halved and sliced thin

⅓ cup minced garlic

2 fresh rosemary sprigs, 3 inches long

4 fresh thyme sprigs

4 flat-leaf parsley sprigs

4 fresh bay leaves

6 whole cloves

2 quarts lamb stock

⅔ cup Marsala wine

¼ pound (1 stick) unsalted butter, cut into ½-inch cubes

Kosher salt or fine sea salt and freshly ground black pepper

ROSEMARY DEMI-GLACE:

2 cups gelatinous beef stock

2 cups gelatinous lamb stock

1 sprig fresh rosemary, 3 inches long

¼ cup Texas Syrah

2 tablespoons unsalted butter

2 shallots, minced

Kosher salt and freshly ground black pepper

Preheat oven to 300°F. Pat the lamb shoulder very dry, using absorbent paper towels. Season the meat on both sides with salt and freshly ground black pepper; set aside at room temperature for 30 minutes. Heat a glaze of canola oil about ⅛-inch deep in a heavy-bottomed 6-quart Dutch oven or roasting pan over medium-high heat. When the surface of the oil is shimmering hot, add the lamb shoulder and sear until deeply browned, about 10 minutes. Turn the meat and brown on the other side until deeply browned. Remove from heat and remove the meat to a platter.

Carefully pour off the fat from the pan, leaving the caramelized meat glaze in the bottom. Arrange all of the vegetables, herbs, and whole cloves in the bottom of the pan. Place the meat on the vegetables and pour any accumulated juices from the platter over the meat. Add lamb stock to cover the meat. Roast in preheated oven 2½ hours, then turn the meat and roast an additional 2½ hours.

While the meat is cooking, make the rosemary demi-glace. Combine the beef and lamb stocks with the rosemary sprig in a heavy-bottomed 4-quart saucepan over medium-low heat. Cook the stocks slowly, stirring occasionally, until they become syrupy and have reduced to about one-fifth their original volume, or about ¾ cup. Add the Syrah and cook to reduce slightly until syrupy consistency returns. Strain the demi-glace, discarding the rosemary sprig. Set aside.

Melt the 2 tablespoons of butter in a heavy-bottomed skillet over medium-high heat. When the butter has melted and the foam subsides, add the shallots and cook until wilted and transparent, about 6 minutes. Whisk in the demi-glace vigorously and season to taste with salt and freshly ground black pepper. Set aside to keep warm. Preheat broiler and place oven rack 6 inches below heat source.

Remove the meat from the pan and cut into serving pieces. Cover with foil to keep hot. Strain the pan juices through a fine strainer or chinois into a bowl, pressing down on the aromatics to squeeze out all liquid. Discard aromatics and wipe the roasting pan clean. Set aside.

Pour 1 cup of the strained pan juices into a heavy-bottomed 2-quart saucepan over medium-high heat. Add the Marsala and cook until reduced by one-third. Remove from heat and vigorously whisk in the butter cubes all at once. Continue to whisk until butter has melted and sauce is smooth and thick. Arrange the serving pieces of meat in the cleaned roasting pan and pour the Marsala glaze over them. Place pan under preheated broiler for 2 to 3 minutes. Take extreme care not to burn the meat. Set aside to keep warm.

To serve the meat, place a portion of the meat on each plate and spoon a portion of the demi-glace over the top, or serve the meat on a platter and pass the sauce separately. Serve hot.

Grilled Double Lamb Chops with Garlic and Cilantro Pesto with Jalapeño

When grilled to a perfect medium rare, the flavor of lamb chops is just irresistible—slightly earthy and subtly rich. So I don't like to mask that marvelous taste with heavy sauces. The pesto adds a bit of zest and a punch of garlic without overwhelming the flavor of the meat. "French-boned" chops have all of the meat removed from the slender top portion of the bone, leaving the bone bare. But some folks, including my husband, find munching on the bones one of the best parts of eating the chops, so feel free to skip buying "frenched" chops.

SERVES 4.

2 french-boned lamb rib racks, each
    8-bone racks
Texas extra-virgin olive oil

Kosher salt and freshly ground
    black pepper

GARLIC AND CILANTRO PESTO WITH JALAPEÑO:
MAKES ABOUT 3 CUPS.

4 bunches fresh cilantro, washed and
dried well

2 bunches fresh mint

⅓ cup minced raw garlic

¼ cup skin-on sliced almonds, toasted

½ cup minced jalapeño

1 cup red wine vinegar

½ teaspoon kosher salt

1 teaspoon cayenne

⅓ cup Texas extra-virgin olive oil,
or more, depending on consistency
desired

Make the pesto first. Combine all ingredients in the work bowl of a food processor fitted with the steel blade. Process until smooth. The mixture should be fairly stiff and spreadable. If you prefer a looser consistency, add additional olive oil. Refrigerate until ready to serve. Serve at room temperature.

Build a hardwood charcoal fire and allow the fire to burn down to the point where the coals are glowing red, covered by a layer of white ash. Or heat a gas char-grill to medium-high heat. Cut the lamb racks into 2-bone portions. You should have a total of 8 double chops.

Glaze both sides of each chop with some of the olive oil. Season each side with salt and freshly ground black pepper. Grill the chops on the first side for about 3 to 4 minutes. Turn the chops and grill for about 3 minutes longer for medium-rare chops. Internal temperature should be 128°F to 130°F. Grill 6 minutes after turning for medium, or to the desired degree of doneness. Serve 2 double chops per person, with a side ramekin of the pesto.

STONE HOUSE VINEYARD AND WINERY

ANGELA AND HOWARD MOENCH have long been enthusiastic about good wine and food. Angela is a graduate of the Cordon Bleu in London and hails from Australia's Barossa Valley, home to some of that country's best wines. But when the pair acquired land on Lake Travis in the Texas Hill County in 1996, they had no intention of planting vines.

Within a year, however, the idea of joining the evolving Texas wine industry was growing on them. In 1999, they planted seven acres of Norton grapes on their property. The Norton is an American hybrid grape that has a long history. It was the result of crossbreeding by Virginian Daniel Norton in the 1820s. Its parents are unknown, except that one was European *Vitis vinifera* and the other local—likely *Vitis aestivalis*.

Having a vineyard in Texas certainly has its challenges, but the Norton has a few advantages with its late bud break (thereby avoiding the late freezes so common in the lake region) and its tolerance of disease pressure, which is a huge factor in vineyards in Texas. Angela says the Norton grape allows her to work with nature, not against it.

The first vintage of Claros, the wine crafted from Stone House's Norton grapes, made a notable debut. It was awarded a Double Gold Medal in the prestigious 2004 Pacific Rim International Wine Competition.

Angela paired two of her wines with one of the most interesting dishes in this book—Tim Byres's Roasted Rabbit Leg with Fig Jam (pages 290–292). The Stone House Riesling, a slightly off-dry wine, is a great play on the flavors of this intricate recipe. The Claros, made from the Norton grape for which the winery has become known, has spicy notes that also complement the dish.

Angela also suggests the Claros with Ross Burtwell's Bison Enchiladas (page 283). The full-bodied wine naturally complements the robust flavors of this dish with the elegance of spicy fruit, soft tannins from the French oak, natural lively acidity, and a long smooth finish. As an alternative, try Angela's Wish, her full-bodied blend of cabernet sauvignon and shiraz.

NORTH AMERICAN BISON

Bison, buffalo, *cibolo* (in Spanish), or *tatanka* ("lord of the plains," in Lakota): whatever name it is called, no other animal has played such a significant role in America's history. Bison were essential to Native American life, providing food, shelter, clothing, and tools as well as spiritual protection. They are the largest terrestrial animals on the North American continent. By the age of seven, the average bull weighs more than 2,000 pounds and stands five to six-and-a-half-feet tall at the shoulder.

Most people know their sad story, though fewer have followed their comeback. At the beginning of the nineteenth century, before Lewis and Clark, the Indian wars, the railroads, and other threats to their existence, there were estimated to be 40 to 60 million bison roaming the plains. Before the end of the century, there were fewer than 1,000 animals. Today, however, because of conservation efforts by ranchers, Native Americans who maintain herds, and the public parks such as Yellowstone or Texas's own Caprock Canyons State Park that protect them, bison numbers are thought to be around 400,000 and growing.

Today's bison fall into one of two categories, defined by genetics as well as geography. When the Transcontinental Railroad was built in the mid-1800s, the bison were split into what became known as the Northern and Southern herds. The Southern herd included animals from Texas, eastern New Mexico, eastern Colorado, Kansas, Oklahoma, and southern Nebraska. Southern Plains bison tend to have a smaller bone structure than those in the Northern herd and have shorter hair, traits that allow them to tolerate a warmer climate.

The Texas Parks and Wildlife Department maintains the largest herd of Southern Plains bison as part of Caprock Canyons State Park in the Texas Panhandle. It includes the last vestiges of the herd started in the 1880s by Texan Charles Goodnight, one of the most prosperous cattlemen in the American West. But it was a newly prosperous media mogul who saved the herd when inbreeding threatened to wipe it out. Ted Turner owns the largest private bison herd in the world, some 55,000 head, which roam on his 14 ranches in seven states. Significantly, some of Turner's bison have ties to the original Goodnight herd. Turner donated three bulls to the Texas herd, providing the genetic diversity that the herd so desperately needed. The herd is growing again at a steady pace, ranging on 10,000 acres of land that their ancestors roamed tens of thousands of years before them.

In recent years, bison meat has been rediscovered by Texas chefs, who praise it for its delicious taste and low fat, and it appears on menus around the state. Two producers in Texas are growing sustainable herds of bison for meat production.

THUNDER HEART BISON

THE SHAPE RANCH, owned by Hugh Fitzsimons and his wife, Sarah, is near the Mexican border southwest of Carrizo Springs. The remote property is covered with mesquite, prickly pear, and native grasses. It's rugged land, crisscrossed with rutted red dirt roads, and there are no fences. So, as you bounce down the roads in ranch manager Freddy Longoria's pickup truck, it seems quite natural to see a pod of bison emerge from the brush.

The Fitzsimons family acquired the land in the 1930s and raised cattle there until 1998, when the land was apportioned among the Fitzsimons siblings, with Hugh receiving the 13,000 acres that became the Shape Ranch. He wanted to use the land in a sustainable way and not run up a king's ransom in vet bills. He didn't want to raise cattle. His views on today's cattle industry are pretty straightforward: "Most cattle end up in feedlots, and we've basically destroyed them with diseases and hormones."

In his book *The Worst Hard Time*, author Timothy Egan describes the bison as "the finest grass-eating creature on four legs." The bison's symbiotic relationship with the land allows Hugh to raise them as wild animals. He provides only water and grass and doesn't interfere in their life cycle.

When Hugh sent his first bison to the slaughterhouse, he found the meat was so soaked with adrenaline released when the wild creature was loaded into a trailer and hauled away to the trauma of the slaughterhouse that it was literally inedible. He built an abattoir on the ranch, which is operated under USDA inspection. Now the animals (usually four-year-old bulls) are field-harvested and processed on the ranch within an hour of being killed. Thunder Heart Bison is certified Animal Welfare Approved, the only bison ranch in the United States to meet the stringent and exacting requirements of the AWA.

Hugh used to ship to high-end chefs all over the country, including New York's Daniel Boulud, but the demand in Texas was very high. He also felt that to really fulfill his mission, he should keep the meat local. Now he sells only to Texas restaurants. It's also available at Austin farmers' markets.

Bison Enchiladas

The Cabernet Grill in Fredericksburg is owned by Ross Burtwell, a talented chef and staunch advocate of all Texas foods and beverages. He was the first chef in Texas to dedicate his entire wine list to Texas wines. This recipe for Ross's Bison Enchiladas is one of the most popular dishes on his menu, with the assertive flavor of Veldhuizen Family Farm's Texas Gold Cheddar matching the robust flavor of the bison to create a rich and delicious combination.

SERVES 6.

1 cup canola oil
12 white corn tortillas
2 pounds Bison Machaca
  (see recipe below)
1½ cups (6 ounces) shredded
  Veldhuizen Family Farm Texas
  Gold Cheddar

1½ cups Green Chile Crema
  (see recipe below)
1 cup Pickled Red Onion Slaw
  (recipe follows)
1 cup Serrano Pico de Gallo
  (recipe follows)
Minced cilantro

BISON MACHACA:
MAKES 2 POUNDS.

2 tablespoons canola oil
2 pounds bison stew meat, trimmed
  of fat and sinew
⅓ cup diced yellow onion
1 carrot, peeled and halved lengthwise
1 celery stalk, halved lengthwise
2 garlic cloves, minced
1 tablespoon medium-hot chili
  powder
1 tablespoon toasted, then ground,
  cumin seeds

1 teaspoon dried Mexican oregano
3 fresh bay leaves, minced
1 teaspoon freshly ground black
  pepper
2 teaspoons kosher salt
2 cups beef stock, preferably
  homemade
1 pasilla chile, seeds removed, toasted
½ cup peeled and diced heirloom or
  homegrown tomatoes

GREEN CHILE CREMA:
MAKES 2 CUPS.

2 tablespoons canola oil
½ cup minced shallots
½ cup Texas Chardonnay
2 cups Mexican crema, or substitute
  whipping cream

½ teaspoon Cholula Hot Sauce
½ cup finely chopped, blistered, and
  peeled poblano chiles
Kosher salt and freshly ground black
  pepper

PICKLED RED ONION SLAW:

MAKES 1 CUP.

1 medium red onion, sliced very thin, preferably on a mandoline

½ cup thin-sliced red cabbage

½ cup shredded carrots

1 jalapeño, seeds and veins removed, minced

Juice of 1 lime

2½ tablespoons Texas extra-virgin olive oil

1 tablespoon sugar

Pinch of Mexican oregano

Kosher salt and freshly ground black pepper

SERRANO PICO DE GALLO:

Ross likes food that bites back, so he leaves the seeds in the serrano chiles when he makes this pico de gallo. If you'd like a little less heat, remove the seeds and veins from the chiles.

MAKES ABOUT 1 CUP.

½ cup ¼-inch-dice yellow onion

½ cup ¼-inch-dice homegrown Roma tomatoes

2 serrano chiles, minced

¼ bunch cilantro leaves and tender top stems, minced

1 tablespoon Texas extra-virgin olive oil

Kosher salt and freshly ground black pepper

Begin by making the pickled red onion slaw. Toss all ingredients together in a medium bowl and season to taste with salt and pepper. Let sit at room temperature for 1 hour. Check seasoning, adjusting as desired. Use immediately or refrigerate, tightly covered.

Make the bison machaca. Preheat oven to 350°F. Heat the canola oil in an ovenproof, heavy-bottomed 14-inch skillet over medium-high heat. When the oil is hot, add the bison meat and sear on all sides. Remove meat from pan and set aside.

Add the onion, celery, and carrot to the pan and cook to brown and sear the vegetables. Add all seasonings and sauté briefly. Add the stock, scraping up browned bits from the bottom of the pan with a spatula. Return the meat to the pan and add the pasilla chile and tomatoes. Cover pan and place in preheated oven. Cook for about 3 hours, or until the meat begins to fall apart. Remove from heat and allow the meat to cool in the broth. Strain the meat, reserving the broth. Discard carrots, celery, and pasilla chile.

Shred the meat by hand, removing any pieces of fat or gristle that may remain. Add the braising liquid back to the meat.

While the meat is cooking, make the serrano pico de gallo. Mix all ingredients together in a small bowl and season to taste with salt and pepper. Refrigerate until ready to use.

Make the green chile crema. Heat the canola oil in a heavy-bottomed 2-quart saucepan over medium-low heat. Add the shallots and cook slowly until they are wilted and translucent, stirring often. Do not allow them to brown. Add the wine and increase heat to medium high. Cook to reduce the wine to about 2 tablespoons. Add the Mexican crema and reduce to 1½ cups. Remove the pan from heat and pour the mixture through a fine strainer, pressing down on the solids to extract all liquid; discard shallots.

Return the sauce to a clean saucepan over low heat and add the hot sauce and poblano chiles. Whisk to incorporate and adjust seasonings as desired with salt and pepper. Keep warm while preparing the enchiladas.

Preheat oven to 350°F. Place the cup of canola oil in a heavy-bottomed 10-inch skillet over medium-high heat. When the oil is hot, dip the tortillas, one at a time, using chef's tongs, into the hot oil for just a few seconds to soften them and make them pliable. Drain well on paper towels and allow them to cool until they can be handled.

To assemble the enchiladas, divide the machaca evenly between the tortillas, spreading it the length of the tortillas just to the side of the center. Top each with a portion of the shredded cheese. Roll up enchiladas and place them, seam side down, in a single layer in a baking dish. Bake in preheated oven for about 10 minutes, or until warmed throughout.

Serve 2 enchiladas per person, topping each serving with a portion of crema, then a little pile of the slaw. Top with a spoon of the pico de gallo and garnish with a scattering of minced cilantro. Serve at once.

PEDERNALES CELLARS WINERY

ESTLED IN THE HILLS overlooking historic Stonewall in the heart of the Texas Wine Country, Pedernales Cellars has a very workable philosophy: Keep it simple, keep it traditional, and produce some of the most distinctive wines in Texas—wines that exemplify the boldness and resilience of the state itself.

The winery was founded in 2005 by David Kuhlken and Fredrik Osterberg to expand the vineyard that David's parents started in the early 1990s, supplying grapes to a number of then-fledgling Hill Country wineries. David and Fredrik left successful careers in software and banking, respectively. David is the winemaker, while Fredrik handles the business end of the operation.

Fredrik notes, "We feel very lucky to be part of something special happening in Texas. The Texas wine industry is really coming into its own. As Texas wineries continue to cultivate the varietals that thrive best in the state, Texas will only continue to gain recognition for quality wine."

One of those varietals is tempranillo, a grape that originated in Spain's Rioja region. Pedernales Cellars began producing tempranillo in 2006. Another varietal made for the challenges presented by the Texas terroir is viognier, from the southern Rhone Valley of France. Its ability to thrive in diverse soil types and the hot Texas climate, as well as its ability to withstand late freezes and drought, make it an excellent grape as a stand-alone white with big fruit flavors or for blends. Pedernales Cellars bottled its first Viognier in 2007, and like Tempranillo, it has emerged as a star varietal for the winery.

The Pedernales Cellars Texas Tempranillo is a great match for the Grilled Bison Tenderloin with Balsamic-Horseradish Aioli (pages 286–288), as is the Pedernales Tempranillo Reserve. The former

is available through general distribution, but the reserve is available only at the winery.

Rabbit dishes can make for tough wine pairing, but the Hasenpfeffer (pages 288–290), with its hefty dose of black pepper, pairs well with the Pedernales Cellars GSM, a blend of grenache-syrah-mourvèdre. Or for an over-the-top pairing, try the estate blend Pedernales Block One, which is available only at the winery—but worth the trip!

Grilled Bison Tenderloin with Balsamic-Horseradish Aioli

Because it does so little work during the bison's lifetime, the tenderloin muscle is the tenderest of any cut available. Hardwood-grilled bison tenderloin is a tender and extremely flavorful choice for a medium-sized crowd, and it's a great conversation maker! I "borrowed" this delicious sauce from my good friend Kevin Henning, an avid hunter, who served it alongside a perfectly grilled elk tenderloin. If you opt to serve the tenderloin simply sliced on a platter, place a bowl of the sauce alongside. I like to serve the tenderloin with Creamy Mushroom Grits (see recipe on page 374).

I developed the procedure for grilling the tenderloin using a pristine whole bison tenderloin from Lucky B Bison. Lucky B, located in Bryan, was founded in 1983 by Reagan Brown, a former commissioner of the Texas Department of Agriculture, and his wife, Gladys. The pair initially saw the ranch as an investment in a small cattle operation, but on further thinking about operating yet another cattle ranch, they felt that bison would be a more sustainable alternative, even though cattle are certainly king in Texas. Reagan Brown died in 1999 as the result of a tractor accident on the ranch. His daughter Beverly and her husband, Donnis, carry on his spirit of pride for the herd. They continued to expand their herd and today maintain it at around 45 animals.

SERVES 8.

1 bison tenderloin, about 4 pounds, trimmed of fat and silverskin
Grilling Paste (see recipe below)
Balsamic-Horseradish Aioli
  (recipe follows)

GRILLING PASTE:
½ cup granulated garlic
¼ cup Lawry's brand seasoning salt
¼ cup ground black pepper
⅓ cup light brown sugar
1½ teaspoons minced fresh thyme
1 teaspoon minced fresh rosemary
2 shallots, minced
½ cup MSG-free beef base paste
¼ cup sherry wine vinegar

BALSAMIC-HORSERADISH AIOLI:
MAKES ABOUT 2¼ CUPS.
2 large garlic cloves
3 egg yolks
3 tablespoons aged balsamic vinegar
2 heaping tablespoons prepared
  horseradish
1 tablespoon Dijon mustard
1 teaspoon freshly ground black
  pepper
1 cup Texas extra-virgin olive oil
1 cup canola oil
Kosher salt

Begin by making the balsamic-horseradish aioli. Place the steel blade in the work bowl of a food processor. With processor running, drop the garlic clove through the feed tube to mince. Stop machine and scrape down sides of bowl. Add the egg yolks, balsamic vinegar, horseradish, mustard, and pepper to the processor bowl. Process until the mixture is light and fluffy and the yolks are light lemon-yellow in color, about 5 minutes. Combine the olive and canola oils. Again with the processor running, add the combined oils in a slow, steady stream through the feed tube until all has been added. Process an additional 15 seconds to form a strong emulsion. Transfer the aioli to a storage container with a tight-fitting lid and refrigerate for up to 2 days.

Make the grilling paste. Combine all ingredients in a medium bowl and stir to blend well, making sure all ingredients are thoroughly incorporated. Refrigerate in a tightly covered container until ready to use. You may not need all of the paste for the tenderloin. The remainder may be refrigerated for up to 2 weeks in a tightly sealed container for use on other red meats.

To grill the tenderloin, first tie it at 1½- to 2-inch intervals, using butcher's twine, to maintain its shape. Rub the tenderloin all over with a thick layer of the grilling paste. Place on a baking sheet lined with foil and set aside at room temperature for 1 hour.

If possible, use a barbecue grill or pit with an external thermometer so you can carefully monitor the temperature inside the pit. I recommend using a hardwood charcoal fire. For bison I like to use mesquite hardwood charcoal because it has a sweeter and more delicate flavor than either hickory or oak. But be aware that mesquite tends to burn hot, so monitor your meat carefully. If you can get your hands on some red wine-barrel chips, soak them in water for an hour or so and throw them on the fire. They add a delightful depth of flavor, and the fire smells wonderful! Allow the coals to burn down to the point where they are glowing red, covered by a layer of white ash.

When the temperature in the pit reaches a steady 250°F, place the tenderloin in the pit. Cook, turning often, for about 30 to 35 minutes for medium rare. As the meat cooks, spread additional grilling paste on it. Use an instant-read meat thermometer to check the temperature. When it reaches 125°F, remove the tenderloin to a platter and loosely cover with foil. Set aside to rest for 15 minutes. The meat will continue to cook from the heat inside. The *resting* period allows the juices, which have been driven to the center of the meat by the heat, to redistribute throughout the entire piece of meat. Using a sharp knife, cut the tenderloin into ½-inch thick slices on the bias and serve with the aioli.

Hasenpfeffer (German Peppered Hare)

This is a grand dish with a complex flavor. One of my earliest good food memories is that of my father and grandfather going rabbit hunting. When they would come home bearing several rabbits, I knew that a big pot of my grandmother's delicious Hasenpfeffer would be on the table in a few hours. If you don't have a hunter in the house, you can find dressed rabbit at specialty markets. Or better yet, check with livestock producers at your local farmers' market, as many are raising rabbit for meat. Traditionally, Hasenpfeffer is served with spaetzle and braised red cabbage.

SERVES 4 TO 6.

1 rabbit, about 3 pounds, dressed and cut into serving pieces*
Marinade (recipe follows)
½ cup all-purpose flour, seasoned with 1 teaspoon kosher salt and

1 teaspoon freshly ground black pepper
8 slices applewood-smoked bacon, cut into ½-inch dice
½ cup finely chopped shallots

2 large garlic cloves, minced

4 whole allspice berries, ground

⅛ teaspoon ground cloves

1 heaping teaspoon minced
fresh thyme

½ teaspoon minced fresh rosemary

2 teaspoons freshly ground
black pepper

1½ cups beef broth, preferably
homemade

½ cup apple brandy

1 tablespoon red currant jelly

4 tablespoons unsalted butter,
softened and blended thoroughly
with 4 tablespoons all-purpose
flour, until no traces of flour remain

1 tablespoon minced flat-leaf parsley

MARINADE:

2 cups dry red wine

2 cups sliced onion

4 fresh bay leaves, minced

4 juniper berries, crushed

Begin by marinating the rabbit. Combine marinade ingredients. Arrange rabbit pieces in a single layer in a baking dish. Add the marinade and turn the rabbit to coat all sides. Cover and refrigerate overnight, turning the pieces several times.

Remove rabbit from marinade and set aside. Strain the marinade through a fine strainer, discarding the solids; reserve liquid. Pat rabbit dry and dredge the pieces in the seasoned flour, coating well and shaking off excess flour; set aside.

Cook the diced bacon in a heavy-bottomed Dutch oven over medium-high heat until it has rendered its fat and is crisp. Remove bacon with a slotted spoon and drain on paper towels; set aside. Reserve bacon drippings in the pan. Add the rabbit pieces to the pan in batches, cooking on both sides, turning once, just until golden brown, about 6 minutes. Place rabbit on a plate and set aside. Add the shallots, garlic, allspice berries, cloves, thyme, rosemary, and black pepper to the pan and sauté, stirring often, until shallots are very wilted and transparent, about 7 minutes.

Add the reserved marinade liquid, beef broth, and apple brandy to the pan, scraping up the browned bits from the bottom of the pan with a spatula. Return rabbit pieces to the pan, cover, and simmer for about 1½ hours, or until rabbit is fork tender.

Remove the rabbit pieces from the pan; set aside to keep warm. Stir the red currant jelly into the sauce and stir until jelly is melted. Bring the sauce to a full boil, then begin to add pieces of the butter and flour mixture, stirring well after each addition, until sauce reaches the desired consistency. It should be about medium thick like cream gravy. Stir in the minced parsley and return rabbit to the pan. Serve hot.

----

* To cut up a whole rabbit, break the joints of the forelegs from the body at the shoulder and remove with a sharp knife. Disjoint the hind legs at the hip and cut them off. Cut hind legs at the knee joints. Remove the loin from the rib section, then cut the rib section in half. Trim off the lower portion of the rib sections, which are mostly bone, using kitchen shears.

Tim Byres's Roasted Rabbit Leg with Fig Jam

Tim Byres is the co-owner and chef of Dallas's acclaimed SMOKE. He is passionate about cooking all kinds of meats by various methods, especially fire. The meats at SMOKE are cooked slowly over hardwood coals, and he often prepares meats not ordinarily used, delighting his customers with new and delicious tastes.

Rabbit was a staple on the tables of the Texas frontier, and an increasing number of local farms are responding to the increased demand for the lean protein by raising hormone-free rabbits on a diet of all-natural feeds. Tim Byres sources his rabbit from the JuHa Ranch in Barry. While Tim uses only the legs in this fabulous recipe, the rest of the animal can be used to make a delicious paté or terrine; or poached and baked into a rabbit pie, much like a chicken pot pie; or cut into serving pieces and added to a batch of Hasen-pfeffer, a traditional German rabbit stew (see recipe on pages 288–290).

SERVES 4.

FIG JAM:
20 dried Mission figs, about 2 cups
1 cup dry red wine
¼ cup water
1 ancho chile, toasted, stem and
   seeds removed
¼ cup dark brown sugar

RABBIT:
4 rabbit legs
4 thin slices Parma or Serrano ham,
   or cured ham sliced paper thin
4 pieces (each about 4 × 6 inches)
   caul fat

VEGETABLE BASE:

1 tablespoon plus 1 teaspoon Texas extra-virgin olive oil, divided

3 large garlic cloves, peeled, stem end removed, sliced paper thin

4 red new potatoes, boiled whole until medium-tender and cooled, then sliced ⅜-inch thick

1 small white onion, cut into ½-inch dice

2 jalapeños, quartered, stems, veins, and seeds removed, cut into ½-inch dice

3 large limes, halved

TO FINISH:

¼ cup sour cream

Kosher salt

1 teaspoon coarsely ground pink peppercorns

½ bunch picked cilantro sprigs

In a small, heavy-bottomed saucepan, combine the dried figs, red wine, water, ancho chile, and brown sugar. Bring to a simmer, cover, and cook for about 15 to 20 minutes, or until figs are very tender.

While the figs are simmering, using a small, sharp knife, slit open the thigh of the rabbit legs and remove the thighbone. Conservatively season the inside of the thigh with kosher salt.

When the figs are tender, remove 8 of them from the pan and set aside. Transfer the remainder of the figs and liquid to a high-speed blender and puree; set aside. You should have 1 cup of jam. Cut off the stems of the reserved 8 figs and slice the figs in half lengthwise. Lay 4 fig slices in each thigh and wrap the flesh of the thigh around the figs.

Lay the legs, seam side down, crosswise, in the center of each slice of ham. Wrap the ham around the thigh. Then lay the legs, ham seam side down, on the pieces of caul fat. Wrap the entire leg completely in the fat. The goal here is to cover and seal the seams. Preheat the oven to 350°F.

Season the legs sparingly with kosher salt, remembering the salty ham inside. Add 1 tablespoon of the olive oil to a heavy-bottomed 12-inch sauté pan over medium-high heat. Lay the wrapped rabbit legs in the pan and sear on all sides until golden brown.

Remove legs from the sauté pan and place them on a baking sheet. Transfer the baking sheet to preheated oven and cook to an internal temperature of 155°F on an instant-read thermometer.

While the rabbit legs are roasting, add the sliced garlic to the hot sauté pan in which the legs were seared. Sauté the garlic just to brown lightly, taking care not to burn it. Remove the garlic with a slotted spoon and set aside. Add the precooked potatoes to the hot pan, making sure each potato lies flat, touching the pan. Season to taste with kosher salt. Sauté until the potatoes are golden brown on both sides. Remove potatoes and set aside to keep hot.

Add the remaining teaspoon of olive oil to the hot pan and allow the oil to get very hot, rippling on the surface. Add the onion and jalapeños at once and season with kosher salt. Don't stir the vegetables; allow the onion to caramelize, but not burn, and the jalapeño to roast. Once the vegetables have browned on one side, toss or flip and brown them on the other side.

Add the browned garlic back to the pan and add the juice of half a lime. Stir rapidly to deglaze the pan, scraping up all browned bits from the bottom. Remove pan from heat.

When the rabbit legs are done, remove them from the oven and cover loosely with foil; set aside to rest for 10 minutes. (They will continue to carry-over cook to the perfect internal temperature.) Cut the thigh portion of each leg into ½-inch slices, but keep them intact and the legs separate.

To plate and serve the dish, spoon 1 tablespoon of the fig jam on each serving plate. Lay slices of the potatoes on the fig jam, then top the potatoes with 1 tablespoon of sour cream. Spoon ¼ of the onion/jalapeño mixture over the potatoes on each plate. The layering of the flavors is important so that each bite contains perfectly balanced sweet, salty, tangy, heat, and acidity. The cool sour cream is melted by the hot vegetables and, along with the jam, creates a rich sauce. Arrange the rabbit legs on top of the vegetables, fanning the sliced thigh meat out slightly, but leaving the slices overlapping. Season each leg with kosher salt, ¼ teaspoon of the pink peppercorns, and a squeeze of lime. Garnish with some of the cilantro.

BROKEN ARROW RANCH

THE BROKEN ARROW RANCH in Ingram was founded in 1983 by Mike Hughes and his wife, Elizabeth. The Hugheses traveled frequently and noticed that venison and other wild game meats were prominent on European restaurant menus but not so in Texas. Mike also knew that large numbers of exotic species had been imported to Texas ranches for hunting purposes and that these animals had proliferated to the point that they were overgrazing Hill Country ranchlands. It was not a sustainable situation for either the animals or the land.

Being a driven man, Hughes began a campaign to create a legal venison industry in Texas and the United States. There were no laws allowing such a business to exist, nor were there laws preventing it. He met with Texas legislators to see about classifying exotic (nonnative) animals as livestock, which meant they could be bought, sold, and inspected for meat. He worked with Texas Parks and Wildlife game wardens to clarify hunting laws as they pertained to exotic animals. Finally, he met with the Texas and US Departments of Agriculture officials to convince them that field harvesting and mobile processing of animals could be done safely and within the existing framework already established for brick-and-mortar processing plants. In the end, Hughes built the first mobile processing unit, then applied for a grant of inspection. The unit met all

of the requirements, and nothing said it couldn't be on wheels, so the Texas Department of Agriculture gave it the stamp of approval. The processing unit was driven to the ranch, and Hughes began harvesting exotic deer and wild boar.

Broken Arrow is the only supplier of "wild" venison in the nation. The company employs professional hunters who harvest free-range game, using techniques that reduce stress in the animals, resulting in a better-quality meat, from more than 100 Texas ranches, which comprise about a million acres. The game grazes on native vegetation, giving the meat the complex natural flavors not found in strictly farm-raised animals. In addition to venison, Broken Arrow supplies wild boar and black antelope (nilgai) to chefs all over the country.

When Hughes decided it was time to retire, his son, Chris, purchased the company from his parents in 2010. Chris had literally grown up in the business, helping his dad at trade shows doing product demonstrations and hosting chef retreats at the family's ranch in Ingram. In 2012, the company processed more than 240,000 pounds of venison and wild boar, shipping their meats to 49 states and Washington, D.C. Broken Arrow meats are purchased by small-town cafés and Michelin-starred restaurants. In addition, the company maintains a large retail trade through its website.

John Sheely's Grilled Broken Arrow Ranch Rack of Venison with Shallot–Black Cherry Compote and Fall Vegetable Hash

Chef John Sheely, a native Houstonian, came to cooking not exactly by choice but by default. During high school in the Memorial area of Houston, he worked part-time in fast-food restaurants to earn spending money. On a spring-break ski trip to Colorado, the chef-to-be set his sights on returning to the region to be a "ski bum." After graduating from high school, John did move to Colorado to indulge his passion for skiing. He fell in love with

Vail, where, to support his skiing, he turned again to the food business. Too young to work up front in restaurants that served alcohol, he fortuitously ended up in the kitchen of several of Vail's top dining establishments. Sheely remained in Colorado for 18 years and eventually purchased his own restaurant, L'Ostello, which he operated for 2 years. By the mid-1990s, he decided he had skied to his heart's content and was ready to return to Houston to open a restaurant. In August 1995, he found a spot on Houston's west side, where he debuted the Riviera Grill, which became a favorite with Houston diners.

In January 2002, after shuttering Riviera Grill, Sheely opened the Mockingbird Bistro. Sheely finally had the restaurant he had always wanted—a place with a casual feel where he himself would like to "hang out." He refers to the Mockingbird Bistro's menu as "Texas Provence" cuisine, or "country French meets Texas market." Sheely updates the menu seasonally so he can use the freshest, Texas-sourced ingredients possible. "At Mockingbird Bistro we pride ourselves in partnering with local farmers and ranchers. This enables us to act on a local level while keeping our eye on the bigger prize, which is global sustainability. We are committed to providing our guests with the freshest high-quality seasonal products and also supporting local farmers and food producers."

SERVES 4.

¼ cup balsamic vinegar

3 cups dry red wine

1 cup molasses

1 tablespoon Worcestershire sauce

¾ teaspoon kosher salt

1½ teaspoons freshly ground
    black pepper

1 tablespoon grapeseed oil

2 Broken Arrow Ranch venison racks,
    about 1¼ pounds each, 4 chops
    each, frenched

Shallot–Black Cherry Compote
    (recipe follows)

Fall Vegetable Hash (recipe follows)

SHALLOT–BLACK CHERRY COMPOTE:
SHALLOTS:

¾ pound shallots, peeled and
    halved lengthwise

1½ tablespoons Texas extra-virgin
    olive oil

Kosher salt and freshly ground
    black pepper

BLACK CHERRIES:

2 cups water

¼ cup red wine vinegar

1 cup port wine

1 cup dried tart black cherries

2 pounds frozen or canned unsweet-
    ened pitted cherries, juice reserved

⅔ cup honey

1 cinnamon stick

FALL VEGETABLE HASH:

3 tablespoons Texas extra-virgin olive oil

½ pound Texas 1015 onions, finely chopped

½ pound sweet potatoes, peeled and cut into ½-inch dice

½ pound butternut squash, peeled and cut into ½-inch dice

½ pound rutabagas, peeled and cut into ½-inch dice

½ pound turnips, peeled and cut into ½-inch dice

1 cup apple cider

¼ pound thickly sliced pancetta, cut into ¼-inch dice and seared until crisp

Kosher salt and freshly ground black pepper

Begin by making the compote. Preheat oven to 350°F. In a medium, ovenproof sauté pan, toss the shallots with olive oil to coat and season to taste with salt and pepper. Roast in preheated oven until deep brown in color and very tender, stirring occasionally for about 30 minutes. Remove from oven and set aside.

For the black cherries, combine the water, vinegar, port wine, and dried cherries in a large saucepan. Bring to a boil and then simmer until liquid is reduced to ¼ cup, about 15 minutes. Stir in remaining ingredients and simmer for about 1 hour, until cherries are tender and sauce is thick. Cool, then stir in the roasted shallots. Can be made up to 2 days ahead of time. Reheat before serving.

Make the vegetable hash. Preheat oven to 400°F. In a large ovenproof sauté pan, add olive oil and sweat the onions for 5 minutes, but don't let them brown. Add the diced vegetables and sauté for another 10 minutes over medium-high heat, tossing or stirring occasionally. Put the pan into preheated oven and roast the vegetables for about 20 minutes, or until tender. Remove pan from oven, then pour in the cider. Simmer over moderately high heat until the cider has almost evaporated, about 10 minutes. Stir in pancetta. Season to taste with salt and pepper. The hash can be refrigerated overnight and reheated when ready to serve.

For the venison, preheat the oven to 450°F. In a bowl, combine vinegar, red wine, molasses, Worcestershire sauce, salt, and pepper.

In a large, nonaluminum ovenproof skillet, heat the grapeseed oil until almost smoking. Set the venison racks bone side up in the skillet. Sear them over high heat, turning once, until browned, about 2 minutes per side. Put the skillet in preheated oven and roast about 20 minutes, brushing the racks several times with the wine and molasses glaze, until the meat is rare and an instant-read thermometer inserted in the meat reads 125°F. Remove from oven, cover with foil, and let rest for 10 minutes. Season with salt and pepper. Slice and serve with the vegetable hash and shallot–black cherry compote.

Chicken-Fried Venison with Hatch Chile Cream Gravy

The chicken-fried steak, or CFS, as it often affectionately known in Texas, can be found in diners, dives, and cafés in every town in Texas big enough to have an eatery. The steak is usually plate-sized, with its gravy dripping off the edges. Upscale restaurants serve fancified versions with complex sauces, but the authentic Texas version is made from beef round steak pounded thin, breaded, and fried until crisp and golden brown and topped with a plain cream gravy made from the pan drippings, flour, and milk. There are as many stories about how and where the CFS originated as there are Texans, but it's generally agreed that the dish got its chicken-infused name because it's breaded with flour and dipped in an egg and milk wash in the same manner chicken pieces are breaded before frying. The dish also resembles the schnitzels prepared by early German immigrants to the Hill Country region.

Floyd Bell, a longtime friend of my husband, is a hunter, and his bounty, combined with his love of fishing, provides a freezer full of healthy protein for the Bell household year-round. Even if you're not a hunter, Texas-based Broken Arrow Ranch offers range-harvested game meats. Floyd makes his chicken-fried steaks from venison backstrap, while his wife, Martha, makes the gravy. I'm telling you, it's so good, it'll make you weep. I've taken the liberty of adding some Hatch chiles to Martha's gravy, as I love the earthy, smoky taste of the chiles with the flavor of venison. CFS is generally served with a big side of mashed potatoes, and Texans cover the potatoes with the gravy, too. You just can't get much better than this!

SERVES 4 TO 6.

FOR THE VENISON:

3 pounds venison backstrap, trimmed of any fat and tendons

Whole milk for soaking

3 cups all-purpose flour tossed well with 2 teaspoons kosher salt, 1½ teaspoons baking powder, 2 teaspoons freshly ground black pepper, 1 teaspoon cayenne, 1½ teaspoons granulated garlic, and 1½ teaspoons paprika

3 eggs beaten into 3 cups evaporated milk

Vegetable shortening for pan frying

HATCH CHILE CREAM GRAVY:

⅓ cup bacon drippings, or substitute canola oil if you must

3 slices applewood-smoked bacon, cut into ½-inch dice

2 Hatch chiles, blistered, peeled, seeded, and cut into ½-inch dice

⅔ cup all-purpose flour

1 teaspoon finely ground black pepper

6 cups whole milk

2 teaspoons chicken base

Kosher salt

Begin by making the steaks. Cut the venison on the bias into slices about 1-inch thick. Using a meat mallet or a rolling pin, pound the pieces of meat until they are between ¼- and ½-inch thick, taking care not to tear holes in the meat. Place in a baking dish and add whole milk to cover the meat. Cover with plastic wrap and refrigerate about 4 hours.

Drain the meat well, then pat dry, using absorbent paper towels. Dredge the steaks in the seasoned flour, coating well and shaking off excess flour. Dip them into the egg wash, coating well on both sides, then dredge them again in the flour, coating both sides well and shaking off excess flour. Place the breaded steaks in a single layer on a platter lined with parchment paper and refrigerate until ready to cook.

To cook the steaks, melt enough shortening in a heavy-bottomed 12-inch skillet, preferably cast iron, to reach about 1¼ inches in depth. Heat to about 350°F. Fry the breaded steaks in preheated shortening. Cook in batches, taking care not to crowd the oil. Fry about 6 minutes, turning once, or until a crisp, golden brown batter has formed. Drain steaks in a single layer on a wire rack set over a baking sheet. Set aside to keep warm while frying the remaining steaks.

When the steaks have all been fried, place the baking sheet with steaks on the wire rack in a warm oven to remain hot.

Make the cream gravy. Pour off all the drippings from the pan, but leave the browned bits in the bottom of the skillet. Return skillet to medium heat and add the bacon drippings or canola oil. When fat is hot, add the bacon slices and cook until almost crisp. Add the Hatch chiles and cook until bacon is crisp, about 5 minutes more. Add the flour all at once, whisking to blend well into the oil. Cook, stirring constantly, for 3 to 4 minutes. Add the pepper, whisking to blend. Add the milk and chicken base; whisk until smooth, scraping up browned bits from bottom of pan. Bring the gravy to a full boil to thicken; boil about 1 minute. Lower heat and season to taste with salt and additional pepper, if desired. Thin gravy with additional whole milk, if needed. Keep warm.

To serve, place the steaks on individual plates and top with a liberal portion of the gravy.

HILMY CELLARS

HILMY CELLARS, located on the bustling Highway 290 corridor just east of Fredericksburg, is one of the state's newest wineries, and founders Erik and Neldie Hilmy embody the "new face" of Texas wine. A self-taught winemaker, Erik Hilmy made his first vintage at age eight, fermenting some fruit juice with yeast in the family refrigerator. Neldie truly believes Erik was a winemaker in a former life.

Although 90 to 95 percent of Hilmy's grapes come from the Texas High Plains AVA, those grown at the winery see no chemicals or pesticides. Natural compost is processed on the property and used in the vineyard. Guinea hens, chickens, and a few peacocks roam freely among the vines, eating problematic bugs. There is no expensive deer-proof fencing, usually a necessary expenditure for Hill Country vineyards, because three Great Pyrenees dogs keep the vineyards deer-free. Goats keep the unplanted property well mowed. It's pretty much a "circle of life" operation.

Erik Hilmy employs a similarly natural phi-losophy in the blending room, relying on instinct rather than convention. One of his original wines, titled "Politics & Religion," was a unique blend of merlot and mourvèdre, a blending not legally allowed in France. He refers to it as "the poster child for what can be done with wine in Texas." It's hard not to envision a bright future for this young, innovative winemaker with the courage to test the limits of Texas terroir.

I paired Hilmy's Tempranillo Rosé with the Dai Due Farmers' Market Wild Boar Tacos with Herb Salsa (pages 307–308), with excellent results. This rosé is no Whispering Angel but rather a totally different and delightful style unto itself. There's a lot of alcohol at 14 percent, but when chilled, as a wine like this should be, the alcohol is less forward. The tempranillo lends a certain garrigue, or soft-leaved scrubland nuance, characteristic of the Mediterranean region's limestone soil, and some hefty leather and a bit of spice. In the mouth, the wine is filling and subtly sweet. This is a wine that will pair well with spicy fare.

INWOOD ESTATES VINEYARDS

DAN GATLIN AND his wife, Rose Mary, built the Inwood Estates Vineyards winery and tasting room in Dallas in 2005. When their first two wines were released a year later, they were immediately embraced by wine enthusiasts around the state. At the time, the most expensive wine in Texas was $21, and very few bottles could be found in restaurants. Today more than 200 Texas restaurants feature Inwood Estates wines.

Dan's parents owned a large retail beverage operation in Dallas, so he was exposed to fine wines at an early age as he traveled the world with his father, observing firsthand the operations at old European wineries. He watched the development of the wine industry in California. The company was sold after his father's death, and it was then that Dan began a decades-long odyssey to determine whether Texas could produce fine wines.

The research spanned some 460 miles and 30 grape varietals in five vineyards. He established his first vineyard in 1981 (at the time there were only five or six vineyards in the state). Gatlin's early experiments revealed that Texas wines would be heavily influenced by their terroir. Texas soil has an extremely high mineral content, particularly calcium, and closely resembles the soil in Europe. Dan refers to Texas dirt as "calcium on steroids." "This minerality, which affects different wine varietals in various ways, is the most important element in making wine in Texas," he said. "Texas winemakers are always seeking to heighten the fruit characteristics of grapes grown here." So, he concluded that Texas cabernet must be blended with other varietals, in the style of Bordeaux, to produce a well-rounded wine.

The palomino grape was another of Gatlin's early experiments. Widely planted in Spain, where it is used primarily in sherry and simple white table wines that are rarely imported to the United States, palomino grown in Texas has a paradoxical combination of crisp minerality and uncommon intensity of flavor from its low yields of less than one ton per acre. Chardonnay (25 percent) proved to be a perfect blending varietal for palomino, as it added complexity and reduced the intensity of the palomino. Gatlin felt this would be an important consideration in a market unaccustomed to white wines that are big and expansive. "The resulting wine became an anomaly in the wine world, where it is believed that a great white wine can't be produced in a hot climate," Dan noted enthusiastically.

On his experience with tempranillo, Gatlin relates, "Although ours was technically the second Tempranillo ever released in Texas, we were the very first planting in the High Plains AVA. From the initial 4,500 vines planted at Newsom Vineyard, 80,000 tempranillo vines went into the ground in that AVA the next spring after our first release in 2006. Today it is believed there are over 1 million tempranillo vines in the High Plains AVA. (Bobby Cox [one of the state's leading authorities on Texas wines] and I speculated about this recently.) I would think that this is the most important development in the entire Texas wine industry since it began. If this had never happened, the Texas wine industry would never have reached the critical mass it enjoys today."

Dan recalls that "in 1977, Charlie Wagner of Caymus Vineyards told me that nobody would ever pay $25 for Napa Valley Cabernet. That shows us how difficult it was for the existing wine world to accept even the best California wines after a full decade of concentrated effort." He adds, "It will be just as difficult for Texas, but Tempranillo has advanced our cause greatly."

In the fall of 2009, Dan and Rose Mary established a second winery and tasting room at The

Vineyard at Florence, 50 miles northwest of Austin. In the spring of 2013, a third winery and tasting room were opened on the banks of Grape Creek on the 290 wine corridor just east of Fredericksburg.

The Inwood Cellars "Cornelious" 100% Tempranillo is a grand match to the John Sheely's Grilled Rack of Venison with Shallot–Black Cherry Compote and Fall Vegetable Hash (pages 294–296). Tempranillo, when bottled unblended, has soft tannins and a red fruit profile, so it favors cherry-raspberry-strawberry flavors.

Pair the Inwood Cellars Tempranillo-Cabernet Blend with the Smoked Wild Boar Leg with Blackberry Mustard Sauce (pages 302–304). The wine has earthy tannins with extracted body and is the most consistently spicy wine in the Inwood lineup. It complements the paprika, cumin, chili powder, and coriander in the pork rub.

Smoked Wild Boar Leg with Blackberry Mustard Sauce

Wild hogs are overrunning parts of Texas. Farmers and ranchers are delighted to have hunters harvest the destructive critters from their pastures, where they dig furiously, destroying foliage and grasses. The best wild hogs are the smaller ones, weighing in at less than 30 pounds. My husband likes to trap the wild hogs and feed them table scraps and corn for a few weeks before harvesting them. This step adds a little fat to the hogs and sweetens up the meat. The legs are especially good. The sauce that I developed to go with the smoked leg is rich and complex but not overtly spicy, adding a slightly sweet, fruity/tangy, subtly spicy dimension to the deep smoke of the meat. The sauce is somewhat time-consuming, but it can be made ahead of time and can even be frozen for a couple of weeks. Thaw and reheat before serving. Sweet potatoes, cooked however you wish, are a good side for wild boar.

5-pound Broken Arrow Ranch bone-in
wild boar leg
Brine (see recipe on pages 256–257).
Double the recipe.
Pork Rub (see recipe below)
8 applewood-smoked bacon slices
Blackberry Mustard Sauce
(recipe follows)

PORK RUB:
MAKES ABOUT 1 CUP.
½ teaspoon smoked paprika
1 tablespoon medium-hot chili
powder
2 tablespoons light brown sugar
1 tablespoon toasted, then ground,
cumin seeds
1 tablespoon toasted, then ground,
coriander seeds
2½ tablespoons Mexican oregano
2½ tablespoons granulated garlic
2 tablespoons kosher salt
2½ teaspoons minced lime zest

BLACKBERRY MUSTARD SAUCE:
MAKES ABOUT 6 CUPS.
4 ancho chiles, seeds, stems,
and veins removed
2 pasilla chiles, seeds, stems,
and veins removed
3 chiles de arbol
3 tablespoons canola oil
6 homegrown Roma tomatoes,
chopped
1 small white onion, chopped
2 large garlic cloves, minced
12 ounces fresh blackberries, or
substitute frozen berries, thawed,
pureed until smooth
1 quart chicken stock, preferably
homemade
2 tablespoons whole-grain mustard
2 tablespoons freshly squeezed lime
juice
2 tablespoons Texas wildflower honey
Kosher salt

Make the brine and brine the boar leg, refrigerated, in a covered container for 24 hours.*

Prepare the rub by combining all ingredients; set aside. To smoke the boar leg, remove it from the brine and pat dry all over with absorbent paper towels. Rub it all over with the pork rub, using all of the rub. Lay the bacon strips over the meat. Build a hardwood fire in your smoker, using oak or hickory for rich smoke flavor, with a little pecan wood thrown in for sweetness. Allow the temperature in the pit to settle in between 200°F and 225°F. Fill the drip pan in the smoker with water. Place the meat on the cooking rack and smoke for about 1½ hours per pound, or until the meat reaches an internal temperature of 180°F. This will be about 6 hours. It is important to maintain a temperature of 200°F to 225°F in the smoker and to keep the water pan filled with water so that the steam will keep the meat moist. When the meat reaches 180°F, cook for 1 more hour, until the temperature registers around 190°F. Remove meat and wrap it tightly in foil. Set aside to rest 20 minutes before slicing.

Make the blackberry mustard sauce while the meat is smoking. Combine the chiles in a bowl and add boiling water to cover. Place a plate directly on the chiles to keep them submerged. Set aside for 30 minutes, or until the chiles are very soft and pliable. Drain well and roughly chop the chiles; set aside. Heat the canola oil in a heavy-bottomed 3-quart saucepan over medium-high heat. Sauté the chopped chiles, tomatoes, onion, and garlic, stirring often, until the tomato juices have evaporated and the onion is cara-melized, about 35 minutes. Add the pureed blackberries and reduce heat to medium. Cook until liquid has reduced to a syrupy consistency, about 25 minutes. Add chicken stock, raise heat to medium high, and simmer for 35 minutes, or until liquid is slightly thickened. Remove pan from heat and puree the sauce mixture in a blender, in batches if needed. Do not fill the blender more than halfway with the hot liquid and be sure that the top is on securely. Begin on low speed, increasing gradually to high. Add the mustard, lime juice, and honey and blend well. Season to taste with salt. Taste the sauce and adjust seasonings as desired. It should be ever so slightly tart and sweet. Reheat sauce when ready to serve.

Remove the meat from the foil and place on a cutting board. Remove and chop the flavorful bacon strips. Cut the meat across the grain into thin slices, using a sharp knife while holding the meat in place with a carving fork. Scatter the chopped bacon over the sliced meat and pass the sauce separately.

----

* Brining the boar leg will require a fairly large container. If your refrigerator will not accommodate the container, cover it securely with a tight-fitting lid and place it in an ice chest with a layer of ice on the bottom of the cooler, then pack ice all around the container. Maintain the ice, emptying out water as needed, during the brining period.

Wild Boar and Chorizo Meat Loaf

Good meat loaf can be a cook's best friend. It's a quick and easy main dish that can be assembled ahead of time and baked while you get the rest of dinner ready, even leaving time to enjoy a glass of wine. It can also be a very boring and tasteless creation if not seasoned boldly and made with a distinctive blend of good-quality meats. This version combines some tasty, traditional Texas flavors with Mexican-style chorizo and a glaze of spicy chipotle chiles with a hint of sweetness from agave nectar. Definitely not your grandmother's meat loaf, unless your grandmother was a two-fisted ranch cook.

SERVES 4 TO 6.

----

2 tablespoons canola oil

1 large yellow onion, cut into ¼-inch dice

1 red bell pepper, blistered and peeled, stem, seeds, and veins removed, cut into ¼-inch dice

1 poblano chile, blistered and peeled, stem, seeds, and veins removed, cut into ¼-inch dice

2 large jalapeños, seeds and veins removed, minced

3 large garlic cloves, minced

2 teaspoons toasted, then ground,
  whole cumin seeds
2 teaspoons toasted, then ground,
  whole coriander seeds
2 teaspoons dried Mexican oregano
1 teaspoon kosher salt
1 teaspoon crushed red pepper flakes
1 pound ground wild boar
1 pound good-quality fresh Mexican-
  style chorizo, casings removed
2 tablespoons minced cilantro

2 eggs well beaten with ½ cup
  evaporated milk
2 cups fresh bread crumbs
⅔ cup ketchup (made without high-
  fructose corn syrup)
1 tablespoon amber agave nectar
3 canned chipotle chiles in adobo
  sauce, minced
2 teaspoons adobo sauce from
  chipotle chiles

Preheat oven to 350°F. Spray a 13 × 9-inch baking dish with nonstick cooking spray; set aside. Heat the canola oil in a heavy-bottomed 12-inch skillet over medium heat. When oil is hot, add the onion, bell pepper, poblano chile, jalapeños, and garlic; sweat until onions are wilted and transparent, but not browned, about 7 to 10 minutes. Add the cumin, coriander, oregano, salt to taste, and crushed red pepper, stirring to blend well. Cook, stirring often, 2 more minutes. Remove from heat and transfer to a large bowl.

Add the boar meat, chorizo, cilantro, egg and milk mixture, and bread crumbs. Stir with a large wooden spoon to thoroughly blend the ingredients. Using your hands, form the mixture into an approximately 10 × 6-inch rounded loaf. Be sure to compact the loaf tightly so that there are no gaps. Place in the prepared baking dish. In a small bowl, mix together the ketchup, agave nectar, chipotle chiles, and adobo sauce. Spread the mixture over the meat loaf. At this point the meat loaf can be refrigerated for up to a day, covered with plastic wrap, if you wish to make it ahead of time.

Bake in preheated oven for about 1¼ hours, or until the juices run clear when the meat loaf is pierced with a small knife. The internal temperature should read 160°F on an instant-read meat thermometer. Remove from oven and tent loosely with foil; set aside to rest for about 10 minutes. Cut into slices 1-inch thick and serve hot.

Dai Due Farmers' Market Wild Boar Tacos with Herb Salsa

Most shoppers who frequent the SFC (Sustainable Food Center) Farmers' Market in downtown Austin, held every Saturday at Republic Square, know all about the delicious tacos, biscuits and gravy, various sandwiches, and other treats available at the Dai Due booth. The wild boar taco is one of my personal favorites, with its heavenly drizzle of fresh herb salsa.

Dai Due owners, the husband and wife team of Jesse Griffiths and Tamara Mayfield, traveled Europe, working on family farms and eating fresh local foods. Their travels greatly influenced the direction of their future in food. At their first supper club in 2006, the pair sourced every ingredient for the meal from local farmers' markets. The dinner was a smashing success, and more were scheduled. The one that I attended included fresh bluegill, which Jesse caught in the creek below the house.

Jesse is also an avid hunter who teaches classes ranging from day-long seminars to three-day weekends in the Texas Hill Country, where students learn how to hunt, butcher, cook, and cure feral hogs and deer, with a little fishing in the mix! If you go hunting with Jesse and do get a hog, this is a great recipe to try.

SERVES 4.

2 pounds bone-in wild boar shoulder, or fatty boar ham
Salt and freshly ground black pepper
12 corn tortillas
1 onion, sliced thin
Cilantro, coarsely chopped

HERB SALSA:
1 bunch cilantro, chopped
3 sprigs fresh Mexican oregano, chopped
6 green onions, chopped
1 green garlic stalk, or substitute 1 tablespoon chopped fresh garlic
Juice of 2 limes
Kosher salt
¾ cup safflower oil
Cayenne

Preheat oven to 225°F. Season the wild boar with salt and pepper, place in a roasting pan, and cover tightly with foil. Roast in preheated oven 6 hours, or until the meat is falling-apart tender. Remove from the oven and set aside to cool. When the meat has cooled enough that you can handle it, shred the meat, mixing it with the accumulated pan juices. Set aside to keep warm.

To make the herb salsa, combine the cilantro, oregano, green onions, garlic, lime juice, and salt in a blender. Blend until well pureed, then add the oil in a steady stream through the top of the blender until the salsa is very smooth. Add additional oil if needed. Season with cayenne to taste, beginning with about ⅛ teaspoon and adding more for a spicier salsa.

To assemble the tacos, heat the tortillas briefly in a very hot, dry skillet, just until they are pliable. Add a portion of the shredded pork, top with some of the salsa, and pile on the onion and cilantro. Chow down!

GRASSLAND OASIS FARM

F RED LYSSY ALWAYS remembered what his father told him as a boy: "This is good land, son, and we must take care of it." Although conventional ranching was his family heritage, Fred recognized the grim realities of the modern feedlot system and the nutritional deficiencies of today's conventionally raised food. He realized that in order to truly care for the land, he should be a farmer of grass and forage and, by extension, livestock.

Fred and his wife, Amber, learned that raising multiple species would utilize their land more efficiently. Their Grassland Oasis Farm in New Braunfels is home to cattle, goats, and sheep, as well as pastured pigs and chickens. They choose heritage breeds, and with the exception of the goats, the animals are harvested at a mature age so they can fatten on forage from the blackland soil along the San Antonio River. It's a process that allows the Texas terroir to shine through!

Fred was amazed when he saw how something as simple as rotational grazing could improve the land and the health of the animals. He studied and then implemented biodynamic and permaculture practices soon after, which have helped weather brutal South Texas droughts.

Today, the Lyssys' mission is to educate, as well as inspire, consumers and other farmers about sustainable farming practices. They carry this message to the farmers' markets with their products, spreading the word one steak at a time.

Carne Guisada de Cabrito (Mexican Goat Stew)

Carne guisada is a very traditional Tex-Mex stew. It can be made from whatever bits of meat are on hand but is transformed into a sublime dish when made with goat. You can also use venison or wild boar with delicious results. Cabrito, or baby goat, was a northern Mexico delicacy that migrated into Texas when Mexicans moved north to work the huge ranches in South Texas. Their cooking became known as *Norteño* cooking and is a distinct regional cuisine, separate from interior Mexican or Tex-Mex cooking. Melissa Guerra, a member of one of the large ranching families near McAllen, wrote a splendid book on the subject of *Norteño* foods, *Dishes from the Wild Horse Desert: Norteño Cooking of South Texas*.

Serve over white rice, and to make it a real Tex-Mex feast, make a batch of Pan de Campo, or "camp bread" (see recipe on pages 101–102).

SERVES 6 TO 8.

CARNE GUISADA:

¼ cup leaf lard, or substitute canola oil

4 pounds goat stew meat, trimmed of all fat and tendons

Kosher salt and freshly ground black pepper

1 large green bell pepper, cut into ½-inch dice

1 medium yellow onion, cut into ½-inch dice

3 cups beef stock, preferably homemade, divided

¾ teaspoon toasted, then ground, cumin seeds

¾ teaspoon toasted, then ground, coriander seeds

¼ teaspoon ground ginger

2 fresh bay leaves, minced

4 medium garlic cloves, peeled and roughly chopped

3 whole allspice berries

4 whole black peppercorns

1 tablespoon Maseca Masa, or other tortilla flour

1 tablespoon all-purpose flour

¼ cup water

Cooked white rice

CHILE PUREE:

1 ancho chile

1 pasilla chile

5 guajillo chiles

1 small white onion, peeled and roughly chopped

4 large Roma tomatoes

Place all of the chile puree ingredients in a heavy-bottomed 3-quart saucepan. Add water to cover and bring to a boil. Turn heat down and simmer until chiles are soft and pliable and onion is very tender, about 15 to 20 minutes. Drain the chile mixture and set aside until cool.

Preheat oven to 350°F. Melt the lard or heat the canola oil in a heavy-bottomed 14-inch skillet over medium-high heat. Season the goat meat with salt and black pepper. When fat is hot, add the meat and cook, stirring often, until meat is well browned. Using a slotted spoon, transfer the meat to a small, deep-sided Dutch oven. Return the skillet to medium-high heat and add the green bell pepper and onion. Cook, stirring often, to lightly brown the onion, about 7 minutes. Remove bell pepper and onion and add to roasting pan with the goat meat. Drain any remaining fat from the skillet but reserve the meat glaze in the bottom of the pan; set aside.

Add 2 cups of the beef stock to the meat and vegetables in the Dutch oven and cover pan tightly with aluminum foil. Roast in preheated oven for 1 hour, or until the goat meat is very tender.

Place the skillet with the meat glaze back over medium-high heat and add the remaining cup of beef broth. Work quickly to loosen the browned meat glaze from the bottom of the pan. Add the cooked chile-vegetable mixture and the cumin, coriander, ginger, bay leaves, garlic, allspice berries, and peppercorns. Pour mixture into the container of a high-speed blender, a little at a time, and puree until smooth, starting on low to avoid spillovers. Repeat until all of the mixture is pureed. Pour the chile puree through a fine strainer set over a medium-sized bowl. Using the back of a wooden spoon, stir the pulp in the strainer to remove all possible chile puree, until only the seeds and skins remain in the strainer. Set the chile puree aside until meat is done.

Remove the meat and vegetables from the pan, using a slotted spoon, and set aside. Pour the broth from the roasting pan through the strainer, stirring the pulp again. Discard pulp; transfer the strained broth and the chile puree to a deep-sided 4-quart braising pan over medium-high heat. Whisk the masa mix and all-purpose flour into the water, blending well so that no lumps remain. Bring the broth to a full boil and stir in the masa mixture to thicken the chile sauce. Lower heat to a simmer and add the goat meat and vegetables to the sauce. Cook, stirring often, just to reheat the meat. Serve over hot rice.

WORLD CHAMPIONSHIP BBQ GOAT COOK-OFF

THE FIRST TEXAS goat cook-off was held in Brady, the self-proclaimed Goat Capital of Texas, in 1973. That contest attracted 16 competitors. Today, more than 200 teams from all over the state, and some from around the country, vie for the title "World Champion BBQ Goat Cooker." Cookers and spectators crowd the little town of 5,500 on the northern fringe of the Texas Hill Country, filling every available motel room and campground. The estimated goat population in McCullough County is 10,000, and goat production there is a $1.5 million annual industry.

The competition is serious, and it's all about the taste of the goat. Goats must come from the same source in Brady, and they must be cooked whole. No garnishes or sauces are allowed on plates presented to the judges. The goat may be marinated and basted, and of course every team has a "secret rub," but it usually comes down to the team's skill at barbecuing and smoking the goat to tender perfection. As a judge of the competition in 2012, I was positively amazed to experience the vast diversity in taste among 206 boxes of barbecued goat meat, which ranged from bland and tough, to tender, juicy, and mouthwatering! Just as amazing were the various barbecue rigs—from simple barrel pits to huge, streamlined, custom-made cookers. And showmanship abounded, with one team from Georgia dressed in togas; others wore team T-shirts and baseball caps. Some simply wore their favorite jeans.

The goats used in the competition, and the best for cooking, are 30 to 40 days old, often known as *cabritos*. The ideal weight for cooking is 10 to 12 pounds. Don't buy a goat that weighs more than 12 pounds. As goats mature, the meat develops a musky, stronger flavor and becomes quite tough. Melissa Guerra, a noted authority on the *Norteño* foods of South Texas, likens the taste of goat to

that of dark turkey meat. I would agree, adding only the distinction of *rich* dark turkey meat.

Pan-Seared and Braised Goat Chops in Rustic Chile Pan Sauce

Goat is the most widely consumed meat on earth—eaten by 75 percent of the world's population. As a Texan, I'm a bit confused about why goat meat isn't more readily available. I live in Central Texas, and there are meat goats in every pasture—lots of them. Much the same all over the state. So why is there no goat meat in the butcher's case at my supermarket? I began to ask this question of goat raisers and was surprised by the consensus of opinion. Most of the goats raised for meat in Texas are shipped to Mexico or the Middle East, where the meat is in great demand. Being an ardent lover of the slightly earthy but delicious taste of goat meat, I have set about to change this.

One thing to remember about cooking goat is that because it is so lean, there is little fat to keep the meat moist during various cooking methods. So the meat is usually best when cooked by moist cooking methods like braising or stewing. Barbecued goat, however, is incredibly tasty, but it is important to marinate the meat before grilling or smoking it and baste often over low and slow heat.

SERVES 4.

---

2 large homegrown Roma tomatoes

4 large garlic cloves, peeled

1 small white onion, quartered

2 tablespoons Texas extra-virgin olive oil

8 Grassland Oasis goat loin chops, about 2½ pounds, seasoned all over with kosher salt or fine sea salt and freshly ground black pepper

2 tablespoons unsalted butter

2 ounces Texas Pride shiitake mushrooms, stems removed, roughly chopped

¼ teaspoon dried Mexican oregano

½ teaspoon toasted, then ground, cumin seeds

2 pasilla chiles, stems and seeds removed, torn into small pieces

1 fresh white corn tortilla, torn into several pieces

3 cups chicken stock, preferably homemade, or more as needed

½ cup toasted hulled pepitas (pumpkin seeds), divided

1½ teaspoons kosher salt

½ teaspoon freshly ground black pepper

2 teaspoons agave nectar

1 tablespoon minced cilantro

Place the whole tomatoes, garlic, and onion quarters in a heavy-bottomed 12-inch skillet over medium-high heat. Dry-roast the vegetables, turning often, until the tomato skins are blistered and charred. The tomatoes will begin to collapse and steam. The onion and garlic should be slightly charred and give off a roasted aroma. Transfer ingredients to a bowl and set aside to cool. Clean the skillet and return to stove.

Trim any fat from the edges of the goat chops; set chops aside. Heat the olive oil over medium-high heat. When the oil is hot, sear the seasoned goat chops until browned on both sides, about 4 minutes total. Remove and repeat with remaining chops. Do not overcook the chops. They should still be rare at this point. Set aside. Discard the oil from the skillet, but leave the browned bits on the bottom of the pan.

Return the skillet to medium-high heat and add the butter. When the butter melts and sizzles, add the mushrooms and sauté until they are lightly browned, about 5 minutes. Add the oregano, cumin, pasilla chiles, and torn tortilla to the pan. Sauté, stirring often, about 4 minutes. Add the reserved seared tomato mixture and the chicken stock to the skillet. Bring to a boil, then lower heat, and cover the pan. Simmer about 30 minutes. Remove from heat and set aside to cool slightly.

When the skillet has cooled, transfer the contents and 2 tablespoons of the toasted pepitas to the container of a high-speed blender. Place the lid on the container and put a towel over the lid. While holding the lid on the blender, begin pureeing on low speed to prevent a splashover. Gradually increase speed to high, pureeing until almost smooth, but leaving a bit of grainy texture. Preheat oven to 350°F.

Pour the puree back into an ovenproof skillet over medium-low heat, adding additional chicken stock if the sauce is too thick. Season to taste with salt and pepper; add the agave nectar, stirring to blend well. Place the seared goat chops in the pan and transfer to preheated oven. Cook about 45 minutes to 1 hour, or until the chops are very tender.

When ready to serve the dish, remove the chops and set aside to stay hot. Stir the cilantro into the sauce, blending well. Cook for 2 minutes.

To serve, place 2 chops on each serving plate. Spoon a portion of the pan sauce over each portion and garnish with a scattering of the remaining pepitas. Serve hot.

David Garrido's Coffee-Chipotle Marinated Beef Tenderloin with Red Beet and Black Truffle Sauce

Austin chef David Garrido, owner of Garrido's Restaurant, won first place with this recipe in the 2011 Edible Texas Wine Food Match. Garrido and other Texas chefs are creating new dishes based on traditional ingredients like chiles and beef, combined with ingredients borrowed from other cultures. The resulting flavors are exciting and innovative but have their roots in the Texas soil. In this dish, the espresso enhances the earthy flavor of the grass-fed beef, while the chipotle lends a smoky note. The fig balsamic,

reduced in the sauce, adds a hint of musky sweetness that brings out the earthiness of the beets. The black truffle adds its own unique flavor, and the arugula and queso fresco add freshness and texture to create a truly complex-tasting plate. David, who has been cooking in Austin for more than 20 years, likes to characterize his cooking style as "Modern Mexican" but credits his grandmother's kitchen in Mexico as his inspiration.

SERVES 4.

8 grass-fed beef tenderloin fillets,
    4 ounces each
3 tablespoons Texas extra-virgin
    olive oil
¼ cup instant espresso granules,
    ground to a fine powder
1 tablespoon ground chipotle
    chile powder
Sea salt and freshly ground
    black pepper
3 cups baby arugula
½ cup queso fresco*

**RED BEET AND BLACK
TRUFFLE SAUCE:**
2 tablespoons olive oil
2 tablespoons finely diced shallots
1 cup small-dice peeled red beets
1 cup fig balsamic vinegar
1 cup veal stock, preferably
    homemade
¼ cup sliced black truffle
2 tablespoons black truffle oil
Kosher salt and freshly ground black
    pepper

Begin by making the red beet and black truffle sauce. Heat the olive oil in a heavy-bottomed 2-quart saucepan over medium heat. Add the shallots and cook for 1 minute, or until they are limp and transparent. Add the beets and fig balsamic vinegar; cook for 10 minutes, or until reduced by half. Add veal stock and bring to a boil. Transfer to a blender and add truffle and truffle oil. Puree until smooth. Season to taste with sea salt and freshly ground black pepper. Return to saucepan and keep warm over very low heat.

  For the tenderloin, combine the olive oil, ground espresso, and chipotle powder, blending well. Coat the tenderloins with the mixture on all sides. Season with salt and freshly ground black pepper. Set aside and heat char-grill to high heat.

  When grill is hot, cook the tenderloins for about 3 to 5 minutes on each side for rare to medium, or to desired doneness. Transfer fillets to individual serving plates. Garnish with fresh baby arugula and queso fresco. Spoon a portion of the sauce over each serving. Serve with grilled, julienned vegetables.

* Queso fresco translates to "fresh cheese." It has a crumbly texture and slightly acidic flavor, making it a good cheese to serve on a variety of dishes, including cooked rice. It is the most common cheese in Mexico, where it is often made from raw cow's milk and is used to stuff chiles or in quesadillas. It is available in most Mexican markets or some upscale specialty markets, but one of the best examples available in the United States is produced by Mozzarella Company in Dallas.

FAIRHAVEN VINEYARDS

LOCATED IN HAWKINS, some 20 miles north of Tyler, Fairhaven Vineyards is one of the most watched in Texas because owner R. L. Winters is dedicated to producing wines from French American and American hybrid grapes (i.e., chambourcin, not cabernet sauvignon). But Winters is much more than a winemaker working with obscure varietals; he's also part historian, part plant breeder, and guardian of some of the rarest vines in Texas.

When he began his research into hybrids, Winters stumbled onto the T. V. Munson varietals and became fascinated with the commercial potential for these very tough, disease-resistant vines. He has built one of the largest collections of Munson hybrids, some 2,000 vines, in the state. Noted wine authority Dr. Russell Kane refers to Winters's vineyard as "a living history of Texas wine heritage. What heirlooms are to tomatoes, Munson varieties are to grapes."

Winters believes much of the real developmental work regarding wine grapes that are suitable for Texas production was done by Munson 150 years ago. These hybrids have had few advocates since they were rediscovered in the mid-1980s. The industry has been slow to realize their potential,

largely because the only information about them is historical, and there are few sources for plantable Munson hybrid vines. As such, there is no large-scale production of wine made from these grapes. However, at least one variety that Winters sells—lomanto—is in high demand, and he hopes it will lead to more demand for these vines. The 2009 Lomanto from Winters's Heritage Series was the first wine made from an American hybrid grape to win an international award since 1873.

Looking ahead, Winters is fairly confident that he can reconstruct more of Munson's lost varieties, although his main thrust will be to try to determine where Munson's breeding sequence was going. "Simply put," Winters says, "my goal is to produce a new series of super-hybrids using T. V. Munson's genetics as a base. No need to reinvent the wheel here."

Pair the Fairhaven Lomanto Reserve, a blue-black, earthy, and rustic wine, with David Garrido's Coffee-Chipotle Marinated Beef Tenderloin with Red Beet and Black Truffle Sauce (pages 315–316). Winters notes that beef and Lomanto are a match made in heaven. The wine is at once dark, brooding, and mysterious, with a distinct wild character (from the Salado grape). The tartness of the American vitis balances out nicely with spicy foods. The wine embraces the rustic profile of the dark coffee and chile marinade, following through with the earthy notes of the beet and truffle sauce.

Pair Fairhaven's Chambourcin, a purple-red, fruit-driven wine, with the Pan-Seared and Braised Goat Chops in Rustic Chile Pan Sauce (pages 313–315). The wine has a wonderful fruity character that lends itself well to this type of dish. Winters's whole-cluster, two-stage fermentation produces a wine that has the unique characteristic of reinforcing delicately spiced foods, such as this dish, without dominating the palate.

KIEPERSOL ESTATES

IEPERSOL ESTATES WAS established in 1954 in the Eastern Transvaal of the Union of South Africa. Dirk de Wet established Kiepersol Tevrede (meaning "satisfied") with the intention of raising generations of families there in a self-sufficient mixed farming operation. But in 1994, Dirk's son, Pierre de Wet, immigrated to the United States with his two young daughters and reestablished Kiepersol Estates south of Tyler, where today three generations of the family live and run a winery, a restaurant, and an elegant, European-style bed and breakfast.

De Wet harvested the first vintage in 2000, and Kiepersol wines were immediately embraced by the local community. As demand grew, more grapes were planted. Today there are 61 acres of vineyard, making it one of the largest in Texas.

Pierre says he "regards wine as nature's blessing, which, when picked, has been imprinted with the hallmarks of each season—summer's warmth, fall's ripening—turning a perishable product into joy embodied and preserved." Great philosophy. I've found myself remembering it each time I open a bottle of wine.

Each year just prior to harvest, the De Wets scout the vineyard and select those vines that have the perfect balance of fruit, flavor, and color to produce their Barrel No. 33 blend. Each vintage of this wine has been superb, and each has great aging potential. This is a wine to be savored with red meats, and I especially like it with lamb.

Pair Kiepersol Syrah with both the Flame-Grilled Rib Eyes with Java Rub and Buckaroo Butter (pages 319–320) and Maiya's Flat Steak on a Bed of Radicchio (pages 320–322). The Syrah is a wild and free-spirited wine grown in the intense climate of Kiepersol's East Texas vineyard. It's full-mouth, jammy fruit-forward style complements rich, grass-fed rib eyes, blending the natural with the natural, perfect for old-world styling. Also, for the sophisticated palate, the wine exhibits some coffee notes, which pick up the same notes in the java rub.

Flame-Grilled Rib Eyes with Java Rub and Buckaroo Butter

I think it's a safe bet to say that no matter how many food trends, immigrant cultures, or dietary discoveries come along, beef will remain numero uno on the Texas table. Beef became synonymous with Texas with the mega cattle ranches and legendary cattle drives of the late 1800s. Texans are devoted to that heritage, and chances are that if you smell compelling smoke in any Texas neighborhood on a Saturday night, it's a big, succulent rib eye steak giving off that glorious aroma.

SERVES 4.

4 grass-fed rib eye steaks, 12 ounces each
Java Rub (see recipe below)
Applewood chips for grilling, soaked in water for 1 hour
4 tablespoons Texas extra-virgin olive oil
Buckaroo Butter (recipe follows)

JAVA RUB:
⅔ cup espresso coffee beans, ground to a very fine powder
3 tablespoons kosher salt
1½ tablespoons ancho chile powder
1 tablespoon medium-grind black pepper
1 tablespoon toasted, then ground, coriander seeds
1 tablespoon granulated garlic
1 tablespoon onion powder
1 tablespoon light brown sugar
¼ teaspoon ground cinnamon

BUCKAROO BUTTER:
MAKES ½ POUND.
1 cup (2 sticks) unsalted butter, cut into small dice and softened
1 heaping tablespoon minced flat-leaf parsley
1 teaspoon minced lemon zest
1 tablespoon Worcestershire sauce
1 teaspoon Cholula Hot Sauce
¼ teaspoon kosher salt
1 teaspoon freshly ground black pepper

Place 3 cups applewood chips in a bucket and cover with water; set aside by the barbecue grill. Begin by making the java rub. Combine all ingredients in a small bowl and whisk to blend well. Store in an airtight container. Save the leftover rub for the next rib eye cookout.

Make the buckaroo butter. Place the butter cubes in the work bowl of a food processor fitted with the steel blade. Add all remaining ingredients and process until smooth.

Shape the butter into a cylinder by rolling it in parchment paper. Twist the ends of the parchment paper to seal, place in a zip-sealing plastic bag, and freeze. Cut off individual portions of the butter as needed, returning the rest to the freezer.

To grill the steaks, whisk 4 tablespoons of the rub into 4 tablespoons of Texas extra-virgin olive oil, blending well. Rub the paste into all sides of the steaks and set aside on a wire rack at room temperature for about 30 minutes. (The air-drying will produce a nice crust on the steaks to seal in their meaty juices.) Cut 4 slices of buckaroo butter, each ½-inch thick, and allow them to come to room temperature. Build a hardwood charcoal fire. Drain the applewood chips and wrap them in foil; poke holes all over the foil. When you light the fire, set the package of chips on the grilling rack and close the lid of the pit. When the fire has burned down to the point where the coals are glowing red, covered by a layer of white ash, scoot the chip package to one side of the grilling rack.

Place the steaks on the pit and grill about 5 minutes per side for medium rare, turning at a 45-degree angle halfway through grilling, then at a 90-degree angle to the first marks, on each side to make nice, crosshatched grill marks on the steaks. Just before the steaks are done, place a slice of the buckaroo butter in the center of each, allowing the butter to almost melt into the steaks. Transfer to individual plates and serve with steak knives.

Maiya's Flat Steak on a Bed of Radicchio

Maiya Keck, chef/owner of Maiya's Restaurant in the West Texas town of Marfa, cites the eight years of her childhood that her father lived in Rome as the formative years of her love of food. When she visited him, they went out to restaurants for every meal. "My food sensibility is Roman—a classic sensibility—you eat food that is fresh, with the ingredients that are seasonal. That ceremony of feasting with friends and being served in a public space became an ingrained part of my childhood," Maiya recounted.

When Maiya moved to Marfa in 1994, it was an isolated town of 2,000 people but full of light and space. There were just a couple of Tex-Mex cafés, a few dusty bars where even dustier cowboys would hang out, and one grocery store that didn't stock much. But it was a place totally uncorrupted by the homogenization of the rest of the country, and Maiya loved it. When she decided to open the restaurant, sourcing food was a challenge. Food purveyors initially would ask, "What is that?" with furrowed brows, when she ordered items like fennel, Parmigiano-Reggiano cheese, white anchovies, watercress, and squid bodies. Most food-service items in Marfa at the time came in #10 cans. Trying to get wine to West Texas was tricky,

too. However, bringing fresh ingredients to the high Chihuahuan Desert got easier every year as more of the public demanded healthy, fresh food. Tourists began to come to the area. Farmers planted specialty produce for the restaurant. A couple moved to Marfa and started a goat farm, eventually producing quality goat cheeses. Ranchers raised heritage grass-fed beef.

Everything on Maiya's menu is made completely from scratch in the restaurant's kitchen. Maiya has fostered a philosophy in the kitchen that anything worth doing is worth doing well, no matter how small the task. She sums it up nicely: "It's all about ingredients, time, temperature, and using your heart. You have to use your heart when you cook—you make every dish the way you feel it deep down. That and using the best, fresh ingredients are really the secrets to good cooking."

This is one of Maiya's signature dishes, a simple masterpiece that showcases her flair for combining fresh flavors and textures.

SERVES 4.

4 Prime or Choice Black Angus rib eye steaks, 8 ounces each	1 cup grated Parmigiano-Reggiano cheese
1 large head radicchio (red chicory)	Kosher salt
Texas extra-virgin olive oil	Chopped flat-leaf parsley
1 large lemon, cut into 4 wedges	

Heat a gas char-grill or build a hardwood charcoal fire in a barbecue pit and allow the fire to cook down to the point where the coals are glowing red, covered by a layer of white ash.

Place the steaks between two pieces of plastic wrap, one at a time, and pound them with a flat, untextured meat pounder until they're evenly about ½-inch to ¼-inch thick. Don't remove the fat from the steaks, as it adds wonderful flavor during the grilling process.

Remove the core from the head of chicory and discard. Shred the head into strips about ¼-inch thick. Cover each plate with one-fourth of the shredded chicory, then drizzle with olive oil, squeeze a lemon wedge over each plate, add a pinch of salt, and scatter ¼ cup of the grated cheese over each. Set aside at room temperature.

When the grill is hot, or the coals are ready—when you can hold your flat palm over them for the count of only 3 seconds—put the steaks on the grill rack. The steaks will cook quickly because they're so thin, so just when enough of the fat melts that the steaks come off the grill without sticking, about 2 minutes, turn them and cook to desired degree of doneness, but medium rare is recommended, about another 2 to 3 minutes. Place the steaks on the prepared plates of radicchio and garnish with the chopped parsley. Serve at once.

BRAZOS VALLEY CHEESE

WHEN MARC KUEHL first visited the Homestead Heritage Community near Waco, where many of his cousins lived, he witnessed a very different lifestyle from the one he had in Denver, Colorado. After seeing how people in the community cared for one another, he wanted to be part of it, too.

His cousin Rebeccah, who lived in the community, had been making cheese for several years. She mentioned to Marc that she hoped one day her cheese business would grow. Although he knew nothing about cheese, Marc agreed to help her fulfill her dream. Her father provided the funding, and with support and encouragement from friends, the pair started Brazos Valley Cheese.

Marc recalled those first few months: "I remember not really having the passion for making cheese that Rebeccah did. That changed one weekend while I was selling our cheeses at the Austin Farmers' Market. After handing samples of cheese to some customers, they became very excited that I actually was the one who made the cheese. I never thought anyone would be excited because of something I had done. When I realized that people really appreciated the cheeses, I gained a new resolve to make the best-quality cheese we could."

Brazos Valley makes several types of cheese from raw cow's milk. "We appreciate the value of a small dairy herd that feeds on grass instead of being crowded into an industrial dairy operation. The healthy cows we get our milk from are not given hormones, steroids, or antibiotics."

After eight years in business Marc reflected: "I appreciate where we have come from. Considering we started by getting milk in 4-gallon buckets that we had to haul 45 miles each way in the back of a pickup, to now processing over 1,500 gallons per week, I'm amazed at the way our business has grown. Today Brazos Valley cheeses are still sold at farmers' markets but are also available at Whole Foods."

Brazos Valley Cheese has received several awards from the American Cheese Society, including first place for its Eden, second place for its Brie, and third place for its Cheddar.

Grilled Grass-Fed Beef Tenderloin Steaks with Aged Brie and Shiitake Mushroom Sauce

The tenderloin is the tenderest cut of beef because it is the muscle of the steer that gets the least amount of exercise. The muscles that the animal uses most, like the round, are tougher cuts of meat, although very flavorful. Steaks cut from the whole, trimmed tenderloin are perfect for steak lovers who like to eat their steak with a fork. But this is true only if you cook the meat no further than medium rare. Why pay a premium price for tenderness, then cook the meat until it becomes tough? The tenderloin also has the mildest flavor of any other cut, another result of little exercise. Therefore, tenderloin steaks are usually served with a sauce or a butter glaze to enhance their flavor.

When I first tasted the Brazos Select cheese from Brazos Valley Cheese, which is aged for six months, I was captivated. The cheese is a bit firmer than a runny young Brie but has a taste that is almost indescribable. It's a creamy, mold-ripened, Brie-style cheese that's painted with Brazos Valley's house-made sorghum syrup, wrapped in mesquite wood, and garnished with a big grape leaf. The cheese is earthy and rich, with a medium-creamy texture. There's a vast difference between *aged* cheese and simply *old* cheese, so this cheese has none of the ammonia-like characteristics of the piece of Brie hiding under layers of other stuff in the fridge that you forgot about for a few weeks.

After savoring the taste for a few minutes, I immediately thought of beef, realizing that this cheese would make a fabulous mate to a delicate cut of beef, matching and intensifying the beef's umami-savory, grass-fed flavor. Then mushrooms entered the mix as my mind's tongue was formulating a sauce—and not any mushroom, but one with a similarly earthy taste. Shiitake jumped to the forefront, and I jotted down a skeleton of a recipe so that I wouldn't forget any of the components. I added shallots and just a hint of rosemary for its woodsy/earthy taste notes; rich, savory beef demi-glace to brace up the beefiness; and a shot of good Texas bourbon to give it pizzazz. Later that week I purchased a lovely whole beef tenderloin from the farmers' market and cut it into steaks about 2 inches thick from the large end of the tenderloin. I prepared the recipe from my notes, and my tasters, including my husband, who considers himself a connoisseur of beef, declared it a definite keeper.

SERVES 4.

STEAKS:

4 grass-fed beef tenderloin steaks, cut from the large end of the tenderloin, about 2 inches thick, 6 to 8 ounces each

Texas extra-virgin olive oil

Kosher salt and freshly ground black pepper

BRIE AND SHIITAKE MUSHROOM SAUCE:

3 tablespoons unsalted butter

3 ounces Kitchen Pride shiitake mushrooms, stems removed and discarded, caps sliced

1 large shallot, minced

¼ teaspoon minced fresh rosemary

1 cup beef demi-glace*

4 ounces Brazos Select aged Brie, rind removed and discarded, cut into 1-inch cubes

2 tablespoons Rebecca Creek Texas bourbon

Kosher salt and freshly ground black pepper

Begin by making the sauce. Melt the butter in a heavy-bottomed 10-inch skillet over medium heat. When the foam subsides, add the mushrooms, shallot, and rosemary. Cook, stirring often, until the mushrooms are lightly browned, about 5 minutes. Add the demi-glace and cook to reduce by one-fourth, about 5 minutes. Add the cheese and stir just until cheese has melted. Whisk in the bourbon and season to taste with salt and pepper. Cover the sauce and set aside to keep warm while grilling the steaks. Gently reheat, if needed, and stir well before serving.

To grill the steaks, heat a gas char-grill to medium-high heat. Brush the steaks all over with some of the olive oil. Season on both sides with salt and pepper. When the grill is hot, place the steaks on the grill rack and cook for about 3 to 4 minutes per side, for medium rare, or to an internal temperature of 125°F, using an instant-read meat thermometer. Turn the steaks only once. Remove from the grill and set aside to rest for 5 minutes. The meat will continue to cook from carryover heat, raising the temperature about 5°F.

To serve, place the steaks on individual serving plates and spoon a portion of the sauce over each steak. Serve at once.

----

* Beef demi-glace is a sauce made by combining equal parts veal or beef stock and sauce espagnole (brown sauce) and then reducing it to the consistency of a light syrup. The reduction usually amounts to about one-fourth the original volume and must be accomplished slowly. It is a time-consuming process, but thankfully there are options, so don't be tempted to use just beef stock in this recipe. Whole Foods markets sell frozen demi-glace that is a good product. For those who live in Houston, Revival Market also sells frozen demi-glace of excellent quality. You can also find a concentrated demi-glace, produced by the Better Than Gourmet brand, in upscale supermarkets.

Franklin Barbecue's All-Natural Smoked Angus Brisket

It's an undisputed fact that barbecue in Texas means beef brisket. Prior to December 2009, finding the best barbecue in Texas meant making a trip either east or west from Austin to Lockhart, Taylor, Luling, Driftwood, or Llano. But then Aaron Franklin and his wife, Stacy, opened Franklin Barbecue in a converted trailer in Austin, and it quickly became a barbecue mecca with pilgrims from, well, from everywhere. The line out front dissipates only when they run out of barbecue, usually by early afternoon.

Today, Franklin Barbecue operates in a brick-and-mortar building. Although many say that the meteoric success of Franklin Barbecue is unprecedented in the history of Texas barbecue, it's been well earned. Aaron grew up in Bryan, where he worked at his father's barbecue place. When he moved to Austin, he worked for John Mueller, of the legendary

Mueller Barbecue family in Taylor. But Aaron arrived at his own particular "style" of barbecuing by experimenting on a little Old Smokey grill in his backyard, inviting friends over to taste the results. Aaron's approach to barbecuing requires patience and attention to detail. Most pit-masters cook their briskets for 6 to 7 hours on a hot fire—around 500°F. Aaron cooks his for about 18 hours at 270°F. It's a technique that results in a succulent, tender hunk of beef with a reddish-pink smoke ring, the hallmark of great barbecue, of about half an inch. Franklin's barbecue sauce is also legendary, but of course, it's served on the side, after the brisket is done. When the Franklins first opened their trailer, it was situated behind a coffee roasting business, and fresh brewed espresso seemed to Aaron like it would be a good ingredient in a barbecue sauce for brisket—and by golly, he was dead right.

Before you start smoking brisket, Aaron recommends purchasing a smoker with a separate firebox so the meat doesn't cook over direct fire, but slowly by hot smoke. He recommends pits by Pitts & Spits, Oklahoma Joe's, and New Braunfels Smokers. A pit with an external thermometer is handy; otherwise, use an oven thermometer set on the cooking rack. A thermometer is essential. His preferred woods for use in the pit are post oak and hickory because they impart the best taste to the meat and burn clean. My own note is to never, ever use charcoal lighter to start your fire! It gives off a vapor of petroleum-like taste that will flavor the meat.

SERVES 10 TO 12.

10- to 12-pound well-marbled beef
    brisket, preferably all natural

½ cup kosher salt
½ cup coarsely ground black pepper

AARON'S ESPRESSO BARBECUE SAUCE:
MAKES ABOUT 3½ CUPS.

¼ cup apple cider vinegar
¼ cup distilled white vinegar
2 tablespoons Worcestershire sauce
3 tablespoons brewed espresso
½ cup water
2 cups ketchup (made without high-
    fructose corn syrup)

⅛ teaspoon ground cumin
2 tablespoons chili powder
2 teaspoons freshly ground black
    pepper
Kosher salt

Begin by bringing the meat to room temperature. This will take 2 to 3 hours. Never leave meat out at room temperature longer than 4 hours for food safety concerns. While the meat is coming to room temperature, build your fire. Put kindling wood and paper sprinkled with vegetable oil in the separate firebox and light the fire. Once the

kindling is burning well, add the logs. Let the temperature in the smoking chamber rise to between 225°F and 250°F.

Meanwhile, trim the exterior fat on the brisket to between ¼- and ½- inch thick. Fill a throwaway foil pan with water and place it under the cooking grill, locating it as close to the firebox as possible. Combine the salt and black pepper, tossing to blend well. Rub the meat all over with the mixture. When the temperature in the smoking chamber is right, place the brisket, thickest end toward the fire box, with the fatty side up, on the grill. Allow 45 minutes per pound cooking time, maintaining a steady temperature in the smoking chamber.

Check the fire every 20 minutes or so, adjusting the vent, flap, and firebox door to keep the heat even. Replenish the water as needed. Now, here's the hard part for most backyard barbecuers who seem to have a deeply rooted need to *mess* with the meat while it's cooking. Aaron admonishes that you should not poke the meat with a fork, and "Do *not turn* it." Rather, cook it the entire time with the fat cap on top so that as the fat melts, it seeps lusciously into the meat, making it moist and tender.

When an instant-read meat thermometer inserted in the thickest part of the brisket registers 195°F to 203°F, the brisket is done, but Franklin says it's best to take it off the heat a little sooner, as it will continue to cook from the internal heat. The meat should have a nice crispy *bark* on all sides but be very tender inside, offering no resistance to a metal skewer plunged into the thickest part. Let the meat rest, covered loosely with foil, about 20 to 30 minutes before slicing so that all the juices redistribute throughout the entire piece of meat.

While the meat is cooking, make the barbecue sauce. Combine all ingredients in a heavy-bottomed 2-quart saucepan over medium-high heat. Whisk to blend well and cook, stirring often, for about 7 to 8 minutes, or until mixture is slightly thickened. Remove from heat and refrigerate until ready to use. Serve at room temperature or gently reheat.

To slice the meat, place it, fat side up, on a cutting board. Trim off the surface fat. Cut the nose end loose from the layer of fat under it, and cut out that fat layer. Cut both pieces of meat into slices ¼-inch thick, across the grain. (Thin slices will be more tender than thick ones.) Serve hot with sliced onions and hamburger dills. Pass the barbecue sauce separately.

TEXAS HILLS VINEYARD

GARY AND KATHY GILSTRAP, pharmacists by trade, owned a drugstore/pharmacy in Galena, Kansas, and a software company—both of which they sold in order to become semiretired. While traveling in Europe, they became interested in wine, and more particularly, the making of wine. The Gilstraps brought a scientific, nontraditional perspective to winemaking in Texas.

Gary, a hands-on, blue-jeans kind of guy, works in the vineyards, as well as the production room. His chemistry background gives him an occasional advantage. For example, he introduced N-pHuric—a mixture of urea and sulfuric acid—as a stabilizer in his irrigation system, which helps get micronutrients into the vines and avoid the usual buildup of limestone in the soil. When the harvested grapes are on their way to becoming wine, Gary uses tannins to round out the wines to achieve a good acid balance. Once the wines are in the barrel, he uses micro-oxygenation—a process of injecting a carefully calibrated amount of oxygen into the wine—which results in a shorter barrel-aging time and reduces the chance of bacterial contamination that can occur with extended barrel aging. Micro-oxygenation enables more control over the fermentation process—maintaining the viability of the yeast and reducing the production of undesirable sulfides. Wines that are barrel-aged using this technique taste as though they've been barrel-aged for twice as long as they actually have.

From the beginning, the Gilstraps have used only grapes grown in Texas, and their wines are produced at the Texas Hills production facility in Johnson City. They source some fruit from growers in the Texas High Plains and the Hill Country, but, Gary says emphatically, "If the grapes are grown in California, they certainly won't make wine that tastes like Texas!"

Texas Hills Vineyard's Kick Butt Cab (Newsom Vineyard) is Gary's first choice for Franklin Barbecue's All-Natural Smoked Angus Brisket (pages 327–329). He also recommends their Toro de Tejas (Newsom Vineyard Tempranillo) with the dish.

For the Shiner Bock Braised Short Ribs with Maple-Balsamic Glaze (pages 332–333), pair Texas Hills Vineyard Malbec (Newsom Vineyard), Toro de Tejas Tempranillo (Reddy Vineyard), or Merlot (Texas Hills Vineyard).

A very satisfying pairing for the Texas Farmhouse Pot Roast with Ancho Chile Pan Sauce (pages 337–338) is the Texas Hills Vineyard Cabernet Franc or the Sangiovese. The Texas Hills Sangiovese is also a spot-on match for the Roasted Fresh Tomato and Basil Soup (pages 66–67). This pairing illustrates an old rule of thumb: Look to the ethnic origin of the dish, which in this case is Italian, then pair a wine from the same region. In the same vein, I also like the Texas Hills Barbera with this soup.

Hellfire and Damnation Barbecue Sauce

My opinion on the subject of barbecue sauce is that you never have enough recipes for good ones. And this is a good one. Because I've always loved to grill and barbecue, it was one of the first recipes I ever created, way before I went to culinary school. Friends have loved it over all the years and encouraged me to produce it commercially, which I did for a while, but that's another story. I consider it to be a quintessentially *Texas-style* barbecue sauce. Good on any kind of meat, and it keeps forever in the fridge. The recipe makes a lot, but once your friends taste it and find out you have extra, well, it won't last long!

MAKES 2 QUARTS.

4 tablespoons unsalted butter

4 green onions, minced, including green tops

2 tablespoons granulated garlic

¼ cup dark red, medium-hot chili powder

1 tablespoon finely ground black pepper

6 cups ketchup (made without high-fructose corn syrup)

⅓ cup firmly packed light brown sugar

½ cup granulated sugar

1 cup apple cider vinegar

¾ cup bock-style beer

⅓ cup dry red wine

1½ teaspoons dried Mexican oregano

1 teaspoon red (cayenne) pepper

½ cup Worcestershire sauce

2 tablespoons Tabasco, or to taste

Combine all ingredients in a 4-quart soup pot. Stir over medium heat until butter has melted. Simmer, covered, for 1 hour. Cool and store in refrigerator until ready to use. Reheat desired amount before serving.

Shiner Bock Braised Short Ribs with Maple-Balsamic Glaze

Beef short ribs are mighty hard to beat in the flavor department. They do require a long, slow braising to render them to their tender best, but the results will not disappoint. This version, in which the short ribs are braised in Texas-made Shiner Bock beer, produced at the Spoetzl Brewery in Shiner, with aromatic veggies and a hint of spice and leathery notes from ancho chiles is one of my favorite dishes for winter.

SERVES 6 TO 8.

TO BRAISE THE RIBS:
4 pounds meaty grass-fed beef short
    ribs, cut into 2-inch portions
Kosher salt, freshly ground black
    pepper, and sweet paprika
Texas extra-virgin olive oil
2 medium onions, roughly chopped
4 large garlic cloves, peeled and
    chopped
2 medium carrots, peeled and
    sliced thin

2 celery stalks, chopped
2 cups Shiner Bock beer
1 cup beef stock
3 ancho chiles, seeds and stems
    removed
2 rosemary sprigs

MAPLE-BALSAMIC GLAZE:
½ cup pure maple syrup
2 cups good-quality balsamic vinegar
2 rosemary sprigs
1 tablespoon prepared horseradish

Season the ribs all over with salt, pepper, and paprika. Place in a single layer on a baking sheet, cover with plastic wrap, and set aside at room temperature for 30 minutes.

Preheat oven to 350°F. Pat the ribs dry with absorbent paper towels, but don't rub off the seasonings. Add some additional black pepper. Heat a glaze of olive oil in a heavy-bottomed, deep-sided 14-inch skillet over medium-high heat. Sear the ribs until well-browned, turning often. Repeat until all ribs are browned. Be sure not to crowd the pan; the ribs should not touch. Place the ribs in a single layer on a sheet tray. Pour off and discard all but about ¼ cup of the fat from the pan. Return pan to heat and sauté the onions, garlic, carrots, and celery, seasoning them with salt and pepper, until the vegetables are browned and wilted, about 8 minutes.

Add the Shiner Bock and bring to a full boil, scraping the bottom of the pan to release all the browned bits. Add the stock, ancho chiles, and rosemary sprigs; cook an additional 5 minutes. Pour the vegetable-beer-stock mixture into a baking pan large enough to accommodate all of the ribs in a single layer. Place the ribs on top of the vegetables. Cover the pan tightly with foil and bake in preheated oven for 4 hours, or until the ribs are fork tender.

While the ribs are braising, make the glaze. Combine maple syrup, balsamic vinegar, rosemary, and horseradish in a saucepan; whisk to blend. Cook over medium heat until reduced by ⅔ and very syrupy. Remove from heat and set aside.

Remove the ribs from the pan and set aside to keep warm. Strain the braising liquid, discarding the vegetables. Skim fat from surface. Place liquid in saucepan and cook to reduce by half.

Serve the ribs in a pool of the reduced pan juices. Place the glaze in a squeeze bottle and squiggle a portion over each serving.

Perini Ranch Steakhouse Grilled Prime Rib

The Perini Ranch Steakhouse and its owner, Tom Perini, have become icons in Texas. Tom started out as a rancher and cattleman but fell in love with chuckwagon cooking around 1973. He opened the Perini Ranch Steakhouse on the family ranch at Buffalo Gap in 1983. The restaurant was an instant success, featured in media all the way from Texas to the *New York Times* and *Gourmet* magazine.

Tom has been invited to cook at the James Beard House and for President George W. Bush, President Vladimir Putin of Russia, and President Jiang Zenin of China at then-President Bush's ranch in Crawford.

In 2004, Perini, together with Dr. Richard Becker of Becker Vineyards, founded the Buffalo Gap Wine and Food Summit, Inc. The summit strives to cultivate appreciation of fine wine and food through industry discussion and education. The event is held yearly during the third weekend of April on the scenic grounds of the Perini Ranch Steakhouse. The summit is attended by luminaries in the wine and food industry from across the nation and Europe. The *New York Times* referred to the summit as "the culinary event of the year in Texas." Noted French chef and author Jacques Pepin, a dedicated attendee, describes his feelings on the summit: "If you want to have fun, learn about food and wine, and share great food and wine with friends, the Buffalo Gap Wine and Food Summit is the place—there's nothing like Texan hospitality."

COOKING PRIME RIB:

The prime rib is the most regal cut on a steer. Actually, the cut is called a "standing rib roast." The *Prime* designation refers to the USDA grading of the cut. Prime has the most marbling, meaning it will be the most tender and moist, followed by USDA Choice grade. Prime, of course, is the most expensive grade but will produce an incredibly delicious cooked product. The entire rib roast has 13 ribs, with 7 of those contained in the "rib" cut. When purchasing a rib roast, opt for the smaller end of the rib portion, which will be the most tender. Buy the roast with the bones on, as the bones add flavor during cooking, but be sure to have the butcher remove the chine and feather bones to facilitate carving the cooked roast. Allow 1 rib for every 2 people you wish to serve.

Temperature and timing are critical to the success of grilling a standing rib roast. Allow 12 to 14 minutes per pound cooking time for medium rare for a 4-bone roast at 350°F, plus about 20 minutes for initial searing of the meat.

SERVES 8.

4-bone (bone-in) beef standing rib roast, about 7¾ pounds
Prime Rib Rub (recipe follows)
Perini Ranch Steakhouse Horseradish Sauce (recipe follows)

PRIME RIB RUB:
1 cup kosher salt
2 cups coarsely ground black pepper
⅓ cup cornstarch
⅓ cup granulated garlic
½ cup dried oregano

PERINI RANCH STEAKHOUSE
HORSERADISH SAUCE:
2 ounces prepared horseradish

8 ounces sour cream
1 teaspoon finely chopped
  flat-leaf parsley

Begin by making the rub. Combine all ingredients in a medium-sized bowl and toss to blend well. Using your hands, massage the rub into all surfaces of the meat, coating well, including the bones. Let the meat come to room temperature for 1 hour.

Make the horseradish sauce by mixing the horseradish and sour cream, blending well. Refrigerate until ready to serve. Garnish with the chopped parsley before serving.

Build a hardwood charcoal fire in a barbecue grill with an indirect fire pit, or build the fire in one side of a standard pit. Allow the coals to burn down to the point where they are glowing red, covered by a layer of white ash. If you wish to add some smoke flavor, soak oak chips in water for 1 hour, then drain and add them on top of the charcoal.

Place the meat directly over the hot coals and sear all sides of the meat to form a good crust. When all sides have been browned, move the meat off the direct heat, bone side down.

Cook for 1 hour without raising the lid on the pit. Quickly turn the roast over, bone side up, and grill an additional 30 to 50 minutes with the pit closed, or until an instant-read thermometer inserted in the thickest part of the meat, not touching bones, reads 120°F for medium rare. Always remove the roast 10°F before it reaches the desired temperature, as the meat will continue to cook while resting. Removing it at 120°F will give you a perfect 130-degree, medium-rare roast after resting. Continue to cook if you'd like the meat more well done.

Remove the meat to a cutting board and cover loosely with foil. Let the meat rest for 20 to 30 minutes to allow the juices to redistribute evenly throughout the meat. Carve the bones off the meat, then slice the meat to desired thickness, and serve with the horseradish sauce. You can slice the bones into individual portions and serve them also, or save them for a mighty tasty snack another time!

Texas Farmhouse Pot Roast with Ancho Chile Pan Sauce

Beef chuck is a very flavorful cut of meat, albeit a tough one that needs to be braised. Pot roast has long been a farmhouse kitchen standby and a favorite "hot plate of the day" dish at mom-and-pop diners. This version is slightly gussied-up with red wine for richness in the brothy sauce and ancho chiles for a little kick of spice. Be sure to spoon lots of the sauce over each portion and serve with your favorite rustic bread for sopping up the broth.

SERVES 4.

-----

3 pounds grass-fed beef chuck roast

Kosher salt and freshly ground black pepper

¼ cup bacon drippings or canola oil

4 medium red new potatoes, about 1 pound, unpeeled, quartered

1 large onion, peeled, halved, and cut into slices 1 inch thick

3 carrots, peeled, halved lengthwise, and cut into 2-inch pieces

4 celery stalks, halved lengthwise and cut into 2-inch pieces

6 large garlic cloves, peeled and quartered

2 large ancho chiles, whole

6 large thyme sprigs

10 flat-leaf parsley sprigs

1 cup dry red wine, such as Cabernet Sauvignon, divided

3 cups beef stock

1½ teaspoons freshly ground black pepper

2 cups fresh or frozen green peas

2 heaping tablespoons cornstarch whisked into ¼ cup cold water

Preheat oven to 350°F. Pat meat dry on all sides, using absorbent paper towels. Season on both sides with salt and pepper, patting the pepper into the meat; set aside. Heat the bacon drippings or canola oil in a heavy-bottomed roasting pan or Dutch oven over high heat. When the fat is hot, add the meat and cook to sear on both sides, turning once. The meat should have a nice crisp crust on both sides. Remove meat to a platter, using chef's tongs.

Add the potatoes to the hot fat and cook, tossing often, until lightly browned. Add onions, carrots, celery, garlic, ancho chiles, thyme, and parsley. Sear the vegetables and seasonings, tossing often, until onion is wilted and transparent, about 7 minutes. Return the meat to the pan and pour ⅔ cup of the wine over the meat and vegetables. Cook until wine is reduced to a glaze, about 5 to 7 minutes. Add the beef stock and black pepper; cover pan and place in preheated oven. Cook for 2 to 2½ hours, or until meat is fork tender and can be pulled apart with a slight tug of a fork. Remove meat and vegetables to a baking dish and add the peas. Cover and return to oven, leaving the chiles, herb sprigs, and small vegetable pieces in the pan juices in roasting pan. Cook for 10 minutes.

Return roasting pan or Dutch oven to high heat and stir in the remaining ⅓ cup wine. Cook to reduce slightly, about 15 minutes. Bring the pan juices to a boil and stir in the cornstarch mixture. Cook just until slightly thickened, about 3 to 4 minutes. Strain the brothy sauce through a fine strainer into a bowl, pressing down on the chiles, herb sprigs, and vegetable scraps to extract as much flavor from them as possible. Discard chiles, herbs, and vegetable scraps. Taste sauce for seasoning, adjusting as needed. Keep the sauce hot.

To serve, place equal portions of the vegetables in individual soup plates or pasta bowls. Top each serving with a portion of the meat. Spoon a liberal portion of the pan sauce over each serving. Serve hot.

BASTROP CATTLE COMPANY

Pati Jacobs and her brother, Cleve, owners of Bastrop Cattle Company, set out to prove that they could offer high-quality meat—free of hormones, antibiotics, and chemicals, and grass-fed—and treat the animals and the people who raise them fairly. The pair have their own cattle, but they also work with other families in Bastrop and neighboring counties. In return for a guaranteed price that far exceeds that of the auction barn, the ranchers agree to place their herds under a continuous monitoring program. "Because our ranchers are earning a fair price, they really strive to raise top-quality beef," says Pati.

All of the ranches, including the Jacobs's ranch, raise heavily Angus-crossed cattle. Calves are fed on pasture grass, cow's milk, and, in winter, grass hays such as coastal bermuda. Ranchers must submit for inspection the labels from any supplements used with the cattle, such as supplemental minerals, salts, or range cubes, to ensure that no animal by-products are present in the supplements.

All of Bastrop Cattle Company's meat is hung and dry-aged for the appropriate amount of time, then cut, vacuum-sealed, and commercially hard-frozen. This is the best and safest method for preserving the freshness of the meat. The taste is generally mild, with a smoky-nutty flavor.

"We're very lucky," Pati said. "We have a band of really loyal customers who buy our meat week in and week out. It makes me feel very good to know that we are one more producer offering quality healthy, drug- and chemical-free food to our neighbors."

LLANO ESTACADO WINERY

LLANO ESTACADO IS the second-oldest winery in Texas. It began in 1976 when two professors at Texas Tech University, Bob Reed and Clinton "Doc" McPherson, set out to discover what the fertile soil of West Texas would bear. The winery has succeeded far beyond even its founders' dreams.

Llano Estacado is generally regarded as the winery most responsible for this state's current wine renaissance. It was the first officially bonded winery to open its doors following Prohibition. The winery walked away with an unprecedented Double Gold Medal (meaning that the decision to award the gold was unanimous) for its 1984 Chardonnay at the 1986 San Francisco Fair wine competition. In 1988, it received its first award at an international competition, winning a Gold Medal for the 1985 Cellar Select Cabernet Sauvignon. The accolades and awards have continued over the decades, and the winery currently produces more than 165,000 cases per year.

In 1993, Greg Bruni signed on to become vice president/winemaker at Llano Estacado. Bruni brought a wealth of knowledge to the Texas wine industry. (His family had founded the esteemed San Martin Winery, where Greg began working in the cellar.) When he first visited the winery and the Texas High Plains, he saw the same challenges that existed years ago in California. He relished the idea of becoming a key player in the future of Llano Estacado. Bruni is a very hands-on winemaker, personally overseeing all aspects of the winemaking process. If he's not in the cellar or the lab, then he's most likely in a vineyard or overseeing a harvest of grapes grown for Llano Estacado at one of the vineyards in the Texas High Plains AVA.

CEO Mark Hyman joined Llano Estacado in 1994, following a successful career in wine marketing beginning in the early 1980s. Since his arrival, the winery's sales have more than tripled. He feels that he is definitely in the right place at the right time and that Texas has the potential to become one of the world's leading wine-producing regions.

Greg Bruni recommends the Llano Estacado Cellar Reserve Tempranillo as his favorite pairing with the Perini Ranch Steakhouse Grilled Prime Rib (pages 335–337). The wine has enough tannin to support the rub and meat texture without overpowering it. This tannin effect is amplified with the horseradish sauce—the more tannin, the hotter, more textural, and lingering the aftertaste of the horseradish becomes. This wine was oak-aged for only 16 months, so it still has a hint of bright red cherry that works as an accent. The texture of the meat carries the heavier grape tannins of the Tempranillo very well. Because the wine was aged in more neutral barrels, the barrel flavors do not interfere with the pungency of the herbal rub.

For the Grilled Grass-Fed Beef Tenderloin Steaks with Aged Brie and Shiitake Mushroom Sauce (pages 324–326), Greg recommends the Llano Estacado Texas High Plains Sangiovese as his number-one pairing, with the Llano Estacado Viviano red blend as his number two. "This was a wrestling match for me," said Greg. "From a flavor perspective, there is a lot going on with this dish. The sauce changes the texture and flavor of this delicate cut of meat yet retains the meat's tenderness and delicate attributes." Greg noted that the Sangiovese seemed to add a mouthwatering savory element, and its medium body and light tannin profile did not interfere with the textural complexity of the mushrooms. Aromatically, two years of oak aging added a very slight "high tone" of smoky oak/Spanish cedar that played well with the shiitake and did not work against the rosemary. In short, it supports the dish without dominating.

7

SIDES
and A FEW
MEATLESS
DISHES

★

Which menu description is more enticing—Grilled Center-Cut Pork Loin Chop with Smashed Potatoes and Sautéed Vegetables or Seasoned and Grilled Center-Cut Heirloom Pork Loin Chop with Jalapeño Corn Pudding and Green Beans Seared with Garlic and Peppered Bacon? What's "also on the plate" is as important as the main dish. I am always impressed when a restaurant has a different side dish for each entrée. This tells me that the chef has carefully orchestrated every plate to be a harmony of flavors that were carefully paired to provide the ultimate taste experience.

Plan your side dishes as carefully as you plan the entrée. Fresh-from-the-ground potatoes are certainly wonderful, but there are many other root vegetables that are nutritious and equally delicious. Turnips, parsnips, rutabagas, kohlrabi, and beets are starches with great, earthy flavors, and they can be cooked by a variety of methods, far more than could be covered in a single chapter! Brussels sprouts are divine and can even make a tasty slaw when cut into fine julienned strips. Spinach isn't the only "green" that makes a good side dish either. Try Swiss chard, kale, collard, turnip, mustard, and beet greens. Even some of the salad greens can be quickly pan-sautéed to make appealing sides.

Grains like quinoa and faro are delicious and very nutritious. Couscous can be flavored to fit the entrée. Orzo (a rice-shaped pasta) and the various aromatic strains of rice are also great alternatives to potatoes.

For a change of pace occasionally, try preparing a meatless meal. The choices are limited only by your imagination. And chances are, you'll discover that you didn't miss the meat! Make it fresh, and make it tasty, and the whole plate will sing in three-part harmony.

Rosa's Mex-Mex Rice

I learned so much more than I could ever relate about preparing real Mexican food from Rosa Ramirez, a former member of my kitchen team from Guanajuato, Mexico. Rosa's rice is incredibly flavorful and has a lovely red clay color, which makes it great for perking up any plate with dull colors. It's a must-have with Carne Guisada de Cabrito (see recipe on pages 310–311). Don't skip the step of frying the raw rice in the shortening or lard, as it adds a flavor that is integral to Rosa's dish. And Rosa, by the way, always used lard.

SERVES 6 TO 8.

6 cups hot water

½ teaspoon kosher salt

3 Knorr brand tomato bouillon cubes

1 Knorr brand chicken bouillon cube

2 large Roma tomatoes, roughly chopped

2 garlic cloves, peeled

1 slice of a large white onion, 1-inch thick

¼ cup solid shortening or leaf lard

2 cups long-grain white rice

Combine the water, salt, tomato and chicken bouillon cubes, tomatoes, garlic, and onion in the container of a blender. Puree until smooth; transfer to a bowl and set aside.

Melt the shortening in a heavy-bottomed 4-quart saucepan over medium-low heat. When shortening is hot, add the raw rice and cook, stirring frequently, to lightly brown the rice, about 15 to 20 minutes. Do not let the rice stick to the pan. When the rice is golden in color, pour the pureed tomato mixture into the pan and stir to blend well. Cover pan and bring to a boil. As soon as the liquid begins to boil rapidly, turn the heat to the lowest setting. Cook, covered, about 20 to 25 minutes, or until all liquid has been absorbed. Stir to fluff the rice. Serve hot.

Thompson Family Thanksgiving Sweet Potato Casserole

Few people realize that the South's beloved sweet potato is not, in fact, a *potato* at all. Nor is it related to the *yam*, with which it is often confused. A sweet potato is a rooted tuber that is first cousin to the morning glory vine. However we classify sweet potatoes, they've become an institution in the South, where they're boiled, baked, fried, and made into delicious pones as in this recipe. What a bonus that the sweet potato is also very nutritious, containing more than twice the recommended daily allowance of vitamin A, as well as healthy doses of potassium, calcium, and vitamin C. To retain the greatest possible amount of nutrients, always cook the sweet potato with its skin on, then peel after it has cooled enough to handle.

SERVES 6 TO 8.

POTATO MIXTURE:

3 large sweet potatoes, about 27 to 30 ounces total, unpeeled

¾ cup butter, softened and cut into ½-inch cubes

¾ cup sugar

½ teaspoon kosher salt

3 eggs, beaten

½ cup evaporated milk

1 tablespoon vanilla extract

½ teaspoon cinnamon

TOPPING:

¾ cup firmly packed light brown sugar

¼ cup unsalted butter, softened and cut into ½-inch cubes

¼ cup all-purpose flour

⅔ cup chopped pecans

Preheat oven to 400°F. Lightly butter a 13 × 9-inch baking dish; set aside. Set the sweet potatoes in a second baking dish; bake in preheated oven for about 40 to 45 minutes, or until you can insert a fork into the flesh with ease. Remove the sweet potatoes and set them aside for a few minutes until they are cool enough to handle. Lower oven temperature to 375°F. Peel the skin from the potatoes and place the potatoes in a large bowl. Mash the potatoes thoroughly. Add butter, sugar, salt, eggs, evaporated milk, vanilla, and cinnamon, stirring to blend well and melt the butter. Turn the mixture into a prepared baking dish.

To make the topping, combine brown sugar, butter, and flour in the work bowl of a food processor fitted with the steel blade. Process until smooth and fluffy. Add the pecans and process just to blend, using the pulse feature and leaving the pecan pieces fairly intact.

Spread the topping over potato mixture. Bake in preheated oven until set and lightly browned on top, about 45 minutes. Serve hot.

Texas Goat Cheese and Cilantro Mashed Potatoes

For a new twist on plain old mashed potatoes, try this flavor-packed version. Even people who claim to hate goat cheese love them.

SERVES 4.

1 pound small new potatoes, unpeeled and quartered

2 tablespoons unsalted butter

½ small onion, cut into tiny dice

4 ounces plain Texas goat cheese, preferably Water Oaks Farm, or substitute another mild-flavored plain goat cheese, cut into small pieces

1 heaping tablespoon minced cilantro

¼ teaspoon freshly ground black pepper

¾ teaspoon kosher salt

Place potatoes in a heavy-bottomed 3-quart saucepan. Add cold water to cover. Bring to a full, rolling boil over medium-high heat and cook for 20 minutes, or until potatoes are very soft.

While potatoes are cooking, melt butter in a heavy-bottomed 8-inch skillet over medium heat. Add onions and sauté, stirring often, until wilted and transparent, about 5 minutes. Remove from heat and set aside.

Drain potatoes in a colander, shaking off all water, and quickly return them to the hot pan. Add the sautéed onions and any residual butter in the skillet, goat cheese, cilantro, pepper, and salt. Mash the potatoes with a potato masher, leaving them slightly lumpy. Be sure the other ingredients are evenly mixed into the potatoes.

Herbed Spaetzle

Spaetzle is a traditional German side dish composed of small curdlike, egg-based dumplings. You'll often find it paired with various schnitzels or roast pork at German restaurants, though it's a tasty side that can be added to a non-German meal, too.

Spaetzle can be made using a plain metal colander, or "spaetzle makers" can be purchased at specialty cookware shops like Der Kuchen Laden in Fredericksburg, which carries quite an array of bakeware and gadgets used in German cooking. You may want to use a different fresh herb, depending on the other flavors in the meal. Flat-leaf parsley always adds a nice note to spaetzle and would pair well with any meat.

SERVES 6 TO 8.

3 cups all-purpose flour

1 teaspoon kosher salt

½ teaspoon freshly ground black pepper

½ teaspoon freshly ground nutmeg

1 teaspoon minced fresh sage

3 eggs, well beaten

1 cup whole milk

1½ gallons chicken stock, preferably homemade

2 tablespoons very soft unsalted butter

⅓ cup dry bread crumbs, optional

Sift the flour, salt, pepper, and nutmeg together into a large bowl. In a separate bowl, whisk the sage, eggs, and milk together, blending thoroughly. Pour the egg mixture into the dry ingredients and whisk until smooth, with no lumps of flour remaining. Add more milk or flour in small amounts as needed to make the batter thick and elastic, yet pourable. Set aside.

Bring the chicken stock to a full, rolling boil in a heavy-bottomed 6-quart pot over medium-high heat. Working in batches of about 1½ cups of batter at a time, pour the batter through a colander with holes about ⅛ to ¼ inch, or a spaetzle maker, allowing small bits to drop off into the boiling stock. Work quickly to get all of the batter into the stock, then cook for about 1 minute, or until the spaetzle rises to the top. Remove with a wire skimmer or finely slotted spoon to a bowl; cover to keep warm while you cook the remaining batter.

When all of the spaetzle has been cooked, quickly strain it through a fine strainer and return to a dry bowl. Add the very soft butter and bread crumbs, if desired. Gently stir to melt the butter into the spaetzle and incorporate the bread crumbs, taking care not to break the delicate dumplings. Serve hot.

FREDERICKSBURG FARMERS MARKET

EACH WEEK I LOOK FORWARD to Thursday, when the Fredericksburg Farmers Market is open. I like to arrive a few minutes early to watch the vendors setting up their tents and booths—farmers unloading produce from their trucks, meat vendors hauling in their many coolers, and many others setting up their wares. I love the color of the farmers' market—vegetables and fruits of many hues, chiles of every description.

On a recent trip to the market, after the bell rang at 4:00 p.m., signaling the opening, I first stopped to drop off my favorite 35-year-old chef's knife to be sharpened at Mr. Holmgren's booth. He can put an edge on a knife that makes it better than new! The chef of the week, who happened to be Ross Burtwell from Fredericksburg's much-loved Cabernet Grill, was handing out tasty goodies. Who could resist? Then I moseyed to Josh Raymer's space to buy a couple of loaves of genuine hearth-baked breads. Josh brings his huge hearth oven on wheels to the market each week and prepares pizza to order.

Next a stop at Twin County Lamb to purchase a beautiful shoulder of lamb and chat with proprietors Lloyd Wendel and Isabelle Lauzierre. Isabelle had some beautiful hand-crafted soaps that she had made from goat's milk. Even though they weren't on my list, I decided to treat myself to a couple of the fragrant bars. A nice little chicken from Marianna at Peeler Farms completed my meat shopping.

I picked up a few peaches, the last of the season, from Gary Marburger of Marburger Farms. Couldn't pass up a couple of the vibrant purple-lobed Sicilian eggplants that Gary Rowland grows at Hairston Creek Farm, or a bit of artisan goat cheese from Chrissy Omo at CKC Farms. Some zucchini and a small Black Diamond watermelon topped off my trusty market bag.

Then, with the last items crossed off my grocery list, I could enjoy the best part of the market and one of the reasons it's been such a special addition to the Fredericksburg community. First I bought a juicy and delicious grass-fed beef slider hot off the grill from Angela Mancino at the Sunset Grill spot, and a glass of wine from Gary Gilstrap at Texas Hills Vineyard, the featured winery of the week. I got a space at one of the picnic tables that line the center of the market and sat down to listen to the live music and chat with fellow foodies, catching up on the latest happenings in the burg.

Farmers' markets like this one are much more than a place to buy groceries. They are community gatherings where you can learn about (even taste) nutritious, natural foods grown by folks who live all around you.

Mixed Greens with
Smoked Pork Jowl in Potlikker

"Greens are good for you." Southerners have heard that since they started eating solid food. But not everybody knows that greens are just plain good. Once associated with "the poor class" in the South, greens have come into the limelight in recent years. I was raised in a household where nothing that smelled offensive while cooking was ever cooked. When I married a southern country boy, I weighed 96 pounds. Mealtime was not something I had been raised to savor. After discovering the pleasures of the table in my mother-in-law's home, I knew I would never again weigh 96 pounds.

One of my favorites was greens. I just couldn't seem to get enough of them or the rich, flavorful broth in which they were cooked. To my further delight, it was not only permitted, but expected, that when you had eaten all of the greens, you would pick up the bowl and drink the broth right from the bowl. Potlikker, I was told, was the real reason that you cooked the greens, and the flavor of the broth was a measure of the cook's skill. Folks are serious about potlikker in the South. Huey Long, one of a long list of Louisiana's flamboyant politicians, once staged an all-night filibuster on the floor of the US Senate on the subject of authentically made potlikker. Franklin D. Roosevelt suggested that the issue be referred to the Platform Committee at the 1932 Democratic National Convention. In defense of the southern spelling of the word, Lieutenant Governor Zell Miller of Georgia sent the following message to the *New York Times* in response to an article that it printed in 1982:

> *I always thought the* New York Times *knew everything, but obviously your editor knows as little about spelling as he or she does about Appalachian cooking and soul food. Only a culinarily-illiterate damnyankee who can't tell the difference between beans and greens would call the liquid left in the pot after cooking greens "pot liquor," instead of "potlikker" as yours did. And don't cite Webster as a defense because he didn't know any better either.*

The choice of "seasoning meat" is a personal one. You can use plain old bacon, cut into tiny dice, or salt pork, or my personal favorite, smoked pork jowl. You can find it in markets in most small towns, in markets in Mexican or African American neighborhoods, and increasingly at artisan charcuterie markets.

2 bunches fresh collard greens

2 bunches fresh mustard greens

2 bunches fresh kale

2 medium onions, halved lengthwise, then sliced

2 small turnips, peeled, halved lengthwise, then thinly sliced

8 ounces smoked hog jowl, rind removed, cut into tiny dice, or substitute other seasoning meat

1½ tablespoons sugar

½ cup Tex-Mex-style picante sauce

1 heaping tablespoon MSG-free chicken base paste

1 tablespoon kosher salt

2 teaspoons freshly ground black pepper

Place all greens in the sink and fill to the brim with water. Let the greens stand for 15 minutes. Carefully remove greens from the water without disturbing the sandy silt that has settled to the bottom. Wash the leaves under running water. Tear leaves into small pieces, removing and discarding the tough center ribs. Place torn greens, onions, turnips, and seasoning meat in a 10- to 12-quart pot; add water to cover the greens. Stir in sugar, picante sauce, chicken base, salt, and pepper. Bring to a boil over medium-high heat; boil 5 minutes. Reduce heat and simmer, stirring occasionally, for 2 hours. Taste for seasoning; adjust as necessary. The greens should have lots of liquid left; add additional water if needed. Serve hot in bowls with plenty of potlikker.

Hoffman Haus Spinach and Cheese Tart

Fredericksburg has a lot to offer visitors: quaint shops, German heritage, great restaurants, an awarding-winning brewery, good music venues, dozens of nearby wineries, and more than 400 bed-and-breakfast establishments. Hoffman Haus is one of the best and most varied. There are rustic cabins; elegant and romantic suites; upstairs rooms over the Great Hall, where guests are met by the cordial staff when checking in; individual houses; and even a large Sears and Roebuck kit farmhouse from the era in the late 1890s when you could buy a kit to build a house from the Sears catalog! It's a fascinating place—all set on a beautifully landscaped piece of property just a block off Main Street yet with the feeling of being miles away from town. The best part of a stay at Hoffman Haus is breakfast. No store-bought sweet rolls and coffee here. There's a complete commercial kitchen where your hosts, Leslie and Hugh Washburne, prepare a tantalizing hot breakfast that is packed into picnic baskets and delivered to your door hot and fresh to enjoy in the privacy of your own room without having to get gussied up.

This delicious dish, loaded with fresh spinach and great Texas cheeses, is one of their most popular breakfast dishes. I love it because it can be prepared completely ahead of time, refrigerated, and then baked just before serving. Sliced wedges of the crustless tart also make a great side dish with a meat entrée, or the tart can be served as a meatless entrée on its own, say, with a mixed green salad.

SERVES 6 TO 8.

20 ounces fresh spinach leaves, blanched, drained, and squeezed very dry
2 green onions, sliced thin, including green tops
5 eggs, well beaten
½ cup Mexican crema
½ teaspoon Texas Pete Hot Sauce
2 tablespoons melted and cooled butter
1 teaspoon kosher salt
4 ounces (1 cup) shredded Brazos Valley Havarti cheese

4 ounces (1 cup) crumbled Texas goat feta cheese, such as CKC Farms
Pinch of freshly grated nutmeg

FOR MUSHROOMS:
4 tablespoons (½ stick) unsalted butter
1 large portobello mushroom, cut in half and then cut into thin slices on the bias
Kosher salt and freshly ground black pepper

Preheat oven to 350°F. Butter a 12-inch round quiche dish* and set aside. Mix all ingredients, except mushrooms, in a mixing bowl.

Turn out into prepared quiche dish and bake, uncovered, in preheated oven for 30 minutes, or until lightly browned on top and set.

While the spinach dish is cooking, melt the half stick of butter in a heavy-bottomed 10-inch sauté pan over medium-high heat. Add the sliced mushrooms and cook, stirring often, until slices are lightly browned and wilted. Season to taste with salt and pepper. Set aside to keep warm.

To serve, slice the tart into wedges and place a portion on each serving plate. Arrange a slice of the mushrooms over the top of each wedge. Serve hot with your favorite breakfast meat and pastry.

* You can also bake the tarts in 8 individual 5-inch gratin dishes. Serve the individual servings with an underlining plate.

Fresh Greens and Goat Cheese Gratin

My husband, Roger, grows beautiful greens—Swiss chard, curly mustard greens, spinach, beets, turnips, collard greens, and bok choy, among others—so I'm always looking for new recipes in which to use his garden's bounty. I especially love Swiss chard, as does my sister, Sandy. The texture is similar to that of spinach, which makes it a very versatile green. Sandy, who is also an avid gardener as well as a great cook, created a version of this dish one night when she had a few friends over for a casual dinner. Texas farmers' markets offer a plethora of fresh greens in the spring and fall.

SERVES 4 TO 6.

3 tablespoons Texas extra-virgin olive oil

1 small portobello mushroom, cut into ½-inch dice

½ small red onion, peeled and sliced lengthwise in thin julienned strips

4 garlic cloves, minced

1 large bunch fresh spinach, stems removed, washed, dried, and torn into bite-size pieces

1 large bunch Swiss chard, stems removed, washed, dried, and torn into bite-size pieces

1 blistered and peeled red bell pepper, cut into ½-inch dice

4 slices prosciutto, sliced paper thin and finely chopped

Kosher salt and freshly ground black pepper

2 eggs, well beaten

2 tablespoons fresh bread crumbs

2 tablespoons Mexican crema

4 ounces crumbled, semi-firm Texas goat cheese

⅓ cup panko bread crumbs tossed with 2 tablespoons additional olive oil, 1 heaping teaspoon grated lemon zest, and 2 tablespoons grated Pecorino Romano cheese

Preheat oven to 350°F. Spray a 10-inch oval gratin dish with nonstick spray; set aside.

Heat the olive oil in a heavy-bottomed 12-inch skillet. When the oil is hot, add the portobello and cook on medium-high heat until lightly browned, about 5 minutes. Add red onion and garlic; cook, stirring occasionally, until onion is wilted, about 5 minutes. Add the spinach, Swiss chard, red bell pepper, and prosciutto to the skillet, tossing to moisten; cook, tossing often, until greens are wilted, about 5 minutes. Season with salt and pepper to taste.

While greens are cooking, whisk the eggs, bread crumbs, Mexican crema, and goat cheese together in a large bowl, blending well. Add the greens to the bowl and stir to mix into the egg and cheese mixture, incorporating all ingredients thoroughly. Turn out into a prepared gratin dish and scatter the panko mixture over the top. Bake in preheated oven for 20 to 25 minutes, or until golden brown and bubbly. Serve hot.

Roger's Brisket Beans

Most Texans never met a bean they didn't like, and my husband, Roger, is no exception. He is always concocting new bean recipes. He also cooks a lot of brisket. A brisket that has been slow cooked over a low fire for many hours will develop a charred crust, known as the *bark* in barbecue jargon. This bark, which is part meat and part fat, is sometimes trimmed away and discarded when the brisket is sliced for serving. But it has a great taste and crisp texture—a treat for whoever is trimming the brisket. One day as Roger was trimming a brisket and putting the finishing touches on yet another pot of beans, he hit upon the idea of tossing some of the bark in with the beans. Some of the pieces contained tender, juicy fat that melted as the beans cooked, creating a thick, creamy sort of gravy. The results were sensational—best pot of beans he ever cooked. Now we save all the brisket trimmings to make Roger's brisket beans. We sometimes serve bowls of them as a meal, along with a side of coleslaw and cornbread. Now that's Texas country eating at its finest!

SERVES 10 TO 12.

1½ pounds dried pinto beans

¼ cup canola oil

2 medium onions, chopped

3 large garlic cloves, minced

2 celery stalks, chopped

1 large poblano chile, blistered, peeled, seeded, and cut into ½-inch dice

1 can (15 ounces) diced fire-roasted tomatoes and their juice

1 can (15 ounces) diced Ro-Tel Diced Tomatoes & Green Chilies

1 meaty ham hock

8 ounces reserved brisket trimmings, finely chopped

2 quarts chicken stock, preferably homemade, or more if needed

Freshly ground black pepper

Kosher salt

1 tablespoon minced cilantro

Chopped onions for topping, if desired

Sort through the dried beans to remove any stones, chunks of dirt, or bad beans; set aside. Heat the canola oil in a heavy-bottomed 10-quart pot over medium-high heat. Add the onions, garlic, celery, and diced poblano chile. Cook, stirring often, until vegetables are wilted and transparent, about 10 minutes.

Add the fire-roasted tomatoes and Ro-Tel tomatoes, stirring to blend. Add the beans, ham hock, and brisket trimmings. Add chicken stock to cover by 2 inches and season to taste with pepper. (Don't add salt to dried beans until they are tender, or they will remain tough and hard.) Bring the liquid to a full boil. Lower heat and cook at a brisk simmer for about 25 minutes, stirring often. Add additional chicken stock as needed to keep the beans covered slightly. Lower heat, cover and cook for about 1 hour, or until beans are very tender and a thickened gravy has formed.

Skim off any fat from the surface of the beans. If you'd like a thicker gravy for the beans, remove 1½ cups of beans and liquid and puree in a blender until smooth. Stir back into the pot to thicken the gravy. Remove the ham hock and trim off the meat. Chop the meat into small dice and return to pot. Season to taste with salt, if needed. Add the cilantro and stir to blend. Remove from heat and serve hot in bowls, topped with chopped onions, if desired.

German Potato Salad

This dish, although served hot or warm, is referred to as potato "salad." I like to serve it with barbecue during the colder months when the thought of a cold side dish makes me shiver.

SERVES 6.

2½ pounds small red new potatoes, unpeeled

6 smoked bacon slices, fried until crisp and crumbled, drippings reserved

1 medium onion, chopped

1½ tablespoons all-purpose flour

¼ cup light brown sugar

1 teaspoon paprika

½ teaspoon celery salt

½ teaspoon freshly ground black pepper

⅓ cup apple cider vinegar

⅔ cup hot beef stock, preferably homemade

1½ tablespoons minced flat-leaf parsley

Scrub the potatoes well and slice into bite-size pieces. Place potato slices in a 4-quart saucepan and add cold water to cover. Bring the potatoes to a boil, then simmer for 20 minutes, or until potatoes are tender, but not mushy. Drain into a colander, shaking off excess water, and place in a large bowl. Set aside to keep warm.

Heat the reserved bacon drippings in a heavy-bottomed 12-inch skillet over medium heat. Add the onion and cook until it is wilted and transparent, about 7 minutes. Stir in the flour all at once, blending well. Cook, stirring, for 3 to 4 minutes. Add the brown sugar, paprika, celery salt, pepper, vinegar, and hot beef stock. Bring to a full boil and stir until thickened. Stir in the crumbled bacon. Pour the dressing over the potatoes, add parsley, and stir to coat the potatoes thoroughly with the dressing. Serve hot or warm.

Hill Country Potato Salad

Potato salad is requisite at any Texas barbecue worth its smoke. It's also likely to show up at backyard burger cookouts, so I like to have three or four really good recipes for potato salad so I can switch 'em up. I particularly like this one because it has a good kick of heat from pickled jalapeños and Cholula Hot Sauce, which has a flavor that I find particularly complements Texas foods.

SERVES 6 TO 8.

5 cups unpeeled, sliced red new
    potatoes, about 2½ pounds

3 boiled eggs, chopped

1 small yellow onion, cut into
    ¼-inch dice

2 large celery stalks, cut into
    ¼-inch dice

2 green onions, chopped, including
    green tops

1½ cups real mayonnaise, preferably
    homemade

⅓ cup "ballpark-style" yellow mustard

½ cup chopped pickled jalapeños

1 teaspoon Cholula Hot Sauce

2 tablespoons minced flat-leaf parsley

1¼ teaspoons toasted, then ground,
    cumin seeds

1½ teaspoons freshly ground black
    pepper

1½ teaspoons kosher salt

Place the potatoes in a heavy-bottomed 4-quart pot and add cold water to cover. Bring to a boil, then cook for about 20 minutes, or until potatoes are tender, but not mushy. Drain in a colander, shaking off excess water. Combine potatoes, boiled eggs, onion, celery, and green onions in a large bowl; set aside.

In a separate bowl combine the mayonnaise, mustard, jalapeños, hot sauce, parsley, cumin, pepper, and salt. Whisk until smooth. Fold the dressing into the potato mixture, blending well. Refrigerate until well chilled. Serve chilled, or at room temperature.

Baked Garden-Fresh Tomatoes with Spinach Stuffing

If you're looking for a colorful and delicious side dish, look no further. This is a great one for a "company" meal served on Grandmother's china. If you grow your own tomatoes and you have a variety of colors of tomatoes to use, the dish really makes an impression. The tomatoes can be put together in advance and baked just in time to serve. The spinach filling for the fresh tomatoes has a note of Creole-French intrigue, provided by just a hint of Herbsaint, a robust anise-flavored liqueur produced in New Orleans.

SERVES 8.

4 large homegrown or heirloom
  tomatoes
Melted unsalted butter

Kosher salt
Spinach Stuffing (see recipe below)

SPINACH STUFFING:
20 ounces fresh chopped spinach
  leaves, blanched, drained, and
  squeezed very dry
2 tablespoons unsalted butter
2 large garlic cloves, minced
2 green onions, finely chopped,
  including green tops
2 tablespoons all-purpose flour
1 cup whipping cream

1 tablespoon Herbsaint, or other
  anise-flavored liqueur
½ teaspoon kosher salt
¼ teaspoon freshly ground black
  pepper
¼ teaspoon red (cayenne) pepper
3 eggs, well beaten
½ cup dried bread crumbs, tossed
  with 3 tablespoons grated
  Parmesan cheese

Preheat oven to 350°F. Halve the tomatoes crosswise. Carefully scoop out and discard pulp and seeds, taking care not to puncture the outside skin. Cut a very thin slice from the bottom of each tomato half, so that it will sit flat without tipping over. Place the tomatoes in a baking dish. Brush the inside of each tomato shell with some of the melted butter; salt and pepper each to taste. Set dish aside.

Press all moisture out of the spinach. In a heavy-bottomed 10-inch skillet over medium heat, melt the 2 tablespoons butter. Add the spinach, garlic, and green onions. Sauté for 5 minutes, then add the flour, stirring to blend well. Cook, stirring constantly for 3 to 4 minutes. Add the whipping cream, Herbsaint, and seasonings. Bring to a boil and stir until slightly thickened. Remove from heat and cool slightly. Stir in the beaten eggs. Spoon a portion of the mixture into each tomato half and top with some of the bread crumb and cheese mixture. Bake in preheated oven for about 25 to 30 minutes, or just until the filling is firmly set and tops are bubbly. Serve hot.

Braised Red Cabbage and Bacon with Apples and Onions

Braised red cabbage is another of the delicious traditional dishes brought to Texas by German immigrants who settled in the central part of the state. It's hearty and a perfect side for a German meat dish, but it's so good that I don't limit it to German meals. You can also turn it into a one-dish meal by adding sliced Polish sausage or kielbasa when you add the onions.

SERVES 4 TO 6.

- 6 applewood-smoked bacon slices, cut into ½-inch dice
- 1 small head red cabbage, about 1 pound
- 2 Granny Smith apples, cored and cut into 1-inch dice
- 1 teaspoon kosher salt
- 1 tablespoon freshly squeezed lemon juice
- 1½ teaspoons firmly packed light brown sugar
- ¾ cup chicken stock, preferably homemade
- 1 small yellow onion, chopped
- ¼ teaspoon freshly ground black pepper
- 1 tablespoon red wine vinegar

Cook the bacon in a heavy-bottomed 10-inch skillet over medium heat until it is crisp and has rendered its fat. Using a slotted spoon, remove the bacon pieces and set aside. Reserve the drippings in the skillet.

Quarter the cabbage and shred it coarsely, discarding the tough center core. Rinse the cabbage, then place in a 6-quart soup pot with the apples, salt, lemon juice, brown sugar, and chicken stock. Bring to a boil, then lower heat, and cover pan. Simmer for 15 minutes, stirring a couple of times.

Heat the reserved bacon drippings over medium-high heat. When drippings are hot, add the onion and sauté until lightly browned, about 10 minutes. Stir occasionally. Add the onion to the cabbage along with the pepper, vinegar, and reserved bacon. Cook, covered, for an additional 15 minutes, or until the cabbage is very wilted. Serve hot.

French Green Beans with Garlic and Peppered Bacon

While there will always be a soft spot in my heart for a big pot of green pole beans cooked to delicious down-home death in chicken broth with fatty bacon for a couple of hours, crisp, pan-seared French green beans are a deserving side for a perfectly grilled steak, or on the Thanksgiving table. Their proper French name, *haricots verts*, threw my new, rough-around-the edges cowboy husband, Roger, into a tailspin the first time I brought home some of the seeds I had found in the big-city garden shop in Houston. But he loved me, so he planted them, along with his beloved pole beans. He was amazed at their bountiful crop. One row yielded enough beans that we were able to eat our fill of them fresh and still have enough to blanch and freeze to provide a supply of them until the next spring. Now he's a devoted fan of "those fancy, French-ified beans."

SERVES 4 TO 6.

----

1 pound fresh French green beans, tipped and tailed

10 peppered bacon slices, cut into small dice

2 tablespoons Texas extra-virgin olive oil

10 garlic cloves, peeled and minced

Kosher salt

Prepare a large bowl of ice water containing lots of ice cubes; set aside. Bring a large pot of salted water to a full boil over high heat. Add the beans all at once and cook, stirring gently, for 2 to 3 minutes. Quickly drain the beans into a colander, shake to remove the hot water, and plunge them into the ice water to stop the cooking. Allow them to cool completely, then drain, shaking off as much water as possible, and set aside.

Cook the diced bacon in a heavy-bottomed, preferably cast-iron, 12-inch skillet over medium-high heat until bacon is crisp and the fat is rendered. Add the olive oil and stir to blend. Add the green beans and garlic to the pan, tossing with chef's tongs to coat the beans with the fat and oil blend. Salt to taste. Cook, tossing constantly, just until the beans are good and hot and the garlic is fragrant, about 3 to 4 minutes. Don't allow the garlic to brown. Serve hot, being sure that each serving includes some of the bacon and garlic.

ATKINSON FARM

MIKE ATKINSON IS the fourth generation to work the family farm in Tomball. After graduating from college in 1974, Mike returned home and began working on the farm. At the time they raised mainly vegetables—tomatoes, peppers, eggplants, green onions, and radishes—for wholesale. In 1988, Mike's grandfather passed away; two years later, his dad decided to retire. Mike bought the farm from his parents and added mustard and collard greens, turnips, and beets. He continued to sell his crops on the wholesale market, until one day his wife suggested they open a produce market of their own.

Their market was successful and doubled in size each year. They added additional varieties of vegetables. In 2006, a friend urged them to start taking their vegetables to the farmers' markets. Today, Atkinson Farm is a regular vendor at Houston's Urban Harvest Eastside Market, where regular customers include a number of prominent Houston chefs. They also have booths at several other Houston farmers' markets but still sell some of their crops to wholesale companies and directly to a few grocery stores.

Mike buys the best-quality seeds he can get. As soon as vegetables are harvested, they are rinsed, washed, and stored in the cooler. He lets his crops mature on the bush or vine to extract maximum flavor. They harvest every day and plant, seasonally, twice a week to keep up with the demand. The vegetables at various farmers' markets are never more than one day old and never trucked more than 30 miles from the farm.

"All of the many different people that we've met growing and selling fresh local produce have been a great inspiration to my family," said Mike. "We hope that we can continue to do this for a long time."

Scalloped Green Tomatoes with Texas 1015 Onions

Onions are the leading vegetable crop in Texas. Growers produce mostly sweet yellow varieties, so, of course, to maintain the state's bragging rights, it was natural that a Texan would develop the sweetest onion in the United States. The Texas 1015 onion, named for its optimum planting date of October 15, was adopted by the state legislature as Texas's Official State Onion in 1997. The onion was developed in the early 1980s by Dr. Leonard Pike, a horticulture professor at Texas A&M University, after 10 years of research, endless testing, and a million dollars in cost.

Texas 1015 onions are grown only in the Rio Grande Valley in South Texas, in a specific terroir that produces the mild-flavored, exceptionally sweet onion. In this dish, I paired the onions with homegrown green tomatoes (Brandywines, but other varieties will work). Serve it with a simple meat or fish main dish.

SERVES 4 TO 6.

6 large homegrown heirloom green tomatoes, cored and sliced into ⅜-inch slices

1 large Texas 1015 onion, peeled and halved from stem to root, then sliced thin

4½ tablespoons unsalted butter

4½ tablespoons all-purpose flour

1¼ cups whole milk

2 teaspoons whole-grain mustard

¾ cup chicken stock, preferably homemade

1½ teaspoons kosher salt

¼ teaspoon cayenne

2 large jalapeños, seeds and veins removed, minced

1½ cups (6 ounces) shredded Veldhuizen Family Farm Green's Creek Gruyere Cheese

TOPPING:

¾ cup panko bread crumbs

3 tablespoons melted unsalted butter

2 teaspoons minced lemon zest

½ teaspoon kosher salt

Preheat oven to 350°F. Layer the green tomatoes and onion in a 4-quart casserole dish; set aside.

Melt the 4½ tablespoons butter in a heavy-bottomed 3-quart saucepan over medium heat. When the foam subsides, add the flour all at once and stir until smooth. Continue to cook, stirring constantly, until the roux is very light beige in color. Add the milk, mustard, chicken stock, salt, cayenne, and jalapeños. Whisk vigorously until the mixture is smooth and thickened, about 4 minutes. Add the shredded cheese and whisk until cheese is completely melted and the sauce is smooth and glossy.

Pour the cheesy sauce evenly over the tomatoes and onions. In a small bowl, toss together the panko bread crumbs, melted butter, lemon zest, and salt. Scatter the topping over the casserole and bake in preheated oven for 1 hour, or until golden brown and bubbly. Serve hot.

Oven-Roasted Brussels Sprouts with Onion and Garlic

Brussels sprouts, as one might surmise, are believed to have originated in Belgium, where they have long been regarded as the country's official vegetable. During the Roman Empire, chefs imported the nutritious green rosettes to create delicacies for the emperor's tables.

Many people claim to dislike brussels sprouts because of a strong, pungent taste. As the sprouts age on the plant, and in the grocery store's vegetable bins, the taste becomes quite strong and does not pair well with seasonings. The best place to buy brussels sprouts is at the farmers' market, where you know they will be only hours out of the soil and picked by farmers who know exactly when the buds are at their prime. Look for the smallest, bright green buds, selecting those with very tight heads and no loose leaves. Pass over those heads that are beginning to open up, or certainly those with yellowing leaves.

SERVES 4 TO 6.

1 pound fresh brussels sprouts
1 medium yellow onion, cut into
  ½-inch dice
1 large garlic clove, minced

2 tablespoons Texas extra-virgin
  olive oil
Kosher salt and freshly ground
  black pepper

Preheat oven to 375°F. Line a baking sheet with foil; set aside. Trim the stems off the sprouts right at their base, but take care that you don't actually cut into the sprout, or it will fall apart when cooked. Cut each sprout in half lengthwise. Combine the sprouts with the onion, garlic, and olive oil in a bowl. Toss to blend well, then season to taste with salt and pepper.

Turn the mixture out onto the prepared baking sheet and bake in preheated oven for 25 to 30 minutes, or until the sprouts are crisp-tender. Serve hot.

BOGGY CREEK FARM

CAROL ANN SAYLE and her husband, Larry Butler, are icons in Austin's local food movement and have been the subject of countless regional and national features. But it takes a lot of work to become a famous farmer, even in East Austin.

Their property was once the plantation of James and Elizabeth Smith, pioneers from North Carolina, who built a house on the fertile bottomland north of the Colorado River, in the winter of 1840–41. Sam Houston, first president of the Republic of Texas, was a dinner guest at the Smiths' new home in 1841.

The original house was still standing, barely, when Carol Ann and Larry bought the land in 1992. They restored the house and cleared the trash, junk cars, and tall weeds from the yard. They named it Boggy Creek Farm in honor of the creek just across the road. The first crop was lettuce, planted in January 1993.

But the couple had already spent a decade growing vegetables. In 1981, they bought some mostly wooded land near Larry's hometown of Gause, in Milam County, Texas, and grew their own food. They couldn't make a living from the small plot, however, because there were no nearby markets.

However, between the oil and real estate busts of the 1980s, Carol Ann's art career was stagnant and Larry, a real estate broker, had turned from selling houses to remodeling them. By 1991, the couple decided that by farming, at least they would eat! They had the Gause farm certified organic and started their first tomato crop. There were no growers-only farmers' markets in Austin at the time, so they set up a card table in front of Wiggy's Liquor on West 6th Street. They also took their tomatoes to the original Whole Foods Market in Austin, creating a relationship that continues to this day.

In 1994, Carol Ann and Larry opened their on-farm market. Today, hundreds of people, including many of the city's leading chefs, are addicted to visiting the East Austin farm every Wednesday and Saturday morning. "We're able to harvest all through the market, so people can buy the freshest produce possible, since the fields are mere minutes from the farmstand," said Carol Ann. "Folks walk around, see the crops in the field and the chickens. Customers spend hours sitting on the benches by the chicken pen communing with 'the girls,' while children play in the dirt pile under the shade of a pecan tree. Many people report that their stress level goes down the minute they turn onto our bumpy driveway."

Carol Ann summed up her philosophy of farming: "Farmers can never give up. We may be pessimistic in the present time, but we are always optimistic that the next season will be splendid. We also know, on the other hand, if we are enjoying a great year, we better save our money. We'll need to spend it the following year, which often is a 'correction year.'"

Their marketing strategy has always been simple: produce the best, freshest organic produce and hope people will spread the word. They never advertised, but the local press quickly embraced them, especially Virginia Wood, food editor of the *Austin Chronicle*, and radio gardening personality John Dromgoole.

Boggy Creek Farm has grown over the years, and as Carol Ann looks back, she muses: "I guess you need a lot of gumption to break from 'modern life' to become farmers. Perhaps a shortage of common sense, too. Then throw in the ability to enjoy physical work—and not think of it as demeaning—with a passion for a life to be spent primarily outdoors in all kinds of weather, combined with the goal of feeding people good food, grown without pesticides, herbicides, and fertilizers, and a conviction that piling up money in the bank does not always equal meaningful success nor happiness. Since we had all of those qualifications, we did it."

Seared Boggy Creek Spinach with Shiitake Mushrooms and Garlic

Austin's Boggy Creek Farm has the most delicious, not to mention gorgeous, spinach in Texas. When I buy Boggy Creek's spinach, I want to taste its delicious flavor unadulterated by a lot of other ingredients, so this is the dish I usually make. It's a simple and easy side to pair with a steak or other grilled meats or fish.

SERVES 4 TO 6.

¼ cup Texas extra-virgin olive oil

6 ounces Texas Pride shiitake mushrooms, sliced, or substitute sliced white button mushrooms

5 large garlic cloves, peeled, trimmed, and sliced thin

2 bunches fresh spinach, stems removed, torn into bite-size pieces

Kosher salt and freshly ground black pepper

5 or 6 drops aged balsamic vinegar

Heat the olive oil in a heavy-bottomed 12-inch skillet over medium heat. Sauté the mushrooms until they are wilted, about 5 minutes. Add the garlic cloves and cook, stirring constantly, until they are very lightly browned, about 3 minutes. Add the spinach, tossing constantly with tongs. Cook just until it is barely wilted, about 3 to 4 minutes. Season to taste with salt and freshly ground black pepper. Scatter 5 or 6 drops of the aged balsamic vinegar over the spinach and toss quickly to incorporate. Don't overdo the balsamic. Just a hint is perfect. Serve at once.

Linda Allen's Ribboned Squash

Linda Allen is a talented, self-taught cook who owns Linda Allen's Fine Foods and Linda Allen Catering in Wimberley. The menu at Linda Allen's Fine Foods changes weekly, offering a variety of both delicious takeout foods and sit-down options that can be enjoyed along with live music on the patio in the summer and around the fireplace in the colder months.

Linda's food, and this dish in particular, showcases the simple goodness and vibrant colors of fresh vegetables and herbs.

SERVES 6 TO 8.

6 zucchini

6 yellow squash

Texas extra-virgin olive oil

2 tablespoons minced garlic

½ cup basil leaves, cut into thin strips

Kosher salt

Freshly ground black pepper

Freshly squeezed lemon juice

4 diced homegrown tomatoes

Slice the squash into thin ribbons, lengthwise, using a mandoline or other type of slicing box like a Benriner slicer (my favorite). Or you can use a vegetable peeler to make the slices, but they won't be as consistent. Heat a few tablespoons of the olive oil in a large, heavy-bottomed skillet over medium-high heat and add some of the garlic. Cook the squash in small batches so that they actually sauté, which can only be done with high heat and a pan that is not crowded. If you crowd the pan, the squash will simply steam and release their juices.

Add some of the basil, a bit of the salt and pepper, and a teaspoon or so of the fresh lemon juice to each batch. Toss with chef's tongs until the squash begin to soften. Throw in a handful of the diced tomatoes, toss together briefly, then remove all the vegetables with a slotted spoon. Place in a bowl and set aside. Repeat with remaining squash and other ingredients until all has been cooked. Be careful not to overcook the squash, which should still have a good bit of crunch. Mound on a platter and serve hot.

Creamed Yellow Squash

Squash is a true Native American vegetable. It is generally believed to be the first dish that Native Americans taught the first white settlers how to cook. Stems, rinds, and seeds found in the Ocampo Caves in Mexico's Tamaulipas mountains date the gourd's use in the region to 3000 BC. The ancient Indians called squash "the apple of God."

Whatever circuitous route brought it to Texas, yellow squash is definitely a summer staple on the tables of the Lone Star State. Just two or three plants can supply a family with enough squash to eat from summer to fall. The delicate-flavored vegetable is made into soups, battered and deep-fried, sautéed in butter, eaten raw in salads, used as a crudité with dips, stuffed, and baked into a multitude of creamy dishes such as this one. Even the blossoms are stuffed with various fillings and often deep-fried.

This recipe was created from a taste memory from my childhood. When I stayed with an elderly neighbor couple one weekend, they picked fresh squash from their garden and made a casserole. I'd never eaten squash, as it was not a vegetable that my mother ever cooked. I was enchanted by the dish, which had an undertone of flavor that I had never experienced. I liked it a lot, although it would be a couple of years before I discovered, through yet another new taste enlightenment while eating Tex-Mex at Houston's old El Fenix, that the mystery flavor was cumin. When selecting yellow squash, opt for the smallest ones, which are the most tender and flavorful. Larger specimens are often tough and woody, and the flavor dissipates in proportion to the girth of the vegetable.

SERVES 4 TO 6.

----

8 small to medium yellow squash, about 2 pounds total
8 cups chicken stock, preferably homemade
3 tablespoons unsalted butter
1 small onion, cut into ½-inch dice
3 cloves roasted garlic, mashed to a pulp
⅔ cup whipping cream

½ teaspoon Texas Pete Hot Sauce
½ teaspoon dried Mexican oregano
½ teaspoon toasted, then ground, cumin seeds
½ teaspoon kosher salt
2 eggs, beaten
½ cup fine, dry bread crumbs
¼ cup grated Parmesan cheese

Butter an 8-inch-square baking dish; set aside. Preheat oven to 350°F. Trim and discard the stem ends from the squash. Pour the chicken stock into a heavy-bottomed 6-quart pot. Bring to a full boil over high heat. Add the whole squash to the pan, reduce heat to medium, cover, and simmer until the squash are very soft, about 20 to 25 minutes. Drain squash thoroughly, reserving the chicken stock for another use, if desired.

Place the squash in a large bowl. Using a potato masher, mash the squash until it is thoroughly broken up, but still somewhat lumpy. Add the butter, onion, and garlic. Stir until the butter is melted. In a separate bowl combine the cream, hot sauce, oregano, cumin, salt, pepper, and eggs, whisking to blend well. Stir the egg mixture into the squash, combining well. Pour the mixture into the prepared baking dish. Combine the bread crumbs and cheese. Scatter over the squash and bake in preheated oven until golden brown and bubbly on top, about 30 minutes. Serve hot.

Jalapeño Corn Pudding

Because corn has become such an integral part of our cuisine, sometimes we forget that early colonists tried to grow the wheat and barley they had known in England, failed, and would have starved if not for the *maize*, or corn, that the Indians taught them to grow and use. We especially love corn in the South, where we use it in many forms, from grits to creamed corn to cornbread, hushpuppies, or just like Mother Nature made it, on the cob. This tasty pudding, with a little hit of jalapeño, makes a great side dish to just about any pork or poultry entrée.

MAKES 8 (4-OUNCE) RAMEKINS.

2 tablespoons unsalted butter

2 small shallots, finely chopped

2 large fresh jalapeños, seeds and veins removed, minced

1 small green bell pepper, finely chopped

2 cups cream-style corn

1 cup whole-kernel corn

2¼ teaspoons sugar

½ teaspoon kosher salt

¼ teaspoon freshly ground black pepper

1 teaspoon Tabasco

3 additional tablespoons unsalted butter, melted

4 eggs, well beaten

1½ cups whipping cream

Preheat oven to 350°F. Butter 8 ramekins and set them in a large baking dish; set aside. Melt the 2 tablespoons of butter in a heavy-bottomed 10-inch skillet over medium-high heat. Sauté the shallots, jalapeño, and green bell pepper until shallots are wilted and lightly browned, about 10 minutes. Turn out into a large bowl and stir in all remaining ingredients, blending well. Ladle the mixture into prepared ramekins. Place the baking dish on oven rack and add hot water to the baking dish to come halfway up the sides of the ramekins. Bake in preheated oven for about 45 minutes, or until the custard is firm and a knife inserted in the center comes out clean. Unmold the custards onto serving plates. Serve hot.

Creamy Mushroom Grits

Grits have a down-home reputation, but they can be gussied up to blend seamlessly into even upscale meals. This creamy, savory version is nice to serve with roasted or grilled red meats, including game, pork, lamb, and poultry.

SERVES 6 TO 8.

8 tablespoons (1 stick) unsalted butter
2 large shallots, minced
6 ounces Texas Pride shiitake
    mushrooms, stems removed, sliced
1½ teaspoons minced fresh thyme
2 garlic cloves, minced
3 cups whipping cream

3½ cups chicken stock, preferably
    homemade
½ teaspoon kosher salt
½ teaspoon freshly ground black
    pepper
2 cups quick-cooking (*never* instant)
    grits

Melt the butter in a heavy-bottomed 6-quart saucepan over medium-high heat. When the foam subsides, add the shallots, mushrooms, and thyme. Cook, stirring often, until shallots are wilted and mushrooms are slightly browned, about 7 minutes. Stir in the garlic and cook for 1 or 2 minutes. Do not allow the garlic to brown. Add whipping cream and chicken stock; bring to a boil. Add salt and pepper. Slowly whisk in grits and reduce heat. Cook 15 to 20 minutes over low heat, stirring frequently. Serve with beef or game meat, pork tenderloin medallions, lamb chops, or other meat or poultry.

Soft Polenta with Jalapeño and Onions

Polenta is a very tasty, but much underused and often misunderstood, side dish. A grain milled from corn, polenta is often featured in Italian cooking but makes a great side for red meats, including game, pork, and poultry. I often stir in a bit of minced cilantro right at the end of the cooking process, if the flavor of cilantro will complement the other flavors in the meal. This is a great pairing for the Shiner Bock Braised Short Ribs with Maple-Balsamic Glaze (pages 332–333).

SERVES 6 TO 8.

¼ pound (1 stick) unsalted butter

2 fresh jalapeños, seeds, stem, and
veins removed, minced

1 medium onion, chopped

2¼ cups chicken stock, preferably
homemade

2¼ cups whipping cream

1½ cups quick-cooking polenta

Kosher salt

1 tablespoon minced cilantro

Melt the butter in a heavy-bottomed 4-quart saucepan over medium heat. When the foam subsides, add the jalapeño and onion. Sauté, stirring often, until the onion is very wilted and transparent, about 7 minutes. Add the stock and whipping cream and increase the heat to medium high. Bring to a full boil, then add the polenta all at once. Cook, whisking constantly, until the liquid has been absorbed and polenta is thickened, but still soft and pourable. Remove pan from heat, whisk in salt to taste, and add the cilantro. Serve hot.

Grilled Mozzarella and Sun-Dried Tomato Pesto Panini

The panini sandwich provides an ideal solution to serving a hot dish to several people at the same time. The sandwiches can be assembled ahead of time, grilled in the panini grill slightly ahead of time, and kept warm in a low oven for up to 30 minutes. I especially like to serve this particular panini with tomato-basil soup. The two seem to harmonize like Willie and Waylon. Panini grills are sold in cookware sections of most department stores, culinary shops, and restaurant equipment stores in all sizes and price ranges. For the best performance, purchase a fairly heavy-duty grill with nonstick grilling plates and one that will accommodate at least two sandwiches at a time.

MAKES 6 SANDWICHES.

FOR THE PANINI:

12 pieces focaccia bread, each
4 inches square and ½-inch thick

Olive oil for glazing bread

Sun-Dried Tomato Pesto
(recipe follows)

½ small red onion, sliced thin

Aged balsamic vinegar in a squeeze
bottle

8 ounces fresh whole mozzarella,
cut into slices ¼-inch thick

SUN-DRIED TOMATO PESTO:

MAKES 2 CUPS.

½ ounce basil leaves

½ ounce flat-leaf parsley leaves

3 ounces sun-dried tomatoes,
  roughly chopped

3 large garlic cloves

1 ounce toasted pine nuts

¼ cup sliced kalamata olives

Pinch of crushed red pepper flakes

¾ cup Texas extra-virgin olive oil

⅓ cup grated Parmesan cheese

Pinch of kosher salt and black pepper

Make the pesto first. Combine all ingredients in the work bowl of a food processor fitted with the steel blade. Process until smooth. Turn out into a bowl and set aside, or store in a tightly covered container in the refrigerator until ready to use.

Place the bread slices in two rows of 6 each on a work surface, cut sides down. Brush the bottoms of each slice with olive oil. Turn cut sides back up. Spread 6 of the breads liberally with the pesto. Top each with a scattering of the red onion. Drizzle a few drops of the balsamic vinegar over the red onion, then top each with some of the mozzarella slices. Place remaining 6 breads on top, cut sides down.

Grill each sandwich in a panini grill until the bread is crisp on the top and bottom and marked well, the filling is warmed, and the mozzarella is melted. Slice in half diagonally and serve at once, or they can be kept warm for up to 30 minutes in a low oven.

Smoked Mozzarella and Tomato Frittata

When it's been a long, busy day and suddenly I realize that it's time for dinner, I often turn to eggs. Because I have a backyard full of happy hens, I always have fresh, all-natural eggs on hand. One of our favorite egg dishes is a frittata. It's so mindlessly simple to prepare, and you can add whatever ingredients you have on hand to conjure up a tasty supper in no time at all.

This is one of our favorites, with some wonderful Scamorza cheese from Paula Lambert's Mozzarella Company. The cheese, her signature fresh, handmade mozzarella, is lightly smoked over pecan shells, then hand-formed into balls. It would make just about anything taste good. I add a little basil and parsley (flat-leaf only, please) from the herb garden and some Parmesan. But the starring role goes to my husband's unbelievably delicious heirloom tomatoes, which I slice and arrange over the egg base just before the frittata goes in the oven. Just toast some good rustic bread, and you have yourself a nice little feast with very little work. I sometimes serve this dish for brunch also. To make your meal ultimately satisfying, chill a bottle of Texas Viognier.

MOZZARELLA COMPANY

WHEN PAULA LAMBERT founded the Mozzarella Company in 1982, almost no one in Texas had heard of *fresh* mozzarella. But Paula had a dream. It began when she was 25 and went to Italy to study Italian for the summer, but stayed five years. She fell in love with the country—the art, the food, the geography, the wine, the people, and especially their way of life. In 1973, she returned to the United States and married a man from Dallas whom she had met in Italy. The couple returned to Italy often for vacations. By 1982, Paula wanted to start a business linked to Italy so she would have an excuse for going back. It didn't take long to determine that what she loved most about Italy was the food—like fresh mozzarella.

So she spent a few weeks at a little mozzarella factory near Perugia where she had often bought cheese. Mozzarella Company opened soon after in a storefront building in Dallas's Deep Ellum neighborhood, just east of downtown. At first, she made only fresh mozzarella and ricotta. Paula tried selling to retail stores, but it was a difficult sell because no one had ever heard of fresh mozzarella and certainly didn't know what to do with it. So she tried selling to local restaurants, but most of them had never heard of fresh mozzarella, either. She approached some well-known chefs across the country. These chefs *did* appreciate her cheeses, and she's very proud that most of them are still customers today. Many are now considered to be among the founders of American regional cooking.

Over the years, Paula has added dozens of cheeses incorporating Texas flavors and published two cookbooks. Some of her first employees are still with the company, and they still have the little storefront in Deep Ellum where it all began.

3 tablespoons Texas extra-virgin
    olive oil

½ small white onion, cut into
    ¼-inch dice

2 large garlic cloves, peeled and
    sliced thin

1 tablespoon minced fresh basil

2 teaspoons minced flat-leaf parsley

6 large eggs, preferably free range

⅓ cup tepid water

½ teaspoon kosher salt

1 teaspoon Cholula Hot Sauce

1 cup (4 ounces) shredded
    Scamorza cheese

3 tablespoons grated Parmesan
    cheese

2 large heirloom or other homegrown
    tomatoes, about 1 pound, cores
    removed, cut into ¼-inch slices

Additional kosher salt and freshly
    ground black pepper

Preheat oven to 350°F. Heat the olive oil in a 12-inch, nonstick skillet with an ovenproof handle. When the oil is hot, stir in the onion, garlic, basil, and parsley. Cook, stirring often, until the onion is wilted and transparent, about 3 minutes. While the onions are sautéing, whisk the eggs with the tepid water, salt, hot sauce, and both cheeses until very frothy. Raise heat to medium high and pour the eggs into the skillet. Stir just to diffuse the onion mixture, then stop stirring and let the eggs cook just until they begin to brown at the edge of the pan, about 5 minutes. Lay the sliced tomatoes around the pan in a single layer and season to taste with salt and pepper.

Transfer the pan to preheated oven and bake the frittata until the eggs are completely set and the top is bubbly, about 20 minutes. Remove from oven and use a heatproof, nonstick spatula to loosen the edges of the frittata, then carefully slide it onto a platter. Slice into wedges and serve hot.

Grown-Up Grilled Cheese Sandwich

I've never met anyone who doesn't love a grilled cheese sandwich. When I was a kid, the gooey concoction was a summer lunch staple, and I've never grown tired of it. Over the years I've worked to create a sublimely delicious version of the classic grilled cheese sandwich, unlike the Velveeta version of my childhood, although there are fond memories associated with those pretend-cheese sandwiches. But it wasn't until I discovered the unbelievably delicious, handmade raw-milk Gruyere cheese made by Veldhuizen Family Farm in Dublin that I reached the epiphany of grilled cheese sandwiches. They market the cheese under the name Green's Creek Gruyere.

For the ultimate grilled cheese sandwich experience, try it with a mug or bowl of Roasted Fresh Tomato and Basil Soup (see recipe on pages 66–67.)

MAKES 4 SANDWICHES.

2 medium-sized fresh jalapeños

1½ sticks (12 ounces) unsalted butter, melted

8 slices artisan rustic white bread, each ½-inch thick

8 slices Veldhuizen Family Farm Green's Creek Gruyere, each ¼-inch thick

8 cilantro sprigs, tender top stems and leaves only

Using a sharp, small paring knife, cut off the stem ends of the jalapeños. Working from the open end of the chiles, use the paring knife to ream out the seeds and veins, leaving the chiles whole. Slice the chiles into very thin rounds; set aside.

Using a pastry brush, liberally butter one side of each bread slice. Lay the slices, buttered side up, on a baking sheet; set aside. Heat a heavy-bottomed 12-inch skillet over medium heat. When the pan begins to heat, lay 2 slices of the bread, buttered side down, in the skillet. Top each with 2 slices of the cheese, a few of the jalapeño slices, 2 sprigs of the cilantro, then another slice of the bread, buttered side up. Cook until the bottom slice of bread is golden brown and the cheese is beginning to stick to the bottom bread slice, about 3 minutes. Don't allow the bread to brown too deeply. It should be golden brown and crisp to the touch.

I notice that many home cooks tend to smash grilled cheese sandwiches with the spatula while they're cooking, but please resist the urge to do this. One of the heavenly features of the grilled cheese sandwich is that when you take a bite you first encounter the buttery, crisp crust; then the soft, airy texture of the artisan bread; then the gooey, delicious cheese from both the top and the bottom of the sandwich.

Using a metal spatula, flip the sandwiches and brown the other side just until golden brown. The cheese should be melted onto both slices of the bread. Set aside to keep warm while grilling the other 2 sandwiches. Slice in half diagonally and serve warm.

Molly McCook's Scott Farms Brandywine and Green Tomato Tart

Molly McCook is the executive chef and co-owner of Fort Worth's Ellerbe Fine Foods. Named after Molly's grandparents, and inspired by the farm-to-fork restaurants in California where she developed her career, Ellerbe Fine Foods features this simple, delicious tart during tomato season. Molly sources the heirloom Brandywine tomatoes and green tomatoes from Scott Farms in Cisco. The success of the dish comes from the quality of the ingredients, so be sure to use the best-quality tomatoes you can find, preferably homegrown. If you can't find the heirloom Brandywines, then substitute another homegrown variety, but be sure to use fresh thyme and good Mascarpone cheese. The tart makes a good luncheon or other light meal when served with a simple, vinaigrette-dressed salad of local greens and chilled Texas Roussanne.

SERVES 4.

PASTRY:

2 cups all-purpose flour

½ teaspoon kosher salt

1 stick (4 ounces) chilled unsalted
    butter, cut into 1-inch cubes

1 egg

2 tablespoons cold water

FOR THE FILLING:

⅓ cup Mascarpone cheese

1 tablespoon minced fresh thyme

1 large Brandywine tomato, sliced
    ¼-inch thick, or substitute another
    large variety of heirloom tomato

2 green tomatoes, sliced ¼-inch thick

½ teaspoon kosher salt

¼ teaspoon freshly ground black
    pepper

Zest of 1 large lemon

To make the pastry, combine the flour and salt in a bowl. Cut the butter into the flour, using a fork or your fingers, until the mixture is the consistency of cornmeal. In a separate bowl, whisk together the egg and water. Make a well in the center of the flour mixture and pour the egg into the well. Work the flour mixture and liquid together to form a dough. Lightly flour a work surface and roll the dough out to approximately ½-inch thickness. Transfer the dough to an 8-inch removable-bottom tart pan, or onto a baking sheet lined with parchment paper. Preheat oven to 425°F.

Spread the bottom of the dough with the Mascarpone cheese, leaving a 1-inch border if you are not using the tart pan. Sprinkle the minced thyme over the cheese. Season the tomatoes with salt and pepper, then begin to layer, alternating the red and the green, over the Mascarpone. Scatter the lemon zest over the tomatoes. If you are baking the tart on the baking sheet, carefully fold the bare edge of the dough over the outer edge of the tomatoes to form a crust. Bake the tart in the preheated oven about 25 to 30 minutes, or until the crust is golden brown. Remove from the oven and gently drain the excess liquid from the tart and discard. Slice into wedges and serve hot.

EAGLE MOUNTAIN FARMHOUSE CHEESE

WHEN DAVE EAGLE, a practicing attorney and owner of Eagle Mountain Farmhouse Cheese in Granbury, began to research cheesemaking earnestly, he concluded that the hardest part of starting the operation would be sourcing high-quality raw milk. As great wine begins with great grapes, great cheese begins with great raw milk. Dave wasn't raised on a farm. He knew absolutely nothing about cows, so he looked for an established dairyman with whom he could partner. He met Mike Moyers of Sandy Creek Farm, which runs a herd of purebred Brown Swiss Dairy cows. Brown Swiss milk is one of the most coveted by cheesemakers because of its high percentage of protein and butterfat. The cows at Sandy Creek are openly grazed on natural grasses in North Texas. Dave's meeting with Moyers was timely in that Moyers was in the process of setting up his dairy as a "Grade A, Raw for Retail" dairy. (In Texas, consumers can legally purchase raw milk, provided that the dairy has its "Grade A, Raw for Retail" license and that the consumer travels to the dairy to purchase the milk.) Eagle Mountain Farmhouse Cheese was born in 2009.

Among its assortment of handcrafted raw cow's-milk cheeses is Birdville Reserve, an award-winning natural-rind cheese made in the Trappist tradition. It has become a favorite of many chefs. Eagle Mountain also makes Granbury Gold, a young Gouda-style cheese. It's mild, creamy, and buttery, with hints of nuttiness on the palate. Granbury Vintage is the company's aged Gouda, which is aged four to seven months, becoming sharper and more complex as it ages.

Dave remains a practicing attorney, but his current focus is the Food Safety and Modernization Act of 2011 and its potentially negative impact on small farmers and other artisan food producers. He is working to repeal the provisions of this act. In his own words, "Now is the time for the people of this country to regain control of our food system. The best way to begin this process is to demand local products made by local producers and to vote with our dollars to get the government out of our kitchens."

Refried Black Bean and Avocado Salsa Quesadillas with Eagle Mountain Granbury Gold Cheese

Quesadillas are one of my favorite finger foods for informal get-togethers. They can range from light nibbles to substantial and filling for those times when the grazing foods will also serve as the meal for the event. This version would most likely fall somewhere in the middle, as it contains no meat. The flavor, however, is sensational, and the dish will be a favorite among guests. The Eagle Mountain Granbury Gold is a rich, deeply flavored, handmade Gouda-style raw cow's-milk cheese. You can also use flour tortillas, if you prefer, as I sometimes do, to make the quesadillas. I only wish that every Texan could experience the incredibly thin, light-as-air flour tortillas that Hilda's Restaurant in Fredericksburg makes by hand every day. They actually have *flavor*, and it's wonderful. Hilda's also cuts the tortillas into chips and fries them to serve with her great salsa at the tables. Too, too good! As an added bonus, the refried black beans in this recipe can double as a side dish with Mexican entrées or with simple grilled meats.

MAKES 16 PIECES.

8 white corn tortillas, or thin flour tortillas
Refried Black Beans (see recipe below)

8 ounces (2 cups) shredded Eagle Mountain Granbury Gold, or another aged Gouda-style cheese
Avocado Salsa (see recipe below)

REFRIED BLACK BEANS:
1½ cups cooked black beans, undrained
1 small onion, chopped fine
2 large garlic cloves, minced
1½ teaspoons toasted, then ground, whole coriander seeds

1½ teaspoons toasted, then ground, cumin seeds
¼ teaspoon cayenne
Juice of 1 lime
½ teaspoon kosher salt
¼ cup bacon drippings or fresh leaf lard

AVOCADO SALSA:
½ small red onion, sliced thin
3 green onions, chopped, including green tops
5 Roma tomatoes, cut into ½-inch dice
2 Hass avocados, cut into ½-inch dice

3 serrano chiles, seeds and veins removed, minced
½ cup minced cilantro
Juice of ½ large lime
Kosher salt

Begin by making the refried black beans. They can be made a day ahead of time and refrigerated until ready to assemble the quesadillas. Combine all ingredients except the bacon drippings in a heavy-bottomed 3-quart saucepan over medium heat. Cook, stirring often, until the mixture is very thick and the onion is very mushy, about 30 minutes. Using a potato masher or a flat wooden masher, mash the black beans until almost smooth. Set aside.

Melt the bacon drippings or lard in a heavy-bottomed 10-inch skillet, preferably cast iron, over medium-high heat. When the fat is hot, pour in the mashed beans and begin stirring. Cook, stirring frequently, until the mixture is very thick and creamy and the beans have absorbed the fat. Don't allow the beans to stick to the bottom of the skillet. Set aside to cool slightly, or refrigerate if you will assemble and cook the quesadillas later.

Make the salsa. Combine all ingredients in a bowl, adding the salt to taste, then stir to blend. If you are making the salsa ahead of time (up to 4 hours), don't add the salt, as it will cause the tomatoes to weep and make the salsa soggy. If you wish to make it ahead of time, add the salt just before serving.

To assemble and toast the quesadillas, spray a flat comal or cast-iron skillet with nonstick spray. Spread each tortilla with a portion of the refried black beans. Heat the comal or skillet over medium-high heat until hot. Lay as many tortillas as will fit in the skillet or on the comal. Place equal portions of the shredded cheese on one-half of each tortilla. Cook until the cheese just begins to melt, and then place a portion of the salsa on top of the cheese on each tortilla. Fold the top half of the tortilla down over the salsa and turn the quesadilla over, toasting the other side until the cheese is almost completely melted.

Remove and repeat with remaining tortillas until all have been cooked. Cut each folded and cooked tortilla in half and serve.

8

LONE STAR
SWEETS

★

★

With the multiethnic heritage of food in Texas, it stands to reason that the state's cuisine would also have a rich heritage of desserts. Desserts were a European tradition introduced to Mexico by the Spanish, who brought milk, eggs, and almonds into the culture, along with the general knowledge of how to make sweetmeats and custards. And Mexico had long embraced the use of chocolate. Over the years, indigenous Mexican fruits like bananas, and nuts like pepitas (pumpkin seeds), were added to the state's dessert repertoire as Mexican culture spread into Texas. Mexican cooks contributed their unique pastries and desserts—pan dulce and rich flans, rice puddings, bread puddings, candied fruits, empanadas made from sweetened sweet potatoes, rich fried pastries called churros, the paper-thin fritters called buñuelos, and fragile shortbread cookies, as well as rich, gooey *cajeta*, a deeply browned caramel often laced with sherry.

The German and Czech settlers brought with them centuries-old traditional sweets—kolaches made with the fruits they found in their new home; streusels made with paper-thin pastry filled with fresh fruits; and kuchen, rich yeast cakes that were often filled with local peaches and apples. Many Germans and Czechs established bakeries in the areas where they settled. The offerings from these bakeries were embraced by the general population in the area.

As the plantation lands on the eastern coast and the deep South became overfarmed and less productive, the residents moved west, seeking fertile new land. This migration brought a rich tapestry of cooking styles from England and France, as well as the style of cooking that had evolved in the region and became known as "Southern food," along with their traditional desserts. Pies, layer cakes, trifles, tarts, and rich custards were introduced and adapted to the ingredients found in Texas. Texas native pecans replaced other types of nuts.

A hearty style of cooking evolved as farms and, later, ranch kitchens were established, creating a style of desserts for the hardworking cowboys, who were meat-and-potatoes eaters. These were hearty, comfort-food dishes made from readily available local ingredients—bread puddings and pies made from local fruits and nuts and, in the fall, many desserts made from pumpkins.

The recipes in this chapter reflect the heritage of the early Texans of many ethnic groups. They range in nature from simple dishes like ice creams and sorbets, fruit crisps, and pies, to more complex and impressive presentations. Of course, all desserts should be eaten in moderation, with a nod to the calories and fat that they harbor. But then, what is life without a little indulgence occasionally? One of my favorite sayings is, "Life is short. Eat dessert first!" And a note on the preparation of dessert recipes. The genre of dessert preparation ranges into a bit of food science. Working with chocolate, flour, sugar, eggs, and the other ingredients used in making desserts requires careful and precise procedures. So, it's important when preparing recipes for the various desserts that you measure the ingredients exactly as listed, and follow the directions in the body of the recipe to ensure success. Many of the ingredients used in preparing desserts are costly, seasonal, and perhaps hard to source. You wouldn't want to risk wasting them by not following the directions!

Innovative Texas chefs and home cooks alike often combine elements from several ethnic derivations into one dessert. The taste of these culturally layered sweets reflects the sum of their time-honored techniques and ingredients. Today, it's simply what we know as Lone Star Sweets.

VAL VERDE WINERY

FRANK QUALIA EMIGRATED from Italy to Mexico before venturing northward into Texas with his family. He settled in Del Rio, comparing it to an oasis in an otherwise arid land. Qualia brought with him a long family tradition of winemaking and soon realized that the Lenoir grape was the one best suited to the area. He began to make wine for his family and friends, and word of the quality of his wines began to spread. In 1883, he opened the Val Verde Winery, and today it is the oldest bonded winery in the state of Texas.

The winery survived Prohibition by making wines for the church. Local doctors also prescribed the wines for many of their patients. The family continued to make wine for their personal consumption and also grew table grapes for neighbors.

Frank Qualia passed away in 1936, and his son, Louis, took over the winery and vineyards and began to expand the operation. In 1933, in response to requests for a white wine, Louis planted herbemont, which, like Lenoir, is a drought- and disease-resistant grape that thrived in northern Mexico, though Louis's plantings were the first in Texas.

In 1973, Louis passed the winery to his son, Thomas, and his wife, Linda. Thomas and Linda's son Michael manages the winery, and daughter Maureen Qualia is the consulting winemaker. The Val Verde Vineyards continue to grow Lenoir and herbemont grapes but also purchase other Texas grapes to make their wines.

The Val Verde Don Luis Tawny Port, made from the Lenoir grape, is the winery's most successful bottle, with numerous medals over the years in major competitions. On those occasions when you don't want a full-fledged dessert, try a glass of this port with some toasted Texas pecans to finish off your meal.

Mexican Fresh Apple Cake with Leche Quemada

This cake has a rich and exotic flavor. Leche quemada, or "burnt milk" sauce, similar to *cajeta* (caramel), can be bought in the markets in Mexico with various spices and with or without sherry. One of my former co-workers, Rosalina Ramirez, who is from the state of Guanajuato, coached me on the development of this particular recipe. When she made a trip home to Mexico, she brought back several varieties of commercially prepared leche quemada. I preferred the ones with sherry. The sherry-less sauce is intensely sweet, but adding the fortified wine cuts it beautifully. In this recipe I have used Madeira, because I find it to have more depth of flavor than sherry. Apples that are slightly past their prime eating stage are perfect for this recipe. They break down into the perfect consistency.

SERVES 12 TO 14.

CAKE:

4 medium-sized Granny Smith apples, peeled, cored, and diced
2 tablespoons honey
2 cups water
4 tablespoons (½ stick) unsalted butter
1½ cups sugar
4 eggs
1 tablespoon vanilla extract
2 teaspoons ground cinnamon
2½ cups cake flour, sifted
2 teaspoons baking soda
¼ teaspoon salt

⅔ cup chopped pecans
Rich vanilla ice cream

LECHE QUEMADA:

½ cup sugar
2 cups sweetened condensed milk
¼ teaspoon cinnamon
¼ cup Madeira
2 teaspoons vanilla extract
4 tablespoons unsalted butter, cut into 1-inch cubes
⅔ cup whipping cream
3 additional tablespoons Madeira

Preheat oven to 375°F. Grease a 9 × 13-inch baking dish; set aside. Combine the diced apples, honey, and water in a medium-sized saucepan and cook about 25 minutes, stirring often, or until the water has evaporated and the apples are very pulpy, almost like chunky applesauce. Set aside to cool slightly.

  In the bowl of a stand mixer, cream the butter and sugar at medium speed until light and fluffy, about 5 minutes. Add the eggs, one at a time, scraping down sides of bowl after each addition. Add vanilla and cinnamon; beat just to blend. Sift together the cake flour, baking soda, and salt. Add the flour mixture to the mixer in thirds, stopping to scrape down sides of bowl after each addition. Do not overbeat. Add the reserved apple mixture and the pecans; beat just to incorporate.

Turn the mixture into the prepared baking dish and bake in preheated oven for 25 minutes, or until a metal skewer inserted in middle of cake comes out clean. Remove from oven and set aside to cool.

To make the leche quemada, place the sugar in a 6-quart saucepan over medium-high heat. (The large pan size is necessary to prevent overflow when liquid is added to the hot caramel.) Cook until the sugar has melted and a rich, dark caramel has formed, about 320°F on a candy thermometer. Combine the milk, cinnamon, the ¼ cup Madeira, and vanilla; add to the caramel all at once. The mixture will spit, sputter, and bubble furiously. The caramel will harden. Take care that none of the mixture splashes out on you. Lower heat and stir the mixture until it is smooth and caramel has melted. Remove from heat and cool to lukewarm. Whisk the butter into the lukewarm sauce until well blended. Rapidly whisk in the whipping cream and additional 3 tablespoons of Madeira. To serve, slice the cake into squares. Top each with a scoop of ice cream and drizzle some of the leche quemada over the top.

Lemon Pound Cake

This is a very tasty and moist pound cake. It's a great dessert with a refreshing zing of lemon that serves a lot of people. It's especially good when topped with some mashed, fresh seasonal berries and their juice. It makes a great dish to tote along on a picnic.

SERVES 15 TO 16.

CAKE:
2 cups all-purpose flour
2 teaspoons baking powder
1 teaspoon salt
1 cup (2 sticks) unsalted butter, softened
2 cups sugar
3 eggs

Minced zest of 1 large lemon
1 cup sour cream

LEMON GLAZE:
¼ cup unsalted butter, melted
2 tablespoons freshly squeezed lemon juice
1 cup powdered sugar, sifted

Preheat oven to 325°F. Thoroughly butter and flour a 10-inch bundt pan; turn pan upside down and rap on the edge of the sink to remove excess flour. Set pan aside.

Sift flour, baking powder, and salt into a medium bowl; set aside. In the bowl of a stand mixer, cream the butter and sugar at low speed until well blended, then beat at medium speed until mixture is very fluffy, about 5 minutes. Beat in the eggs, one at a time, scraping down sides of bowl after each addition. Add lemon zest and blend. By thirds, add the flour mixture to the butter and sugar mixture alternately with the sour cream and beat at medium speed, scraping down sides of bowl after each addition. Pour the batter into the prepared bundt pan. Bake in preheated oven until a metal skewer inserted in center of cake comes out clean, about 1 hour. Cool in the pan for 10 minutes. Turn cake out onto platter and cool for another 10 minutes.

Meanwhile, prepare the lemon glaze. Whisk all ingredients together until smooth. Drizzle the glaze evenly over the top of the cake while it is still hot. Let the cake cool completely before slicing.

PURE LUCK FARM AND DAIRY

IN 1979, SARA SWEETSER bought 11 acres and an old homestead on Barton Creek to raise her daughters, Gitana and Amelia. The fertile pasture had been one of many tomato farms in the area in the 1930s. In 1983, Sara met and married Denny Bolton. They had two more daughters, Claire and Hope. Sara named her growing farm Pure Luck, saying that it was pure luck that it worked! Pure Luck was one of the first farms in Texas to be certified organic by the Texas Department of Agriculture.

The sisters often explain that although their mother originally bought the land as a home where she could raise them, slowly, organically, it grew into a business. While taking care of a friend's goats, Sara decided she wanted to raise goats and make cheese. She made some for family and friends, and it was so well received that in 1995 she decided to start a Grade A goat dairy. Amelia joined Sara in the cheese plant in 1997 and has been there ever since. After starting with the simple pure chèvre, Pure Luck has expanded to several other cheeses over the years.

Sara Sweetser Bolton passed away on November 9, 2005, a victim of cancer. Her legacy continues as the business thrives, and Pure Luck cheeses continue to excel in national competitions.

Gitana recently reflected on the nature of the farm, the family, and the land, and she says she was struck by something more. While the farm has been the family home since she was four, the goats have been there for *generations*. They know the land, and they know the family. They teach their kids the best stomping grounds, how to walk a particularly rocky trail. Gitana says that to discuss Pure Luck's terroir, you must hold close to their cultural reality, the family inheritance of the land, both for the people and the goats.

Amelia married Ben Sweethardt in 2007. They are raising their son, June, on the farm, where he soaks up the value of the land, the goats, the work, and his home. Under Amelia's guidance the goats are cared for with kindness and joy. She manages the herd and continues to make the cheese. Ben runs all deliveries and works to keep the farm in good repair.

Claire and Hope both live on the farm. Claire works full-time in the cheese plant. Hope continues to find just the right mix of energy, calm, joy, and entertainment with her animal friends. Gitana works part-time, but in the important job of keeping the books, teaching workshops, and just filling in where needed.

Hudson's on the Bend Hopelessly Blue Cheesecake

Kelly Casey has been the executive chef of Austin's acclaimed Hudson's on the Bend Restaurant since 2010, though she started in the kitchen in 2001. Although Hudson's on the Bend is renowned for a creative menu focused on wild game and fresh seafood, Kelly's unbelievably delicious cheesecake is a sought-after menu item. The delicate tangy earthiness of Pure Luck's Hopelessly Bleu (goat) cheese and the slightly sweet graham and pecan crust is a beautifully balanced expression of Texas Hill Country soil. Even avowed haters of blue cheese fall in love with this amazing dessert.

SERVES 16.

PECAN CRUST:

½ cup sugar
1 cup graham cracker crumbs
1 cup Texas San Saba pecan pieces
½ cup butter, melted

CAKE BATTER:

4 ounces Pure Luck Hopelessly Bleu
    cheese, or substitute another soft,
    mild-flavored blue goat cheese
2 pounds cream cheese, softened
1½ cups sugar
4 eggs
½ cup whipping cream
1 tablespoon vanilla extract

Preheat oven to 350°F. Make the pecan crust. Combine sugar, graham cracker crumbs, and pecans in the work bowl of a food processor fitted with the steel blade. Pulse until it forms chunky crumbs with bits about the size of crushed oats. Add the melted butter in a slow, steady stream through the feed tube, adding just enough to make the mixture form a ball when squeezed in your hand. Press the crumbs into the bottom of a 10-inch, springform cake pan. Bake in preheated oven for 10 minutes. Set aside on a wire rack to cool. Lower oven temperature to 300°F.

To make the cake batter, mix the blue cheese and cream cheese in a stand mixer with the whisk attachment. Scrape the bowl. Add the sugar and beat to blend. Scrape the bowl again, then add the eggs, whipping cream, and vanilla. Beat to combine well. There may still be visible lumps of blue cheese, but that's okay. Pour the batter over the prepared crust. Place the pan in a large baking dish and set on middle rack of preheated oven. Add boiling water to come halfway up the side of the cake pan and bake for 2 hours. Turn the oven off and leave the cake in the oven for 1 hour to prevent cracking on the top. Remove cake from the water bath and cool completely on a wire rack. Refrigerate, in the pan, until well chilled before slicing. To serve, remove side of springform pan and place cake on a platter. Slice into wedges and serve.

Olive Oil Cake with Blackberries and Chantilly Cream

The origin of this delightfully different cake is not clear. I first tasted, and loved, it at the Olives Olé Festival hosted by the San Antonio chapter of Les Dames d'Escoffier International. Chapter member June Hayes shared the recipe with me; then I investigated several recipes for olive oil cakes, each of which was a bit different; tested several; and came up with this version, paired with blackberries. June used strawberries, which are also quite good, but I really, really like the earthy flavor of those juicy spring blackberries paired with the bold, resinous nuances of the fresh rosemary. The resulting moist, yet light texture of the cake made my mouth very happy.

SERVES 8 TO 10.

1 pint fresh blackberries, or you may substitute strawberries

3 tablespoons sugar

½ cup freshly squeezed orange juice

1 cup all-purpose flour

¼ teaspoon baking powder

¼ teaspoon baking soda

½ teaspoon kosher salt

3 large eggs, at room temperature

1 cup sugar, divided

¾ cup Texas extra-virgin olive oil

¾ cup whole milk

1½ teaspoons each lemon and orange zest

1½ teaspoons minced fresh rosemary leaves

Good-quality orange marmalade, at room temperature

Chantilly Cream for serving (see recipe below)

Rosemary sprigs and reserved blackberries as garnish

CHANTILLY CREAM:

2 cups well-chilled heavy cream

2 heaping tablespoons chilled sour cream

2 heaping tablespoons powdered sugar

1 tablespoon vanilla extract

The day before you will serve the cake, place the blackberries in a bowl. Pick out 20 perfect berries for garnishing the cake servings and refrigerate. If you are using strawberries, remove the leafy tops and slice the berries. Scatter the 3 tablespoons of sugar over the berries and mash them to release some of their juice, but don't completely puree them. Cover and refrigerate overnight.

Preheat oven to 350°F. Lightly oil the bottom of a 9-inch cake pan. Line the bottom of the pan with a parchment paper circle, then oil the parchment paper and sides of the pan with olive oil; set aside.

Place the orange juice in a small saucepan over medium heat. Cook to reduce the juice to ¼ cup.

Combine the flour, baking powder, baking soda, and salt in a bowl, tossing to blend well; set aside. In the bowl of a stand mixer with the beater attachment, combine the eggs and sugar. Beat until the mixture is fluffy and light lemon-yellow in color, about 5 minutes, stopping to scrape down sides of the bowl occasionally. Add the olive oil and reduced orange juice; beat to blend well.

Combine the milk, citrus zest, and rosemary. Add to the batter in thirds, alternating with the flour mixture, beating just to blend after each addition and scraping down sides of bowl.

Turn the batter out into the prepared cake pan and gently rap the pan on a work surface a couple of times to remove any air bubbles. Bake in preheated oven for about 35 minutes, or until a cake tester or wooden skewer inserted in the center comes out clean. Remove from oven and cool in the pan on a wire rack for 10 minutes. Run a thin, sharp knife around the edges of the pan to loosen the cake, then invert the cake onto a serving platter. Gently peel off the parchment paper round. Using a pastry brush, glaze the top of the cake liberally with the orange marmalade. Allow cake to cool completely before serving.

While the cake is baking, make the Chantilly cream. Combine all ingredients in the bowl of a mixer fitted with a wire whisk. Beat until the cream is slightly stiff. It should be soft enough that it will drape invitingly down the sides of the cake slices onto the plate.

To serve, cut the cake into desired-size wedges. Place a large dollop of the Chantilly cream over each slice. Then top with a portion of the berries and syrup. Garnish each serving with a couple of the reserved whole berries and a rosemary sprig. Enjoy.

Slow-Burn Brownies

The chipotle chiles in these brownies create a really nice, back-of-the-throat glow—a surprise after a few bites. The malted milk balls add a nice crunch and evoke long-ago Saturday-afternoon matinees at the picture show. The topping is actually a chocolate ganache, which can also be used as a glaze for cakes or to make the luscious gooey centers for truffles. The brownies are delicious to eat just as they are, but they can be transformed into an upscale presentation with a scoop of good vanilla ice cream and caramel sauce drizzled over the top, perhaps some chopped pecans, too.

MAKES ABOUT 16 BROWNIES.

BROWNIES:

1 large canned (not the whole can) chipotle chile, packed in adobo sauce

1 tablespoon adobo sauce from canned chipotles

3 eggs

1 tablespoon vanilla extract

¼ cup dry instant espresso granules

1½ cups sifted all-purpose flour

1 teaspoon kosher salt

1 teaspoon baking soda

2 ounces (2 squares) unsweetened chocolate

½ pound (2 sticks) unsalted butter, softened

¾ cup sugar

¾ cup firmly packed light brown sugar

1 cup semisweet chocolate morsels

1⅓ cups chopped malted milk balls

CHOCOLATE TOPPING:

6 ounces bittersweet chocolate

¾ cup whipping cream

To make the brownies, preheat oven to 350°F and place oven rack in center position. Spray a 9 × 13-inch baking dish thoroughly with nonstick vegetable spray. Line the dish with parchment paper, pressing it into the vegetable spray so that it will stick. Now spray the parchment paper; set dish aside.

In the work bowl of a food processor fitted with the steel blade, combine the chipotle chile, adobo sauce, eggs, vanilla, and instant espresso. Process until mixture is smooth and well blended. Turn out into a bowl and set aside.

Sift together the flour, salt, and baking soda; set aside.

Place the unsweetened chocolate in top of a double boiler over simmering water and stir until melted. Remove top of pan from heat and set aside.

Place the butter in the bowl of an electric mixer and cream until soft and fluffy. Add the sugar and brown sugar; beat until well blended, about 1 minute. Add the reserved chipotle chile mixture and beat to blend. Add the melted chocolate and mix well. On low speed, add the sifted dry ingredients in thirds, stopping to scrape down sides of bowl after each addition. The batter will be thick. Turn the batter out into a bowl.

Fold in the chocolate morsels and chopped malted milk balls. Turn the batter out into the prepared baking dish and smooth the top with a rubber spatula. Bake in preheated

oven for about 30 to 35 minutes, or until a skewer inserted in center comes out clean. The brownies will be soft, but don't overbake them. They're very fudgy. Cool in the pan on a wire rack, then invert onto a baking sheet. Carefully peel off the parchment paper. Set aside to cool while preparing chocolate topping.

Combine the bittersweet chocolate and cream in a small, heavy-bottomed saucepan over heat on the low side of medium. Cook, stirring, until chocolate melts and mixture is very smooth and uniform in color. Do not allow the mixture to get too hot, or come anywhere near boiling. Chocolate will "break," and the cocoa butter will separate from the chocolate liquor, resulting in a grainy, unusable mess, at temperatures around 130°F. Remove from heat. Pour the topping over the cooled brownies, starting at the center. Coat the top and sides. Set aside until the topping sets. Slice brownies into desired-size squares and serve.

Chocolate Lava Cakes with Texas Whiskey Sauce

This is the dessert of choice for chocoholics. Rich and gooey and wonderful on their own, but combined with whiskey sauce, the little cakes are downright heavenly, or should I say, sinful? Timing is everything in the success of this dessert, so be sure to use a kitchen timer when baking and "resting" the cakes.

SERVES 6.

Sweetened whipped cream as garnish
Mint sprigs or fresh strawberries or
    raspberries as garnish

WHISKEY SAUCE:
1 cup (2 sticks) unsalted, butter,
    softened
1½ cups firmly packed dark
    brown sugar
2 eggs, beaten until frothy
½ cup Texas whiskey, such as
    Rebecca Creek

CAKES:
Softened unsalted butter, for
    greasing ramekins
¼ cup cocoa powder blended with
    ¼ cup raw sugar
1½ sticks unsalted butter
9 ounces bittersweet chocolate
3 eggs
3 egg yolks
⅓ cup sugar
⅛ teaspoon kosher salt
3 tablespoons all-purpose flour

Begin by making the whiskey sauce. Using a stand mixer with beater attachment, cream the butter and sugar until very light and fluffy, about 7 minutes. Transfer the mixture to the top of a double boiler over simmering water. Cook for about 20 minutes, whisking often, or until the mixture is silken smooth and comes away from the sides of the pan cleanly when whisked. It seems like nothing is happening as you whisk, but suddenly this base for the sauce magically comes together into a silken mass. Whisk ¼ cup of the hot butter mixture into the beaten eggs, then another ¼ cup. Whisk the warmed egg mixture slowly into the remaining butter mixture over the heat. Cook until thickened, about 4 to 5 minutes, whisking constantly. Whisk in the whiskey, blending well. The sauce may be kept warm over hot water until ready to serve, or it can be stored in the refrigerator. Gently reheat, whisking vigorously 3 or 4 times before serving to restore the smooth consistency.

Preheat the oven to 450°F. Line a baking sheet with parchment paper; set aside. Butter six (6-ounce) ramekins on bottom and sides. Coat the ramekins with the raw sugar-cocoa mixture. Tap out excess on the side of the sink. Place ramekins on prepared baking sheet and set aside.

Combine the butter and chocolate in the top of a double boiler over simmering water. In the bowl of a stand mixer, beat the eggs and extra egg yolks with sugar and salt at medium-high speed until thickened and light lemon-yellow in color, about 7 minutes.

Whisk the chocolate-butter mixture until smooth. Whisk the flour into the chocolate, blending well. Add the chocolate mixture to the egg and sugar mixture, beating just to blend. Spoon the batter into the prepared ramekins, smoothing the tops. Bake in preheated oven 11 to 12 minutes, or just until the sides of the cakes are firm. The centers will still be soft. Reheat the whiskey sauce in the double boiler while cakes are baking. Remove baking sheet from the oven and allow cakes to cool in the ramekins for 2 minutes, then invert quickly onto individual serving plates, letting them stand for about 1 minute before unmolding. Spoon some of the whiskey sauce around each cake, then top with a generous dollop of the sweetened whipped cream. Garnish with mint sprigs or berries and serve at once.

Texas Hills Vineyard Sangiovese Sorbet

Sorbet is such a delightful creation. It can be a palate cleanser between courses or the perfect light dessert at the end of a heavy meal. For a summer luncheon, I like to serve it alongside an entrée salad. Sorbet can be made from just about any fruit that is fresh and seasonal, but wine sorbets are especially wonderful. You can even make them from sparkling wine. Select a wine varietal that pairs with the main course of the meal to make the sorbet. This recipe was created by chef Ross Burtwell, owner of Fredericksburg's Cabernet Grill, for a vintner's dinner that he hosted in honor of Texas High Plains grape growers Neal and Janice Newsom. The wines that night were wonderful, but the sorbet was so unique that it prompted me to ask Ross to share the recipe. Although the egg white might seem strange, don't leave it out. Egg white adds a nice creaminess to sorbet and helps prevent crystallization when the sorbet is frozen.

MAKES 1 QUART.

1 bottle Texas Hills Vineyard
    Sangiovese
1 cup water
1½ cups granulated sugar

1 sprig fresh rosemary, 3 inches long
Zest and juice of ½ large lemon
1 tablespoon raw egg white

Combine all ingredients except egg white in a heavy-bottomed 2-quart saucepan over high heat. Bring to a full boil, then lower heat and simmer for 10 minutes.

Remove pan from heat and strain the liquid through a fine strainer into a bowl. Discard rosemary and lemon zest. Place the bowl of the wine mixture over a bowl of ice water and whisk until completely cool. Vigorously mix in the egg white until the mixture is somewhat frothy.

Pour into ice-cream maker and process according to the manufacturer's instructions. Transfer to a storage container with a tight-fitting lid and freeze until firm before serving, about 4 hours.

Biga on the Banks Sticky Toffee Pudding with Custard Sauce

Biga on the Banks chef/owner Bruce Auden was born in North London and moved to the United States when he was 17 to begin a career in the culinary arts that has garnered national recognition. Among his many accolades, Auden has been named one of the "Ten Best New Chefs in America" by *Food and Wine* magazine and has received five nominations for the James Beard Award, Best Chef Southwest. His restaurant, as its name implies, is located on San Antonio's famed river and has become a legend with San Antonio residents and visitors to the city alike. He's an innovative cook driven by local ingredients, but legions of fans are grateful he hasn't forgotten his roots, on display in this classic English dessert.

SERVES 6.

CUSTARD SAUCE:

⅔ cup whole milk

½ vanilla bean, split in half lengthwise, seeds scraped out with sharp paring knife

4 large egg yolks

2 tablespoons granulated sugar

Pinch of kosher salt

1 teaspoon honey

PUDDING:

5 tablespoons unsalted butter, softened, plus extra for greasing the ramekins

½ pound whole pitted dates, cut crosswise into slices ¼-inch thick

¾ teaspoon baking soda

⅔ cup boiling water, plus extra for the water bath

1 cup unbleached all-purpose flour

½ teaspoon baking powder

⅛ teaspoon kosher salt

¼ cup dark brown sugar

⅓ cup molasses

¾ teaspoon vanilla extract

1 large egg

TOFFEE SAUCE:

2⅓ tablespoons unsalted butter

⅓ cup light brown sugar

3 tablespoons heavy cream

Pinch of kosher salt

GARNISH:

18 fresh raspberries

Prepare the custard sauce. Bring the milk and vanilla seeds and pod to a simmer in a medium saucepan over medium-high heat. When the milk begins to simmer, reduce the heat to low. Whisk the egg yolks, granulated sugar, and salt together in a medium bowl. Whisk 3 tablespoons of the hot milk mixture into the yolk mixture. Slowly whisk the now-tempered egg yolk mixture into the simmering hot milk. Cook, whisking constantly, until the sauce is quite thick and heavily coats the back of a spoon, about 2 minutes. Mixture should register 165°F on an instant-read thermometer.

Pour the custard through a fine-mesh strainer into a clean bowl and stir in the honey. Cover with plastic wrap and refrigerate until needed, or place in the freezer to chill if needed immediately. Custard should be well chilled before using.

To prepare the pudding, adjust an oven rack to middle position and preheat oven to 325°F. Butter six (4-ounce) ramekins and line the bottoms with small rounds of parchment paper. Arrange the ramekins in a small roasting pan lined with a clean dish towel

to prevent them from sliding around in the pan. Combine the dates, baking soda, and ⅔ cup boiling water in a medium bowl and set aside.

Whisk together the flour, baking powder, and salt in a small bowl. In the bowl of a stand mixer fitted with the paddle attachment, beat the remaining 5 tablespoons of butter and dark brown sugar together on medium-low speed until just mixed, about 1 minute. Add the molasses and vanilla and beat just to combine. Scrape down the paddle and bowl using a rubber spatula. Continue to mix on medium low, add the egg, and beat just until blended. Add the date mixture and mix to combine. Slowly add the flour mixture, beating just until blended.

Divide the batter evenly among the prepared ramekins and place them in the prepared roasting pan. Fill the pan with enough boiling water to come halfway up the sides of the ramekins, making sure that you don't splash any of the water into the puddings. Cover the pan tightly with foil, crimping the edges to seal. Bake in preheated oven for about 35 minutes, or until the puddings are slightly puffed and a knife inserted into the center of the puddings comes out clean.

While puddings are baking, prepare the toffee sauce. Melt the butter in a medium saucepan over medium heat. Whisk in the light brown sugar and cook, whisking occasionally, until an instant-read thermometer registers 250°F. Carefully whisk in the cream and salt and bring to a simmer. Be careful, as the mixture will spit and sputter furiously. Whisk just until thickened and smooth. Remove from the heat and transfer to a glass measuring cup. Cover tightly with plastic wrap to keep warm.

To serve, transfer the hot puddings to a wire rack to cool slightly. Run a paring knife around the edges of the ramekins to loosen the puddings. Pour a portion of the cold custard sauce, as desired, into each serving bowl. Invert the ramekins into the center of the custard sauce in each bowl and remove the parchment paper. Pour desired portion of the warm toffee sauce over the top of each pudding. Garnish each with 3 raspberries and serve immediately.

Salted Agave Caramel Ice Cream

I had never been much of an ice-cream fanatic until I tasted salted caramel ice cream that was made right here in Fredericksburg at the Clear River Pecan Company. It was like I had been waiting all my life for just *this* ice cream. I was instantly hooked on the combination of flavors and textures that were pinging around my mouth. The rich, custardy ice cream was the perfect creamy base for the rich caramel. The little nubbins of sea salt put the experience over the top of sensory pleasure! I vowed to re-create the experience using my own agave nectar–based caramel. I did, and found the results to be mighty fine. I love this ice cream simply piled into a bowl or served on top of any apple-based dessert.

CARAMEL:

¾ cup plus 2 tablespoons
   granulated sugar

¼ cup plus 2 tablespoons agave
   nectar

¼ cup water

¾ cup whipping cream

4 tablespoons salted butter, room
   temperature

1½ teaspoons coarse, flaky sea salt,
   such as Adams Reserve Flaky
   Sea Salt

CUSTARD FOR ICE CREAM:

5 large egg yolks

¼ cup sugar

2 cups whole milk

1 cup whipping cream

¾ teaspoon vanilla bean paste

Begin by making the caramel. Combine the sugar and agave nectar in a medium-sized, heavy-bottomed saucepan; stir in the water to blend well. Set over medium-high heat and bring to a simmer, then lower heat to a bare simmer and cook, without stirring, for 30 to 35 minutes, or until the caramel is a rich amber color. You want a dark caramel so the finished product will be a rich caramel color. Take care, however, not to burn the caramel.

Remove pan from heat and slowly stir in the cream. Be careful, as the mixture will spit and sputter and bubble up in the pan. If the caramel clumps, don't worry, just stir it over medium heat and it will slowly remelt. Stir in the butter, incorporating well. The sauce should be satiny smooth. Cool the caramel in an ice-water bath, stirring often, while making the custard for the ice cream. The caramel may be made ahead of time and refrigerated in a tightly covered container. When it is completely cool, stir in the salt, blending well.

To make the ice cream, combine egg yolks and sugar in the bowl of a stand mixer. Beat, beginning on low, and gradually increasing as the sugar is blended, until smooth and light lemon-yellow in color, about 7 minutes. Set aside.

Combine the milk and cream in a heavy-bottomed 3-quart saucepan over medium heat. Heat the mixture until very hot, but not boiling. Remove from heat and temper the egg yolk mixture by whisking ½ cup of the hot milk mixture into the yolks, blending well. Now pour the tempered yolks into the saucepan with the remaining milk mixture and return to heat. Add the vanilla bean paste. Continue to cook, whisking constantly, until the custard thickens. It should coat the back of a spoon fairly heavily. Do not allow the mixture to boil. Remove custard from the heat and pour through a fine-mesh strainer to remove any bits of scrambled egg. Cool the strained custard in an ice-water bath, stirring often, until completely cool, then whisk in the caramel, blending well.

Transfer the custard to the canister of an ice-cream maker and process according to the manufacturer's directions. When the ice cream is finished, transfer it to a container with a tight-fitting lid and freeze for 4 hours before serving.

WATEROAK FARM

WHEN I WAS EXPERIMENTING with the recipe for the Chocolate and Goat Cheese Crème Brûlée (page 412), I wanted a delicate-tasting cheese, and one with a nice, silky texture. The plain chèvre produced by Mark and Pam Burrow at their Wateroak Farm in Robertson County, outside Bryan, was just what I needed. The cheese has a slight tartness that cuts the richness of the chocolate, and its tangy, earthy taste provides an exotic side note of delicate flavor.

I had to ask Mark what makes his cheese so special. He said that at Wateroak they use only glass and stainless containers for their goat milk. Reused plastic containers can harbor residual particles of fat, which become rancid. Also, he keeps the male goats, which give off strong scents, separate from milk-producing females. Finally, he added, "Pam and I enjoy drinking our product. We consume our goat milk on a daily basis. Bottom line here is that we both screen the milk we use for everything. If it doesn't pass both of our taste tests, then it is not used. You have to start with good-tasting milk in order to generate good-tasting cheeses. In the spring it is not unusual for us to be discarding 20 to 30 percent of our milk. Good news is that this lasts for only two to three weeks. After the hormones clear out, then we get to utilize all of the milk."

That attention to detail typifies Texas's new crop of young agrarians, people who really want to farm on a small scale, get their hands in the dirt, and become part of the growing movement toward better food. Pam and Mark handle all phases of the business themselves, from milk production to deliveries. Mark's typical day is 12 to 14 hours, ending "between 11:30 p.m. and 12:30 a.m. Winding down and resting is only about 30 minutes; then I hit the comatose phase for a few hours before I get up and do it all over again."

Chocolate and Goat Cheese Crème Brûlée

I was inspired to create this unusual flavor combination in a crème brûlée by the great goat cheeses that are being produced in Texas. Their textures and flavors vary from cheesemaker to cheesemaker, and it's an interesting taste experiment to make this recipe using cheese from different artisan cheesemakers. The tartness of the goat cheese cuts the richness of the chocolate, and that tangy, earthy taste provides an exotic side note of flavor.

MAKES SIX (6-OUNCE) RAMEKINS.

⅓ cup light brown sugar

2¼ cups whipping cream

4½ tablespoons sugar

3 ounces bittersweet chocolate

2 tablespoons Dutch process cocoa

4 egg yolks

2½ teaspoons vanilla extract

7½ ounces mild-flavored Texas goat cheese, such as Wateroak Farm Plain Goat Cheese

Preheat oven to 250°F. Line a baking sheet with parchment paper. Spread the brown sugar in a thin layer on the prepared baking sheet and place in preheated oven for about 10 minutes. Do not allow the sugar to melt. Remove baking sheet to cooling rack while preparing custard. Raise oven temperature to 325°F. Lightly butter bottom and sides of six (6-ounce) ramekins; set aside.

Combine the whipping cream, sugar, chocolate, and cocoa in a heavy-bottomed 2-quart saucepan over medium heat. Cook until chocolate is melted and sugar has dissolved, whisking often. Remove from heat and set aside to cool. Combine the egg yolks, vanilla extract, and softened goat cheese in the bowl of a stand mixer. Beat, beginning on low speed, and increasing to medium high, until smooth and fluffy, about 5 minutes. Add the chocolate mixture and beat just until smooth.

Divide the mixture among the prepared ramekins and place the ramekins in a baking dish large enough to hold them so that they don't touch. Set the baking dish on oven rack and pour in boiling water to come halfway up the sides of the ramekins. Place a sheet of parchment paper on top of the ramekins. Bake in preheated oven for 1 hour. Carefully remove the baking dish from the oven and remove ramekins from the water. Cool to room temperature, then refrigerate until well chilled, at least 6 hours.

Put the cooled brown sugar in the work bowl of a food processor fitted with the steel blade and process until the sugar is very fine. Set aside.

When the crème brûlée is well chilled, place the ramekins on a baking sheet and divide the brown sugar among the ramekins, spreading an even layer on top of each one. Using a blow torch (like the one you have in the garage), caramelize the sugar, taking care not to burn it. If you don't own a blowtorch, preheat the broiler and place oven rack 3 inches under heat source. Place the baking sheet under broiler and cook just until sugar has caramelized. Take care not to burn the sugar. Allow the sugar to harden for a few minutes, and then serve.

NAVAJO GRILL

Goat's Milk and Vanilla Bean Panna Cotta with Marburger Strawberries Macerated in Texas Riesling

Navajo Grill in Fredericksburg is one of the city's best restaurants, known for its perfect Hill Country ambience, Texas wines, and, most important, outstanding food. Mike Raymer, who bought the restaurant in 1998, brought his son, Josh, into the business as chef/co-owner in 2006. Josh brought a dedication to sourcing fresh, local ingredients. This delicious dessert, made from local goat's milk and finished with fresh strawberries from Fredericksburg's Marburger Farm, was one that Josh prepared for the first Edible Texas Wine Food Match in 2011.

PANNA COTTA:

4 teaspoons gelatin

4 teaspoons water

1 cup buttermilk (not low fat)

2 cups goat's milk

1 cup whipping cream

¾ cup sugar

1 large vanilla bean, split lengthwise

STRAWBERRIES:

3 cups fresh Marburger Farm
  strawberries, quartered

2 tablespoons sugar

½ cup sweet Riesling, such as
  Messina Hof "Angel" Riesling

Mint sprigs as garnish, if desired

Have a large bowl of ice water ready. Spray eight (4-ounce) ramekins with nonstick spray; set aside. In a small bowl, stir the gelatin into the water; set aside. In a large pot, combine buttermilk, goat's milk, whipping cream, and sugar. Scrape the seeds from the vanilla bean and add to the pan, then add the vanilla bean. Warm the mixture, whisking constantly until very warm and sugar has melted. Scrape the gelatin mixture into the pan and cook, whisking, until gelatin is completely melted. Strain through a fine strainer into a metal bowl and place in the bowl of ice water. Whisk until cool. Divide the mixture among the prepared ramekins. Refrigerate until set.

Mash half of the strawberries, then stir together with the remaining quartered berries and the sugar and Riesling until sugar is dissolved. Refrigerate until ready to serve. To serve, unmold panna cotta onto serving plates. Top with a portion of the strawberries and a little of their juice. Garnish each serving with a mint sprig if desired.

MARBURGER FARM

THE MARBURGER FARM, just outside Fredericksburg, is a yearly destination for carloads of people from all over the state. In midspring, folks come to pick their own strawberries from the vast fields at Marburger. You can pick as many as you've got the fortitude to pick. When my sister and I went to the farm to photograph, we picked enough to fill up all the available space in Sandy's car that wasn't occupied by camera equipment or my file boxes. When she returned home, she made strawberry preserves that were heavenly.

After the strawberries have run their course in May, there are big, succulent blackberries, followed closely by delicious peaches. Marburger provides the containers for picking, so you can leave your buckets at home, though lots of folks save the containers from year to year—saves a lot of trees! Most important, you have to go to the farm to get the fruit: they don't ship their peaches or berries anywhere!

415

Puffy Homemade Doughnut Holes with Seeing Double Chocolate Dip

This is one of my favorite desserts because it's so unusual and, of course, because people go wild over it. The doughnut holes are wonderfully puffy and light, so they should be served fresh and warm, but the seeing double chocolate dip, so named because of the nice hit of sherry it contains, can be made ahead and gently reheated. I adapted the doughnut recipe from one created by Jessica Maher, who, along with her husband, Todd Duplechan, owns Lenoir Restaurant in Austin. The dip, or sauce, my creation, is also wonderful on anything that you'd generally serve with a chocolate sauce. It's also perfect with a good Texas Port wine.

MAKES ABOUT 24 DOUGHNUT HOLES.

DOUGHNUT HOLES:

2 tablespoons instant-rise yeast

¼ cup plus 1 teaspoon sugar, divided

¼ cup water (105°F to 115°F)

2½ cups all-purpose flour, or more as needed

½ teaspoon freshly ground nutmeg

2 teaspoons kosher salt

2 eggs

2 tablespoons unsalted butter, softened

Canola oil for deep-frying, heated to 370°F

Turbinado (raw) sugar for rolling the doughnut holes

SEEING DOUBLE CHOCOLATE DIP:

8 ounces good-quality bittersweet chocolate

2 cups whipping cream

1½ sticks unsalted butter, cut into ½-inch dice

½ pound (by weight) powdered sugar

⅔ cup sherry

Begin by making the dip. Combine chocolate and cream in a heavy-bottomed 2-quart saucepan over medium heat. Cook, whisking often, just until chocolate is melted and mixture is smooth. Remove from heat and set aside. Combine the butter and powdered sugar in the bowl of a stand mixer and cream until light and fluffy, about 7 minutes, stopping mixer to scrape down sides of bowl 2 or 3 times to be sure all sugar is incorporated. Turn mixture out into a mixing bowl set over simmering water and whisk until silky smooth, about 7 to 8 minutes. *Note:* The mixture will begin to leave the sides of the bowl as you whisk. It will become very smooth and satiny-glossy. Whisk in the chocolate mixture and cook for 5 minutes, or until mixture is smooth and creamy. Whisk in the sherry and cook, whisking often, for 5 minutes. Serve warm or refrigerate until ready to serve. Reheat gently just until the sauce is warm and pourable.

To make the doughnut holes, gently whisk yeast and the 1 teaspoon of sugar into the water in a 1-cup Pyrex measuring cup. Set aside until the mixture begins to bubble and foam. In the meantime, combine the flour, remaining ¼ cup sugar, nutmeg, and salt in the bowl of a stand mixer with the beater attachment. Beat on slow speed just to combine. Add the yeast mixture and beat, starting on low speed and increasing to medium, just long enough to moisten the dry ingredients. Add the eggs, one at a time, beating to blend and scraping down sides of bowl after each addition. Add the butter and beat to blend well at medium speed.

Turn the dough out onto a lightly floured work surface and knead several times by hand until the dough is very smooth and elastic. If the dough is sticky, scatter an additional tablespoon of flour over it and knead to blend. Transfer the dough to a lightly oiled large bowl and cover tightly with plastic wrap. Set aside to rise in a draft-free spot until doubled in bulk, about 1 hour.

When the dough has doubled in bulk, turn out onto a lightly floured work surface and roll out to a thickness of ½ inch. Using a sharp-edged cutter, cut the dough into 1½-inch-diameter rounds and place on a parchment-lined baking sheet. Make the cuts as close together as possible. Re-roll dough scraps and cut into rounds until all dough has been used. Cover the dough rounds with a second sheet of parchment paper and set aside to rise again for 15 to 20 minutes. Heat the oil in a deep fryer to 370°F.

When the rounds are puffed, begin to fry them 5 or 6 at a time, taking care not to crowd the fryer. Fry for about 45 seconds on each side, or until golden brown and quite puffy. Remove with a slotted spoon and place on a wire rack set over a baking sheet to drain.

Place the turbinado sugar in a shallow baking pan. As soon as each batch of the doughnut holes becomes cool enough to handle, but while they're still fairly hot, roll them in the sugar and return to cooling rack.

To serve, pour a bit of the warm dip into individual small bowls and place in the center of serving plates. Arrange desired number of the warm doughnut holes around the bowls of chocolate and serve at once.

CERTENBERG VINEYARDS AND THE WINES OF DOTSON-CERVANTES

ALPHONSE DOTSON HAS a different story from that of your average Texas vineyard/winery owner. He played offensive tackle for the Oakland Raiders. When he retired from the gridiron, he moved to Acapulco, where he met and married Martha Cervantes. But he never outgrew his childhood fascination with a large grape arbor that grew at his grandfather's house. Year in and year out that old grapevine would lose every last leaf in the fall; then in the spring it would bud out again, soon followed by huge clusters of grapes hanging all over.

Martha was all for his idea that they might grow grapes themselves. After exhaustive research, they found a property in Mason County, where the red Hickory Sands soil was proving to be great terroir for growing high-quality grapes. They planted 30 acres and named the vineyard after that grandfather, Alphonse Certenberg.

Help was hard to find at first, so the planting and tending of vines were an intensely hands-on operation. But that "close-to-the-ground" nurturing paid off, as the vines are healthy and vigorous and produce high-quality fruit, which the Dotsons sell to wineries in the Texas Hill Country. "It's a good thing we love what we're doing, because it is purely hard work," Alphonse recently told me after yet another hand harvest.

Although he works as hard as the typical, anonymous farmer, Alphonse is sometimes called "Texas's Celebrity Grape Grower" because of his days in the NFL. His colorful history, in addition to the quality of the vineyard, has drawn writers from national publications—all of which brought attention to the growing Texas wine industry. But what the couple wanted more than publicity was a small, very personal winery. In 2009, they released the first of their Dotson-Cervantes wines, Gotas de Oro, "Drops of Gold." You can sample it in their tasting room in downtown Pontotoc, a growing center for boutique wineries in Texas.

Dessert wine must be sweeter than the dessert itself. Gotas de Oro, a unique blend of chardonnay and muscat canelli, is a quintessential dessert wine. Pair it with the Rustic Apple Tart with Moscato (pages 420–421) or Kelly Casey's Hopelessly Blue Cheesecake (page 397).

Rustic Apple Tart with Moscato

I created this dish after visiting the Love Creek Orchards in Medina. I purchased some of their Granny Smith and Pink Lady apples and couldn't wait to get home to make something wonderful with them. This free-form apple pastry was the result. It's simple to make, but the flavor is outstanding. Macerating the apples in the sweet white dessert wine, Moscato, lends an exciting dimension of flavor to the creation. For the ultimate experience, top wedges of the tart with salted agave caramel ice cream.

SERVES 6 TO 8.

Chilled, sweetened whipping cream
   or Salted Agave Caramel Ice Cream
   (see recipe on pages 409–410)

APPLE FILLING:
3 large Granny Smith and 3 large
   Pink Lady apples, peeled, cored,
   and sliced about ¼-inch thick
1 teaspoon vanilla bean paste, stirred
   into ⅓ cup Texas Moscato wine, or
   substitute a Texas Muscat Canelli
1 cup sugar
⅓ cup all-purpose flour
1 teaspoon ground cinnamon
1 teaspoon freshly grated nutmeg
½ teaspoon ground allspice
2 tablespoons lemon juice

PASTRY:
1½ cups all-purpose flour
Pinch of kosher salt
1 tablespoon sugar
1½ sticks frozen unsalted butter,
   cut into 1-inch cubes
6 to 8 tablespoons very cold water

STREUSEL TOPPING:
¼ cup light brown sugar
2 tablespoons unsalted butter, melted
Pinch of kosher salt
½ cup all-purpose flour
⅓ cup coarsely chopped pecans

Begin by placing the sliced apples in a large bowl. Pour the Moscato/vanilla bean paste mixture over them and stir to coat all of the apples. Cover with plastic wrap and set aside for 2 hours.

After the apples have macerated in the wine for 2 hours, drain them well and return to the bowl. Add the remaining filling ingredients, stirring to blend well; set aside.

Make the pastry. Combine flour, salt, sugar, and butter in the work bowl of a food processor fitted with the steel blade. Use the pulse feature to combine the ingredients, pulsing until the butter is broken up into pea-sized bits. Add 6 tablespoons of the cold water and process until well blended. The dough should form a ball when a small amount is gathered into your hand. If dough is too dry, add the remaining 2 tablespoons of water, or more if needed. Process just until water is blended. Do not allow dough to form a ball in the processor. Turn crumbly dough out onto a work surface and gather together. Knead 3 to 4 times to form a cohesive dough. There should still be chunks of butter in the dough. Pat dough into a disk, wrap in plastic wrap, and refrigerate 20 minutes. Preheat oven to 375°F and line a 14-inch-wide baking sheet with parchment paper; set aside.

Make the streusel topping. Stir together the first three ingredients, blending well. Add the flour and pecans; stir to blend well. Refrigerate the streusel for 30 minutes until it is firm enough to crumble into small bits.

To assemble the tart, roll the pastry out on a floured work surface into a 14-inch round. Roll the pastry around the rolling pin and unroll it onto the parchment-lined baking sheet. Turn the apple mixture out into the center of the pastry. Working quickly, fold the edge of the dough up around the apples in a sort of pleated fashion, leaving about 4 to 5 inches of exposed apples in the center. Scatter the topping over the entire tart and bake in preheated oven 30 to 35 minutes, or until pastry is golden brown and filling is bubbly, having formed a nice syrup. Slide the tart onto a wire cooling rack by lifting both sides of the parchment paper. Cool to lukewarm, then slice into wedges. Serve in shallow bowls, drizzling desired amount of sweetened whipped cream, or a scoop of ice cream, over each serving.

VOGEL ORCHARD

Peaches came to Central Texas, like so many other delicious things, with the first German settlers in the mid-1800s. The local soil, temperature variations, and altitude combine to form an almost perfect peach-growing climate (if untimely freezes and other inclement weather don't come around). The average peach tree produces three to four bushels (150 to 200 pounds) of peaches each year. Folks come from far and near to buy peaches each summer.

Many of the orchards date back to the early 1900s and have been passed down through generations. The first Vogel peaches were planted by Armand Vogel, who sold them under a shade tree on the road between Stonewall and Fredericksburg. In 1972, the Vogels built a permanent roadside market near the spot where Armand used to sell his peaches.

Armand's son, George, and his wife, Nelda, planted 200 more trees in 1953. The orchard now has more than 7,000 trees and is run by George and Nelda's son, Jamey, his wife, Terri, and their family. They grow some 17 varieties, which begin to ripen around the middle of May. The first peaches of the season are the clingstone variety Starlite White. The first freestones at Vogel Orchard are the Tex Royal, generally available around the end of May. The various varieties continue through the summer until early August.

In addition to peaches, the market sells Methley plums from the family orchard, blackberries, cantaloupes, and other seasonal produce. They also offer a variety of peach-based goodies made by the family—peach ice cream, peach cobbler, Nelda's peach preserves, and peach butter, plum jelly, and fig, blackberry, and pear preserves.

Stonewall Peach Crisp

Although I enjoy fresh peaches all summer, I also stock up our freezer around the end of July when the crop begins to dwindle. Then I can add a peach cobbler or crisp to my holiday menus using my stash of fresh frozen peaches. It adds a welcome taste of summer sun to the holiday table.

SERVES 6.

PEACHES:

5 cups fresh peaches, peeled, pitted, and sliced

½ teaspoon ground cinnamon

3 tablespoons turbinado (raw) sugar

3 tablespoons all-purpose flour

TOPPING:

2 cups mini shredded wheat cereal

1 cup all-purpose flour

1 cup firmly packed light brown sugar

⅓ cup chopped pecans

1½ sticks well-chilled unsalted butter, cut into ½-inch cubes

1 tablespoon vanilla

Preheat oven to 350°F. Spray a 9 × 13-inch baking dish with nonstick spray; set aside. Place the peaches in a medium-sized bowl; set aside. In a small bowl combine the cinnamon, turbinado sugar, and flour. Toss to blend well, then pour the flour mixture into the peaches and toss to mix well, making sure all peaches are coated. Turn the peaches out into the prepared baking dish, smoothing the top evenly; set aside.

To make the topping, place the cereal in the work bowl of a food processor fitted with the steel blade and pulse until it is completely broken up into very small bits. Add remaining ingredients and pulse to blend, taking care to leave the butter in pea-sized bits.

Scatter the topping over the peaches, making sure it extends into the corners and covers the peaches. Bake in preheated oven for about 45 minutes, or until golden brown and bubbly. Cool for 30 minutes before serving. Top each serving with a scoop of good-quality vanilla ice cream for an over-the-top experience.

Fredericksburg Peach and White Chocolate Bread Pudding with Schnapps-Whiskey Sauce and Chantilly Cream

This bread pudding is sensuously delicious with complex layers of flavor. I believe it's a fitting testament to the Fredericksburg peach crop. I prefer to use any variety of the freestone peaches in this recipe rather than the earlier-ripening clingstone varieties (which I love to eat just as they come off the trees, skin and all).

SERVES 12.

BREAD PUDDING:

8 ounces white chocolate, cut into small chunks

2 cups half and half

½ cup (1 stick) unsalted butter, softened

½ teaspoon ground cinnamon

10 ounces day-old croissants, cut into ½-inch pieces

3 eggs

¾ cup sugar

3 cups fresh Fredericksburg peaches, peeled and chopped into bite-size pieces, about 7 medium peaches

½ cup toasted, chopped pecans

1 tablespoon vanilla extract

SCHNAPPS-WHISKEY SAUCE:

1 cup (2 sticks) unsalted butter,
    softened
1½ cups sugar
2 eggs, beaten until frothy
⅓ cup peach schnapps
3 tablespoons Rebecca Creek Fine
    Texas Spirit Whiskey

CHANTILLY CREAM:

2 cups whipping cream, well chilled
¼ cup sour cream, well chilled
¼ cup powdered sugar
2 tablespoons vanilla extract

Preheat oven to 350°F. Butter a 13 × 9-inch baking dish; set aside. In a 2-quart saucepan combine the white chocolate, half and half, butter, and cinnamon. Cook over medium-low heat, stirring often, until smooth. Remove from heat and set aside. Place croissant pieces in a large bowl and stir in the white chocolate mixture, blending well and breaking up the croissants. In the bowl of a stand mixer with the beater attachment, combine eggs and sugar; beat at medium speed until thickened, about 7 minutes. Add the peaches, pecans, and vanilla; beat just to blend. Fold egg mixture into the croissants, blending well. Turn out into the prepared baking dish and bake in preheated oven 45 to 55 minutes, or until a knife inserted in the center comes out clean. Set aside to cool.

To make the sauce, cream butter and sugar in a stand mixer until very light and fluffy, about 7 minutes. Transfer to top of a double boiler over simmering water. Cook 20 minutes, whisking often, until the mixture is silken smooth and comes away from the sides of the pan when whisked. Whisk ½ cup of the hot butter mixture into the beaten eggs, then another ¼ cup. Whisk the warmed egg mixture slowly into the remaining butter mixture over the heat. Cook until thickened, about 4 to 5 minutes, whisking constantly. Whisk in the schnapps and whiskey; blend well. Keep warm over low heat; whisk before serving.

Make the Chantilly cream by combining all ingredients in the bowl of a stand mixer. Beat at medium speed, using the whisk attachment, until the mixture forms loose, floppy peaks. Refrigerate, tightly covered with plastic wrap, until ready to serve.

To serve, slice the warm pudding into squares. Place a portion of the schnapps-whiskey sauce in the bottom of each serving bowl and set a square of pudding in the center. Top with a large dollop of Chantilly cream.

DOS LUNAS CHEESE

Joaquin Avellan was born in Venezuela. His earliest memories were of smells—of food and the earth, in particular. The family moved to Houston when he was a teenager in the 1970s. He quickly fell into a pattern of eating what everyone in America was eating—cured meats on white breads and heavy cheeses on thick pizzas, and gallons and gallons of pasteurized milk, plus a daunting amount of other processed dairy products. He became lactose intolerant, and in his 30s, he shifted back to a healthier, largely organic lifestyle.

In 2009, Joaquin's father, who had retired to Venezuela to start a dairy farm in the foothills of the Andes, needed triple bypass surgery and came to Houston. After the operation, Joaquin accompanied his father back to Venezuela to help with the dairy. At 3:00 a.m. every morning for two months, Joaquin rose and once again inhaled the cherished scents of his childhood on his walk up to the barns to make his father's signature queso fresco. He nibbled his way through the days, surprised that he wasn't intolerant to this cheese made from pure raw milk.

When he returned to the United States, he couldn't get his father's cheese out of his mind. After buying some American queso fresco produced with pasteurized milk, he was shocked at how terrible, almost rancid, it tasted. He began researching sources for raw milk near Austin and met a wonderful dairy farmer in Schulenburg. In his home kitchen, Joaquin tried to replicate his father's cheeses, using the pristine raw milk from Stryk Farm. He was pleased with his results and took some of his early experiments to Antonelli's Cheese Shop, an elegant emporium of artisan cheese. John Antonelli loved the cheeses until Joaquin mentioned they were made with raw milk only a week before. John almost spit out the cheese as he declared, "Please, you must get this cheese out of my shop! Raw milk cheeses must be aged 60 days in America!"

"Wow," Joaquin thought. "Queso fresco, or fresh cheese, certainly isn't by definition *fresh* two months after it's made." But rather than being discouraged, he was inspired. He wanted to recapture the tastes of his childhood and found that by tweaking the recipes and adapting the process, he could make incredibly fresh-tasting cheese that aged for, yes, two months. Joaquin now makes other varieties of cheese, including flavored cheese and Cheddar. "The beautiful Jersey cows at Stryk Farm only eat grass in the open pastures. I also experience great joy knowing that this wonderful milk, after making cheese, yields even more goodness from its whey, from which the creamy and fresh Dos Lunas Ricotta Fresca was created."

Dos Lunas Ricotta and Orange Moscato Tart with Almond Pastry

When I first met Joaquin Avellan and tasted his handmade ricotta, I fell in love—with the cheese, that is, although I have great admiration for Joaquin and his ability to make many types of cheese, all of which are delicious. I set about developing recipes using the rich, almost buttery, ricotta. This tart is one of the best, with the tangy, but delicate cheese acting as a base for the nutty, lemon-flecked crust, the hit of citrus from the orange Moscato wine in the filling, and the topping of fresh strawberries. As a side note, another incredible use for Joaquin's ricotta is as a finger food for cocktail parties. Simply pile a mound of the cheese on a plate and serve it with a bit of fresh honeycomb. Heaven can wait!

SERVES 6 TO 8.

ALMOND PASTRY:
⅓ cup sliced, skin-on almonds
¾ cup all-purpose flour
2 teaspoons minced lemon zest
¼ cup sugar
¼ teaspoon kosher salt
6 tablespoons unsalted butter at
    room temperature
1 egg
1 tablespoon cold water

RICOTTA FILLING:
1½ cups Dos Lunas Ricotta Fresca
5 egg yolks
½ cup sugar
¼ teaspoon kosher salt
½ cup Texas orange Moscato wine
Minced zest of 1 lemon

TOPPING:
1 jar (18 ounces) Texas strawberry
    jam, such as Confituras
Powdered sugar for dusting
1 pound fresh Hill Country
    strawberries, hulled and cut
    lengthwise into thin slices

Prepare and bake the pastry first. Process the almonds in the work bowl of a food processor fitted with the steel blade, until finely chopped. Add flour and pulse 3 to 4 times to blend. Add remaining ingredients and process until dough forms a cohesive ball. Turn dough out into a 10-inch removable-bottom tart tin. Press dough into bottom and up the sides of the tin. Prick dough all over with a fork, including the sides, and place on a baking sheet. Freeze for 1 hour. Preheat oven to 475°F. Bake in preheated oven 10 minutes, or until golden brown. Cool on a wire rack in the tart tin. Reduce oven temperature to 350°F.

In the bowl of a stand mixer fitted with the whisk attachment, whisk the ricotta until very smooth and fluffy on medium speed for about 3 minutes. Add all remaining ingredients and beat until well blended.

Spread the filling in the cooled tart shell and bake in preheated oven until set in the center, about 50 minutes to 1 hour. A toothpick inserted in the center of the tart should come out clean. Transfer the tart pan to a wire rack and cool completely.

While the tart is baking, heat the strawberry jam in a heavy-bottomed 2-quart saucepan over medium heat. When the jam is melted, strain through a fine strainer over a metal bowl. Stir the fruit with the back of a spoon to extract all of the liquid glaze from the jam. Discard pulp; set glaze aside.

When the tart has cooled, dust the edge of the pastry with powdered sugar. Arrange the strawberry slices in concentric circles, slightly overlapping and beginning at the outside edge of the tart. Using a pastry brush, brush the glaze over the strawberries. Set aside until glaze is set. Remove the tart from the tin to a platter. Slice into wedges to serve.

SWEET BERRY FARM

WHEN DAN AND GRETCHEN Copeland developed their "pick-your-own" farm on a picturesque 20-acre property outside Marble Falls in 1999, they had two goals in mind. First, they wanted to offer fresh, seasonal, all-natural berries and vegetables to the public. Second, by making it a pick-your-own operation, they envisioned whole families coming to the farm so that children could see where real food comes from and taste fruit right off the vines, while having lots of space to run and learn about nature. To that end, they made the farm totally family oriented. Their own children, Raelynn and Lacy, helped out when they were kids, and Dan's dad, Max, who retired after 40 years as a local pastor, serves as the farm's greeter. A covered arbor provides a place for families to picnic, if inclined.

A small on-premise store offers dessert—homemade ice cream, made with the farm's fruit, and delicious smoothies and shakes as well as Dan's mom's amazing strawberry preserves.

Then there is the Texas Maze, a four-acre maze in the shape of the state of Texas cut from nine-foot-high sorghum-sudan grass. Within the maze are many paths that lead to Texas "cities" at points that approximate their actual geographical locations within the state. Be aware that navigating the maze can be challenging even for adults.

Sweet Berry Farm produces strawberries, blackberries, tomatoes, potatoes, and pumpkins on a seasonal basis. The farm provides collection boxes, clippers, and even gloves to use while picking blackberries from those thorny bushes.

Sweet Berry Farm Blackberry and Pound Cake Crisps

In May and June, it's blackberry season in Texas. We eat them for breakfast, make jam and lots of these tasty crisps to eat right away, and then we make more to freeze and enjoy on a dreary and cold winter's day, when a reminder of summer is a welcome thing. To make the crisps an experience to remember, pile a scoop of Texas's own vanilla ice cream, made by the Blue Bell Creamery in Brenham, on top of the warm crisps. As it begins to melt and ooze down into the topping, it makes a kind of sauce that's just indescribably good!

SERVES 4.

TOPPING:

1 cup sugar, divided

⅓ cup all-purpose flour

½ cup rolled oats, preferably stone ground

¼ cup firmly packed light brown sugar

1 cup crumbled Lemon Pound Cake (see recipe on page 393)

1 teaspoon minced lemon zest

1 teaspoon vanilla bean paste

¼ teaspoon ground cinnamon

¼ teaspoon ground mace, preferably freshly ground from mace blades

½ stick unsalted butter, softened and chopped into ½-inch cubes

BERRY FILLING:

¼ cup Texas Moscato or Muscat Canelli wine

4 cups freshly picked and rinsed blackberries

3 tablespoons cornstarch

Blue Bell Homemade Vanilla Ice Cream, if desired

Preheat oven to 350°F. Line a small baking sheet with foil and butter four (6-ounce) ramekins. I use ramekins that are marketed as crème brûlée dishes. Place the ramekins on the baking sheet and set aside.

Combine ⅓ cup of the sugar, flour, rolled oats, brown sugar, pound cake, lemon zest, vanilla bean paste, cinnamon, and mace in a medium-sized bowl and toss to blend well. Add the butter cubes and use your fingers to blend them into the topping until the mixture resembles coarse meal. Set the topping in the refrigerator while you prepare the berries.

In a large bowl, combine the remaining sugar, wine, blackberries, and cornstarch, stirring to blend well. Place an equal portion of the berries in each of the prepared ramekins, then add a portion of the topping, scattering it evenly over the berries, and using all of the mixture. Bake in preheated oven for about 35 to 40 minutes, or until topping is browned and crisp and berries are bubbling. Serve warm. If you'd like to make it really decadent, put a small scoop of Blue Bell Homemade Vanilla Ice Cream on top of each serving.

★

SAN SABA PECANS

THE PECAN HAS thrived in Texas for thousands of years, but today no town is more closely associated with the nut than San Saba, the self-proclaimed "Pecan Capital of the World."

In 1875, Englishman Edmond E. Risien was on his way to California, but the huge native pecan trees in San Saba so impressed him that he decided to stay. A cabinetmaker by trade, Risien became an ambassador for the pecan. He was eager to experiment with the nut and offered a prize of five dollars cash for the most perfect pecan brought to his cabinet shop. Many samples were brought, but one in particular stood out from all the other contenders. Although only medium in size, it had a very thin shell and the quality of the kernel was excellent. Riesen asked to see the tree from which it was harvested and was taken to the man's property at the confluence of the Colorado and San Saba Rivers. There, outlined against the sky, stood a once-magnificent tree with but one branch remaining. The man told Risien that he had to cut off the other branches to get the nuts, and that the branch left was the one he stood on to cut the others off.

Risien bought the property and named the variety of pecan from this tree the San Saba. In the annals of Texas pecan history, the one-branched tree, still standing on land owned now by Risien's great-great-grandchildren, who founded the Millican Pecan Company, is known as the Mother Pecan. From nuts he gathered from this one tree, Risien planted more than 400 more and then further experimented with nuts from those trees—developing even better varieties. One of them, the Western Schley, has become the most planted pecan in the world today. In 1888, Risien established the West Texas Pecan Nursery in San Saba—the first in Texas to specialize in pecan stock.

In 1919, the Texas legislature officially declared the pecan the state tree, and in 1921, the major families in the pecan business established the Texas Pecan Growers Association—the state's oldest agricultural organization—in San Saba. R. D. "Buddy" Adams of San Saba Pecan Company estimates that San Saba County produces 6 to 8 million pounds of pecans per year. "But it's hard to say, really," he noted, "because there are so many small growers and home growers who only sell what they don't use themselves or share with family and friends. I think the figure could be as high as 12 million pounds, especially if we still harvested the pecans that fall in the sloughs and on the riverbanks like we used to. I remember back in the '70s and '80s, we used to put tarps and even old parachute canopies on the ground to catch the pecans from the native trees in those areas. But nobody messes with those pecans anymore." Today the large growers use mechanical shakers to shake the nuts off the trees. Mechanical sweepers follow to gather up the pecans.

Most bakers won't use the native Texas pecans because it's too hard to get the nuts out of the shells, even though they have an incredibly rich, delicious taste. One exception is the Blue Bell Creamery in Brenham, producers of Blue Bell Ice Cream. The company insists on original native Texas varieties for any of their products using pecans.

San Saba Texas Pecan Pie

No doubt about it, pecan pie is a Texas institution. Nothing finishes a barbecue better than pecan pie. Some of the best pecans in the country are grown in the upper reaches of the Texas Hill Country around San Saba. I never liked pecan pie much as a kid because it was just too sweet and seemed to me to have a gluelike texture. But to be a chef and food writer in Texas who didn't like pecan pie seemed to be blasphemy, so I began to experiment with the standard corn syrup–based recipes, substituting other types of syrup in place of the corn syrup. When I hit upon agave nectar, it was a winner! Not as sweet, and the texture is softer and looser. The coffee-based tequila liqueur is also a nontraditional ingredient but delicious nonetheless. I created this recipe for a cooking demonstration that I did at one of the best of the many Texas food festivals—the San Saba River Pecan Jam, which celebrates the local pecan industry each fall in San Saba.

MAKES ONE (9-INCH) PIE.

CRUST:

1 stick (¼ pound) unsalted butter, cut into 1-inch cubes
1 cup all-purpose flour
½ teaspoon sugar
¼ teaspoon kosher salt
3 tablespoons to ¼ cup ice water

FILLING:

3 eggs, well beaten
½ cup granulated sugar
½ cup light brown sugar, firmly packed
1 cup agave nectar
2 tablespoons Patron XO Café (tequila/coffee liqueur)
¼ cup melted unsalted butter
1 tablespoon vanilla extract
1⅓ cups chopped San Saba pecans

Preheat oven to 350°F. Make the pastry first. Combine the butter cubes, flour, sugar, and salt in the work bowl of a food processor fitted with the steel blade. Pulse 3 to 4 times to break up the butter into pea-sized bits. With the processor running, add the water until a cohesive dough forms. Do not let the dough form a ball. Turn the crumbly dough out onto a work surface and gather it together. Knead by hand a couple of times, just long enough to make a smooth dough. (But it will still have lumps of unblended butter.) Pat dough into a 6-inch disk, wrap in plastic wrap, and refrigerate for about 20 minutes before using.

Spray a 9-inch Pyrex pie dish with nonstick coating spray; set aside. Roll the dough out to a ⅛- to ¼-inch-thick round and transfer to the prepared pie dish. Flute the edges of the pastry as desired and place in freezer while you make the filling.

Make the filling by combining all ingredients except pecans. Whisk to blend well, then whisk for about 3 minutes until mixture is very smooth and frothy—no lumps or blobs. Scatter the pecans in the bottom of the prepared pastry. Pour the batter over the pecans and bake in preheated oven for about 1 hour and 5 minutes to 1 hour and 15 minutes, or until the crust is golden brown and filling is almost set. The filling should jiggle in the center ever so slightly, and there will be slight cracking on the top of the pie when it's perfectly done. Do not bake until the filling is completely firm.

Cool on wire rack and serve at room temperature. Do not refrigerate pecan pie, as it spoils the smooth, gooey texture.

Bonnie Travis's Green Tomato Pie

Green tomato pie is an old Texas favorite, enjoyed first by farm families who had house gardens that always included many tomato plants. Today, it still helps to have your own tomato patch or be good friends with someone who does. (And then you'll have to make two pies—one for you, and one for the tomato-growing friend!)

This recipe comes from Bonnie Travis, manager of a delightful little eatery in Blanco, Zocalo Eclectic Café. I have combined Bonnie's wonderful pie with another old favorite, boiling water and lard pastry. This is a delicious and flavorful pastry that's fun to make. You can substitute your own favorite pie pastry, if you wish, but this pastry is quite an heirloom itself and its down-home taste really matches the rustic nature of the pie. Be sure to use only fresh leaf lard, the kind you buy at farmers' markets, not the hydrogenated blocks from the supermarket, which, to me, have a rancid and charred flavor.

MAKES ONE (9-INCH) PIE.

Boiling Water Pastry (recipe follows)

1½ cups sugar

5 tablespoons all-purpose flour

1 teaspoon ground cinnamon

⅛ teaspoon kosher salt

3 cups sliced homegrown green
    tomatoes, about 4 to 5 medium
    tomatoes

1 tablespoon apple cider vinegar

Minced zest of 1 lemon

2 tablespoons unsalted butter,
    cut into ½-inch cubes

BOILING WATER PASTRY:

MAKES ENOUGH PASTRY FOR
ONE 9-INCH DOUBLE-CRUST PIE.

¾ cup pure leaf lard

¼ cup boiling water

1 tablespoon whole milk

2½ cups all-purpose flour

1 teaspoon kosher salt

Begin by making the pastry. Place the lard in a large bowl. Add the boiling water and milk. Working quickly, break up the lard with a fork, then whisk vigorously until the mixture is smooth, thickened, and fluffy. It should hold soft peaks. Sift the flour and salt into the lard mixture. Stir vigorously and quickly to form a mass that comes away from the sides of the bowl. Turn the dough out onto a very lightly floured work surface and gently knead to form into a smooth ball. Divide dough in half; press into round disks and refrigerate one disk. Preheat oven to 350°F.

On a floured work surface, roll out the unrefrigerated half of the pastry gently, but with pressure, into a round about 1/16-inch thick. Loosely roll the pastry around the rolling pin, then unroll it over the pie pan. Lift the edges of the pastry all around the pan, allowing the pastry to slide into bottom of pan. Don't stretch the pastry into the pan or it will shrink when baked. Gently pat the pastry into the sides of the pan. Using kitchen shears, trim off excess pastry, leaving a 1-inch overhang at rim of pan. Refrigerate while making filling.

To make the green tomato filling, combine the sugar, flour, cinnamon, and salt in a large bowl, then toss with a fork to blend well. Add the tomatoes, vinegar, and lemon zest; toss to coat all of the tomatoes with dry mixture. Turn the tomato mixture out into prepared pastry, spreading evenly. Dot the filling with the butter cubes; set pie aside.

Roll out the remaining pastry after reflouring the work surface. Roll the pastry around the rolling pin and unroll carefully over the filled pie. Using kitchen shears, trim off excess pastry to the same 1-inch overhang as the bottom pastry. Press the top and bottom pastries together and tuck the overhang under, even with the rim of the pan. Flute the edges, if desired, or press the edge with the tines of a fork. Cut 2 rows of V-shaped steam holes in top pastry. Place the pie on a baking sheet and bake in preheated oven for about 1 hour, or until pastry is golden brown and filling is bubbly. Cool slightly before serving.

Bananas Foster Cream Pie

Everybody loves the famous rich and gooey New Orleans dessert bananas Foster. What a treat it is when the waiter wheels the flambé cart to your table to sauté the heavenly sauce right before your eyes, then adds the bananas and rum, which sets the whole pan ablaze. But face it, few of us are going to try that one at home and risk setting the dining room curtains on fire! So this pie is a wonderful, but equally delicious, compromise—and it's much safer! It combines two much-loved-in-Texas desserts—banana cream pie and bananas Foster. It can also be made ahead of time.

MAKES ONE (9-INCH) PIE.

VANILLA WAFER CRUST:

1 cup finely ground vanilla
    wafer crumbs

1 teaspoon sugar

¼ cup finely ground pecans

⅓ cup melted unsalted butter

FILLING:

3 cups whole milk

1 tablespoon unflavored gelatin

½ cup sugar

¼ cup cornstarch

1 whole egg

3 egg yolks

2 tablespoons unsalted butter,
    room temperature

1 tablespoon plus 1 teaspoon
    vanilla extract

2 large ripe bananas, peeled and
    cut into bite-size slices

¾ cup whipping cream

BANANAS FOSTER TOPPING:

1 cup firmly packed light brown sugar

1 tablespoon ground cinnamon

1½ cups (3 sticks) unsalted butter

1½ cups crème de banana or other
    banana-based liqueur

1½ cups Pecan Street Rum, divided

1 cup chopped pecans

Preheat oven to 375°F. Begin by making the vanilla wafer crust. Combine all ingredients in the work bowl of a food processor fitted with the steel blade. Process until well blended. Turn the crumb mixture out into a 9-inch Pyrex pie pan. Using the back of a large spoon, press the crumb mixture firmly on bottom and up sides of pan. Bake the shaped crust for 6 minutes, then refrigerate until well chilled and firmly set.

To make the filling: Pour ¼ cup of the milk into a bowl and stir in the gelatin. Set aside until all milk has been absorbed and mixture feels spongy to the touch. Heat the remaining 2¾ cups milk in a heavy-bottomed 3-quart saucepan over medium heat just until bubbles appear around the side of the pan, about 8 to 10 minutes. Do not allow the milk to boil. Add the spongy gelatin to the milk and stir until gelatin is completely dissolved.

Meanwhile, combine the sugar, cornstarch, whole egg, and egg yolks in the bowl of a stand mixer with the beater attachment. Beat until thickened and light lemon-yellow in color, about 7 minutes. Add about ½ cup of the hot milk mixture to the egg mixture while beating. Beat to warm the eggs slightly. Now add the warmed egg mixture slowly to the milk in the saucepan while whisking vigorously. Bring the mixture to a boil, whisking constantly. Allow it to boil for about 2 minutes, until thickened. Strain through a fine strainer into a clean bowl and whisk in the softened butter and vanilla, blending completely. Cover the surface of the custard directly with plastic wrap and refrigerate just until the custard has cooled to room temperature. Don't let it become firm.

Remove the cooled custard and stir in the sliced bananas, blending well; set aside. Beat the whipping cream until medium-stiff peaks form. Fold the whipped cream into the banana custard, blending well. Turn the custard out into the prepared and chilled crust, spreading evenly. Refrigerate until filling is well chilled and well set, at least 6 hours.

When you are ready to serve the pie, make the bananas Foster sauce. Toss the brown sugar and cinnamon together with the tines of a fork to blend well; set aside. Melt the butter in a heavy-bottomed 12-inch skillet over medium heat. Add the cinnamon-sugar mixture and cook, stirring, until sugar melts. Add the crème de banana and 1¼ cups of the rum with the pecans; stir to blend well. Cook, stirring often, until sauce is thickened and syrupy, about 20 minutes of hard simmering. Remove pan from heat and whisk in the remaining ¼ cup rum. Set sauce aside until cooled to room temperature. Slice the pie and place slices on individual serving plates. Drizzle desired portion of the sauce over each serving and serve at once.

Coconut-Buttermilk Pie with Sour Cream Pastry

Buttermilk pie is a southern classic that's hard to beat. While I do love upscale desserts with architectural features and dots and splashes of sauce, fruit, and caramel, or chocolate curlicues, when push comes to shove, I'd probably choose buttermilk pie!

MAKES ONE (9-INCH) PIE.

SOUR CREAM PASTRY:

1 cup sifted all-purpose flour

¼ teaspoon kosher salt

½ cup (1 stick) unsalted butter, cut into 1-inch cubes

1 egg yolk, beaten

⅓ cup sour cream

COCONUT-BUTTERMILK FILLING:

½ cup (1 stick) unsalted butter

1⅓ cups sugar

1 tablespoon vanilla extract

3 eggs

3 tablespoons plus 2 teaspoons
   all-purpose flour

¼ teaspoon kosher salt

⅔ cup buttermilk (not low fat)

⅓ cup well-shaken canned
   coconut milk

⅔ cup (firmly packed) sweetened
   flaked coconut

To make the pastry: Combine flour, salt, and butter in the work bowl of a food processor fitted with the steel blade. Process until butter is broken up into pea-sized bits. In a small bowl, combine the egg yolk and sour cream, whisking to blend well. Add the sour cream mixture to the flour mixture in the processor. Process just until blended. Turn dough out onto a lightly floured work surface and gather into a ball, kneading once or twice by hand. Flatten into a round disk, wrap tightly in plastic wrap, and refrigerate for about 20 minutes while preparing the filling.

Preheat oven to 300°F. Cream the butter and sugar in a stand mixer with the beater attachment at medium speed until light and fluffy, about 5 minutes. Add the vanilla and beat to blend. Add the eggs, one at a time, beating well and scraping down sides of bowl after each addition. Combine the flour and salt in one bowl and the buttermilk and coconut milk in another bowl. Add to the mixer in thirds, alternating the two mixtures and scraping down sides of bowl after each addition. Add the coconut and beat just to blend. Set aside.

Roll the chilled pastry out on a lightly floured work surface into a circle about 1/16-inch thick. Roll the pastry loosely around the rolling pin and unroll over a 9-inch pie pan. Do not stretch the pastry to push it into the pan. Lift the edges and let the pastry fall to the bottom and sides of the pan. Pat pastry gently into sides and bottom of pan. Cut off excess pastry at rim, leaving a 1-inch overhang. Fold the excess pastry underneath at the rim and flute the edges as desired, or press with the tines of a fork.

Pour the filling into the pastry and bake for 1½ hours in the preheated oven, or until a metal skewer inserted in center of pie comes out clean. Cool pie on wire rack, then refrigerate to chill thoroughly before slicing, about 6 hours.

FLAT CREEK ESTATE

T HE EVOLUTION OF Flat Creek Estate began when Rick and Madelyn Naber, a few years into an early retirement on Lake Travis in the Texas Hill Country, purchased the only remaining agricultural property in the area. The pair considered several possibilities for the land, but the gently sloping terrain and excellent water source convinced them to start a vineyard.

The varietals in "Helen's Block" are mainly Italian and produce consistent-quality red fruit, as evidenced by their award-winning Super Texan, probably the winery's best-known bottle. Other blocks include syrah, tempranillo, and white varieties such as pinot grigio, pinot blanc, and muscat canelli. Flat Creek also sources grapes grown in other parts of Texas.

Winemaker Tim Drake says the goal at Flat Creek is "to make wines that are unique to Texas and that compete successfully in international competition." Tim related that Texas offers more opportunity for crafting unique wines than he found on the West Coast.

Flat Creek has a large tasting room, which overlooks the scenic vineyards, and includes a restaurant whose menu was built around dishes that pair with the estate's wines.

Flat Creek produces some outstanding dessert wines. Pair the Muscato D'Arnancia with the Dos Lunas Ricotta and Orange Moscato Tart with Almond Pastry (pages 427–428). Use the wine both to prepare the tart and to pair with it. For the Bananas Foster Cream Pie (pages 436–438), try the Blanco Brio, a frizzante-style wine. The San Saba Texas Pecan Pie (pages 432–433) is a nontraditional pecan pie, but it's a good pairing with the Flat Creek Estate Port.

INDEX

RECIPE INDEX